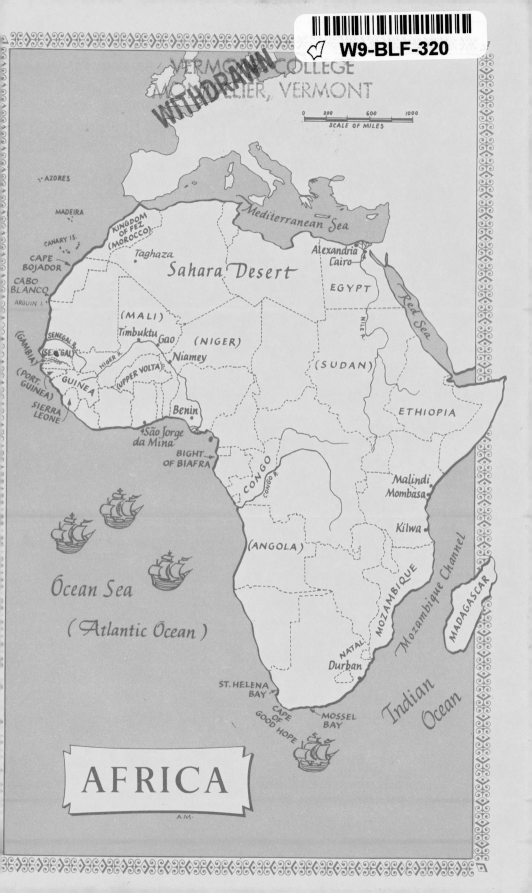

SCALE OF MILES
0   200   600   1000

AZORES

MADEIRA

Mediterranean Sea

CANARY IS.

KINGDOM OF FEZ (MOROCCO)

CAPE BOJADOR

Taghaza

Sahara Desert

Alexandria
Cairo

EGYPT

CABO BLANCO

ARGUIN I.

(MALI)

Red Sea

SENEGAL R.

Timbuktu   Gao

(NIGER)

(SENEGAL)

NILE R.

(GAMBIA)

NIGER R.

Niamey

(SUDAN)

(PORT. GUINEA)

GUINEA

(UPPER VOLTA)

SIERRA LEONE

Benin

ETHIOPIA

São Jorge da Mina

BIGHT OF BIAFRA

CONGO

CONGO R.

Malindi
Mombàsa

Kilwa

Ocean Sea

(ANGOLA)

(Atlantic Ocean)

MOZAMBIQUE

Mozambique Channel

MADAGASCAR

NATAL
Durban

Indian Ocean

ST. HELENA BAY

CAPE OF GOOD HOPE

MOSSEL BAY

AFRICA

A.M.

Books by Louis B. Wright

GOLD, GLORY, AND THE GOSPEL   *1970*

EVERYDAY LIFE ON THE AMERICAN FRONTIER   *1968*

THE AMERICAN HERITAGE HISTORY OF THE THIRTEEN COLONIES   *1967*

THE ARTS IN AMERICA: THE COLONIAL PERIOD   *1966*
(in collaboration with others)

EVERYDAY LIFE IN COLONIAL AMERICA   *1965*

THE DREAM OF PROSPERITY IN COLONIAL AMERICA   *1965*

SHAKESPEARE FOR EVERYMAN   *1964*

THE CULTURAL LIFE OF THE AMERICAN COLONIES   *1957; 1962*

CULTURE ON THE MOVING FRONTIER   *1955; 1961*

THE BRITISH TRADITION IN AMERICA   *1954*

THE COLONIAL SEARCH FOR A SOUTHERN EDEN   *1953*

THE ATLANTIC FRONTIER: COLONIAL AMERICAN CIVILIZATION   *1947; 1959*

THE FIRST AMERICANS IN NORTH AFRICA   *1945*

RELIGION AND EMPIRE: THE ALLIANCE BETWEEN PIETY AND COMMERCE IN ENGLISH EXPANSION, 1558–1625   *1942; 1969*

THE FIRST GENTLEMEN OF VIRGINIA   *1940; 1964*

PURITANS IN THE SOUTH SEAS   *1936*

MIDDLE-CLASS CULTURE IN ELIZABETHAN ENGLAND   *1935; 1959; 1964*

GOLD, GLORY,
AND
THE GOSPEL

GOLD, GLORY, *AND* THE GOSPEL

The Adventurous Lives and Times of the Renaissance Explorers

LOUIS B. WRIGHT

Atheneum New York

1970

Maps by Ava Morgan

TO THE MEMORY OF

Thomas J. Wilson

DISTINGUISHED PUBLISHER, EMINENT SCHOLAR,

AND LIFELONG FRIEND

PREFACE

✠

FOR MANY YEARS THE ALMOST INCREDIBLE DEEDS OF THE Renaissance explorers and conquerors have fascinated me, and I have made notes of their activities since graduate school in the hope that someday I could put together an account of their accomplishments. In this book I have tried to discuss the principal motivations that drove these men to perform miracles. Alas, the magnitude of a definitive study of so vast a subject is self-defeating, and I must be content with a brief and highly selective treatment of only a few of these figures from a past that is growing ever dimmer to most readers.

The genesis of this book dates from a luncheon conversation with the late Thomas J. Wilson, who shared my interest in and enthusiasm for these heroic men of the Renaissance. "Why don't you write a brief book about their motivations, their drive for power, glory, whatever?" he inquired. "We have plenty of big books, plenty of coffee-table books full of pictures, and plenty of learned academic treatises. What readers would welcome is a concise, clearly written narrative of the spectacular accomplishments of the men who conquered the unknown lands and seas in the fifteenth and sixteenth centuries. What made them do it?" Acting on this hint, I have tried to write such a narrative. Obviously, much more could be said about every subject treated. Indeed, much more has been said in many scholarly treatises. But if I have been able to distill the essence from learned works and make it more readily available, perhaps my efforts will serve the need that Tom Wilson discerned.

I am under great obligation to many scholars who have devoted their lives to research in some corner of this field. No one can deal with explorations without incurring a debt to the Hakluyt Society and the men who for more than a century have made valuable travel narratives available with careful notes and explanations. To many writers still active I am also conscious of an indebtedness that I can only pay with an expression of gratitude for their work: J. J. Parry, David B. Quinn, R. A. Skelton, Boies Penrose, Charles McKew Parr, Samuel E. Morison, Amando Cortesão, Charles R. Boxer, and a host of others.

Portuguese names sometimes pose a problem for a work in English. I have used the English form of names that are already well known to readers—as, for example, Prince Henry and Magellan—rather than their Portuguese equivalents. For names not so familiar I have retained the Portuguese forms.

For assistance in the preparation of this manuscript and for useful criticism I wish to thank Elaine W. Fowler and Megan Lloyd, both of whom have given me invaluable help. To members of the Folger Library reading-room staff I also wish to express my appreciation for help beyond the call of duty.

It has been a pleasure and an immense satisfaction to work with the editorial staff of Atheneum Publishers, especially Tony Clark, whose perceptiveness and assistance have eased the final throes of getting this book into print. I have had good advice. The errors and shortcomings are mine.

Louis B. Wright

April 24, 1970

✠

The Quality of the Explorers and Conquerors

LONG BEFORE COLUMBUS SET OUT FROM PALOS ON THAT AUGUST day in 1492, Europe was astir with ideas and with dreams that would transform the world as men had known it for the preceding centuries. An age of intellectual curiosity, an age of questioning, an age of testing old notions and beliefs was beginning. Within a century after Columbus, the ferment that was exerting its influence in his youth would serve as a leaven to change conditions in every country of Western Europe. In some the changes would be gradual; in others they would be revolutionary and cataclysmic. But everywhere life would be different.

The post-Columbian era saw the world suddenly doubled in extent, as the first space age burst upon the consciousness of men. The impact upon European imaginations of the discovery of a vast new space across the Western Ocean can be dimly perceived today by men whose imaginations have been stirred by voyages to the moon. But we should remember that the discoveries in space across the seas, discoveries that astounded sixteenth-century Europeans, were even more dramatic than the discoveries in outer space made by modern astronauts. The explorers of the sixteenth century brought back tangible evidence of their discoveries, evidence that excited and pleased Europeans and stimulated them to further ventures overseas. These explorers also brought back specimens of primitive peoples, human beings perhaps from the Golden Age, merely waiting to be given the Gospel Message to be saved for Christ. Excitement ran through Europe, and few who heard or read of the New World's wonders failed to dream of some adventure or some benefit that the explorations might bring.

Great as were the changes in man's thinking and his outlook in the late fifteenth and sixteenth centuries, we must not conclude that Europeans suddenly began to adopt present-day mental attitudes or to regard the world as we do. Furthermore, not all Europeans responded alike to the new impulses; a Spaniard's attitudes and motivations might differ enormously from those of an Englishman. Although the spirit of the Renaissance left no country of western Europe untouched, everywhere vestiges of medieval thought remained to condition men's actions. Although Martin Luther's teachings might destroy old religious concepts in some areas, they merely served to harden the resolution of others against heresy. The medieval age of faith might give way in Italy before the pagan Renaissance, but secularization made slower progress in the Iberian Peninsula, where Spaniards and Portuguese still conceived of themselves as crusaders ordained to continue the warfare against Islam, to suppress heretics wherever found, and to carry the gospel to the heathen.

The motivations of the explorers and conquerors were complex and are sometimes hard for modern man to comprehend. For example, it is difficult for a dweller in mid-twentieth-century America to understand the profound religious convictions of many of the Spanish conquistadors whose greed for gold was exceeded only by their zeal to convert the Indians. It is almost as difficult to comprehend the attitude of some of these same conquerors whose determination to seek glory by heroic deeds was greater than their eagerness to seize treasure of silver and gold. But fame was a goal that the man of the Renaissance often placed highest in the category of desirable attainments. Hernán Cortés, for example, declared in a letter to his father that he "held it better to be wealthy in fame than in property." This desire for fame, for glory, led to the performance of incredible feats and the display of courage rarely equaled in any period.

Religion was a profound motive for action in the fifteenth, sixteenth, and seventeenth centuries. So accustomed are we to regard the pursuit of material welfare as a primary aim that we forget other incentives that may have inspired our ancestors. The Portuguese and the Spaniards, for example, saw no conflict between the search for treasure and the evangelization of the heathen encountered in that pursuit. Indeed, the two goals were complementary, and both were desirable. Furthermore, the belief was widespread that God would vouchsafe signal favors to those who served Him well. Piety and good works thus became sound insurance against misfortune. This doctrine subconsciously influenced most Christians of the sixteenth and seventeenth centuries, whether Catholic or Protestant. For instance, even when Protestants declared that faith and not works would determine the welfare of men's souls, their books on holy dying advised generous bequests to the Church and to charity to ensure the blessing of God. Neither Catholic Portuguese and Spaniards nor Protestant Dutch and English saw any hypocrisy in invoking God's aid in their struggles for material success. If they did right by God, God surely would do right by them. This they all firmly believed.

The Iberians, particularly, conceived of themselves as crusaders for Christ. They had been engaged in war against the infidels of Islam since the eighth century when the Moors first overran Spain. The Portuguese had succeeded in driving the Moors from their borders in the thirteenth century, but not until January 2, 1492, did Spain win a final victory with the capture of Granada. This ancient conflict with Islam, which made a deep impression on the Iberians, explains their fanatical zeal to continue the warfare against the followers of Mohammed. The unremitting conflict in which no religious compromise was possible also explains their self-appointed role as the protectors of Christian orthodoxy against heresy of any sort. The fountains of the true gospel had to be kept pure and undefiled. If heretics had to burn to ensure this purity, that was a small price to pay for the protection of the Faith.

As Mohammedans believed that those who fell in a holy war against Christian dogs would be immediately translated to heaven, so the Iberian Christians were convinced that God would especially favor those who waged war for the Gospel of Christ. The furtherance of the Faith and the aggrandizement of Portugal or Spain often meant one and the same thing. That was understood; not even God performed miracles in a vacuum. So the Pope in Rome offered plenary indulgences to those who lost their lives in dangerous voyages to Africa, India, or the New World, where the soldiers of the Cross had yet many battles to fight and many souls to save.

If Protestants in England and Holland were somewhat less zealous in their evangelical efforts, they were nonetheless convinced that they too were waging war for the Lord, but with a difference. As they conceived it, their principal obligation was to prevent the Papists from overrunning the New World. Not Islam but the Roman Church became the target of Protestant onslaughts. The success of Spain in creating an empire in America —and in gaining the wealth to carry on the propagation of the Catholic faith both overseas and in Europe—alarmed Protestants everywhere. The English and the Dutch believed that they were ordained to thwart the steady progress of Spain and the spread of the religion that Spaniards so zealously defended. Although Protestants also accepted the obligation to convert the heathen, they showed more enthusiam for smiting the Papists. Thus religion became a deeply felt motivation for Protestants, as well as for Catholics, in their drive for expansion beyond the seas.

The sincerity of both Catholics and Protestants in their religious motivations was genuine and profound. What sounds today like hypocritical rationalization was unquestioned truth to the

xii

men of the sixteenth and seventeenth centuries. When English and Dutch corsairs, engaged in piracy on the high seas, seized Spanish or Portuguese galleons laden with gold and silver or spices from the Indies, they convinced themselves that they were doing the work of God in taking the sinews of war from the followers of anti-Christ. When Portuguese or Spanish traders bought slaves from African kings, or when Spaniards seized Indians and used them for forced labor, they pointed out that their actions provided an opportunity to baptize these heathen and thus to save their souls for eternity. In the eyes of the Spaniards and the Portuguese the exchange of personal liberty for lasting salvation was a bargain. This argument, sincerely believed, remained a justification for enslaving heathen peoples for generations to follow. Even in New England godly merchants of the eighteenth century, making money in the slave trade, convinced themselves that they were serving a missionary purpose. But perhaps the New Englanders' rationalization was less genuine than the convictions of the Spanish and Portuguese of an earlier period.

To the modern world, the cruelties of the explorers and conquerors during the Age of Discovery often excite horror and revulsion. To understand the actions of these men, we must be aware not only of their beliefs but also of the characteristics of the times in which they lived. We do not need to whitewash them, but we do need to view them in relation to their own age. Before we heap obloquy upon the Spaniards for their treatment of the Indians, we might remember that the twentieth century is hardly in a position to cast stones at the sixteenth. It remained for our own age to perpetrate the greatest atrocity of recorded history in the massacre of more than six million Jews by a supposedly Christian nation, all done with technological efficiency unknown in more primitive times.

The Spaniards have suffered from the perpetuation of the "Black Legend" recounting manifold cruelties to the aborigines whom they encountered in the conquest of their American empire. Thousands of Indians perished under forced labor, it is true, but many more died because of the introduction of European diseases: smallpox, measles, influenza, and other ailments. Whether the Indians wreaked an unperceived revenge by conferring upon Europeans a virulent form of syphilis is a matter of controversy among medical historians.

Ironically, the story of Spanish cruelty was dramatically exaggerated by the publications of a Spanish Dominican, Bartolomé de Las Casas, in his laudable efforts to arouse the consciences of the ruling authorities. But Las Casas outdid himself, and his stories were translated by gleeful Protestants eager to damn bloodthirsty Papists. Spanish conquistadors and colonists were not models of gentleness, to be sure, but they were not all as ruthless as legend has made them. One purpose of the present volume is to try to indicate the characteristics of these adventurers in terms of their own century.

In general the actors in the great scenes of Renaissance exploration and discovery were romantics inspired by an intense passion for honor and glory, hungry also for material wealth which would permit the trappings and display that were the visible evidences of glory in the Renaissance. This desire for glory and wealth, combined with a zeal to serve God as well as the earthly sovereign, led to incredible heroics that at times seemed mystically inspired. These qualities were confined to no single nation or people. A phlegmatic Dutchman or a taciturn Englishman might on occasion demonstrate the same romantic dash as the most volatile Latin.

Yet of all the men of the Renaissance, perhaps the Spaniard was more deeply affected than others by romantic influences. Don Quixote was not the only Spaniard of the sixteenth century whose head was turned by reading tales of chivalry. As Irving Leonard has shown in a charming and wise work, *Books of the Brave* (Cambridge, Mass., 1949), the reading of chivalric fiction delighted Spaniards of every degree. The Emperor Charles V avidly devoured these tales; St. Ignatius Loyola, founder of the Society of Jesus, as he waited for a broken leg to knit, whiled away hours reading stories of knightly adventure, which may help to account for the military quality of the order that he created; St. Teresa of Ávila was stirred to action by reading about Amadis of Gaul; and even Spaniards who could not spell out the words in chapbook romances listened with bated breath while some more literate villager read aloud the stories of Amadis, of Palmerin of England, Primaleon, or some other. These tales of impossible adventures, magic, and mystery excited readers and listeners, who sometimes accepted the narratives as true "history" and sought to emulate the heroics described therein. The Man from La Mancha had many contemporaries who were prompted to go on adventure by reading the books that had so addled the good knight's wits. When Bernal Díaz, with Cortés struggling over the mountains toward Montezuma's capital, at last crosses a rise and gazes down on Tenochtitlán gleaming white against the blue water of the lakes, he exclaims that it looks like some enchanted thing described in the story of Amadis of Gaul.

The actual wonders that returning travelers told of the New World were so astounding that would-be adventurers, nourished on descriptions of the strange lands and stranger deeds reported in chivalric romances, found it easy to believe that they too might equal or surpass the glories of fictitious knights. Hence, many a poor Spaniard with little else besides his sword and his courage sailed across the Atlantic and in some instances achieved the unbelievable and the impossible.

A vast literature has developed around these explorers, adventurers, conquerors, and empire-builders, so voluminous that the average reader, even if he had the inclination, would find it difficult to work his way through the maze of books. The narratives are also frequently complicated. For example, the history of the conquest of Peru, with its recurring civil wars and incessant struggles for power among the Spanish leaders, is likely to leave the reader in a confusion as dense as a swamp on the upper Amazon. Hence a book that attempts to provide a succinct account of the more significant developments in the European expansion overseas may be of some value. An effort has been made in the present volume to give more attention to the complex motivations of the adventurers than is commonly found in narratives of their deeds. Obviously, within the compass of one moderate-sized book a detailed history of European expansion into Africa, Asia, and America is impossible. I have tried, instead, to relate important and dramatic episodes that are typical of expansion overseas in various regions from the beginnings to the early years of the seventeenth century. If characteristic accounts of the story of expansion provide some notion of the development as a whole, the purpose of this book will have been achieved.

Contents

INTRODUCTION *The Quality of the Explorers and Conquerors*   ix

   I   *War Against the Infidel and a Foretaste of Profit*   3

  II   *Search for Eastern Christians, African Gold, and Heathen Souls*   12

 III   *The Gold and the Wonders of Guinea*   29

 IV   *The Legacy of Prince Henry: Passage to India*   46

  V   *Portugal Rejects Columbus and Loses a Western Empire*   60

 VI   *Vasco da Gama Opens the Sea Route to India*   83

 VII   *Riches and Ruin in the Indies*   100

VIII   *Magellan's Feat: Spain's Westward Route to the Spice Islands*   128

 IX   *Hernán Cortés, Greatest of the Conquistadors*   160

  X   *Bartolomé de Las Casas and the "Black Legend"*   205

 XI   *The Curse of the Incas and the Wealth of Potosí*   227

 XII   *Competition for El Dorado*   257

XIII   *The Long Struggle Against the Iberian Colossus*   287

XIV   *The "Elect of God"*   329

    Index   353

GOLD, GLORY,
AND
THE GOSPEL

War Against the Infidel and
a Foretaste of Profit

THROUGHOUT PORTUGAL DURING THE SPRING AND SUMMER of 1415 rumors ran and excitement mounted. Some great venture was afoot, but none could tell what the stir was all about. Messengers from King João I had gone out to the nobles of the kingdom and to the masters of guilds in the towns to gather vast quantities of naval stores, munitions, and weapons and to recruit crossbowmen and other soldiers for some service that would redound to God's glory and the country's benefit. Shrewd men coming from court gave out that perhaps the King meant to sweep the Dutch pirates from the seas and make voyages safer for Portuguese merchantmen carrying their salt, fish, olives, and oil to foreign ports. But the real purpose of King João's preparations remained a state secret, hidden from all save the King's sons and a few grave counselors. No one then knew that the outcome of all the activity would set in motion currents that would change the history of the world.

Portugal lay at the outermost verge of western Europe, a narrow land fronting the stormy Atlantic with the mountains of

Spain at its back. In that land lived some million and a half people eager to keep their independence from the domination of Spain and ready to fight again the Moors whom they had driven from their borders nearly two centuries before. When King Fernando died in 1385, he left a daughter, Beatriz, as his only heir. This daughter was married to the King of Castile. The Portuguese were unwilling to risk their fate to a queen who was the wife of a Spanish king; consequently, they looked about them and chose João, the illegitimate son of King Pedro, Fernando's predecessor on the Portuguese throne. João was Master of the religious Order of Avis, and hence the dynasty that he founded is called the House of Avis.

He did not gain his crown without a fight. Castile went to war to claim the throne for Beatriz, but João met and defeated the Spanish army at Aljubarrota, north of Lisbon. His victory was made sure by a contingent of longbowmen sent from England by John of Gaunt, who had a shadowy claim upon the throne of Castile and wanted to see the Spanish weakened. Not only did John of Gaunt send bowmen, but presently he sealed an English alliance with Portugal by giving his daughter, Philippa, in marriage to King João. This marriage had important results for Portugal and the world.

Queen Philippa, with the puritanism always latent in the English, reformed both King João and the court. She became the scourge of philandering courtiers and complaisant ladies. Hundreds were literally dragged to the altar and married. When she caught the King kissing a lady-in-waiting in the palace at Cintra, even João was speechless before the frowns of his wife and could only point in excuse to a motto painted on the ceiling, "Por bem" [for good]. For good or not, the Queen had the whole ceiling painted with the motto, where it can be read to this day. But Philippa proved more than a virago; she won the love and respect of João and became the mother of five sons and two daughters. These sons were Duarte [Edward, named after Philippa's grandfather, Edward III of England], Pedro, Henrique [Henry, called by the English "the Navigator"], João, and Fernando.

4

The three eldest sons were deeply concerned with the warlike preparations being made in Portugal in 1415. They had heard from their mother stories of King Arthur, and they had been taught the virtues of chivalry by the aging Constable of Portugal, Nun'Álvares Pereira. Furthermore, those romances of chivalry that turned Don Quixote's head, *Amadis of Gaul* and others like it, were now becoming popular in Portugal. The young princes, in their early twenties, were eager to go off on some knightly adventure to win fame for themselves and their country. Their zeal had helped induce King João to agree to a new crusade, a crusade in which only Portugal would take the risk and reap the glory. Portugal would once more attack the Moors, smite the infidels, and substitute the Cross of Christ for the crescent of Mohammed. And this time Portugal would fight the Moors on foreign soil. João planned to capture Ceuta, a rich Moroccan city across the Strait of Gibraltar, opposite Algeciras. To Ceuta came spices, pepper, ivory, and gold from across the African desert; to seize this center of Eastern trade would bring a profit to the treasury and add stars to the heavenly crowns of the victors.

Lest the people murmur at new taxes, King João borrowed money and sought funds from his friends to pay the cost of the venture. The prospect for plunder was sufficient to arouse the greed of speculators and to induce soldiers to enlist in the enterprise. To his sons the King parceled out responsibilities. Duarte would take over affairs of state at home. Pedro would recruit lancers and gather supplies in the Alentejo to the southeast; Prince Henry would enlist tough mountaineers in the Trás-os-Montes to the north and find shipping for them at Oporto. Feverishly everyone set to work to get the armada ready.

Foresters searched the hills for tall pines needed as ship masts; for rosin from pitch pines; for spars and for oak timbers that the shipbuilders required. Cattle- and hog-drovers hurried their livestock to the slaughter pens downriver from Lisbon where the butchers dressed beeves and pigs and salted them down to supply the troops with food. Gulls in clouds hovered over the river, gorging on offal as the butchers worked. Fishermen also brought their catches to be salted and dried on scaffolds. The crusaders

5

against the infidels would not fight on empty stomachs.

In Oporto as in Lisbon, the streets rang with the clang of hammers on steel as the armorers made or repaired breastplates, helmets, greaves, swords, and lances. The blacksmiths were equally busy at their forges and anvils fashioning hardware needed by the shipwrights. Sail-makers were in such demand that tailors had to be pressed into service to help in the cutting and sewing of canvas for vessels being readied. Few craftsmen of any kind were idle: Carpenters, coopers, caulkers, and rope-makers labored by torchlight far into the night. Rapidly galleys and supply ships took shape in the shipyards on the Douro River at Oporto and on the Tagus at Lisbon. With the merchant ships already commandeered and refitted, the two rivers bristled with masts like gaunt pines in a burned-over forest.

The fury of these preparations for war did not escape the notice of spies from neighboring lands. Castile, ever the enemy of the House of Avis, naturally worried lest João had designs on its territory; Aragon, farther away, nevertheless wondered if the flotilla being fitted out might not descend on its shores; the remaining little enclave of Moors in Spain, the Kingdom of Granada, had reason for concern that it might be the objective of a planned crusade by the Christian Portuguese. To diplomatic inquiries from these states, João gave bland assurances and nothing more. While his workmen labored, spies speculated but gained no certain clue to the King's intentions.

By early July the expedition was beginning to mobilize. Prince Henry sailed up the Tagus on July 10 with twenty war galleys, gay with banners and pennons. Other leaders brought in their contingents. When all were counted, the fleet numbered 240 craft of all kinds: rowed war galleys, caravels for horses and men, round-bottomed supply ships, trim little pinnaces, ships for every purpose. The human complement consisted of some 30,000 sailors and oarsmen and 20,000 soldiers of various types, including a company of English longbowmen. King João and his sons, intending to smash the infidels, were determined to attack in sufficient force to capture at one blow the Moslems' prize city

6

across the waters on the African shore.

As the fleet was nearing its day of departure, calamity in the shape of a visitation of the plague fell upon Lisbon. Workmen sickened and died; men whispered that this ill omen foretold disaster; worst of all for the King and his sons, the Queen, whose stern faith had done so much to strengthen the dynasty, who had encouraged the crusade, and who had exhorted her sons to go forth and fight for Christ and their country, was struck down by the plague. In her last moments her thoughts were upon the expedition. She asked about the weather, the direction of the wind, and was told that a northern gale was blowing. "It is a favorable wind for your voyage," she is reported to have said, and with that she died.

Lisbon and the country were plunged in grief, and the ships in the harbor, which had been gay with flags, now showed only black draping. The people shivered in panic and were even more concerned when an eclipse of the sun added to their superstitious fears. But Prince Henry demonstrated his innate powers of leadership. He declared that the Queen herself had urged them to sail as they had planned, to do battle in a holy cause, and that no mourning would mar their departure. With that he ordered all the banners to be flung to the breeze and the trumpets to sound in triumph. With this note of cheer, on the flood tide the armada sailed down the Tagus and out to sea. The day was Wednesday, July 23, 1415.

The troubles of the crusaders, however, now began. The seas and the winds at the tip of Portugal, this most westerly point of Europe, where the Mediterranean and the Atlantic meet, are often wild and tempestuous; at other times a calm settles upon the waters and no sail stirs. For a week the fleet was becalmed off Faro, and for some days yet it tacked back and forth until it reached Algeciras during the second week of August. On August 14, the day planned for the attack on Ceuta, the flotilla headed across the strait, made a tentative attack, and withdrew to a less exposed anchorage west of the town. Two days later a storm blew up from the Atlantic; a few vessels dragged their anchors and crashed against rocks; others put out to sea; and the King with part of the fleet returned to Algeciras. After a week the storm abated and the armada reformed. Although several counselors advised the King to abandon Ceuta and seize Gibraltar instead, he ordered the assault on Ceuta for dawn on August 21. This time the Portuguese achieved surprise, for the Moors, having seen the ships depart, had convinced themselves that the fleet had another objective.

Although gigantic foot-soldiers from the Sudan lined the shores, they were poorly armed and proved no match for Portuguese lancers and archers. Slaughtering the defenders in heaps, the invaders swarmed over the walls, carried the castle in a speedy assault, and within a few hours won the city. King João suffered a slight wound that caused him to limp; many others received hurts from rocks thrown by the defenders; but the Portuguese losses were negligible, and they counted only eight of their men killed. The nearest of kin of these could take comfort in their end, for the Pope had announced a plenary indulgence for all who fell in the holy crusade against the Moslems.

In the words of a contemporary chronicler, Gomes Eannes de Azurara, "that most glorious conquest of the great city of Ceuta" was a victory in which "the heavens felt the glory and the earth the benefit." He also added: "And as to the profit of our world from this achievement, East and West alike are good witnesses thereof, since their peoples can now exchange their goods, without any great peril of merchandise—for of a surety no one can deny that Ceuta is the key of all the Mediterranean Sea." [1]

Ceuta, like Rome, occupies seven hills and is situated on a peninsula jutting into the Mediterranean. On clear days the inhabitants of Algeciras can glimpse white houses gleaming on Ceuta's hillsides. When the Portuguese captured it, they found orchards of limes, oranges, and pomegranates, gardens, and green fields

---

[1] *The Chronicle of the Discovery and Conquest of Guinea, Written by Gomes Eannes de Azurara*, trans. and ed. Charles R. Beazley and Edgar Prestage (London, Hakluyt Society, 1896), I, 15–16.

surrounding the town. Within the walls, the white houses of merchants held luxuries never before seen by the common soldiers of Portugal: silken hangings, rugs resplendent in Oriental color and design, sandalwood chests, divans with soft pillows and silk coverlets, ornaments in silver, gold, and ivory, utensils of brass, and dainty foods unknown to the invaders. The markets were stocked with all the luxuries of the East, with silks, fine cottons, and carpets, with spices, pepper, sugar, drugs, dates and confections, oil, rice, wheat—everything, it seemed, that human beings could want. For Ceuta was the port to which Arab traders brought the goods that Africa and Asia afforded.

The troops of King João sacked the town while the panic-stricken inhabitants fled to the surrounding hills, orchards, and fields. The soldiers pillaged every house and market stall, dumping food and grain in the streets in a mad search for gold, silver, and jewels, items easily carried away. Every trooper found something of value or interest. Some wound cloth around their bodies and stuffed scarves and silken garments inside their shirts; others made bundles of loot and slung them over their shoulders on the ends of their lances; the lucky ones concealed in their clothing money, golden ornaments, or jewels. Officials of the King hurriedly sequestered much of the spoils for the royal treasury. They marked for their master sacks of pepper, cloves, and cinnamon and had them loaded on ships before the excited soldiery could scatter them. They saved much silk, ivory, and bales of rugs, as well as rare drugs from the apothecary shops. The King's officers were also eager to find caches of gold, for Ceuta was known to be one of the ports to which caravans from Africa brought gold. King João, like everyone since King Solomon's time, was eager to obtain this African gold, and to discover whence it came.

The soldiers and sailors who sacked Ceuta had never seen a city so rich in treasure. As was the custom in this age, soldiers often fought merely for the sake of the booty found in a captured town. "Free companies" of soldiers from England, Germany, and Italy had long roamed Europe, ready to offer their

9

services in any war that promised spoils. Some of the English archers with King João were troops of this type. Ceuta did not disappoint them. The troops went back to the ships laden with the products of Africa and Asia; they would long talk of the luxuries and treasure they had seen in Ceuta.

When the officers of the King and the soldiers had thoroughly searched the city and gathered up its goods for shipment, King João prepared to return to Portugal. But first he ordered the Great Mosque to be cleansed and purified of the symbols of Mahomet; then the clergy gathered to consecrate it as a Christian church, an outpost against the infidel whence missionaries might go forth to save Africa and Asia for the true faith. For King João and his sons were moved by piety as well as greed.

Leaving a governor, a bishop, and 3,000 garrison troops in Ceuta, the Portuguese returned to Lisbon on September 2. They had been gone forty days, and they had made the first conquest in a long sequence of achievements that would eventually lead to an empire stretching over three continents. No one could yet foresee the full implications of this victory, but Prince Henry's mind seethed with hope and plans. Although only twenty-one at the time of the capture of Ceuta, Henry had shown his ability. Now created Duke of Viseu and made administrator of the new possessions in Africa, Henry had scope for his dreams. He would extend the influence of Portugal, explore the unknown seas around Africa, find the hosts of Christians believed to live in the realm of Prester John—somewhere in Africa or Asia—and deal a death blow to the Moslems once more threatening Europe. He would save many heathen souls and bring prosperity to his homeland. Surely no prince could have had higher motives—at least, not a prince of the fifteenth century.

Henry's responsibility for the security of Ceuta and the western Mediterranean was no light duty that the King had imposed. Ceuta was only thinly garrisoned. Behind it and on both sides were thousands of Moors ready to avenge the attack of 1415. Indeed, three years later Henry had to rush reinforcements and a fleet to Ceuta's defense against a huge army of Moslems, but he managed to reach the city in time to prevent its recapture. For the rest of his life he kept war galleys on the alert off the tip of Portugal to protect shipping and to prevent surprise attacks by sea. In this he was successful.

In 1418 Prince Henry was made "ruler and governor" of the Order of Christ, a religious order that had succeeded the Knights Templars. Sometimes called grand master, Henry retained control of the Order until his death forty-two years later. The revenues from the Order of Christ gave Henry the financial capacity to maintain a force against the infidels and to carry on a consistent program of exploration. The victory of Ceuta had shown the value and promise of both efforts. After Ceuta, no one had to convince the Portuguese, least of all Prince Henry, that they had a great destiny to fulfill. The conquest of Ceuta served as a stimulus and pointed the way to the vast unknown around the fear-inspiring capes of Africa.

Search for Eastern Christians, African Gold, and Heathen Souls

AFTER THE RESCUE OF CEUTA FROM THE MOORISH COUNTER-attack in 1418, Prince Henry established himself not far from Cape St. Vincent on the rocky eminence of Sagres—the "Sacred Promontory" of the ancients. Here, at the southern tip of Portugal, he built an austere residence, more like a monastery than a palace. An ascetic bachelor who even gave up the drinking of wine with his meals, Henry devoted the rest of his life to the promotion of voyages of discovery. These he hoped would reveal the sources of African gold, perhaps find a way to the mysterious realm of Prester John, and bring untold heathens in Africa to Christian salvation. All three motives exercised a strong influence on Henry. If he could unite Western Christendom with the hosts of Christians believed to exist in Prester John's kingdom, Henry thought he might activate a pincer movement to crush in its jaws the dreaded Moslems. Since the beginning of their conquest of Iberia in 711 A.D., Europe had never been rid of

12

the fear of these people. Henry dreamed of eliminating the danger once and for all.

The Iberians—the Spanish and the Portuguese—had borne the brunt of Moslem pressure through the centuries. Although Portugal had conquered the last Moorish stronghold in its southern province, the Algarve, in 1249, the threat of new incursions from Africa always remained. That was one of the reasons for establishing a Portuguese base at Ceuta.

Spain had been slower to rid itself of the Moors. In Henry's time a Moorish ruler still held sway in the Kingdom of Granada. Not until 1492 did Ferdinand and Isabella succeed in conquering Granada and ending Moorish rule within the borders of Spain. The Iberians thus had an inborn fear of Moslem power and a fanatical religious conviction that Christians ought to unite to subdue these infidels.

The Christian reconquest of Iberia had been made easier because the Moors themselves were constantly at war with one another. Although they were all Moslems, they were neither a religious nor a political monolith. The Islamic faith was split into sects, and Moslem rulers, within Iberia and outside of it, showed as much jealousy and hatred of one another as did Christian kings.

By the fifteenth century, however, a new Moslem threat to all of Europe had developed. The Ottoman Turks had become a power to be reckoned with. For two centuries the descendants of tribes that had fled from Khorassan before Genghiz Khan into Asia Minor had been spreading and gathering strength. By 1299 they had established a sultanate with a capital at Iconium in what is now southern Turkey, and for another century they expanded until they endangered all of eastern Europe. So great was the threat from Turkish armies raiding into Europe that King Sigismund of Hungary in 1396 gathered 100,000 Christian soldiers whom he led to defeat against Sultan Bajazet I. Only an attack by Timur (Tamerlane), the Mongol terror, on the eastern borders of Bajazet's realm saved Constantinople from falling into the hands of the Turks. The capital of the shrunken Byzantine

13

Empire was by then virtually isolated and its capitulation, now only a matter of time, finally occurred in 1453. For two centuries war against the Turks was almost continuous in eastern Europe. By 1529 the Turks, under Suleiman the Magnificent, greatest of the sultans, were pounding on the walls of Vienna, but that city, fortunately, held out. The imminent danger to Europe was finally relieved in 1571 when a combined European fleet destroyed the Turkish navy at the battle of Lepanto.

In the first half of the fifteenth century the recognition of the growing strength of the Ottoman Turks gave particular point to Portuguese efforts to mount a crusade against Islam. Although the Ottoman threat was as yet confined to eastern Europe, the Portuguese believed that the time would come when a new wave of Moslems would sweep into North Africa. They would then look across the Strait of Gibraltar for other lands to conquer. What the Moors had once done, the Ottoman Turks could do again. In the meantime it behooved all Christians to unite in a holy war to prevent such a disaster.

While Prince Henry was gathering seamen, pilots, geographers, and mathematicians at his rendezvous at Sagres preparatory to launching voyages of discovery—and perhaps expeditions of conquest—his brother Dom Pedro was making his own plans to find out about the world beyond Portugal and to help in the war against the Turks. In the late summer of 1425 he set out on his travels, going by ship first to England. He would not return to Portugal for three years. From England he went to Flanders and thence through Germany to Hungary and Rumania, where he took service under the banners of Sigismund, now Emperor-elect of the Holy Roman Empire, who was once more at war with the Turks. For two years Pedro remained with Sigismund and then returned to Portugal by way of Venice. He had the opportunity of picking up fresh information, not only about the danger from Islam but also about the need for new contacts with the East, whose products were in even greater demand now that the Turks had disrupted the old trade routes. What information Pedro imparted to Henry on his return to Portugal we can only surmise, but it must have stimulated his brother to push his maritime enterprises. Early in the sixteenth century Dom Pedro became the hero of a popular work of fictitious travels which had a vague basis in the European journey that he actually made.[1]

The nature of Prince Henry's so-called "school" of navigation at Sagres is still a matter of controversy, but it clearly was not a formally organized academy providing instruction in the latest science of geography and navigation. Instead, Henry appears to have sought out Italian, Spanish, Dutch, and even Arab pilots and seamen whose knowledge and experience might be put to good use by Portuguese mariners, whom he was also recruiting. Significantly, he established on the cape both a chapel and an observatory, for he intended to worship God and to study His handiwork. To be certain that he had the best maps and nautical equipment, Henry brought to Sagres cartographers and instrument-makers. Arab and Jewish mathematicians and astronomers also found a welcome in Henry's palace. Henry was not a speculative thinker nor a theoretician. All his efforts were directed to the practical application of everything his seamen could learn, with the result that a contemporary reported that "our sailors went out well taught and provided with instruments and rules which all map-makers should know." [2]

Contrary to popular notions, the west coast of Africa and the Atlantic Ocean beyond the Pillars of Hercules were not altogether unknown. A few daring souls from the time of the Phoenicians onward had occasionally ventured into the Ocean Sea, as the Atlantic was called. Although Arab sailors had explored the Indian Ocean and had traded with the east coast of Africa, they had a fear of the Atlantic and described the region south of Cape Bojador (on the West African coast of what is now the Spanish Sahara) as the "Green Sea of Darkness." Their tales of the horrors beyond this point became a part of Mediterranean folklore,

[1] A detailed and scholarly treatment of the career of Dom Pedro and an account of the famous book purporting to tell of his adventures is found in Francis M. Rogers, *The Travels of the Infante Dom Pedro of Portugal* (Cambridge, Mass., 1961).

[2] C. Raymond Beazley, *Prince Henry the Navigator* (New York, 1895), p. 162, quoting Pedro Nuñes.

15

and terrified sailors kept in circulation reports of seas boiling hot, of waters teeming with serpents, of an ocean of thick and impenetrable slime. Some said that if anyone lived to return from beyond Bojador he would be forever black.

Nevertheless, even as early as classical times an occasional ship had ventured into the Atlantic. Pliny tells of a voyager who found the Canaries about 40 B.C. These were perhaps the "Fortunate Isles" of classical story. In the Middle Ages, Arab navigators, deliberately exploring or blown to sea by storms, apparently had also reached the Canaries and perhaps Madeira. A famous Arabic geographer, El-Edrisi, who took service under Roger II, King of Sicily, in 1154 completed a work called the *Book of Roger* or *The Rogerian Description of the World*. In it Edrisi tells of the travels of eight kinsmen, designated the "Lisbon Wanderers," who sometime before 1147 made a voyage into the Atlantic, found what may have been Madeira, and finally reached an inhabited island where they were captured and a little later set adrift in a boat. Landing on the northwest coast of Africa, they ultimately made their way back to Lisbon with tall tales to tell. A romantic story reports that two English lovers, Robert Machim and Anna d'Arfet, fleeing England for France in 1370, were blown by contrary winds to Madeira. Genoese sailors undoubtedly reached these islands in the fourteenth century, for an Italian chart, the Laurentian Portolano of 1351, plainly shows Madeira. In 1402 two Norman adventurers, Gadifer de la Salle and Jean de Béthencourt, sailing from Rochelle, reached two of the islands in the Canaries. Vowing allegiance to the King of Castile, Béthencourt got himself named king of the islands; but in 1406 he handed them to a nephew, who sold them several times over: to an agent of the King of Castile, to Prince Henry of Portugal, and finally to a second Spaniard, who in turn was forced to sell out to King Ferdinand and Queen Isabella. News of these islands and reports obtained from Arab traders who had gone overland to the west coast of Africa stirred Henry and his men at Sagres to busy themselves with plans for further discoveries.

Europe at this time was suffering from an acute shortage of

16

gold. The cost of the wars in eastern Europe created a fresh drain. But ever since the Crusades the appetite for Eastern luxuries had been growing in Europe, and these luxuries had to be paid for in bullion. For years Venice had been the great mart for the goods of Asia, which her galleys brought back from Alexandria; but these products were constantly increasing in price, and Europeans were hard put to it to find the money for spices, silks, jewelry, perfumes, drugs, and fine cottons of India. Most of the new gold that reached Europe came across the Sahara Desert by caravan from Timbuktu and Gao in what is now Mali and the adjacent regions. This trade was in the hands of the Taureg (a Berber people) and desert Arabs. They demanded a heavy return in European goods for this gold, and at best the trade was uncertain. The need for an easier and cheaper supply of gold was desperate.

From Arabs in Ceuta and elsewhere Henry's agents had picked up information that led him to believe his seamen might reach the African mines by sailing around Cape Bojador. Somewhere down that coast a "river of gold" emptied into the sea, if rumors could be believed. Nothing could be of greater benefit to Portugal and all of Christian Europe than the discovery of a sea route to the mines of African gold. Vague reports had also reached Henry of an African potentate in the interior who might be Prester John. Perhaps his explorers could find both gold and Christians. That would be a double blessing of God. In enumerating Henry's reasons for sending men on voyages of discovery, Azurara, his contemporary and eulogist, asserts that the Prince in all of his years of fighting the Moors "had never found a Christian king nor a lord outside this land [of Portugal] who for the love of our Lord Jesus would aid him in the said war. Therefore he sought to know if there were in those parts [beyond Cape Bojador] any Christian princes in whom the charity and love of Christ was so ingrained that they would aid him against those enemies of the faith." [3]

[3] *The Chronicle of the Discovery and Conquest of Guinea, Written by Gomes Eannes de Azurara,* trans. and ed. Charles R. Beazley and Edgar Prestage (London, Hakluyt Society, 1896), I, 28.

Even the earliest voyages, according to Azurara, had as their objective the discovery of that land in Africa called Guinea whence came the gold. Soon after the return from Ceuta "two noble esquires," members of the Prince's household, "begged him to put them in the way to perform some honorable deed." In answer to their entreaty, Henry "bade them make ready a vessel in which they were to go on a warlike enterprise against the Moors, directing them to voyage in search of the land of Guinea, which he already had purposed to discover." [4] These two adventurers were João Gonçalves Zarco and Tristão Vaz Teixeira, who, instead of reaching Guinea, discovered, in 1418, Porto Santo, one of the Madeira Islands. With them was a friend and nobleman, Bartholomew Perestrello, who carried along a pregnant rabbit that gave birth to her young on the voyage. These rabbits, released on the island, were to prove a disaster.

On their return, the adventurers reported the discovery of a goodly island worthy of being peopled. Enthusiastic over the idea, Henry fitted out a ship with supplies and colonists and sent it back to Porto Santo. Already he probably realized the island's value as a supply point for his ships, for he sent along grain, sugar cane, and malvoisie grapes, native to the island of Crete, to be planted. In time these grapes would produce the famous Madeira wine. The would-be settlers were dismayed to discover on their arrival in 1420 that the rabbits had so multiplied that they had destroyed every sprig of grain sown on Porto Santo. Luckily, Zarco saw on the horizon the dark outlines of land, the main island of Madeira, of which he took possession in the name of Prince Henry. To Madeira the settlers moved and began an occupation that encouraged Henry to think of further colonization.

To Henry's efforts and the explorations of his captains Portugal owes the possession and colonization, not only of Madeira, but eventually of the Azores and the Cape Verde Islands. Henry also wanted to annex and colonize the Canaries, but in this he was thwarted by Spain. About 1432 Gonçalo Velho Cabral discov-

[4] *Ibid.*, II, 244–5.

ered Santa Maria, a large island in the Azores, and soon thereafter embarked Portuguese colonists to settle it. A quarter of a century later, in 1457, Alvise da Cadamosto, an Italian, sailing under Henry's orders, discovered the Cape Verde Islands, and they too became a Portuguese possession. In the colonization of the Atlantic islands Henry was a modern innovator, for not since Roman times had Europeans sent out emigrants to make colonial settlements. In the words of a Portuguese historian, J. P. Oliveira Martins, this activity of Henry's was "something quite fresh, something which was an entirely new thought," and his initiative "served as a type to other nations, who later entered on the same colonial husbandry." [5]

In the meantime Henry was busily at work attempting to establish bases for trade and exploration at Sagres and Lagos, strategically located for both Mediterranean and Atlantic commerce. Azurara mentions his efforts at the end of the chapter describing the capture of Ceuta:

> And because I began this chapter with the taking of a city, I would fain end it with an account of that noble town which our prince caused them to build on Cape St. Vincent [Sagres, rather than the Cape itself], at the place where both seas meet, to wit, the great Ocean Sea and the Mediterranean Sea. But of the perfections of that town it is not possible to speak here at large because when this book was written there were only the walls standing, though of great strength, with a few houses, yet work was going on in it continually. According to the common belief, the Infant [Infante or Prince] purposed to make of it an especial mart town for merchants. And this was to the end that all ships that passed from the East to the West should be able to take their bearings and to get provisions and pilots there as at Cadiz—which last is very far from being as good a port as this, for here ships can get shelter against every wind (except one that we in this King-

[5] J. P. Oliveira Martins, *The Golden Age of Prince Henry the Navigator*, trans. James J. Abraham and William E. Reynolds (London, 1914), p. 230.

dom call the cross-wind), and in the same way they can go out with every wind, whenever the seamen willeth it. Moreover I have heard say that when this city was begun, the Genoese offered a great price for it; and they, as you know, are not men that spend their money without some certain hope of gain.[6]

Actually, whatever Henry hoped to make of the anchorage at Sagres, it was Lagos, some thirty kilometers east of Sagres, that developed into the principal commercial port of the Algarve.

By decree of the Pope, the Portuguese had the exclusive privilege of trading with and colonizing the Atlantic islands (excepting the Canaries) and the regions to be discovered on the coast of Africa. The King of Portugal conferred upon Prince Henry the right to receive the "Royal Fifth"—that is, a fifth of all products and profits from those regions. Henry also had the exclusive right of licensing traders and explorers who went thither from Portugal. Many shipmasters and merchants, members of guilds in Lagos, which became the center of trade with the islands and with Africa, sought to capitalize upon this commerce. The harbor of Lagos, formerly filled merely with fishing boats, soon was a base for trim seagoing craft, armed and ready for any fray.

Henry's exploring activities increased after the death of his father, King João I, in 1433. Someone has suggested that the old King frowned on what he considered harebrained dreams of the empire south of Cape Bojador. Henry's elder brother Duarte, who now became king, allowed the Prince a free hand. When Duarte died on September 9, 1438, leaving his six-year-old son Afonso V as heir, Henry's brother Pedro, acting as regent, urged continued exploration of the African coast. For a little more than ten years, during Pedro's regency, Henry was given every inducement to send out expeditions and to develop trade with Africa. After Afonso reached maturity, he dismissed Pedro, who rebelled and lost his life in a battle with the King's troops in

[6] *Chronicle of the Discovery* . . . *of Guinea*, I, 21.

1449. Although Pedro's death did not curtail official encouragement of Henry's activities, Afonso showed somewhat less enthusiasm for African discovery. Nevertheless Henry continued to send his caravels probing African waters, and his zeal for discovery scarcely flagged.

Long before this, in the year 1433, Henry had armed a barcha and ordered Gil Eannes, one of his squires, to try rounding Cape Bojador. Eannes, frightened by reports of four Flemish sailors who warned of boiling seas and fatal currents, went only as far as the Canaries, where he captured a few of the native Guanches and returned. The next year Henry armed another vessel and sent Eannes again toward Africa. "You cannot find a peril so great that the hope of reward will not be greater," Henry exhorted him. "You tell me only the opinions of four mariners who come from the Flanders trade or from some other ports that are very commonly sailed to, and know nothing of the needle or sailing chart. Go forth then, and heed none of their words but make your voyage straightway inasmuch as with the grace of God you cannot but gain from this journey honor and profit." [7] As Azurara observes, Henry's "admonitions, mild though they were, had much effect on the serious minded." This time, "despising all dangers," Eannes doubled the Cape "and found the lands quite contrary to what he, like others, had expected."

The importance of Gil Eannes' voyage was that once and for all it dispelled the tales of the terrors beyond the Cape. Although he put a boat ashore, he found no evidence of human habitation. But he did bring back a few herbs already known to the Portuguese as "Roses of St. Mary," which Henry and Eannes regarded as a pious and good omen.

Henry hardly gave Eannes time to recover from this voyage before he sent him, with Afonso Gonçalves Baldaya in a second ship, to continue the exploration. Landing fifty leagues beyond Cape Bojador, they found tracks of men and of camels.

Once more Henry ordered Baldaya back to Africa, this time with two horses aboard. Riders were to penetrate the interior

[7] *Ibid.*, I, 33.

and capture, if possible, a native who could tell them about the country. Some 120 leagues beyond Cape Bojador, Baldaya landed the horses and two seventeen-year-old boys as riders, equipped with swords and lances. Seven leagues from shore the boys came upon nineteen natives armed with assagais, the javelins characteristic of many African tribes. Although they attacked the group boldly, the natives retreated behind a point of rocks and the boys had to return to the ship without a captive. One youth received a javelin wound in his foot.

Baldaya improved his opportunity by slaughtering a great lot of seals, called "sea-wolves," that he found on a bank near the shore, and loading his ship with their skins. He had not obtained much information about the country except that it was sandy and rocky and inhabited, so far as he could tell, only by a few poverty-stricken nomads. Farther down the coast he found some fishing nets made of tree-bark thread and took them aboard. "And so Afonso Gonçalves turned back to Portugal," says Azurara, "without any certain knowledge as to whether those men were Moors or Gentiles, or as to what life or manner of living they had. And this was in the year of Jesus Christ 1436." [8]

Not all of the Portuguese were enthusiastic about Prince Henry's explorations, which at this point had been barren of profit and had discovered no heathen craving salvation. Some of his contemporaries murmured that the voyages were a useless expense, though, to be sure, the Order of Christ had paid the bills.

The year after Baldaya returned from his fruitless expedition to Africa, Henry's zeal found expression in a more active campaign. Early in 1436 Pope Eugenius IV proclaimed a crusade against the Moslems. This call coincided with a scheme of Prince Henry's to enlarge the realm of Portugal by seizing lands in the Moroccan Kingdom of Fez; perhaps the Portuguese might make all Morocco theirs. Furthermore, Fernando, Henry's younger brother who had not been old enough to win glory in the capture of Ceuta, now wanted to display his prowess against the infidel. Henry had been disappointed in Ceuta's profits to Portu-

[8] *Ibid.*, I, 38.

22

gal. Instead of becoming a great center of the Eastern trade, Ceuta had seen its commerce wilt after the Portuguese capture. No longer did caravans bring goods and gold across the desert to Ceuta; other cities on the North African coast absorbed the trans-Saharan trade. The occupation of Ceuta showed an annual loss that might be relieved by the seizure of adjacent territory. Since the logical objective was Tangier, grudgingly King Duarte gave permission for an attack.

Unlike the campaign against Ceuta twenty-two years before, this crusade went out ill-prepared and undermanned. When the fleet sailed from Lisbon on August 23, 1437, Prince Henry and Prince Fernando commanded only 6,000 men of the 14,000 that they needed. Even some of the transports that bore them had to be hired for the occasion. The Portuguese had not rallied to the cry of a holy war, and they showed no enthusiasm for this expedition. Their misgivings were well founded. The affair proved an unrelieved disaster.

The Portuguese laid siege to Tangier on Friday, September 13, an ill-omened day. The Moors inside the city walls showed no sign of panic; indeed, they had reason to be cheerful, for reinforcements began to arrive from the desert and presently the besiegers found themselves besieged, virtually cut off from retreat to the sea, pressed by the gathering hordes against the walls of Tangier. When the Portuguese had consumed all their food and were so desperate for water that they sucked damp mud when they could find it, they at last agreed to surrender. By October 17 the terms of capitulation were signed and the tattered remnants of the Portuguese army took to their ships. Prince Henry agreed to free all Moorish captives in Portuguese hands, to avoid attacking North Africa for a hundred years, and to surrender Ceuta. No terms could have been more humiliating. As hostages pending the evacuation of Ceuta, Henry left in the hands of the Moors his brother Fernando and several of his companions.

Despite their terms of surrender, the Portuguese showed no inclination to turn Ceuta back to the Moors. Although Fernando might suffer in his prison cell, the royal family back in Lisbon

23

did not or could not procure his release. Plans for ransom or rescue by military coup failed. Finally, in July 1443, news reached Lisbon of his death and the people proclaimed him a martyr. But Ceuta remained in the possession of Portugal. Promises given infidels need not be kept.

For a few years after the disaster at Tangier, Henry's captains accomplished little. Although they made voyages to the African coast, they obtained nothing more than sealskins and seal oil. Then in 1441, Antão Gonçalves, after loading a cargo of skins and oil, determined to find something better. With nine men, he went ashore and succeeded in taking a camel driver and a black slave woman belonging to a group of desert nomads who managed to evade capture. Before Gonçalves left his anchorage, another of Henry's captains, Nuno Tristão, turned up. With him he brought an Arab interpreter in the hope of communicating with the inhabitants ashore. Tristão was determined to return with a cargo of slaves. By this time, evidently, Prince Henry had decided that human beings—if heathen—might be a profitable commodity.

Going ashore, the Portuguese discovered two encampments and succeeded in capturing ten men, women, and boys, one being a man of some rank who understood Arabic. These people were Azanaghi or Sanhaja (whom Azurara calls Azenegues), a Berber folk, described by the Portuguese as "tawny Moors" to distinguish them from Negroes or "black Moors." The Arab interpreter, whom the Portuguese sent ashore with one of the captive women, was taken prisoner by a horde of Berbers who returned the next day and attempted to ambush the voyagers. Dividing their captives, the two captains set sail, Gonçalves to Lagos and Tristão to make a further investigation down the African coast as far as Cabo Branco, the present Cap Blanc at the northwest tip of Mauretania. At that point, unable to take any more slaves, he too turned back to Lagos.

At last Henry's exploring ships had brought back something that promised to compensate the Order of Christ for all the money spent on previous expeditions. Henry was overjoyed. "I

24

cannot behold the arrival of these ships, with the novelty of the gain of those slaves before the face of our Prince, without finding some delight in the same," Azurara remarks. And he hastens to add that Henry's pleasure was acute because he had become the instrument of salvation for these heathen:

> But thy [Prince Henry's] joy was solely from that one holy purpose of thine to seek salvation for the lost souls of the heathen. . . . And in the light of this it seemed to thee, when thou sawest those captives brought into thy presence, that the expense and trouble thou hadst undergone was nothing, such was thy pleasure in beholding them. And yet the greater benefit was theirs, for though their bodies were now brought into some subjection, that was a small matter in comparison of their souls, which would now possess true freedom for evermore.[9]

In this fashion did the Portuguese justify the beginning of the African slave trade, and this rationalization would persist through the centuries. That Prince Henry sincerely believed that slavery was a small price to pay for salvation we need not doubt. The fifteenth century put a greater premium on salvation than we can readily comprehend. A century and more later, sincere Christians also burned one another at the stake because of disagreements about dogma which imperiled their salvation. The price of salvation might come high in terms of personal suffering; hence Henry and his generation had no qualms about enslaving heathen if thereby they could offer them the hope of heaven. If the heathen had any preferences in the matter, that could be forgotten. The Devil had many wiles to retain his own.

So exhilarated was Henry by the arrival of this small cargo of slaves that he at once dispatched a messenger to the Pope, none other than the Chief Commander of the Order of Christ, Antão Lopes d'Azevedo, to ask for financial support in further voyages to Africa and for indulgences for the participants in these ven-

[9] *Ibid.*, I, 50–51.

tures. In a letter of reply Pope Eugenius IV offered such voyagers "complete forgiveness of all their sins of which they shall be truly penitent at heart and have made confession by their mouth." But the Pope promised not a single ducat toward the expense of the holy enterprise. Salvation, he too believed, would be sufficient reward for the Portuguese navigators and slavers.

Nevertheless, from this time forward, Portuguese activity on the African coast increased rapidly. If not all the captains who went out from Lagos and Lisbon were inspired by the thought that they were serving on a mission of God, they at least knew now that material profit was in sight.

The Moorish chief whom Gonçalves had captured explained that he could be ransomed in Africa for at least ten Negroes, and that two boys in the company were also worth several Negro slaves in exchange. Acting on this hint, Gonçalves took his Berber captives back where they had been taken, on the Rio do Ouro, the name given the estuary in the false belief that it was the fabled "river of gold." The chief promised that he would return with ten blacks, but once he was ashore the Portuguese never saw him again, although a party of Berbers did come to the beach to ransom the two boys for ten blacks, male and female. Gonçalves also obtained a little gold dust, an oxhide shield, and some ostrich eggs, which he proudly took back to the Prince, who had them served up on his table "as fresh and as good as though they had been the eggs of any other domestic fowls." [10]

The little bag of gold dust was as exciting as the first slaves had been. At last, Henry believed, his adventurers were on the trail of the African mines that had provided gold for civilized man since the days of King Solomon.

In the year 1443 Nuno Tristão pushed farther down the African coast in the hope of finding slaves and gold. About twenty-five leagues beyond Cap Blanc he entered a bay containing several small islands. The largest of these is now named Arguin. There he observed numerous natives in canoes and managed to capture as many as he could cram into his caravel. Returning to

[10] *Ibid.*, I, 57.

Lagos "more merrily than at the first" because he did not have to divide his spoils with a fellow captain, Tristão received Henry's praise and convinced the prince that Arguin would make a good base for further slaving expeditions. As yet the Portuguese voyagers had not passed beyond the desert lands, the country of the "tawny Moors." The captives they had taken were dark-skinned, but they were Arabs or Berbers. The "land of the Negroes" the Portuguese had heard about but had not yet found. Nor had they found the "river of gold" despite the name they had given the inlet to the north.

But no longer was Prince Henry criticized for the expense and folly of his explorations. People called him "another Alexander," and Azurara observes that "their covetousness now began to wax greater. And as they saw the houses of others full to overflowing of male and female slaves, and their property increasing, they thought about the whole matter and began to talk among themselves." [11] This talk led to mounting enthusiasm for voyaging to Africa, and adventurers begged the Prince for a license to explore—and to capture slaves.

One of the most daring of these was a member of the Prince's household known to history simply by the name of Lançarote [Lancelot], a name he took from the chivalric romances of King Arthur, then popular in Portugal as in Spain. Lançarote, desiring to do some deed of honor and to make a profit, fitted out six armed caravels and obtained the Prince's license. In fact, Henry was so pleased that he "commanded his banners to be made with the Cross of the Order of Christ, one of which each caravel was to hoist." With Lançarote as chief captain and the other caravels commanded by some of Henry's most competent mariners, the expedition sailed in 1444 and returned from Arguin with a cargo of 235 Moorish captives. Pleased at Lançarote's enterprise, Henry made him a knight.

Slave-raiding was now a business of importance. But though captive families were sometimes scattered, the father remaining in bondage at Lagos and the mother being sold to a merchant of

[11] *Ibid.,* I, 61.

27

Lisbon, Azurara maintains that the Portuguese treated their slaves with humanity. "Suffice it that I never saw one of these slaves put in irons like other captives and scarcely anyone who did not turn Christian and was not very gently treated. . . . And so their lot was now quite the contrary of what it had been, since before they had lived in perdition of soul and body." [12] According to the chronicler, some slaves were even adopted into Portuguese families and others married Portuguese peasants.

The number of slaves who could be absorbed into the economy of Portugal was limited. The day when masses of slaves could be employed in the sugar-cane fields of Brazil still lay years in the future. As yet Prince Henry's captains had captured principally tawny Moors on the Sahara coast. They had still to find the well-watered land of Guinea, the land of the Negroes, and the mines of gold. Prince Henry would not rest until his captains brought back word of that distant region.

[12] *Ibid.*, I, 84.

The Gold and the
Wonders of Guinea

THE FIRST PORTUGUESE BASE IN WEST AFRICA, THE FORT
erected by Prince Henry on the island of Arguin in 1448,
was the beginning of Portuguese colonial expansion and of the
penetration of the Dark Continent. The base was a magnet that
drew merchants and ship captains in increasing numbers. Although slave-raiding continued to be a preoccupation of the Portuguese mariners, other forms of commerce developed at Arguin.
Curiously, considering Portuguese ruthlessness in taking captives
on the Sahara coast, a trickle of trade with the nomads of the
mainland gradually increased. Arab merchants brought gold dust
and black slaves from the regions to the south, which they exchanged for woolen cloth, cloaks, wheat, and other commodities
from Europe. Instead of capturing Moors on this coast, the Portuguese soon found it more profitable to encourage the nomads
and Arab merchants to bring in blacks from the Sudan. Furthermore, precious gold was at last beginning to appear in appreci-
able amounts. Even before the erection of the fort at Arguin, a
Portuguese adventurer, João Fernandes, in 1445 had contrived

to spend seven months with the nomads on the mainland, learning their language and prying into the secrets of their caravan trade. Arguin became a point as hard for the Portuguese to pass as Cape Bojador once had been, but profit, not fear, now was the reason.

Although Prince Henry had the monopoly of this trade and no merchant or mariner could voyage to the coast of Africa or the Atlantic islands without his license, he was not content with the prosperity that African commerce was already bringing to Portugal. He still yearned for greater things, for the knowledge of what lay beyond the utmost reaches of the African coast. For João Fernandes had heard wondrous tales of the riches of Africa, of a land to the south where gold was as common as gravel in the Mondego River at Coimbra, where unicorns and even stranger beasts roamed the forests, where African kings ruled with swarms of slaves to attend them, where perhaps Prester John had his domain. Tales of Africa's wealth and wonders had already become a part of the folklore of the Mediterranean region. The stories that João Fernandes picked up from the nomads of the Sahara merely confirmed what the Portuguese had already heard and wanted to believe. They were certain that some of these wonders would be found in Guinea, a land somewhere farther south than they had sailed. To exploit Guinea, the land of the blacks and of gold, now became an obsession.

To the Portuguese, Guinea was a mysterious land inhabited by strange black people. They did not know its boundaries, but were agreed that it began at the mouth of the Senegal River and stretched an indeterminate distance to the south and to the east, how far no man knew. The name may derive from that of a town in what is now Mali, Jenné [or Djenné], then a thriving center of trade between desert folk and Negroes of the upper Niger River.

Through the long centuries caravans had crossed the Sahara to trade with people who lived beyond the desert. For more than a thousand years three commodities had kept that trade alive: salt, gold, and black slaves. So great was the lack of salt in the Sudan (the name given by the Arabs to the fertile region between the desert and the tropical forests, stretching across the whole of Africa) that this commodity was literally worth its weight in gold in certain areas. Black slaves had also remained in demand for untold centuries. Phoenicians, Romans, Egyptians, and Arabs had possessed slaves brought by traders from Central Africa. The traffic in human souls was the lifeblood of commerce for many transitory African kingdoms in what is now Mali, Upper Volta, and Niger. The rulers of these kingdoms engaged in constant warfare with more primitive tribes in the interior in their insatiable greed for prisoners whom they could sell to the caravans from the north. By comparison with the Arabs and their predecessors, the Portuguese traffic in slaves was trivial and of small account. According to Azurara's chronicle, the total number of slaves captured by Prince Henry's captains up to 1448 amounted to only 927, "of whom . . . the greater part were turned into the true path of salvation." [1]

Slavery has been practiced by most peoples, of whatever color, race, or creed, since the beginning of time. Only within the past two centuries has man been troubled in his conscience by keeping fellow creatures in bondage. It is true that occasionally in an earlier age Christians sometimes objected to enslaving other Christians, but quibbles like this did not prevent the Most Christian King of France from sending captured English prisoners to row for the rest of their lives in his galleys, nor did such scruples bother the Venetians who needed galley slaves of any faith to maintain their commerce. Nevertheless, Christians were more comfortable if they could enslave heathen who could work out their salvation to the profit of their masters. No doubt African kings felt equally virtuous when they enslaved cannibals from the Congo and sold them to the Arabs. At any rate, the slave trade was one of the oldest elements in African commerce. It remained for modern man to define this traffic as an iniquity.

[1] *The Chronicle of the Discovery and Conquest of Guinea, Written by Gomes Eannes de Azurara*, trans. and ed. Charles R. Beazley and Edgar Prestage (London, Hakluyt Society, 1896), II, 288.

From the Arabs and others had come tales of the wealth of African countries beyond the desert. Some of these stories had passed into legend and had grown with the telling. For example, the Arab geographer Edrisi told about one minor potentate who had so much gold that he tethered his horse to a nugget weighing thirty pounds. The size of this nugget increased with generations of story-telling until some Egyptian merchants in the fourteenth century described it as weighing a ton.[2] Such tales passed from trader to trader until merchants and seafarers even in the fishing ports of Scandinavia had heard about the fabulous gold of Guinea.

Another African potentate, Mansa Musa, who ruled the Mandingos in Mali in the first quarter of the fourteenth century, left a heritage of legends that excited Europe for the next two centuries. In his capital at Niani (sometimes called simply Mali), surrounded by a vast horde of slaves, retainers, and concubines, he lived in splendor. An ardent Moslem, Mansa Musa set out in 1324 on a pilgrimage to Mecca with the intention of showing the world of Islam the grandeur of a prince of Mali. Since he had control of rich goldfields, he planned a display of wealth such as no caravan bound for Mecca had ever shown. Setting out from Niani on horseback, he traveled by easy stages via Cairo, showering his largesse as he went. Five hundred slaves, each bearing a staff of pure gold weighing more than five pounds, preceded the monarch. More than eighty camels weighed down with gold brought up the rear. So lavish was the King's distribution of gold as he went through Egypt that it caused an inflation from which, an observer noted twelve years later, the country had not yet recovered.[3]

Mansa Musa's fame spread rapidly throughout the Mediterranean world and endured for many generations. Though he died in 1332, approximately a century before Prince Henry's captains began the exploitation of Africa, stories of this monarch stimulated the search for a coastal contact with his kingdom. The fact

[2] E. W. Bovill, *The Golden Trade of the Moors* (London, 1958), p. 81.
[3] *Ibid.*, p. 88.

32

that he was a devout Moslem did not prevent legend from equating him with Prester John, the mythical Christian ruler. Mapmakers kept his memory alive. A Majorcan cartographer, Angelino Dulcert, in 1339 designed a mappa-mundi which showed, in the center of the Sahara, a king labeled "Rex Melly" seated on a throne. Later world maps continued to portray the King of Mali in the middle of Africa. The Catalan Atlas of Charles V, drawn by another Majorcan, Abraham Cresques, also had a picture of Mansa Musa, scepter in one hand and a gold nugget in the other, with an inscription reading: "The Negro lord is called Musa Mali, Lord of the Negroes of Guinea. So abundant is the gold which is found in his country that he is the richest and most noble king in all the land." [4] As late as 1516, on a map made by Martin Waldseemüller, the man who first called the New World America, Mansa Musa still appeared in royal glory.

The persistent fame of Mansa Musa owed something to the monarch's own sense of publicity. At Mecca he encountered an Andalusian poet, one Es-Saheli, whom he added to his retinue and made a sort of laureate of his reign. He also persuaded the poet to double as an architect when he returned to Mali. While the King was away, one of his generals captured the town of Gao, an important center of trade, which Mansa Musa ordered the poet to refurbish. He also began rebuilding Timbuktu, to which he invited Moslem scholars in an effort to make it a seat of Islamic learning. Since caravans had long been accustomed to come across the desert to Timbuktu and Gao, these traders carried back news of Mansa Musa's innovations and the wealth of his domain, stories that grew ever more exaggerated with the telling.

Diplomatic missions from North African countries also brought back news of the western Sudan. An important Arab reporter was Ibn Battuta, sent by the King of Morocco in 1352 to visit Mali and other regions to the south. When he finally reached the court of Sulayman, a brother and successor of Mansa Musa, at Niani on the upper reaches of the Niger River, he was

[4] *Ibid.*, p. 91.

astonished at the ritual required of the King's subjects seeking an audience. Before presenting themselves to the view of the monarch, they had first to dress themselves in rags; then they had to prostrate themselves and throw dust on their heads as a sign of their humility. Ibn Battuta was impressed, however, with the king's sense of justice and the strictness with which he enforced the laws. One could travel in his domain with complete security. "Neither traveler nor inhabitant in it has anything to fear from robbers or men of violence," the Arab reported.[5]

Not everything, however, pleased Ibn Battuta. The habit of women and girls of going about stark naked, he regarded as indecorous. Nor did he altogether approve of the extent to which the monarch's hospitality extended when welcoming his more primitive subjects. Some cannibals having arrived from the gold fields, Sulayman "gave them as his hospitality-gift a servant, a young Negress. They killed her and ate her, and, having smeared their faces and hands with her blood, they came to the sultan to thank him. I was informed that this is their regular custom whenever they visit his court." [6] Ibn Battuta eventually returned to Fez in Morocco, traveling with a caravan taking back 600 women slaves.

Accounts such as those of Ibn Battuta filtered into the Mediterranean consciousness and kept alive an interest in the mysteries of Africa beyond the Sahara. In 1413, two years before the Portuguese capture of Ceuta, Europeans were astonished and titillated by the arrival in Marseilles of one Anselm d'Isalguier, a native of Toulouse, with a story of having spent years in Gao, then repossessed by the Songhai tribe from whom Mansa Musa's Mandigos had earlier taken it. Accompanying the Frenchman were his wife, described as a "princess," his mulatto daughter, three slave women, and three eunuchs. More than that, he had a stock of gold and jewels reported to be his wife's dowry. At any rate, they all settled down in Toulouse, but not without publicity—particularly after one of the eunuchs set up as a doc-

[5] *Ibid.*, p. 97.
[6] *Ibid.*, pp. 96–97.

tor of physic and acquired the Dauphin of France as a patient.[7]

The story of the citizen of Toulouse and his wealthy Negro wife from Gao further stirred an interest in the gold of Guinea. Thus, by the time of Prince Henry's explorations Europeans were deeply concerned about this African wealth that remained so elusive. Efforts redoubled to find the source of the gold. When Henry's brother Pedro was on his travels, he heard of the wealth of Guinea and became a staunch supporter of the explorations by sea.

The Portuguese zeal for discovery, whetted by the profit from the slaves already brought back from the Sahara coast, led in 1447 to the organization in Lagos of a syndicate to make a renewed effort to exploit the slave trade and perhaps reach Guinea. Dinis Dias and others had already passed the Senegal River, rounded Cape Verde, and brought back reports of the coastline. The head of the Lagos syndicate was Lançarote, who three years before had led a successful slaving raid of six caravels to Arguin and brought back 235 captives. This time Lançarote assembled a veritable armada of fourteen caravels of Lagos, to be joined by twelve others from Lisbon and Madeira. The richest and noblest men of the Algarve joined in the enterprise. Lançarote himself was an aristocrat, wealthy already and highly respected. So was his father-in-law, Sueiro da Costa, Mayor of Lagos, a grandee who had fought in the Battle of Agincourt and in many other campaigns. A member of the syndicate, he commanded one of the caravels. The other captains were men of experience, some of them also of aristocratic background. The flotilla could not have gone out under more respectable auspices. The quality of the membership in this syndicate indicates the high hopes they had of profit and honor from the enterprise.

The certainty of capturing Moors on the islands in the Bay of Arguin led the fleet to stop there to raid both islands and mainland. But afterward six of the caravels, including Lançarote's, set sail for Guinea, because the prince had so commanded him. The others, with their cargoes of slaves, returned to Lagos and Lis-

[7] *Ibid.*, pp. 115–116.

bon. At length Lançarote and his companions reached a point of land where stood two palms, mentioned by Dinis Dias as a landmark between the country of the tawny Moors and the land of Negroes. From the shore came the sweet scent of flowers or fruit, "so delicious that . . . it seemed to them that they stood in some gracious fruit garden ordained for the sole end of their delight," Azurara reported, and then added: "Now the people of this green land are wholly black, and hence this is called Land of the Negroes or Land of Guinea. Wherefore also the men and women thereof are called 'Guineas,' as if one were to say 'Black Men.' " [8]

The voyagers presently observed that they were sailing in a vast stream of fresh water and concluded that they had come upon one of the branches of the Nile, which, according to the highly confused geography of the Middle Ages, wandered mysteriously around Africa. Actually they had reached the mouth of the Senegal River. Spying a hut onshore, a party landed and brought back a Negro boy and his eight-year-old sister, the only captives the explorers made in Guinea on this trip, for the blacks were too numerous and well armed with spears for the Portuguese to risk a landing.

The two children were taken to Prince Henry. The boy was "taught to read and write, with all other knowledge that a Christian should have; and many Christians there be who have not this knowledge as perfectly as he had, for he was taught the prayer of Paternoster, and the Ave Maria, and the Articles of Faith, and the precepts of the Law [of God], and the various works of mercy, and many other things." Henry planned to train him for the priesthood and send him back to Guinea as a missionary. "But I believe," adds Azurara, "that afterwards he died without ever reaching man's estate." [9] The burden of pious learning was too great for the little boy from Guinea. Salvation for his people would have to wait for a stronger vessel of the Lord.

Although Lançarote's group had been unable to capture black

[8] *Chronicle of the Discovery . . . of Guinea*, II, 177.
[9] *Ibid.*, p. 179.

slaves in Guinea, they did not go home empty-handed. On the return they once more raided the region around Arguin and took enough Moors to pay for their voyage. But before they reached Arguin, they landed on an island opposite Cape Verde and found the coat-of-arms of Prince Henry carved upon trees, evidence of a landing made by Dinis Dias.

Although Lançarote brought back neither gold nor a profitable cargo of slaves from Guinea, his reports of "that green land" whetted the appetites of the merchants of Lagos and stirred Prince Henry to promote other voyages. Moreover, it was obvious that the time had come to establish a base for trade and further exploration of Guinea. That resolution led in 1448 to the fortification at Arguin and the eventual elimination of slave-raiding on the Sahara coast in the interest of peaceful commerce. About 1448 Azurara ended his chronicle in praise of Prince Henry's activities, but Henry's own interest did not flag, and some of the more important discoveries came after the close of Azurara's narrative.

Fortunately for our knowledge of Henry's later African achievements, he had as one of his adventurers a highly literate Italian, one Alvise da Cadamosto, merchant of Venice, who, with his brother, arrived at Sagres in August 1454. A query as to whether he could obtain permission to engage in the African trade aroused Henry's interest. Apparently Henry was convinced that Venetians, with their ancient experience in the commerce of the East, would be knowledgeable about exotic products, for he sent his secretary to show Cadamosto sugar, a rosin called "dragon's blood" from Madeira, and other commodities obtained abroad. Anyone going to Africa, the secretary explained, could expect great gain, for, says Cadamosto, "he [the Prince] believed that in these parts they would find spices and other valuable products, and [he] knew that the Venetians were more skilled in these affairs than any other nation." [10] For this

[10] *The Voyages of Cadamosto and Other Documents on Western Africa in the Second Half of the Fifteenth Century*, trans. and ed. G. R. Crone (London, Hakluyt Society, 1937), p. 5.

reason Henry was eager to grant permission to any of that nation to explore Africa.

His faith in Cadamosto was well founded, for the Venetian made valuable observations, appraised commercial prospects shrewdly, and wrote a narrative that still can be read with interest. On his first voyage, in a caravel armed and fitted out by Prince Henry with Vicente Dias as captain, Cadamosto traveled as far as the Senegal and Gambia rivers.

On the way down the African coast Cadamosto stopped at Arguin, and he describes the improved state of trade since the Portuguese had quit raiding the region for slaves. The nomads, he reports, now came to the coast with merchandise from the interior, even from the land of the Negroes to the south. Their principal commodities were black slaves, malaguetta pepper, and gold dust, which they exchanged for silver trinkets, food grain, and cloth of various kinds, including silk and woolens. Cadamosto learned that horses were in great request among the tropical people whose chiefs increased their prestige by riding. Since horses died quickly in the heat and did not breed well, they brought a large price; indeed, one horse could be exchanged for nine to fourteen black slaves, depending upon the condition and spirit of the horse. Acting on this knowledge, Cadamosto bought a few Barbary horses at Arguin and loaded them on his caravel.

More fully than any previous explorer of the African coast, Cadamosto gives concrete details about African life and the trade of the interior, information that he diligently sought for Prince Henry and carefully set down in his journal. For example, in an effort to discover the source of Guinea's gold, he learned about the mysterious "silent trade" of salt for gold somewhere in the swamp region of the middle Niger River.

Then, as now, the Taureg (the veiled Berbers of the desert) loaded camels with great blocks of salt at Taghaza in the middle of the Sahara, a place so hot only black slaves could survive in the salt pits. From Taghaza they plodded across the burning sands until they reached Timbuktu, a journey that Cadamosto says took some forty days by horseback, though modern caravans make better time. From Timbuktu the nomads continued their journey to southeastern Mali, a distance of another thirty days by horseback. There the caravans exchanged their salt cakes for black slaves or gold, and local merchants broke up the salt into smaller chunks and sent carriers into the interior, each bearing a load of salt on his head. When they arrived at a region of "certain waters," probably on the upper Niger, each trader deposited his rock salt on the ground in rows, retired a half-day's journey, and waited. The customers came out of the forest, left a quantity of gold beside each pile of salt, and then vanished. The next day the traders came back, and if they deemed the gold sufficient, they took it and departed; if not, they retired and waited for the gold to be augmented. Thus the trade was carried on by people who never saw one another, either out of fear or tradition.

So great was the need of salt in the hot African climate that the natives would pay any price to get it. As modern workers in intense heat take salt tablets, so the Africans from experience had learned its therapeutic value. Cadamosto explains that otherwise the heat would cause "the blood to putrefy, so that were it not for this salt, they would die. The remedy they employ is as follows: they take a small piece of the salt, mix it in a jar with a little water, and drink it every day. They say this saves them." [11]

Cadamosto's information about the exchange of salt for gold resulted from his effort to find out the location of mysterious "Wangara," the region in Guinea from which the gold came. Although the Italian diligently sought to learn about Wangara, neither he nor any of his contemporaries ever discovered these goldfields; indeed, not until modern times was Wangara identified as the Bambuk and Bure districts "bounded on the north by the Senegal, on the west by the Faleme, on the east by the Niger, and on the south by the Tinkisso" rivers[12] in what is now western Mali and northern Guinea. Some gold also came from the Lobi district on the Black Volta River in Upper Volta. Though these

[11] *Ibid.*, pp. 21–22.
[12] *Ibid.*, pp. xv–xvi.

alluvial goldfields were very productive and the metal was plentiful, the Portuguese had to content themselves with acquiring it through middlemen; search as they might, the secret source eluded them. Nevertheless, they managed in time to develop a remunerative gold trade and to divert much of the flow of gold from the old caravan routes to North Africa.

The first of the native kingdoms to be reached in Senegal, Cadamosto reported, was governed by a ruler who supported himself "by raids, which result in many slaves from his own as well as neighboring countries. He employs these slaves in cultivating the land allotted to him; but he also sells many to the Azanaghi [and Arab] merchants in return for horses and other goods, and also to Christians, since they have begun to trade with these blacks." [13] Thus in a few words the Italian described the characteristic commerce in slaves carried on since early times between local African chiefs and traders willing to transport them great distances across the Sahara Desert to North African markets. With the arrival of Christians on the scene, the unholy traffic would increase.

Although a keen trader, Cadamosto did not confine his interest exclusively to the commercial potentialities of the countries that he visited, for he showed a greater curiosity than any previous explorer sent out by Prince Henry. For example, accepting the hospitality of a ruler named Budomel, whose domain he reached fifty miles below the Senegal River, Cadamosto left his caravel anchored offshore and went some 250 miles inland, where he spent twenty-eight days observing the country and the customs of the people. The Italian's visit was not entirely to satisfy mere curiosity, however, for he hoped to learn about the gold mines. Furthermore, Budomel had promised "to reward him richly" and to give 100 slaves in exchange for the horses that Cadamosto had brought. As a token, before his departure, the chief gave him "a handsome young Negress, twelve years of age . . . for the service of my chamber," whom Cadamosto sent on to the ship.[14] There would be plenty more like her in the chief's villages.

[13] *Ibid.*, p. 30.
[14] *Ibid.*, p. 36.

The Italian's detailed report of this petty kingdom is one of the earliest descriptions of African life by a European. Everything was of interest to him, and he made careful notes of the characteristics of African life that impressed him, of the nature of the country, and of the strange animals that he saw.

Budomel was only one of many rulers of small kingdoms in the vast region of Africa where Cadamosto found himself, but he was typical of such chiefs, and his realm was like others in the locality, a country where the villages consisted of collections of grass huts placed under trees for shade. Budomel himself had no fixed dwelling, but moved from village to village, where he had innumerable wives. In the village that Cadamosto first reached, "Budomel had nine wives and likewise in his other dwellings, according to his will and pleasure," Cadamosto reported. "Each of these wives has five or six young Negro girls in attendance upon her, and it is as lawful for the Lord to sleep with these attendants as with his wives, to whom this does not appear an injury, for it is customary."

Such lasciviousness clearly explains the King's most earnest request of Cadamosto: "Budomel demanded of me importunately, having been given to understand that Christians knew how to do many things, whether by chance I could give him the means by which he could satisfy many women, for which he offered me a great reward." [15] Whether Cadamosto risked the reputation of Christianity by prescribing for Budomel, he does not reveal.

The deference shown an African king astonished the Italian. Though the chief might live in a grass hut, he was careful to maintain an aloofness from his ordinary subjects, "showing himself only for an hour in the morning and for a short while towards evening." He also treated his subjects with haughtiness and demanded abject submission. "Such lords as he [Budomel]," Cadamosto explains, "when granting audiences to anyone, display much ceremony." However highborn the subject might be, he "throws himself down on his knees, bows his head to the ground, and with both hands scatters sand upon his naked shoulders and head." He must not come into the presence of the King

[15] *Ibid.*, p. 38.

41

without first stripping himself "naked save for the girdle of leather they wear." After a time, continuing to scatter dirt on his head, the petitioner draws nearer but always "groveling on hands and knees." Even while relating his business, the client must keep his head bowed and continue to throw dirt on his head and shoulders. The King deliberately appears to take no notice of him, but at length "replies arrogantly in a few words. Thus by this act he shows much haughtiness and reserve. If God himself came to earth, I do not think that they could do Him greater honor and reverence." [16]

In attempting to explain the ability of these local kings to rule so autocratically, Cadamosto remarks that their subjects hold them in infinite dread "since for the most trivial misdeed, he seizes and sells their wives and children. Thus it appears to me that his power exacts obedience and fear from the people by selling their wives and children." [17] The slave trade, in this fashion, helped to keep in power petty magnates who, with a small band of armed retainers, could dominate their subjects by threatening to sell their families into bondage. As Cadamosto points out, this practice was already traditional before the arrival of the Portuguese.

Although the Arabs had long since converted Budomel and a portion of his people to nominal faith in Islam, Cadamosto regarded him as a promising candidate for Christianity. The King was impressed by the "many good and rich gifts" that the Christian God had bestowed on His people, much more than Mohammed had given his. If Cadamosto had been able to produce an aphrodisiac, Budomel undoubtedly would have craved baptism.

Shrewd merchant that he was, Cadamosto observed the products of the country and comments upon them. Although the Africans had tried to grow wheat and other grains obtained from Christians, the climate was too hot and the rainfall too uncertain. Instead, millet and beans grew in abundance, and he describes the times and methods of planting. By tapping a certain palm tree,

[16] *Ibid.*, pp. 40–41.
[17] *Ibid.*, p. 41.

they obtain a sap that makes an excellent and an intoxicating wine. This palm wine Cadamosto professed to like better than his own vintages. He also was delighted by the many fruits growing wild, and by an oil used in food, the source of which he did not discover, but it had the "scent of violets, the taste of our olive oil, and a color which tinges the food like saffron but is more attractive." [18]

Although Cadamosto heard about the animals of Budomel's country, he did not go out into the bush to see for himself. Later he would make further investigations of African fauna. But he reports huge snakes that could swallow a goat, and the ability of the Africans to charm them. From certain snakes they obtained poison for their arrows and spears. The country also abounded in lions, leopards, elephants, giraffes, and other strange beasts. Birds were numerous, and he captured and took back 150 parrots, which he sold in Portugal for half a ducat each.

Still trying to discover gold, Cadamosto visited a market, but was disappointed at the poverty of the people. The wares consisted of small quantities of cotton, cotton thread, coarse cotton cloth, vegetables, oil, millet, palm-leaf mats, weapons, wooden bowls, and other simple utensils. All of the trade was by barter, for they had no money and only a very little gold. "To this market I went," he reports, "to see further strange sights, and also to find out whether any came thither with gold for sale, but altogether, as I have said, there was little to be found." Surely few merchants ever went out with more of the spirit of the observant tourist.

At length Cadamosto ended his visit to Budomel and rejoined his caravel. With two other caravels that turned up at this time, they made their way south, staying within sight of land. Prince Henry had learned from slaves that farther south from Senegal, on the river Gambia, "there was gold in large quantities, and that the Christians who should go thither would become rich." Now Cadamosto and his fellow voyagers went in search of this goldfield.

After a time they did indeed reach the mouth of the Gambia

[18] *Ibid.*, p. 44.

43

River, but the natives met them in canoes and attacked in such force that they could not land. Although the traders parleyed with the Gambians through interpreters, explaining that they had come to buy and sell, the Africans replied that "they firmly believed that we Christians ate human flesh, and that we only bought Negroes to eat them; that for their part, they did not want our friendship on any terms but sought to slaughter us all, and to make a gift of our possessions to their lord, who, they said, was three days distant." [19]

Unable to get anywhere with the Gambians, Cadamosto and his companions had to turn back. The sailors were "pig-headed and obstinate men" who wanted to go home. Lacking their leader's curiosity, they were tired of Africa. Cadamosto might have remembered that they had been sweating it out in the caravel while he was drinking palm wine with Budomel. At any rate, bowing to necessity, Cadamosto sailed for Portugal with his 100 black slaves, his parrots, and other products of Budomel's kingdom. He had not done badly. But on a second voyage he would see more.

The next year, 1456, Cadamosto and a Genoese named Antoniotto Usodimare, who had commanded one of the three caravels on the previous trip to Gambia, fitted out two caravels and in March again sailed from Lagos for Africa with Prince Henry's license and blessing. On the way out, they touched the Cape Verde Islands, but made only a cursory exploration, as they did not want to delay.

Reaching the Gambia, they sailed boldly upstream past the point where the year before the canoes had attacked the caravels. This time they managed to entice a native aboard, load him with gifts, and obtain his help in finding a local king, one Battimansa, whose domain lay about sixty miles up the river. Through their interpreters they parleyed with Battimansa, won his friendship, and conducted a moderately profitable trade. Though Battimansa had some gold, they were disappointed in the quantity. Battimansa preferred to sell slaves, which he had in abundance.

[19] *Ibid.*, p. 60.

The traders obtained some civet—an extract from the civet cat much prized for perfume—a few civet-cat skins, and miscellaneous curiosities. An outbreak of fever in the caravels, however, hastened their departure, and they left Battimansa's country without finding the gold they sought.

Cadamosto, however, with his tourist's eye, had seen some wonders. Wild elephants had actually appeared onshore, but had returned to the forest when Cadamosto put out a boat to get a closer look. Near the mouth of the Gambia a Negro chief who wished to impress the visitors sent out a hunting party to kill an elephant to provide a feast for them. Cadamosto took some of the meat aboard ship, ate a portion, which he found tough and insipid, and had some salted down to take to Prince Henry. He also took elephant hair, an elephant foot, and a portion of the trunk to the Prince, "who received them as a handsome gift, being the first that he had had from the country discovered through his energy." [20] Cadamosto also saw hippopotamuses, which he described in some detail; and he vowed that in Gambia one could find cockatrices and divers other strange creatures.

Leaving the Gambia, the voyagers sailed farther down the coast past several rivers until they reached the Rio Grande (now the Jeba in Portuguese Guinea). At this point their interpreters could no longer understand the native tongues, and the explorers decided to sail for Portugal. They had acquired a reasonably profitable cargo on the upper Gambia; they had some information to report to Prince Henry; and at last, says Cadamosto, "God in his mercy brought us, when it pleased him, safely to port." Thus ends one of the most illuminating narratives of Prince Henry's discoveries. Gold in great quantities still eluded the explorers, but they were finding enough to make the African trade profitable so long as they could supplement gold with black slaves.

[20] *Ibid.*, p. 72.

The Legacy of Prince Henry: Passage to India

THE LAST YEARS OF PRINCE HENRY WERE FILLED WITH SATIS-
faction, for, unlike many dreamers, he lived to see the ful-
fillment of some of his visions; he was pleased that he had been
the instrument for bringing wealth to Portugal and glory to
God. It is true that his explorers had not yet found the kingdom
of Prester John, but he and his countrymen still had hopes of
reaching that mythical realm. Though the Portuguese had not
yet discovered the fabulous gold mines of Africa, they had succeeded in establishing viable contacts with African kings who
turned gold into Portuguese channels. Though they had not
come upon multitudes of people thirsting for the Christian faith,
they had encountered Africans who appeared to be hopeful subjects for conversion. And at last Henry had seen the Moslems
discomfited in North Africa.

The disastrous defeat of the Portuguese at Tangier in 1437
was a searing experience that Henry never forgot; hence, in his
old age he was still eager for revenge and readily accepted the
suggestion of his royal nephew, King Afonso V, that he lead

46

another attack on the Moors. Since the fall of Constantinople in 1453 the Pope had been exhorting all Christian princes to rally for a crusade against the Turks. In 1457 he had sent a legate to Portugal to announce a new crusade, but the Pope's crusade was directed against the Turks in eastern Europe, not against the Moors of North Africa. To the Portuguese these were the most threatening Moslems, and it was against them that Portugal directed its energy, though the Pope offered no help.

Fired with zeal for war against the infidel by the Pope's messenger, however, King Afonso collected a fleet at Lisbon in late September 1458. By early October the vessels arrived at Sagres and Prince Henry took command. The Portuguese objective was a small city near Tangier, Alcácer Ceguer (anglicized to Alcazar). Taking the Moors by surprise, Henry's troops easily captured the town and expelled the Moorish inhabitants, who, however, were allowed to take away their household goods. By fifteenth-century standards, this was benevolent treatment. Now the Portuguese had a second base in North Africa, and Henry returned to Sagres confident that eventually his country would control all the land across from the Strait of Gibraltar. Actually, in 1471, taking advantage of civil war in Morocco, the Portuguese captured Arzila, another town near Tangier, and then Tangier itself. Prince Henry did not live to see this victory. But the Portuguese never established sovereignty over North Africa, and the effort to do so led to utter disaster at the battle of Alcácer Kebir on August 5, 1578, when the Moors killed King Sebastian and annihilated his army, with the result that for more than sixty years Portugal had to accept Spanish rule. That ill day, however, was far in the future, and Prince Henry, after his victory at Alcácer Ceguer, content in his palace at Sagres, could dream of a Christian Africa.

Henry's last days were also cheered by hopeful reports from his captains about their contacts with Guinea. The year before Alcácer Ceguer, Diogo Gomes had commanded three caravels that made a successful trading voyage up the Gambia River. At a place called Cantor, some fifty leagues upstream, Gomes talked

47

with people who told him that gold in great abundance was to be found in the realm of King Bormelli, who ruled the right bank of the river. "They said further," Gomes reported, "that he was lord of all the mines, and that he had before the door of his palace a mass of gold just as it was taken from the earth, so large that twenty men could scarcely move it, and that the king always fastened his horse to it, and kept it as a curiosity." [1] This was the legend of the immense nugget, a legend that had been circulating in Europe for centuries. Gomes was convinced that at last he had a clue to the source of Africa's gold, for he himself had seen Negroes traveling the roads "loaded with gold." His informants told him that east of the Gambia was a region "full of gold mines, and that the men who went into the pits to get the gold did not live long, on account of the impure air. The gold-bearing sand was afterwards given to women to wash the gold from it." This account of the method of retrieving gold from the alluvial deposits was confirmed by other travelers.

Gomes, remembering Prince Henry's zeal to convert the heathen, came back with another report that must have pleased his master. On the Gambia he had encountered a local king whom he calls Nomymans. This ruler had previously made war on Portuguese traders and was uneasy about treating with the latest arrivals. Gomes, however, loaded him with presents and agreed to make a ceremonial visit. In an argument with the King's Moslem chaplain, Gomes so confounded the priest that Nomymans summarily dismissed him and demanded Christian baptism.

The quantity and quality of the Portuguese gifts, evidencing the favor of the Christian God, had made a revolutionary impression on the King. Clearly, he saw a benefit in this new religion. As a missionary Gomes had proved a success, though perhaps he had somewhat overdone it, as he indicated in his own words: "What I said pleased the King so much that he ordered

[1] *The Voyages of Cadamosto and Other Documents on Western Africa in the Second Half of the Fifteenth Century,* trans. and ed. G. R. Crone (London, Hakluyt Society, 1937), p. 95.

48

the Bishop [the Moslem priest] within three days to take his departure out of his kingdom, and, springing to his feet, he declared that no one, on pain of death, should dare any more to utter the name of Muhammad, for he believed in the one God only, and that there was no other God but He, in whom his brother, the Prince Henry, said that he believed." Gomes found himself in a predicament, for the King demanded instant baptism, and, however persuasive his theology had been, Gomes was not ordained to perform such a ceremony. "Calling the Infante his brother, he desired that I should baptize him, and so said all the lords of his household, and his women likewise," Gomes added. "The King himself declared that he would have no other name than Henry, but his nobles took our names, such as Jacob, Nuno, etc., as Christian names. I remained that night on shore with the King and his chiefs, but I did not dare to baptize them because I was a layman." [2] The King had to be satisfied with the promise that Prince Henry would send out a properly ordained priest to complete the conversion of His Majesty and his people. A year later Prince Henry did send two clerics to take care of the spiritual needs of Nomymans. Episodes like this convinced Henry that he might indeed be the means of saving the heathen of Africa.

Full of years, and satisfied that he had served well his country and his God, Henry, Duke of Viseu and Grand Master of the Order of Christ, died on November 13, 1460. Earlier he had provided that at his death the Order of Christ should have one twentieth of all merchandise coming from Guinea, including slaves. Although he had the sole right to the Royal Fifth of the produce of Africa and the Atlantic islands, he died in debt. His own fortune, as well as funds from the Order of Christ, had gone to fit out innumerable caravels that through the years had probed the waters of Africa. He had laid the foundation for Portuguese expansion, not only in Africa but in Asia and South America.

After Henry's death King Afonso took over the right of licensing trade with Africa and the islands. As African commerce

[2] *Ibid.*, pp. 97–98.

continued to develop, Italian as well as Portuguese captains sought licenses. A taste for European goods soon lured African natives to coastal trading stations, where "they carried on their business in peace and friendliness, without those warlike incursions, assaults, and robberies which happened at the beginning," according to João de Barros the chronicler, who himself later commanded one of the important Portuguese bases, that of São Jorge da Mina.[3]

The taste for European goods transformed the attitudes of the natives and made them amenable to the attractions of commerce. Since Europeans would take human beings in exchange for their commodities, now so much desired by the Africans, the native chiefs were more than willing to supply the demand. Nothing was cheaper than human life in the teeming jungles. Barros explains: "These people were always intractable until they grew accustomed to them [European products]. However, after they learnt something of the truth through the benefits they received, both spiritual and intellectual, and articles for their use, they became so well disposed that when ships, sailing from this kingdom, arrived at their ports, many people came from the interior to seek our goods, which they received in exchange for human beings, who were brought here more for salvation than for slavery."[4] Thus blandly, and piously, Barros tells of the expansion of the slave trade. To the African chiefs on the coast the Christian Portuguese were infinitely more beneficial than the Arab slave traders. The Christians had more and better goods than the Arabs could haul across the Sahara, and they were generous in their offers for slaves. Once the coastal chiefs perceived the benefits of the trade, they co-operated enthusiastically with the Portuguese.

Since King Afonso was too busy about affairs of state to give personal attention to Africa, he granted in 1469 a five-year concession of African trade to Fernão Gomes, a merchant of Lisbon, for 200,000 reis a year, with the understanding that Gomes

[3] *Ibid.*, p. 103.
[4] *Ibid.*, pp. 107–108.

should "discover" one hundred leagues farther down the coast each year. The King retained a monopoly of civet, malagueta pepper, and unicorn horns, though Gomes was allowed one civet cat per year. Exempted from his concession were a few sites already granted to others.

A man of great enterprise, Gomes discovered the gold traffic at a place later called Elmina but named by the Portuguese São Jorge da Mina [Saint George of the Mines]. This spot, a rocky peninsula eight miles west of the present town of Cape Coast in Ghana, became one of the most important trading posts on the West African coast. Alluvial gold was abundant in adjacent territory, and farther north on the Black Volta River were the Lobi goldfields. At São Jorge da Mina the Portuguese rapidly developed a rich trade in gold and slaves, which were also abundant. So important a post required adequate fortification, and in 1481 Diogo d'Azambuja began building a massive stone fort that took eighty years to complete. One of his officers was Bartholomeu Dias, who was later to distinguish himself by rounding Africa. To São Jorge da Mina came Christopher Columbus while he was still trying to find support for his own exploration of the Ocean Sea. Much later, in 1637, the Dutch, who had become one of the greatest slave-trading powers, captured and three years later wrung from the Portuguese the cession of the fort. Until the end of the slave trade, the Dutch made this fort one of their most important points of contact with the Ashanti. All of this, however, lay in the future.

Fernão Gomes' ingenuity in finding gold on the Ghana coast so pleased King Afonso that he "gave him a new coat-of-arms of nobility," says Barros, "a shield with crest and three heads of Negroes on a field of silver, each with golden rings in ears and nose, and a collar of gold around the neck, and 'da Mina' as a surname, in memory of its discovery." [5]

Although eager captains continued their probing of the African coast and opened the way for further trade as far as the Bight of Biafra, not until Afonso's son came to the throne in

[5] *Ibid.*, pp. 109–110.

51

1481 as King João II did exploration resume the impetus it had had under Prince Henry. King João quickly demonstrated his capacity by suppressing the powerful nobles and concentrating power in the throne. With a shrewd recognition of commercial possibilities in further exploration, he supported voyages that eventually gave Portugal a world empire. His personal interest in Africa was keen. Before his father's death he had taken over the concession of the African trade, which was rapidly increasing. Gold, ivory, pepper, and slaves poured into Portugal, which became a distributing point to the rest of Europe. The wealth of merchants in Lagos, Lisbon, and Oporto increased, and the royal coffers fattened. King João II could not have been so independent of the nobles if he had not had Guinea's gold in his treasury.

The fortification of São Jorge da Mina received the King's personal attention. When some of his council quibbled about the cost and the great distance from Portugal, he dismissed the complaints by pointing out the profitable trade already established with natives who were eager for Portuguese goods. "Thus with the bait offered by the worldly goods which would always be obtainable there," Barros quotes the King as saying, "they might receive those of the Faith through our doctrine, which was the principal aim," for, Barros continues, "the King considered that the possibility of getting even one soul to the Faith by baptism through the fortress outweighed all the inconveniences. For he said that God would take care of them, since the work was to His praise, that his subjects would win profit, and the patrimony of this kingdom would be increased." [6] King João and his contemporaries saw no conflict of interest between piety and profit; indeed, no better insurance was available than good works done for God, who would be certain to reward those who labored for the salvation of souls. King João was as convinced of his Christian mission as his great-uncle, Prince Henry, had been. And he worked at it with even greater energy and persistence.

The sincerity of the Portuguese belief in their mission to Christianize the heathen even while enslaving them is attested by Barros in citing an instance in the reign of King João III, when

[6] *Ibid.*, p. 115.

the King refused to let slaves be sold to Moslem buyers. The King was concerned because slaves passing into the hands of the infidels "lost the merit of salvation and their souls were damned eternally; accordingly as a very Christian prince, ever more mindful of the salvation of souls than of the profits of his treasury, he ordered the cessation of this trade, although he suffered great loss by this act. . . . For this work, done in His praise, God immediately rewarded the King: because he had placed the salvation of these heathen souls above the gaining of much gold in the slave market, another mine was found below the city of S. Jorge from which have flowed great quantities of gold down to the present time, much exceeding what he would have obtained by the sale of slaves." [7]

With São Jorge da Mina as a base for refitting and as a fortified place of defense, the Portuguese were now in position to extend their domination of Africa. In 1482 King João II sent out another explorer, Diogo Cão, to discover and claim land beyond the Bight of Biafra. Cão carried stone markers properly inscribed to set up on newly claimed territory. On his first voyage he reached the Congo, which the Portuguese called the Zaire, and put up a marker on the left bank before continuing to Angola, where he put up a second marker. Angola, which he claimed for King João, remains a Portuguese possession to this day, and the marker, attesting Cão's discovery, has been found and returned to the Lisbon Geographical Society.[8] On his first voyage Cão kidnapped a few Congolese and brought them to King João, who had them baptized and taught Portuguese. When Cão went back to the Congo in 1484, he returned these new Christians to their homes. So marvelous were the stories they told of the blessings of the Christian world that swarms of their countrymen came craving salvation so that they too might share in these good things. Peaceful trade was established, and King João promised to send priests to look after the spiritual welfare of the Congolese.

Profitable as was the burgeoning African trade, King João II

[7] *Ibid.*, p. 125.
[8] Charles E. Nowell, *A History of Portugal* (New York, 1952), p. 54.

53

had greater aspirations. Although from Africa came some malagueta pepper, the great source of spices lay in Asia. Other luxuries also came from Asia: silk and fine cottons, richly wrought
jewelry, precious stones, exotic confections, drugs, and perfumes. Moreover, Prester John's Christians, who might help in a
war against the Moslems, still remained undiscovered. King João,
with the energy of an efficient administrator, set out to tap this
wealth and find these Christians.

With greater resources than were available to Prince Henry,
João decided to send expeditions by both land and sea to seek
Prester John and the riches of Asia. The Portuguese had collected a considerable amount of information about the Arab
trade with the west or Malabar Coast of India by way of the Red
Sea to Alexandria and about Arab contacts with the east coast of
Africa. If Portuguese ships could get around Africa, they could
sail across the Indian Ocean to the Malabar Coast. No Portuguese navigator had yet rounded Africa, but King João and his
counselors reasoned that it must be possible.

By João's time many stories were in circulation about the
Eastern Christians who had been originally converted by the
Apostle Thomas. As for Prester John, belief was growing that he
was to be identified with the Emperor of Ethiopia. Fresh
attention had been focused on these twin problems by the ecu-
menical zeal of Pope Eugenius IV, who had sought a union between Western and Eastern Christians. In fact, in 1439 he had addressed letters to Prester John of Ethiopia and to the "Emperor
Thomas of the Indians," address undesignated, and had dispatched a mission to try to reach them.[9] As the Portuguese had
since Prince Henry's time proclaimed this search to be one of
their major objectives, King João in 1487 picked two skilled lin-
guists and sent them overland to seek out Prester John and the
Indian Christians. About the same time he ordered Bartholomeu

[9] Francis M. Rogers, *The Quest for Eastern Christians* (Minneapolis,
Minn., 1962), p. 40. Professor Rogers gives an authoritative and detailed
account of the mass of literature concerning the belief in the Eastern
Christians and in the kingdom of Prester John.

Dias to try to round Africa by sea. No longer was trade with petty kings of West Africa sufficient for the Portuguese. They were playing for the highest stakes in commercial and religious realms. More than a year before, in December of 1485, King João had sent an orator to newly elected Pope Innocent VIII boasting of the accomplishments of the Portuguese and announcing that they were about to sail around Africa and make contact with the Christians of India.

The overland messengers whom João selected were Pero da Covilhã and Afonso de Paiva, both of whom could speak Arabic and other foreign languages. Covilhã was well known and trusted by the King's own household, for he had been sent by Prince Manuel to Barbary to buy horses. So fluent was he in Arabic that he could pass for a native. João had sent a previous mission overland, but it had turned back at Jerusalem because, the members reported, without a knowledge of Arabic they could go no farther. This time King João made certain that his mission would not be handicapped by ignorance of the language.

Setting out on May 7, 1487, Covilhã and de Paiva journeyed across Europe to Naples and thence to Rhodes and Alexandria. Laying in a stock of honey, they posed as honey merchants until they both fell ill and their supplies were stolen. Able to travel again, they bought other articles of trade and made their way to Aden, where they separated. De Paiva headed for Ethiopia and Covilhã went on to India. They agreed to rendezvous on a certain date in Cairo, whence they would return together to report to King João. After thoroughly exploring the Malabar Coast, visiting among others the cities of Cannanore, Calicut, and Cochin, Covilhã turned back to Goa and went from there to Hormuz in the Persian Gulf. After some further exploration, he returned to Cairo hoping to rejoin his companion, but learned that de Paiva had died.

In Cairo Covilhã by good luck encountered two Jewish messengers, one a rabbi and the other a shoemaker, sent by King João to find him, deliver further instructions, and bring back such information as he had collected. The King's orders were that if Covilhã had found out everything he had been sent to discover, he could come home and receive a reward; if not, he was to stay and keep searching. Covilhã decided it would be better to stick to his task. By the shoemaker he sent a letter to the King saying that he had discovered ginger and pepper in Calicut but that cinnamon and cloves came from some place beyond, though all these spices could be bought at Calicut. Furthermore, he informed the King that his ships could navigate by the coast of Guinea around Africa to Sofala on the east coast and across to India. After sending this message back, Covilhã took the rabbi on a visit to Hormuz, and from there he himself went on a tour of the Moslem holy cities of Jidda, Mecca, and Medina, the first Christian of whom there is any record who took such a risk in this period. After this foray into forbidden country, Covilhã crossed by sea to the African coast and set out for the court of the Emperor of Ethiopia. A report on Prester John was one of the unfinished pieces of business that King João required to be completed before he would welcome Covilhã back to Portugal.

As it turned out, Covilhã never saw his homeland again. The Emperor of Ethiopia received him, found him useful, and never let him go. He became a respected official in the court, along with other Europeans who were also virtual prisoners. When the Portuguese finally sent a successful mission to Ethiopia, one of its members, Father Francisco Álvares, got Covilhã's story and reported that the exile was overjoyed at seeing him. The expatriate explained "how thirty-three years had passed that he had not confessed because he said in this country they do not keep the secret of confession and he only went to the church and there confessed his sins to God." [10]

Covilhã's adventures, which can be pieced together from Álvares' narrative and from other contemporary sources, rank with the most extraordinary stories of the romantic East.[11] The

[10] *The Prester John of the Indies: A True Relation of the Lands of the Prester John, Being the Narrative of the Portuguese Embassy to Ethiopia in 1520, Written by Father Francisco Álvares*, ed. C. F. Beckingham and G. W. B. Huntingford (London, Hakluyt Society, 1961), II, 369.

[11] For a good summary of Covilhã's exploits, see Henry H. Hart, *Sea Road to the Indies* (New York, 1950), pp. 43–78.

letter that Covilhã sent to King João by the Jewish shoemaker has not survived, but the probability is that either the shoemaker or the rabbi got back with messages reporting on the prospects for trade with India and with Hormuz, a bustling mart in the Persian Gulf. So great was the Portuguese eagerness to keep information from falling into the hands of potential competitors, Italian or Spanish, that maps, reports, and letters of travelers were strictly guarded. Perhaps Covilhã's messages reached the King and his close advisers. Certainly from this time forward King João never relaxed his efforts to tap the riches of the Indies.

To Bartholomeu Dias goes the credit for opening the sea route to India, but as a sixteenth-century Portuguese writer commented, like Moses he was not permitted to enter the Promised Land. Dias, already experienced as an explorer of African waters, was given command of one of the best-equipped expeditions thus far sent out from Portugal; he set sail from Lisbon in August of 1487 with the avowed purpose of reaching India by rounding Africa. To make the voyage he had two well-built caravels and a supply ship; the latter carried as much additional food and equipment as could be stored aboard. Everyone knew that the journey would be long and doubtless hazardous; it must not fail for lack of essential supplies.

The chief pilot was one Pero d'Alenquer, so famous already that the King had given him a patent to wear a special gold chain around his neck and to dress in silk. From time to time he was also called upon to dine with his royal master and to give advice on African matters. All the other officers and pilots in the expedition were men of experience and reputation.

Dias had orders to sail directly for the Congo. Unlike other expeditions, his was not to waste time trading on the African coast but was to proceed southward, setting ashore at various points two Negro men and four Negro women who were being returned to Africa loaded with gifts; they had instructions to spread the word of the Portuguese desire to trade and to induce other Africans to come to coastal points where ships would supply them goods like the gifts carried by the repatriates. These landings did not delay Dias for long.

After passing the Congo, Dias proceeded down the coast, but soon encountered weather so stormy that for thirteen days he had to run close-hauled before the wind. The temperature dropped and the sailors, shivering with cold, began to wonder whether they would ever see land again. At last Dias turned north, and on February 3, 1488, they reached a haven on the southeast coast of Africa. They had rounded the continent in the storm without knowing it. Their anchorage was in Mossel Bay. Thus for the first time a modern European had proved that a voyage around the vast bulk of Africa was possible.

From their ships Dias' men could see black herdsmen minding cattle in a rolling pastureland. An effort to attract them to the shore to trade proved fruitless. When natives attacked a party sent ashore to get water, a shot from a crossbow killed one African, the first casualty from the Portuguese in East Africa.

The expedition sailed from Mossel Bay and slowly made its way eastward along the blunt end of South Africa until they reached Algoa Bay, where Dias put up a stone marker claiming the land in the name of his sovereign. Although he wanted to continue his explorations, his men were restive and eager to turn back; Lisbon was a long way off, and even the supply ship had been left far behind. The sailors grumbled that they might well starve before they ever saw home again. But Dias pacified them with a promise that he would start the return journey after two or three more days' sailing, which brought them to the mouth of the Great Fish River. Northward and eastward stretched the Indian Ocean, the reaches of which would take the Portuguese to the Indies, but Dias was not fated to make that journey. His men would go no farther. So he hoisted sail and, with a fair wind, started home.

The return journey soon brought them in sight of a great cape, the point of land that they had missed in the storm on the way east. Legend says that Dias named the point "Tormentoso" [Stormy] but that King João later changed it to "Cape of Good Hope" because of its promise of a passage to India. Other reports say that Dias himself gave it that favorable name. In any case,

Cape of Good Hope it became.[12] Before leaving this southern tip of Africa, Dias landed and set up another marker. The Portuguese were gradually laying claim to a continent.

After finding the supply ship, which had only three surviving members of its nine-member crew, Dias took off the food and equipment needed by his two caravels and then burned the unseaworthy hulk. On the way up the coast he picked up a few slaves; at São Jorge da Mina he shipped aboard gold collected there by the King's agent; and thence he made his way to Portugal. In December of 1488 he reached Lisbon and anchored in the Tagus.

In Lisbon at this time was a visitor much concerned with marine matters, one Christopher Columbus. In two books in his possession he wrote down comments on the voyage around the Cape of Good Hope and remarked that he was present when Dias reported in detail on his voyage.

Dias had shown the way for another and more famous navigator, Vasco da Gama, to make the passage to India. He himself did not go on that voyage, for what reason no one knows. But later, in 1500, he commanded a caravel in the fleet of Pedro Álvares Cabral destined for India. Driven westward by storms, or perhaps going west by design, Cabral explored the coast of Brazil and claimed it for Portugal before continuing to India. Off the coast of Africa a hurricane swept down on his fleet and sank four vessels, one of which was Dias' caravel. Thus died the pathfinder of the African seas, one of Portugal's most intrepid navigators, whose earlier explorations and the careful data that he brought back had assured the success of later voyagers.

[12] *Ibid.*, pp. 33–42.

Portugal Rejects Columbus
and Loses a Western Empire

WHEN BARTHOLOMEU DIAS GOT BACK TO LISBON IN DECEMBER 1488 after rounding the Cape of Good Hope and pointing the way to India, Christopher Columbus was still hoping to interest King João II in financing a voyage of discovery to the west, across the great Ocean Sea. Convinced that the distance to Asia was vastly shorter than it really is, and that Japan, China, and the "Golden Chersonese" of the ancients (the Malay Peninsula) could be reached by sailing westward, Columbus had become a dedicated man, a "Man with an Idea" as Samuel Eliot Morison describes him in his brilliant study of the Discoverer.[1] To get support for his great idea, Columbus laid siege to the Portuguese monarch certainly as early as 1484. Using his best persuasions, he tried to convince João that he could reach the fabled

[1] Samuel Eliot Morison, *Admiral of the Ocean Sea: A Life of Christopher Columbus* (Boston, 1949). Since the publication of Professor Morison's great work, no one can write about Columbus without being in his debt. My own obligation in this chapter is obvious. Professor Morison's research is supplemented by common sense and a practical knowledge of seamanship, qualities not often found in a historian.

East by a voyage across the Ocean Sea. He gave a plausible account of his reasons for believing that the land of the Grand Khan (China) and the island of Cipangu (Japan), described by Marco Polo as so wealthy that the temples and palaces were roofed with solid gold, were within sailing distance west of Lisbon.

João of course was eager to tap this region of riches and was sufficiently attracted by Columbus' proposal to lay it before his newly created Junta dos Mathemáticos, a committee of experts. They solemnly analyzed the plan submitted in 1484 and rejected it. So far as we know, this was the first of the rejections received by Columbus, rejections that would have discouraged a less stubborn man. Undeterred, however, he continued to hope that he could influence the Portuguese to underwrite a western voyage of discovery.

Christopher Columbus, son of a wool-weaver of Genoa, like many of his countrymen, went to sea as a mere youth. In the spring of 1476 he was aboard a trading vessel flying the flag of Burgundy, one of a merchant fleet off Cape St. Vincent, that was attacked by French and Portuguese naval vessels. When his ship was sunk, Columbus managed to swim ashore at Lagos, where he was kindly treated, and he eventually made his way to Lisbon to join a colony of Genoese resident there. For a time he worked as a map- and chart-maker, along with his brother Bartholomew, who had come to Lisbon under less dramatic circumstances. Genoese merchants, mariners, pilots, and map-makers were so numerous in Lisbon that a few years later Portuguese competitors petitioned the King to ban them from the country.

How much experience Columbus had had at sea before his precipitate arrival at Lagos no one knows, but he had made a voyage to the Greek islands and had probably been on other voyages in the Mediterranean. The year after his arrival in Portugal he apparently shipped on a voyage to Iceland, touching at Ireland on the way. In 1478 his reputation as a merchant mariner was so high that a Genoese firm employed him to sail to Madeira to buy sugar. He also made voyages to Africa and picked up information about winds and ocean currents that later proved useful. As Morison constantly emphasizes, Columbus developed into one of the best navigators and seamen of his day.

Columbus evidently had an excellent reputation in Lisbon, where he spent eight or nine years alternating between going to sea and plying his trade as map- and chart-maker. About 1479 he married Felipa Perestrello, daughter of Bartholomew Perestrello, a prosperous Italian naturalized in Portugal. Bartholomew Perestrello was the explorer who had introduced rabbits on the Madeira island of Porto Santo with such disastrous results and later had been named by Prince Henry to the hereditary captaincy of the island. From this marriage came one son, Diego; Felipa died sometime prior to 1485. Another son, Ferdinand, by an extralegal union, became Columbus' biographer.

Like many others of his generation, Columbus was imbued with a deep sense of piety and a conviction that he ought to do something to free the Christian world from the dangers of Islam. Not merely was he obsessed with the notion of finding a way to the Indies by sailing westward, but he was eager to be the instrument of bringing salvation to the heathen and, says Bartolomé de Las Casas, "he was especially affected and devoted to the idea that God should deem him worthy of aiding somewhat in recovering the Holy Sepulchre." [2] This notion of redeeming the Holy Sepulchre from the infidels was one of the motivations driving Columbus to seek personal wealth from his discoveries, for he dreamed of devoting part of his gain to outfitting a Crusade against the Moslems. The discoveries that he intended were part of a genuinely pious plan.

To Columbus, Portugal was the obvious country to undertake the Enterprise of the Indies, for the nation had already established its priority in exploration. Since the early days of Prince Henry its captains had dared unknown seas and had shown their skill and courage as navigators and explorers. They had already proved that a harvest of heathen could be gathered in Africa and perhaps beyond, that the infidels could be thwarted, and that the

[2] Quoted by Morison, *ibid.*, pp. 45–46.

Christians of Prester John's kingdom might be reached, to join in the fight against Islam. Though King João's astronomers and mathematicians had decided against Columbus' proposal once, the Genoese clung to the hope that the King might see the light and outfit an expedition under his command.

Then Bartholomeu Dias came back from the east coast of Africa in 1488 with proof that the Dark Continent had an end and that Portuguese ships could reach India by sailing around the Cape of Good Hope. With that route assured, King João saw no reason to invest in an adventure so uncertain and speculative as Columbus' scheme. Furthermore, Columbus had made stiff terms. He had demanded that the King fit out three caravels and supply them with trading goods; that he make Columbus a knight, with the hereditary right of his descendants to inherit the title; that he name Columbus Admiral of the Ocean Sea; that he appoint Columbus viceroy and governor of all islands and mainlands discovered; that he permit him to have a tenth of the profits from these lands and allow him an eighth part of the freight space in ships trading to the regions discovered.[3] Morison accepts a hint in Ferdinand's account of his father that these demands were too stiff for King João, who in 1484 turned down Columbus' offer. Be that as it may, these are the terms that later, after much frustration, he wrung from Isabella of Castile and Ferdinand of Aragon, whose marriage had united Spain.

Before Dias' return from Africa, Columbus had decided to seek support for this enterprise in Spain. In 1485, with his little son Diego, he took ship in Lisbon and landed at the small river port of Palos, a short distance up the Río Tinto from the southwest coast of Spain. Nearby was the Franciscan monastery of La Rábida, where he found hospitality and friends, and where he left Diego in charge of the monks. One of the Franciscans was Brother Antonio de Marchena, noted for his knowledge of astronomy and his interest in navigation. He advised Columbus to seek support for his project from the Duke of Medina Sidonia (ancestor of the commander in chief of the Spanish Armada)

[3] *Ibid.*, p. 72.

and, when the Duke was not helpful, to try the Count of Medina Celi, who expressed a willingness to finance the undertaking. But Columbus had decided that it was the part of wisdom to gain royal backing. After all, a mere nobleman might equip caravels, but he could not guarantee the demands that the Genoese navigator intended to make.

Consequently, in January 1486 Columbus journeyed to Cordova in the hope of gaining an audience with the Spanish sovereigns, but they had left for Madrid. For the time being he had to console himself by winning the love of a pretty orphan girl, Beatriz Enríques de Harana, who in the summer of 1488 bore him his son Ferdinand. Though he never formally married Beatriz, in his will he enjoined his legitimate son Diego to pay her an annuity, which was dutifully done. Ferdinand proved a great asset to his father, not merely as his biographer and apologist but as an advocate at court who fought manfully to secure the rights of the legitimate descendants to the promised remunerations from the profits of Spanish exploitation of islands in the West Indies discovered by Columbus.

When the sovereigns at length returned to Cordova in April 1486, Columbus gained an audience and managed to excite the interest of Queen Isabella. But before she would give him an answer, she had to have the opinions of expert counselors. She appointed her confessor, Hernando de Talavera, to head a commission to study the proposals. The commission, which held its meetings at the University of Salamanca, listened patiently to Columbus' explanations of his conception of the map and the narrowness of the Ocean Sea but could not be convinced. The meetings dragged on, and two years passed without an answer.

Columbus had gained his notions of the nearness of Asia from reading Marco Polo and from contemplating the theories of Dr. Paolo Toscanelli, a learned Florentine physician. In 1474 a clerical friend of the physician told the King of Portugal about Toscanelli's views and obtained a letter from the Florentine enclosing a chart that showed China some 5,000 nautical miles west of Lisbon. Cipangu, or Japan, was even closer. Learning about the

Florentine's ideas, Columbus wrote to him and received a copy of his letter of 1474 and the seductive chart. It was this chart, with its foreshortened distance to China, that Queen Isabella's commission could not swallow because it contradicted all the traditional notions of geography based on Ptolemy. Asia could not be so close to Europe, and in that conclusion the commission was correct. No one dreamed, least of all Columbus, that a continent intervened.

But the commission delayed making a report, and Columbus twiddled his thumbs with such patience as he could muster. To keep soul and body together, from the royal treasury he received a small allowance—about the pay of an able-bodied seaman, Morison estimates—but even this was cut off in June 1488. In the autumn, with no answer in sight, Columbus returned to Lisbon with the hope that King João might yet be induced to put an exploring expedition under his command. Dias' return in December ended that hope, and sometime in 1489 Columbus wearily turned his face again to Spain.

For nearly two more years he had to wait for the Talavera commission to report and then got an unfavorable answer. Late in 1490 the learned committee announced that Columbus' plan was not a proper object for royal support; and, among the reasons for rejection, the committee declared that it would take three years to reach Asia and that so long after the Creation it was doubtful whether any worthwhile lands yet remained undiscovered.

In the meantime, Columbus' brother Bartholomew had sought help for the enterprise elsewhere, though his activities remain obscure. Henry VII of England, to whom he applied, showed some interest. After all, the Tudor king's Bristol fishermen and voyagers were already probing the North Atlantic at least as far as Iceland. Rumors of land beyond Iceland were circulating in Bristol and other west-of-England ports. But King Henry's counselors are said to have ridiculed the Genoese's proposals as fantastic, so Bartholomew left England for the court of France. From Charles VIII he got another negative reply. Nevertheless, he re-

65

mained in the French court, employed as a map-maker; apparently the French held out some hope that they might eventually support a voyage of discovery.

Despite the unfavorable report of the Talavera commission, Queen Isabella was unwilling to dismiss Columbus entirely. The Spanish sovereigns were busy warring against the Kingdom of Granada, the last pocket of Moors in Spain. When that campaign was ended, Isabella gave Columbus to believe, she might again listen to his plans for exploration. In the meantime Columbus hung on in Spain and hoped. In the summer of 1491, however, his patience came to an end, and he determined to join his brother Bartholomew in France. Perhaps the two of them could persuade Charles VIII of the validity of their project. Before leaving Spain Columbus went once more to the monastery at La Rábida to reclaim his son Diego. One of the monks, Juan Pérez, who had once been the Queen's confessor, urged Columbus not to leave Spain and promised to obtain for him another audience with the Queen, which he succeeded in doing. Late in the summer Isabella sent Columbus a summons to appear at Santa Fe, a new city outside Granada erected as a base of operations against the Moorish city, which the Christian forces were then besieging. She also sent a sum of money so that Columbus could outfit himself with a new suit of clothes and hire a mule for the trip. Once more Columbus used his best arguments with the Queen and once more she referred them to a committee. And again Columbus waited.

In the meantime Granada surrendered; the last outpost of the Moors in Spain was in the hands of Christians. Whatever his own anxiety, Columbus could at least exult in this victory over the infidels. He marched in the victory parade and doubtless believed that in such sanguine circumstances the sovereigns would look with favor upon him.

He was doomed to disappointment. This time the technical committee apparently approved of his proposal, but the Grand Council of the realm, which had the final say, rejected Columbus' demands for honors and compensation as too exorbitant.

66

The sovereigns themselves finally said no, wished him well, and dismissed him. Columbus now had no recourse but to mount his mule and take his departure for Cordova. Perhaps Beatriz could offer some consolation while he decided what next to do.

Plodding along the bleak mule track that led from Santa Fe toward Cordova, with a chill wind blowing from the mountains, Columbus needed more to warm his spirits than the words of his faithful friend Juan Pérez, the monk from La Rábida who accompanied him. To the sovereigns of the four most powerful countries of western Europe he had offered a way to the wealth of the Indies, and the little men around the sovereigns had ridiculed him and rejected his ideas. The riches of the East might have enabled them to mount another crusade to wrest the Holy Sepulchre from the hated Moslems, yet none had the imagination to seize the opportunity. So little was the faith of men who occupied the high places of the world that they could scoff at his enterprise of the Indies, nod wisely, and throw in his face antiquated maxims about geography from Aristotle, Ptolemy, and St. Augustine. St. Augustine! As if that worthy father of the church knew anything about navigating the Ocean Sea. Such must have been the ruminations of Columbus as he took the road to Cordova.

The future had never appeared darker to Columbus. As he looked back at a horseman spurring toward him, he might have thought him a highwayman coming to snatch the last coins left from the Queen's gift. That would have completed his misery. But the horseman pulled up with a message from Queen Isabella herself: Her Majesty instructed Columbus to return to Santa Fe. What the summons meant he did not know; he could only obey.

An official of the court, Luis de Santangel, with more imagination than most, had been impressed by Columbus. At the last moment he had spoken with the Queen and had urged her to look with favor upon the persistent Genoese. He was surprised "to see that her Highness, who had always shown a resolute spirit in matters of great pith and consequence, should lack it now for an enterprise of so little risk, yet which could prove of so great service to God and the exaltation of His Church, not to speak of very great increase and glory for her realm and crown; an enterprise of such nature that if any other prince should undertake what the Admiral offered to her, it would be a very great damage to her crown and a grave reproach." [4] In short, Santangel's argument prevailed. Isabella ordered Columbus back to the court at Santa Fe and presently apprised him of the acceptance of his proposals. Details had yet to be worked out.

The story that Queen Isabella pawned her jewels to outfit Columbus' first voyage is a late myth. It is true that she offered to borrow on the Crown jewels if necessary, but money was found without this expedient. The Spanish monarchy agreed to the demands that Columbus had earlier made of the Portuguese, and he hurried to Palos to fit out three vessels for the expedition for which he had struggled these many years—longer than it took Ulysses to get back to Ithaca. Now created Admiral of the Ocean Sea, viceroy and governor general of lands yet to be discovered, with the authority of the crowns of Castile and Aragon to back up his requisitions of ships and supplies, Columbus could ask for little more.

The port of Palos had in some fashion offended the Crown, and for that offense the sovereigns, on April 30, 1492, issued an order commanding that within ten days of the receipt of the order the town must prepare and equip, at its own expense, two caravels for the use of Columbus in a voyage "toward certain regions of the Ocean Sea." With instructions to charter a third caravel, Columbus reached Palos on May 22 and set to work to organize his little fleet. By the end of July he had three vessels equipped and ready for a year's voyage, with an adequate complement of some ninety men. The Admiral himself, as Captain-General of the fleet, chose the Santa María as his flagship. The other two caravels were the Niña and the Pinta.

No precise information is available for the size of the three ships, but from evidence that has been found for the Niña Morison deduces that she was a one-deck vessel with an over-all

[4] Ibid., p. 102.

length of about seventy feet, a beam of some twenty-three feet, and a depth of hold amidships of about nine feet. Clues as to the exact dimensions of the other two are lacking, but the Admiral's flagship was the largest of the three, and the *Pinta* was probably slightly larger than the *Niña*.[5] The *Niña*, Columbus' favorite of the three vessels, started out with only a lateen rig, but in the Canaries her rigging was altered to give her a square rig like the other two.

For second in command of the *Santa María* Columbus named her owner, Juan de la Cosa, master. The *Pinta* had as captain Martín Alonso Pinzón, with his younger brother Francisco Martín as master. The captain of the *Niña* was another Pinzón, Vicente Yáñez. Although excellent seamen and useful in the voyage, the Pinzóns later made trouble for Columbus and tried to take credit to themselves for the success of the expedition. Martín Alonso proved the most difficult and on occasion was insubordinate. One must always remember that Columbus was an Italian commanding Spanish seamen, who would naturally resent a foreigner. That made Columbus' feat all the more remarkable.

At last preparations were complete, and Columbus' three little ships sailed from Palos half an hour before sunrise on Friday, August 3, 1492. Before dawn the commander and his men had performed their religious rites by making confession and taking communion. Then, going aboard, Columbus gave the command "in the name of Jesus" to weigh anchors. This pious phrase, conventional but nonetheless sincere, is still used in the Portuguese fishing fleet on the Grand Banks as the captain sends out his dorymen. The crews of Columbus' fleet felt the need of divine help, for they were setting out on an unknown sea, and what lay before them none could tell.

Columbus, like Prince Henry, had in him something of the crusading spirit of the Middle Ages. The riches of the fabled East were important in his thinking, but he also fancied himself a warrior for Christ. At the beginning of his *Journal* of the First Voyage he noted that the Spanish sovereigns "had made an end

[5] *Ibid.*, p. 115.

to the war with the Moors who ruled in Europe." He recalled to Ferdinand and Isabella that across the seas were subjects of the Grand Khan and other heathen who stood in need of salvation and redemption from idolatries into which they had fallen because the Pope had not answered a request for missionaries. He was pleased that Their Majesties had seen fit to send him, Christopher Columbus, to observe "the manner in which may be undertaken their conversion to our Holy Faith." [6] This apostolic zeal was genuine and had a large place in the motivations that drove this inspired Genoese to endure the hardships and dangers of four voyages across the Ocean Sea.

As Columbus' flotilla drifted with the tide down the Río Tinto and Río Saltés out to the open sea, the three ships were not alone. Other craft heavily burdened with humanity were also putting out from shore, laggard vessels bearing Jews being expelled from Spain. By royal decree, ships taking Jews into exile, following a decision for their expulsion made on March 30, were ordered to sail by August 2, but some had not yet been able to clear the harbors. Like others of his age, Columbus doubtless regarded this heartless expulsion as another evidence of the sovereigns' religious zeal, and he probably shared their belief that this was a work of virtue. Nevertheless, the expulsion caused inconvenience in all the ports, which were cluttered with ships taking distraught people away from a homeland they had known for centuries. Columbus could not foresee that he was on his way to discover a land that would one day offer freedom to the race persecuted by religious bigots of the fifteenth century.

Once at sea, Columbus set his course for the Canaries, which he reached on August 12. While waiting to repair a damaged rudder on the *Pinta* and add a square sail to the *Niña*, the commander improved the opportunity by visiting a beautiful widow, Beatriz de Peraza, who ruled the island of Gomera. Although tradition reports a romance between them, love did not delay him longer than the shipwrights took to complete their work; Columbus was a man with great singleness of purpose. On Sep-

[6] *Ibid.*, pp. 153–154.

tember 6 the expedition hoisted sail and headed into the western sea.

The story of the long voyage has been often told, but never better than in Morison's narrative. Making careful observations, Columbus kept two logs, one for himself and one for the mariners to see. He was fearful lest they mutiny if they realized how far from home they had really come. A religious routine that would have done credit to a monastery was followed on board, for Morison maintains that mariners in the great days of sail "were the most religious of all workers on land or sea," [7] and Columbus, being particularly pious, saw to it that the Almighty was frequently and earnestly invoked. The watch began the day with a recitation of the Paternoster and the Ave Maria. With the changes of the watch came other invocations. And all hands turned out after sunset for evening prayers and the singing of the Salve Regina. If observances of religious offices and the personal prayers of the commander could prevail, the expedition would be a success.

In reality, fortune did smile on the First Voyage. The weather was unusually good for September and early October. In this particular year no autumn hurricane threatened and the trade winds were constant and favorable. But the expanse of ocean was immense, and the men wondered whether they could ever find westerly winds to take them back to Spain. The distance was greater than Columbus himself had imagined, and although he was following what he thought was the latitude of Japan, that island proved elusive. At sunset on September 25, Martín Alonso Pinzón saw what he thought was land and gave a cry that excited the crews with hope. But when morning came, no island was visible; a cloud bank had fooled him.

Tension increased each day. The men were worried and restless. On October 7, after a week of brisk sailing ever farther to the west, the *Niña*, out in front, fired a gun and signaled that she had sighted land. This too proved false, and the men became more dejected than ever. To be sure, great flocks of birds over-

[7] *Ibid.*, p. 171.

71

head and floating weeds and cane seemed to signify land somewhere, but they could not find it. Finally, on October 10, seamen on the *Santa María* who had been grumbling openly mutinied and demanded that they turn back. How Columbus quelled the rebellious crew the record does not explicitly state, but he apparently promised that if they did not make a landfall within two or three days, they would begin their return.

By October 11 signs of land multiplied. Someone spotted the flowering branch of a tree; another saw a carved stick float by; canes, bits of board, land plants, and birds obviously from land cheered the men, who were straining their eyes to catch sight of a coastline, for the sovereigns had promised 10,000 maravedis to the one who first made the discovery. About 10:00 P.M. Columbus called out that he had seen a light, which, he later recalled, was "like a little wax candle rising and falling." [8] When a seaman a bit later cried out that he saw a light on land, Columbus' page shut him up, saying his master had already seen it. That first glimpse of light, no larger than a candle's gleam, gave Columbus a claim to the prize money, which he eventually collected.

Shortly after 2:00 A.M. on October 12 sailors in the *Pinta* saw shining in the bright moonlight the white sand of a beach and called out, "Land, land!" This time no cloud bank was fooling them. Since they were clearly a few miles offshore, all three ships shortened sail and waited for daylight before attempting to find an anchorage. When they could see well enough to navigate closer to shore, they entered a shallow bay and dropped anchors. They could see the white sand of a coral island glistening in the first rays of sunlight. Soon visible were naked people staring at the three vessels as if they were giant birds from heaven.

The landing was made with a certain amount of pomp and ceremony. Dressed in their best clothes, Columbus and the officers from all three ships were rowed ashore with banners flying. Planting a royal standard in the sand, they knelt and gave thanks to God for safely guiding them across the seas. They then rose, and Columbus named the island San Salvador after the Sav-

[8] *Ibid.*, p. 224.

72

iour and formally took possession of the land in the names of Ferdinand and Isabella. The natives looked on in wonder.

Las Casas quotes Columbus' *Journal* to show his opinion of these people: "In order that we might win good friendship, because I knew that they were a people who could better be freed and converted to our Holy Faith by love than by force, I gave to some of them red caps and to some glass beads, which they hung on their necks, and many other things of slight value, in which they took much pleasure." The natives were entranced with the strangers and later came swimming out to the ships with parrots, skeins of cotton thread, darts, and other objects of their making. So gentle, intelligent, and well-made were these people that Columbus quickly decided they would make good servants. Already he was contemplating letting them exchange their liberty for their salvation—in other words, making slaves of them. "They ought to be good servants and of good skill," he comments, "for I see that they repeat very quickly all that is said to them; and I believe that they would easily be made Christians because it seemed to me that they belonged to no religion. I, please Our Lord, will carry off six of them at my departure to Your Highnesses, so that they may learn to speak." [9] These gentle people, whom Europeans were to equate with dwellers in the Golden Age, were Taino tribesmen and vastly different from the fierce and cannibalistic Caribs who sometimes raided them. Haiti, Cuba, Jamaica, the Bahamas, and a few other islands were the principal areas occupied by Tainos.

For two days the sailors refreshed themselves on San Salvador, now sometimes called Watling's Island, and traded with the natives for food and souvenirs; then the fleet sailed in search of Japan. For Columbus was certain that he had hit upon an island offshore from Cipangu, which plainly showed in that position on Toscanelli's map. Since the San Salvadoreans had displayed a few bits of gold, which they wore as nose plugs, the search now was on for gold. Had not Marco Polo said the temples in Japan were roofed with gold? The natives whom Columbus took aboard in-

[9] *Ibid.*, p. 230.

73

dicated that gold was to be found on islands farther away.

For more than two weeks Columbus and his men explored the Bahamas in search of gold. At some islands natives appeared wearing gold nose plugs, but always the newcomers received indications that the gold came from some more distant place. They heard of an island that the Indians called Cuba; perhaps it might be Cipangu. At any rate, they would go there. On October 28 they sailed into a safe harbor on the north shore of Cuba, which Columbus named Juana after Don Juan, heir to the Spanish throne.

After exploring the coast of Cuba for a time and questioning the natives, Columbus decided that he was on the outskirts of Cathay and prepared to send a mission to the Grand Khan. His messengers, including the Jewish interpreter Luis de Torres, marched into the interior of Cuba, but they found neither Chinese nor gold. What they did find was tobacco, a commodity that one day would prove more profitable than the mines of New Spain. They observed the native Cubans smoking cigars, which excited their interest, though not yet to the point of imitation.

After exploring Cuba and outlying islands, Columbus on December 6 set sail for the southeast; somewhere in that direction, Indians had told him, lay an island where gold was abundant. Some time before, Martín Alonso Pinzón had sailed away in the *Pinta,* perhaps in an effort to outwit his commander in finding that island. Columbus first made port at what is now Carénage in Haiti, on the island that the Spaniards called Española, soon to be Latinized to Hispaniola. The seamen were greatly impressed by the good looks of the women, who, like others they had seen, went stark naked, but as yet they found no quantities of gold. As they continued to explore the coast of Hispaniola, the increasing number of gold ornaments worn by the natives gave hope that at last they were coming to the country of the gold mines. At any rate, the country was pleasant, the people gentle, and Columbus wrote in his *Journal* for his sovereigns' eyes the hope that they would fortify the place and set the natives to work; for, he commented, "they are fit to be ordered about and made to work, to sow and do aught else that may be needed, and you may build towns and teach them to go clothed and to adopt our customs." [10] Not once did Columbus betray the slightest doubt that slavery for the heathen whom he had discovered would be good for them if they could be baptized as Christians.

Searching the coast of Hispaniola, Columbus sailed eastward with the *Santa María* and the *Niña*. No one knew where Martín Alonso Pinzón in the *Pinta* might be. On Christmas Eve they had rounded Cape Haitien and were sailing inside the barrier reef when, just after midnight, the *Santa María* ran aground. This indeed was a sorry Christmas gift for the Admiral. All efforts to float the vessel proved unavailing, and Columbus and the crew went aboard the *Niña*, that stout little ship that never failed him. Indians sent by a friendly cacique (the Cuban name given by the Spaniards to Indian chieftains) helped unload the stricken craft, and so honestly did they watch over the stores taken ashore that nothing was stolen.

Into the gloom of this dismal Christmas came one bright glimmer: The natives on shore came bearing pieces of gold bigger than any Columbus had seen. For hawk bells and beads the Admiral could obtain gold that might solace Queen Isabella for the loss of her ship. Perhaps God had seen fit to wreck the *Santa María* here so that the Admiral could discover mines of gold.

The gold the Indians brought so encouraged the seamen that Columbus had no trouble enlisting thirty-nine volunteers to remain at the settlement now proposed. With timbers from the *Santa María* the men erected a fort; and Columbus named this first town established in the New World La Navidad, in honor of the birthday of Christ—the day of their precipitate arrival.

Although Columbus had not found the golden roofs of Japan or the splendid palaces of the Emperor of China, he had found some gold on islands off the coast of Asia, as he thought. He had also found heathen whom he believed were ripe for salvation and for service to the Crown of Spain. Time was now running out.

[10] *Ibid.*, p. 290.

and he knew that he must soon depart. So, taking leave of the settlers at La Navidad, he finally hoisted sail on Friday, January 4, 1493. Winds were contrary, and he had only reached the vicinity of Monte Cristi on January 6 when the long-lost *Pinta* hove into sight. Martín Alonso Pinzón made excuses, but it was clear that he had gone off in search of gold—and had actually found a gold-bearing region in northern Hispaniola. After ten more days of desultory sailing along the coast of Hispaniola, the two caravels on January 16 upped anchors and, taking advantage of a brisk westerly wind, set their course for Spain.

On the homeward voyage the ships caught the prevailing westerlies and bowled along at a great rate until February 12, when in the region of the Azores they ran into heavy weather with thunderstorms and tempestuous winds. By February 14, with a full gale blowing, Columbus and the crew of the *Niña* decided that only divine help could keep them from foundering. If God would only spare them, they would go on pilgrimages to various holy shrines—Santa María de Guadalupe in Estramadura, Santa María de Loreto in Ancona, and Santa Clara de Moguer at Palos. They drew lots to see who would go where, and to Columbus himself fell the duty of going on two pilgrimages. As the weather continued desperate, the whole crew vowed that if God should let them see dry land, they would all march in their shirts to the nearest shrine of the Virgin.

On February 18, when at long last the winds relented and the mountainous seas diminished, Columbus sighted an island and an anchorage; he had reached Santa María in the Azores. Learning that a church dedicated to the Virgin was convenient to the harbor, Columbus sent half his crew ashore to satisfy their vows while the others minded the ship. To the shock of the sea-weary pilgrims, the Portuguese inhabitants fell upon them and made them prisoners, surely the most inhospitable treatment the mariners had experienced since they sailed from Palos. After several days of threats and diplomacy, Columbus managed to obtain the release of his crewmen and sailed out into another terrible storm. But by daybreak of March 4, when the *Niña's* sails had been torn

76

to ribbons, she found herself at the mouth of the Tagus River and made for Lisbon. Columbus managed to reach an anchorage opposite the present site of the Tower of Belém. He was safe at last from tempests, but would he be safe from the envious Portuguese when they heard that he had discovered a new route to Asia for the sovereigns of Spain?

Columbus' trepidation over King João's reception of the news was well grounded. That monarch had reason for concern over the success of a voyage that he had deliberately let his rivals underwrite. But João put a good face on it and invited Columbus to court. Some of the King's advisers, however, privately recommended that this Genoese employee of Spain be quietly assassinated. Such a measure João vetoed.

Ironically, the master of a Portuguese warship whose officers came to examine Columbus' papers was Bartholomeu Dias. When Dias had returned from his successful voyage around the Cape of Good Hope, Columbus had been in Lisbon to witness his arrival; now Dias had to welcome Columbus after an even more momentous discovery.

Though King João was bitter over his own folly in not subsidizing Columbus, he showed the Admiral much honor, ordered new sails and equipment supplied to the *Niña*, and even had him visit Queen Leonor and report to her on the wonders of the New World. At length, on March 13, João allowed Columbus to sail in the *Niña* for Spain. Two days later the caravel anchored at Palos. Close behind her came the *Pinta*. Martín Alonso Pinzón had first made port on the northern coast of Spain and had sent a messenger overland to the sovereigns requesting that he be permitted to come and report on the discovery. His presumption received a royal rejection, and, disappointed and sea-worn, Pinzón died soon after landing at Palos. But his kin and his partisans long afterward continued to plague Columbus.

Queen Isabella and King Ferdinand were holding court at Barcelona when Columbus docked. Immediately he sent a messenger on the 800-mile journey to report his arrival; while he awaited permission to come to court himself, he went to Seville for

77

Easter Week. A letter from the sovereigns soon came inviting him to Barcelona, where he arrived sometime after the middle of April. His journey, accompanied by a small retinue and six of ten Indians he had kidnapped and brought back, created a nine days' wonder in the towns through which they passed. The Indians carried cages of parrots and were decked out in beads, baubles, and gold ornaments to show the promise of the newly discovered lands.

The sovereigns received Columbus like a grandee of Spain, as indeed he now was. Confirmed in his titles, certain, as he believed, of wealth and honor, and assured of royal support for another voyage of discovery, the Admiral's cup of joy ran full. Elated by success, he immediately laid before the rulers of Spain a plan for the colonization of Hispaniola and other islands. Neither Columbus nor the sovereigns realized the extent of the empire that this first voyage had made possible.

The spread of the news of Columbus' success served to deepen the concern of King João II of Portugal over Spain's potential expansion. The Portuguese had first conceived of the exploitation of the East, and João was determined not to let this new discovery spoil his well-laid plans. His concern deepened when a Spanish Pope, Alexander VI, with a stroke of the pen drew a line from pole to pole one hundred leagues west of the Azores and the Cape Verde Islands: all lands west of that line would belong to Spain; lands not possessed of any Christian prince east of the line would belong to Portugal. The demarcation line was drawn in the second of two bulls called *Inter caetera*. This division did not suit King João, who believed that he had a right to lands south of the latitude of the Canaries. Other European countries were later to complain about the papal disposition of the world, and King Francis I of France would remark sarcastically that he wanted to see the will of Father Adam to learn how he had apportioned his patrimony. Finally, on June 7, 1494, Spain and Portugal signed the Treaty of Tordesillas, by the terms of which the line of demarcation was moved 370 leagues west of the Cape Verde Islands. This line cut through the hump of Brazil, and

78

consequently Portugal claimed the right to settle that portion of the New World.

With diplomatic problems settled, Spain set about exploiting Columbus' discovery. The Admiral himself commanded three more expeditions, with the dual purpose of exploration and colonization. Volunteers flocked to join the Second Voyage, composed of seventeen ships and between 1,200 and 1,500 men including a full complement of priests being sent to convert the heathen. Indeed, the sovereigns gave Columbus explicit instructions to labor in this holy work. The expedition sailed from Cádiz on September 25, 1493, and on November 3 made a landfall in the Leeward Islands.

Making a landing on the island later known as Guadeloupe, the Spaniards encountered fierce Caribs who were so addicted to cannibalism that they made a habit of raiding Taino villages and fattening boys and girls for the pot. Morison gives an account of a later victim of the Caribs, a Spanish friar, upon whom the Indians feasted with such ill effects that they were violently sickened and forever after would eat no Spaniard captured wearing clerical dress.[11] On Guadeloupe the mariners saw ample evidence of Carib cannibalism. After sailing through the Caribbean and touching the Virgin Islands, the fleet on November 27 anchored off La Navidad in Hispaniola.

To Columbus' distress, disaster had overtaken the settlement. Greed for gold and women had been the ruin of the colonists, who had fallen to fighting among themselves. Seeing their chance, the Indians had made an onslaught, killed them all, and burned the fort. From this melancholy place Columbus decided to move eastward, nearer the reputed goldfields, and finally made a landing in eastern Hispaniola at a place that he named Isabella, in honor of the Queen.

After making settlements in the interior of Hispaniola and imposing a tribute of gold upon the Indians, he continued explorations of Cuba and Jamaica before sending home the major part of the fleet. Gold he had found, but not in the quantities that he had

[11] *Ibid.*, p. 405.

hoped for. Nevertheless, by driving the natives to the utmost, he managed to procure a small quantity of the precious metal. Every native over fourteen years of age was required to produce a hawk bell full of gold dust every three months. Those who failed were hunted with hounds, and so desperate were some of the Indians that they poisoned themselves. In March 1496 Columbus in the *Niña*, with another caravel for consort, returned to Spain. In the meantime the capital of Hispaniola was moved from Isabella to Santo Domingo. The Admiral had proved less successful as a governor of a colony than as a navigator.

With further promises of gold and the salvation of the heathen, Columbus persuaded the sovereigns to fit out the Third Voyage, which sailed from Seville down the Quadalquivir on May 30, 1498. This time Columbus first reached the mainland of America, on the coast of Venezuela, where he believed he had discovered the Earthly Paradise. Although he found women wearing pearl necklaces, the misfortune that dogged him kept him from exploiting the pearl fisheries between Margarita and the mainland, from which Alonso de Hojeda later brought back bushels of pearls. The Third Voyage ended in calamity, for when Columbus landed at Santo Domingo he found that rebels had attempted to overthrow the rule of his brothers Bartholomew and Diego, who had been left in charge of the colony. In the summer of 1500 the sovereigns of Spain sent out Francisco de Bobadilla as commissioner to settle complaints of the colonists against the Columbus brothers. In his wisdom, Bobadilla arrested Columbus and sent him home in chains. Thus low had the glory of the Admiral fallen.

On his return, the sovereigns treated him with compassion and freed him from imprisonment. Obviously he and his brothers had failed as colonial administrators, but Queen Isabella especially felt kindly disposed toward the discoverer of the new lands. Indeed, in the spring of 1505 the sovereigns authorized a fourth and, as it turned out, last voyage of discovery for Columbus. On May 9, from Cádiz once more the Admiral sailed, this time with a fleet of four caravels. He still hoped to find a way to Cathay and the wealth of the Indies. He still believed that he had been exploring the outskirts of Asia.

The Fourth Voyage was an even greater disaster than the Third. The end of June found the Admiral and his little fleet off Santo Domingo with a hurricane blowing up. Ready to depart was a flotilla of thirty sail being sent back to Spain by the new royal governor, Nicolás Ovando, who churlishly refused Columbus' request to enter the harbor. The hurricane caught the fleet and annihilated all except one old tub, which, ironically, carried gold that belonged to Columbus as his share of profits from mining on Hispaniola. Columbus' fleet survived the hurricane, and he later spent months exploring the coast of Central America, searching vainly for a strait that would lead him to Cathay. To the end he believed that China lay not far away if he could only find the way. Finally, with only two vessels left, both riddled with worms until they leaked like sieves, Columbus had to run them aground on the north shore of Jamaica, where he was marooned for a year and five days. Rescued at last, he got back to Spain in a chartered vessel on November 7, 1504.

After four perilous voyages Columbus had somehow missed the gold and the pearls of the Indies, but he had added a new dimension to the world and to the realm of Spain. Although he had failed as a colonial administrator, he had pointed the way to Spain's imperial destiny. Others would reap the rewards of his discoveries, but the fame of the great enterprise would be his. Although the Spanish monarchy could not suffer him to remain as governor-general and viceroy of the new dominions, the stipulation that he would have a share of the gold mined in Hispaniola made him and his heirs comparatively wealthy—if not wealthy enough to mount a Crusade, at least sufficiently rich for his family to remain grandees of Spain. Racked with rheumatism and worn out with exertion, on May 20, 1505, Columbus died in the city of Valladolid, where he had followed the royal court. In his will he left a sum for use in freeing the Holy Sepulchre from the infidels.

Even in death Columbus would or could not lie quietly in one

81

spot. Interred first in Valladolid, the body was taken in 1509 to the Carthusian monastery of Santa María de Cuevas in Seville, where later his son Diego was buried. In 1541 Diego's widow transferred the remains of both father and son to Hispaniola and had them buried in the Cathedral of Santo Domingo. When that island was ceded to France in 1795, the bones were again disinterred and removed to the Cathedral of Havana, Cuba. When Cuba won its independence after the Spanish-American War of 1898, once more the bones were dug up and this time transferred to a handsome tomb in the Cathedral at Seville. But in 1877, during restoration of the Cathedral of Santo Domingo, workmen had unearthed a small lead box containing bones and an inscription declaring that these were remains of Christopher Columbus, the discoverer.[12] So the bones under the sarcophagus in Seville may be merely those of Diego, the Admiral's son.

Christopher Columbus, the great pathfinder, showed the way across the Ocean Sea—if not to the wealth of Asia, at least to the gold of Mexico and Peru. Fate did not permit him to reap the riches vouchsafed the conquistadors who came after him, but it was he who started the migrations across the Atlantic that have not yet ended.

One dark stain spoils Columbus' escutcheon: It was he who first suggested the enslavement of the Indians, the gentle Tainos who had befriended him. Not once did he reveal any compunction over reducing to slavery these people and other Indians, like the more hostile Caribs. For this the editor of his *Journal*, Bartolomé de Las Casas, whose father had sailed with the Admiral, condemned him. Columbus, however, had insisted that, though the Spaniards might enslave the Indians, they must also baptize them in the Christian faith. In some hereafter they would achieve peace and freedom.

[12] Björn Landström, *Columbus* (New York, 1966), p. 190.

Vasco da Gama Opens the Sea Route to *Asia*

WHILE COLUMBUS WAS STRUGGLING TO GET A FLEET TO-gether for his Third Voyage across the Ocean Sea, an-other navigator, his equal in seamanship, determination, and courage, was making preparations for an epic voyage that would lead eventually to the establishment of a Portuguese empire in the East. Vasco da Gama, a Portuguese aristocrat, was organiz-ing a fleet to sail around Africa to India, following the lead of Bartholomeu Dias and other explorers.

Vasco da Gama came of a highly respected family. His father was the chief administrative officer in the town of Sines, which looks out from the Algarve upon the stormy Atlantic. Born about 1460, Vasco spent his early years in Sines, which he re-membered with such nostalgia that he later sought to become lord of the town. For his education he was sent to the ancient city of Évora, where the Romans had erected a temple to Diana and where King Duarte had built a handsome palace. At some point in his youth Vasco must have gone to sea and learned the art of navigation, but the records are silent. Clearly, however, he had come by this knowledge from experience, for there was then no other way. Perhaps King João II had sent him on unrecorded expeditions, for we know that his family stood high in royal favor.

The King in 1494 had issued orders for timber to be cut in the forests of Leiria for the building of stout ships able to withstand tempests certain to be encountered on a voyage to India. After six years, during which he was too distracted with troubles at home and abroad to pursue the Indian quest, King João again was turning his attention to the opening of a sea route to the Indies. He did not intend to let the discoveries of that upstart Genoese, Columbus, thwart Portugal's bid for a commercial empire in the East. Realizing that much depended upon the success of the next voyage around Africa, the King appointed the veteran Bartholomeu Dias to supervise ship construction, for Dias knew best the type of vessel required for so long and difficult a voyage. To command the expedition the King chose a trusted friend, Estavão da Gama, Vasco's father. But before the ships were ready both the King and the intended commander were dead.

At João's death, on October 25, 1495, the Duke of Beja, the Queen's brother, came to the throne as Manuel I. He inherited because João's only legitimate son and heir, Afonso, four years before had been thrown from a horse and killed. Although the new King lacked the force and ability of João II, he inherited a stable and prosperous kingdom and reaped the benefits of his predecessor's sound administration; as a result, he is called Manuel the Fortunate.

One of the inherited assets was the plan for the expedition to India. Not all of the new King's councilors, however, approved of so risky an undertaking. They pointed out that the dangers and cost of a voyage to so distant a land made any profit doubtful. Furthermore, if successful, Portugal's scheme to divert the spice trade from the route through Alexandria, where the Venetians were long established as the principal carriers, would disrupt Mediterranean commerce. It might bring on the hostility of both Egypt and Venice, and endanger the peace and security of Portugal. To such predictions of disaster, Manuel turned a deaf ear and ordered the fleet prepared. And he appointed Vasco da Gama to command it.

Dias had built two vessels of the best oak that he could find. Like Columbus, he had learned that square-rigged ships were best for the Atlantic, and he had so rigged these craft, giving them each three masts. Special care was taken with the caulking to minimize leaks, and the bottoms were painted with pitch, tallow, and fish oil to keep out the dreaded teredos, the worms that had riddled Dias' supply ship on his voyage around Africa. Two other vessels were purchased to serve as supply ships. The two three-masted ships were named the *São Gabriel* and the *São Rafael*. One of the supply ships, a lateen-rigged craft purchased in Lagos, was called the *Berrio;* the name of the fourth vessel has been lost to history. Supplies to last three years if necessary were loaded aboard, along with extra sails and tackle. Trade goods that the African explorers had found useful—striped cloth, coral, glass beads, hawk bells, red hats, mirrors, and trinkets of various sorts—made up part of the cargo. The ships were well armed for that day, each carrying twenty guns, some of which were one-pounder "bombards." These bombards could be taken in the ship's boat if a landing party found use for them. The crews were all armed with a variety of weapons including crossbows, lances, and cutlasses. This voyage would not fail if advance planning could prevent it.

The flagship was the *São Gabriel;* for captain, da Gama chose Gonçalo Álvares, an experienced navigator, with Pero D'Alenquer as pilot, for D'Alenquer had already rounded Africa with Dias. Vasco da Gama's brother Paulo went along as captain of the *São Rafael,* with João de Coimbra as pilot. The captain of the *Berrio* was Nicolau Coelho, with Pero Escolar as pilot. The captain of the other vessel was Gonçalo Nunes, with an unnamed pilot. Some of these men were to distinguish themselves in later voyages. In addition to clerks, supercargoes, and other ship's officers, da Gama took along three interpreters who could

85

speak Arabic, African dialects, and Hebrew. He was prepared to do business in these languages and perhaps to use the sacred tongue of the Old Testament with Eastern Christians whom he might encounter. One curious group mustered by da Gama for dangerous duties consisted of about a dozen men convicted of capital offenses who might win the King's pardon if they served faithfully on this voyage. Since they were going to be executed anyway, they could afford to take a chance on being slain in Africa or Asia on some mission too hazardous for other men to undertake. One of these men, João Machodo, later rose to an important administrative post in Goa during the regime of the viceroy Afonso d'Albuquerque.[1] Da Gama's total ships' complement numbered somewhere between 140 and 170 men.

The pious motives so frequently mentioned by Prince Henry and even by King João II were less emphasized by King Manuel I, though they were not entirely forgotten. If Christians could be found in the East, they would doubtless be useful. But King Manuel and Vasco da Gama had their minds on trade, and if the slaughter of Moslems proved helpful to the exploitation of Eastern commerce, so much the better. Da Gama was ready with bombards, crossbows, fire bombs, and lances to further the

[1] Henry H. Hart, *Sea Road to the Indies* (New York, 1920), p. 110. Hart gives a succinct account of Vasco da Gama's career and has attempted to reconcile inconsistencies in the early accounts. Many of the contemporary documents concerned with da Gama's exploits evidently perished in the earthquake of 1755 or have since been lost. The early Portuguese chroniclers differ in their descriptions of da Gama's voyages, sometimes varying widely as to dates and places visited. The one surviving eyewitness account of the first voyage is an anonymous *Roteiro* or journal kept by some unknown participant on that voyage. It is printed as *A Journal of the First Voyage of Vasco da Gama, 1497–1499*, trans. and ed. E. G. Ravenstein (London, Hakluyt Society, 1898), and it is referred to simply as "the *Roteiro*." An account by Gaspar Correa, written in India sometime before 1583 as part of his *Lendas da India*, has been published as *The Three Voyages of Vasco da Gama and His Viceroyalty from the Lendas da India by Gaspar Correa*, trans. and ed. Henry E. J. Stanley (London, Hakluyt Society, 1869). Correa's narrative of the first voyage has many variations from the *Roteiro* and mentions only three ships instead of four sailing from Lisbon.

The great poem of Luis de Camõens, *The Lusiads*, first published in 1572, makes Vasco da Gama the hero of an epic of nationalism.

86

Portuguese penetration of India. His orders from the King stated the monarch's hope for fame and wealth, with perhaps some conversions as well in India and other regions of the East:

In those places, even though they be situated far distant from the Church of Rome, I hope in the mercy of God that not only may the faith of our Lord Jesus Christ His son be proclaimed and received through these our efforts and that we may obtain the reward thereof—fame and praise among men —but in addition kingdoms and new states with much riches, wrested by force of arms from the hands of barbarians.[2]

The adventurers sent out by King Manuel thus received a royal hint to be ruthless, and ruthless they invariably were.

Even so, religion was believed to be good insurance against disaster, and few seamen going on such a voyage would have dared go unshriven. Vasco da Gama was no exception, and he and his brother Paulo, with the other officers, spent a night-long vigil in the little chapel at Belém before sailing. There they confessed their sins and prayed for success in their great undertaking.

All of the forenoon of July 8, 1497, da Gama's four ships lay anchored in the Tagus off Belém with their pennants fluttering in the breeze. Crews were collecting on the shore for final leave-taking as the lamentations of weeping women rent the air. Vasco da Gama led officers and men to the chapel for a final religious service in which the priests invoked God to show mercy to the men and bring glory and honor to the banners of Portugal. Each man was assured of absolution of his sins if he lost his life on the voyage. With that, they went aboard and cast off. A flag bearing the red cross of the Order of Christ, given to da Gama by the King, was unfurled, and the wind billowed the sails, each of which displayed the same cross of Christ. Like Columbus, Vasco da Gama omitted no pious devotion that might ensure the blessing of the Almighty on his own great Enterprise of India.

The fleet followed the usual route to the Canaries and Cape

---

[2] Hart, *Sea Road*, p. 118.

87

Verde Islands and thence to the coast of Africa. On the first leg of the journey they had the company of a ship commanded by Bartholomeu Dias, who was sailing to São Jorge da Mina. After reaching Sierra Leone, da Gama boldly turned westward and made a great arc before swinging again to the southeast. By chance or from some inkling of the wind currents he hit upon the route followed in later years by sailing ships headed for the Cape of Good Hope. Beset by contrary winds, da Gama's ships were storm-tossed and out of sight of land until November 1, when a lookout spotted the outlines of a coast. But because of bad weather they could not reach an anchorage until November 4, when they sailed into an inlet that da Gama named St. Helena's Bay. There they careened their ships, made repairs, filled their water casks, and loaded firewood. For a time the native Bushmen were friendly, but under provocation they turned hostile. In going to the rescue of some of his men being attacked on shore, da Gama stood up in his boat and received an arrow wound in his leg. With no further opportunity of profiting from this anchorage, he hoisted sail and left the bay. It was to be the fate of the Portuguese on this voyage, as on others to follow, to antagonize most of the people with whom they came in contact. Da Gama proved an extraordinary navigator, but he lacked the arts of diplomacy.

St. Helena's Bay was only some 125 miles north of the Cape of Good Hope, which da Gama rounded on November 22. A few days later he anchored in Mossel Bay. From the Hottentots on shore he bought an ox for a few trinkets and feasted on roast beef. At this point, apparently (though it may have been somewhat later), da Gama ordered all the goods on the supply ship transferred to the other three vessels and ordered the now useless craft burned. Although the chronicler, Gaspar Correa, tells a story of the ransacking of a ship commanded by Nicolau Coelho (which he calls the São Miguel) sometime later in January and says it was burned for its nails, his account is erroneous. Coelho commanded the Berrio, which survived to make the return trip to Portugal. As at St. Helena's Bay, the Portuguese soon

88

offended the natives, who had at first been friendly, and da Gama saw them tearing down the stone markers erected on shore as he sailed away.

Pushing against adverse currents and contrary winds, the ships made slow progress up the east coast of Africa. By Christmas Day they had gone no farther than the site of the city of Durban. In memory of the birth of Christ, they named the country Natal. Pressing on through the Mozambique Channel, by the last week in January of 1498 they made a landing at the mouth of the Quilimane River and found a native wearing a silk cap obviously of foreign origin. With this evidence that traders from across the Indian Ocean had reached Africa, da Gama and his men were encouraged. What Arab sailors had done, they could do.

To prepare for the last lap of their voyage, they spent more than a month in the harbor on the Quilimane River careening and repairing their ships. Although an attack of scurvy laid many of the sailors low, they managed to procure fresh vegetables from the natives and by February 24 were again healthy and ready to sail. A few days later they cast anchor in the harbor of Mozambique Island and found a town inhabited by Arabs, half-breeds, and African natives who had adopted the Moslem faith. They were now definitely in the region that traded with the Malabar Coast of India and with Arabian ports to the northeast.

Da Gama began picking up information about the winds and ocean currents and determined to find an Arab pilot who might guide him across the Indian Ocean. He had arrived on the east coast of Africa at an opportune time, for the monsoon blows toward India from April to September. In the winter, from December to February, it blows from India toward Africa.[3] Soon da Gama could take advantage of this favoring wind to carry him to India.

This alternation in the direction of the monsoon had been of untold benefit to Arab traders and seamen: They let the east wind blow their dhows to Africa in the winter; then, after trafficking with the natives until the winds changed, they blew

[3] *Ibid.*, pp. 139–140.

back across the Indian Ocean in the spring or summer. The Prophet Mahomet himself could not have ordered the weather better for commerce between Africa and the Asian coast, and the Arabs made the most of it. Long since, they had established centers of trade along the African coast; the missionaries of the Prophet had converted the natives to the religion of Islam, and, at least in the towns, the Africans had taken on some of the civilized ways of the Arabs.

The East African trade was profitable to both Arab merchants and African chiefs with whom they bartered. From the Africans the Arabs obtained gold, ivory, and slaves. The traffic in human souls was the most lucrative element in the commerce with Asia. Slaves were in great demand in Arabia, Persia, and India, and the coastal chiefs always had an abundant supply of captives obtained from the interior. Tribal wars were waged for the prime purpose of capturing victims who could be readily bartered. One of the most profitable branches of this nefarious traffic was the production of eunuchs, who brought premium prices from wealthy Arabs, Indians, and Persians with harems to guard. Innumerable young African males were emasculated to supply this market.[4] The East African trade in slaves, which had existed for untold centuries, has never been completely wiped out, and even in recent years it has been of concern to the United Nations.

Observing several Arab dhows at Mozambique, da Gama realized that pilots might be available there. He finally succeeded in hiring two, but they turned out to be rascals and deserted at Mombasa, the next port reached. The ruling Sheik of Mozambique was friendly enough so long as he thought the visitors were Moslems, but when he discovered they were Christians, he became hostile. Da Gama, however, took the initiative and ordered a landing party to attack the town. In the harbor Paulo da Gama captured a loaded canoe manned by four Negroes and two Arabs; its cargo of cloth, perfumes, and household goods he confiscated. Using no diplomacy and resorting to torture when necessary to extract information from captives taken on the

4 *Ibid.*, pp. 141–142.

coast, Vasco da Gama soon gained a reputation for ruthlessness and cruelty that preceded him as messengers carried the news of the strangers' approach.

When the fleet reached Mombasa, the Sheik, at first pretending friendship, sent a gift of fruit and food aboard, but armed Mombasans swarming around the ships aroused da Gama's suspicion. After several attempts of the natives to board the ships, da Gama sailed for Malindi, a port farther up the coast, where he hoped to find a pilot. As he left Mombasa, he captured a Moslem vessel containing a quantity of foodstuffs, gold, and silver. Thus he repaid the Mombasans for their attempts at thievery.

On Easter Sunday, April 15, da Gama reached Malindi and found a friend in that town's ruler, who hated the Sheik of Mombasa and was looking for an ally, whom he thought he had found in the Portuguese. To show his friendliness, he sent to the ships gifts of nine sheep and a quantity of pepper and spices. Furthermore, despite da Gama's obtuseness in sending to the King of Malindi a return gift of bells and beads and other cheap trade goods brought along for the natives to the south, this potentate remained on amicable terms and put on a show of fireworks in celebration. Officers from four Indian ships anchored at Malindi paid the Portuguese courtesy visits. All was going well, but da Gama was impatient to be on his way and the promised pilot had not yet appeared. To hurry matters, he seized a servant of the King as hostage and sent word that he must have a pilot immediately. Wonder of wonders, he received a pilot, and not just any pilot, but the best pilot in the Indian Ocean—one Ahmad ibn Majid, the author of numerous rutters (or sailing directions), some of which still exist.[5] To this pilot's skill and fidelity must go some of the credit for the success of the final episode of the voyage to India.

Now, with the monsoon blowing from the west and a pilot to show them the way, the ships of Portugal had nothing to hinder their crossing the Indian Ocean. Leaving Malindi on April 24, they reached land north of Calicut on the Malabar Coast on May

[5] *Ibid.*, p. 155.

20, 1498. For nearly a year—just nineteen days short of a full twelve months—the indomitable leader had driven his ships across trackless seas and had at last brought up on the long-wished shores of India, the land of infinite riches. His task now was to lay the foundation for peaceful commerce, and for that task Vasco da Gama was something less than adequate.

Calicut, now called Kozhikode in the modern state of Kerala, sprawled along fingers of water in the marshy delta of a river infested with crocodiles. Ocean-going vessels had to anchor off-shore and unload their cargoes into small boats or canoes for transportation into the city. Despite its unfortunate location, Cal-icut was a prosperous city, with merchants who had grown wealthy from trade in silks, cottons, jewelry, spices, and drugs—luxury products that Arab and Indian vessels transported to the head of the Persian Gulf, whence they were carried overland by caravan, or to the upper reaches of the Red Sea for transshipment to Cairo and Alexandria. The ruler of Calicut in 1498 was called the Samorin (sometimes spelled Zamorin), a member of the Nairs, the caste of warriors. The Samorin lived in great state, surrounded by servants. He ate from silver dishes, and even the cup that a page always held for him to spit in after chewing betel was richly jeweled. To this potentate da Gama sent messengers, accompanied by a Spanish-speaking Arab named Monçaide, whom they had met by chance. The Samorin re-ceived the messengers kindly and invited da Gama to his court; he also sent a gift of fine cloth. All seemed to be going well.

Accompanied by a bodyguard of his own men, borne on a palanquin carried by six stout bearers, da Gama on May 28, 1498, made the journey to the court of the Samorin, who re-ceived him graciously and expressed a willingness to send an em-bassy to Portugal. But shortly after da Gama's visit the atmos-phere of friendliness changed. Arab merchants who realized the significance of the establishment of shipping between India and Portugal poisoned the Samorin's mind. To make matters worse, the gifts that da Gama attempted to send the Samorin—a handful of cheap trade goods—were so paltry that the Samorin's officers would not convey them to court. Friction quickly developed. For a few days da Gama was kept on shore under guard, but after some of the Portuguese merchandise was landed and offered for sale, he was permitted to return to the fleet anchored in the roadstead of Pandarani, a few miles north of Calicut. Though neither the Moslem merchants nor the Hindus showed much interest in the goods that da Gama had brought, a little desultory trade was carried on, and the Portuguese acquired some spices and jewels. Finally, the Samorin refused to allow da Gama's men to reload the unsold goods and held the men themselves prisoners. At this juncture da Gama seized eighteen hostages from boats that had rowed out to the fleet and threatened to behead them if his own men were not released. Ultimately, having retrieved his men but not his goods, on August 29 he hoisted sail for Portugal, taking with him five hostages. The Arab interpreter, Monçaide, begged to go along because his life had been threatened for aiding the Portuguese. Since his help had been invaluable, he was welcomed aboard; later in Portugal he was baptized a Christian. Da Gama's expedition, which had come in search of Christians, could count at least one convert to its credit.

Thus ended the first efforts to establish trade between Portugal and India. Although da Gama had procured with difficulty only small amounts of spices and other merchandise of the East, he had learned something about conditions that would affect future relations between the Portuguese and the Indians. He had also proved that the sea route to India was feasible. Now he would take back all the information he had collected to King Manuel and the merchants of Lisbon.

Despite da Gama's unhappy experiences with the Samorin of Calicut, that autocrat sent a letter to King Manuel expressing a desire to trade with Portugal. Calicut, the Samorin assured the King, was "rich in cinnamon, cloves, ginger, pepper, and precious stones" and he desired in exchange "gold, silver, corals, and scarlet cloth." [6]

[6] *A Journal of the First Voyage*, p. 75.

One curious misconception that da Gama and his men acquired on their first visit was that the Hindus were Christians, albeit somewhat odd Christians. The Portuguese had visited some of their temples, which they took to be churches, and they had seen images that they thought were Christian symbols. Even when the Portuguese saw their first Hindus on the Indian ships at Malindi, the unknown author of the one journal, or *Roteiro*, of the voyage declares that these strangers shouted "Christ! Christ!" [7] On arrival at Calicut, the Portuguese, in answer to queries as to why they had come so far, replied that they were "in search of Christians and spices," [8] and they soon convinced themselves that they had found both. On his way to visit the Samorin, da Gama had stopped at a temple that the *Roteiro* describes and adds:

In this church the captain-major said his prayers and we with him. We did not go within the chapel, for it is the custom that only certain servants of the church, called quafees, should enter. . . . They threw holy water over us, and gave us some white earth, which the Christians of this country are in the habit of putting on their foreheads, breasts, around the neck, and on the forearms. They threw holy water upon the captain-major and gave him some of the earth, which he gave in charge of someone, giving them to understand that he would put it on later.[9]

If da Gama had known that the "white earth" was composed of holy cow dung, dust, sacrificial ashes, and the ashes of sandalwood, he would have been even less eager to apply it.

Before attempting to cross the Arabian Sea on the return journey, da Gama sailed north along the coast of India to the Anjediva Islands, where he repaired his ships and, in the course of his stay, fought off pirates. While in the Anjedivas he received a stranger who, under torture, confessed that he had been sent by a pirate

[7] *Ibid.*, p. 45.
[8] *Ibid.*, p. 48.
[9] *Ibid.*, pp. 54–55.

94

to spy on the ships. Da Gama carried him a prisoner to Portugal, where he turned Christian, took the name Gaspar da Gama, and proved useful as an interpreter in subsequent expeditions to India.

Storms, unfavorable winds, and dead calms plagued the fleet as it tried to make its way back to Africa; scurvy attacked the crews, and thirty men died; pirates again attacked, but were driven off. Not until January 7, 1499, did the fleet limp into Malindi and receive a friendly welcome from the King. After taking on fresh food and other supplies, da Gama pushed on. A week later the fleet was anchored among shoals south of Mombasa, where da Gama decided that he would have to abandon the *São Rafael* because he did not have enough able-bodied mariners to man three ships. The *São Rafael* had been damaged in a storm in the Arabian Sea; furthermore, her captain, Paulo da Gama, was now a very sick man. So, after removing all equipment, supplies, and the figurehead of the vessel (now preserved in the church of the Jeronimos at Belém in Lisbon), da Gama sorrowfully burned the ship and set sail in the two surviving craft, the *São Gabriel* and the *Berrio*. On March 20 the ships rounded the Cape of Good Hope and by April 16, with favoring winds, reached the vicinity of the island of Santiago in the Cape Verdes. There a storm separated the *São Gabriel* and the *Berrio;* Nicolau Coelho in the latter ship continued on course for Lisbon, which he reached on July 10, 1499, but Vasco da Gama in the flagship was delayed.

Deeply troubled by the illness of his brother Paulo, which he now believed fatal, Vasco decided to place the slow-sailing *São Gabriel* under the command of one of his officers, João da Sá, while he chartered a faster caravel to take his brother home. But as Paulo grew rapidly weaker, Vasco decided to land on Terceira in the Cape Verdes. There Paulo died a day later, and Vasco was able to bury him in the church of São Francisco. The great navigator, who unflinchingly faced all the horrors that the seas could send, could not bring himself to commit the body of his beloved brother to the deep; for this reason he sent others on

95

to Lisbon with news of the successful voyage to India while he took time to land his brother on Terceira, where he could die and be buried on Portuguese soil.

The records of Vasco da Gama's arrival in Lisbon have been lost, and later accounts are contradictory. The early chroniclers date his arrival anywhere between August 29 and September 18, 1499. E. G. Ravenstein, editor of the *Roteiro*, accepts August 29 as the date on which he reached Lisbon and September 8 as the day of a triumphal reception ordered by King Manuel.[10]

In the meantime João da Sá had brought in the *São Gabriel* with the remainder of the crews that had sailed two years before. Of all the men and officers who had knelt to be blessed by the priest before embarking in the four ships on July 8, 1497, fewer than half survived to see the Tagus again. Mothers, fathers, and wives of those lost on the voyage took what solace they could from the recollection that their loved ones had received a plenary absolution of sins. But that was cold comfort to those who mourned. From this time forward, ships coming back from India might bring the material wealth of the East, but each fleet would return with diminished numbers of ships and men until Portugal was drained of its manpower. As yet, however, Manuel and the merchants did not know the price that Portugal would pay for prosperity and an empire.

As soon as the King received news of the return of Vasco da Gama's ships, he wrote to the sovereigns of Spain, Ferdinand and Isabella, to apprise them of Portugal's good fortune. In October 1497, after Vasco da Gama had sailed for India, Manuel had married Isabel, daughter of Ferdinand and Isabella, and presumably he thought his royal in-laws would rejoice in the successful outcome of the Indian venture. His letter emphasized the hope that his Eastern "Christians" would be re-converted and would aid in the annihilation of the "Moors." Manuel recognized the importance of attacking the economic bases of the Moslems' prosperity by destroying their spice trade with Europe. In his letter Manuel noted that the Portuguese had brought back a quantity of spices,

[10] *Ibid.*, p. 95.

including cinnamon, cloves, ginger, nutmeg, and pepper, as well as other kinds, together with the boughs and leaves of the same; also many fine stones of all sorts, such as rubies and others. And they also came to a country in which there are mines of gold.

As we are aware that your Highnesses will hear of these things with much pleasure and satisfaction, we thought well to give this information.

It is doubtful that Ferdinand and Isabella rejoiced overmuch at their son-in-law's prospects of making Portugal an imperial power. But Manuel appealed to Queen Isabella's deep sense of piety by stressing the evangelistic work that lay ahead:

And your Highnesses may believe, in accordance with what we have learned concerning the Christian people whom these explorers reached, that it will be possible, notwithstanding that they are not as yet strong in the faith or possessed of a thorough knowledge of it, to do much in the service of God and the exaltation of the Holy Faith, once they shall have been converted and fully fortified [confirmed] in it. And when they have thus been fortified in the faith there will be an opportunity for destroying the Moors in these parts. Moreover, we hope, with the help of God, that the great trade which now enriches the Moors . . . shall . . . be diverted to the natives and ships of our own kingdom so that henceforth all Christendom in this part of Europe shall be able in a large measure to provide itself with these spices and precious stones.[11]

Thus the Portuguese would carry on the work of God and enrich themselves with a collateral benefit to the rest of Christian Europe.

The prospect of an empire in the East had already worked on King Manuel's imagination, and he magnified his own titles to comport with new honors and dignities. In a letter to the Cardinal Protector of Portugal, Jorge da Costa, dated August 28,

[11] *Ibid.*, pp. 113–114.

97

1499, apprising him of the successful eastern voyage, King Manuel begins:

> Most Reverend Father in Christ, whom we love much as a brother. We, Don Manuel, by the Grace of God King of Portugal and of the Algarves on this side and beyond the sea in Africa, Lord of Guinea and of the Conquest, the Navigation, and Commerce of Ethiopia, Arabia, Persia and India, we send to recommend to your Reverence . . . very great news.

He would be pleased if the Cardinal would bring the matter before the Pope and get a further confirmation of Portugal's rights in Asia:

> His Holiness and your Reverence must publicly rejoice no less and give many praises to God. Also, whereas by Apostolical grants we enjoy very fully the sovereignty and dominion of all we have discovered, in such manner that little or nothing else seems needed, yet would it please us, and we affectionately beg that after you shall have handed our letters to the Holy Father and the College of Cardinals, it may please you—speaking in this as if from yourself—to ask for a fresh expression of satisfaction with reference to a matter of such novelty and great and recent merit, so as to obtain his Holiness' renewed approval and declaration in such form as may appear best to you, Most Reverend Father, whom Our Lord hold in His keeping.[12]

Moved by holy ardor, King Manuel also set about building the great church of the Jeronimos at Belém on the site of the chapel where da Gama and his officers had stood vigil on the night before their sailing. This structure is a monument of that architecture now known as Manueline which one so often encounters in Portugal. In time the bodies of Vasco da Gama and the poet who immortalized him, Luis de Camões, would be enshrined there.

Vasco da Gama, like Columbus, was not shy about demanding

[12] *Ibid.,* pp. 114–116.

adequate rewards for his feat. He received immediately a substantial royal pension and somewhat later was styled Admiral of the Sea of India. He also demanded that he be made lord of his home town of Sines, with its revenues and taxes. Unhappily, Sines already belonged to the religious Order of Santiago, whose Grand Master was Jorge de Lencastre, Duke of Coimbra, bastard son of King João II, a man not given to relinquishing profitable real estate. Although King Manuel issued letters patent to Vasco da Gama as seignior of Sines and offered the Order of Santiago another town in exchange, the Grand Master flatly refused to move. In consequence, da Gama and the Order of Santiago engaged in an unseemly row. For years da Gama continued his efforts to get hold of Sines, and in 1507 he even went so far as to take up residence in the town and begin building as if he owned it. Faced with an intruding would-be seignior, the Duke of Coimbra demanded that King Manuel remove da Gama; in this embarrassing dilemma the King had no recourse, and on March 21, 1507, he ordered the navigator to leave Sines on pain of dire punishment. To recompense the miffed explorer, the King made him Count of Vidigueira, increased his pension, and gave him other privileges including the right to hunt in certain royal preserves.[13]

After his return from India, Vasco da Gama had taken a wife, and for a time he settled down in Évora. He had shown the way to the Indies; let others exploit the discovery. The voyage to the other side of the world was arduous and dangerous; for a season he would enjoy the good life in Évora. But Vasco da Gama would not always remain a stay-at-home, and the call of the sea would again bring him from retirement. In the meantime King Manuel would busy himself with another expedition, larger and better supplied than the first. The spices, the gems, and the gold of India and the islands beyond must be brought to Lisbon to enrich the Portuguese and to frustrate the Moslems.

[13] Hart, *Sea Road*, pp. 204, 234–235.

99

Riches and Ruin in the Indies

A S A MARK OF HONOR TO VASCO DA GAMA FOR HIS SUCCESSFUL voyage to India, King Manuel I gave him an alvará, or irrecoverable commission, declaring that during his lifetime he could be chief captain of any fleet going to India. The alvará declared "that in the said armadas he has to go in person, and in them to serve us, and when he thus wishes to take the said captaincy, we may not place in them nor appoint another chief captain save him because of his honor." [1] But da Gama, newly married, was eager to enjoy life for a time ashore and King Manuel was impatient to reap the profits promised by Asiatic commerce. Since da Gama did not wish to exercise his option of leading another fleet around the Cape of Good Hope, the King appointed a thirty-two-year-old nobleman, Pedro Álvares Cabral, to command an armada of thirteen vessels that sailed from the Tagus on March 9, 1500, bound for India.

All of the vessels except two were provided by the Crown; one of the ships was equipped by Italian merchants in Lisbon and another was owned by a Portuguese nobleman. Some of the best

[1] William B. Greenlee, *The Voyages of Pedro Álvares Cabral* (London, Hakluyt Society, 1938), p. xl, note 5.

captains in Portugal, including the veteran Bartholomeu Dias, commanded vessels. Despite the hardships and dangers that da Gama's returning seamen had reported, volunteers flocked to enlist in this new voyage. The lure of adventure and wealth and stories of the voluptuous women of India induced young Portuguese to seek berths in Cabral's ships.

Before the fleet sailed, Bishop Diogo Ortiz officiated at a solemn pontifical mass and blessed the fleet. The King himself, and half Lisbon besides, came to see the voyagers depart. Cabral received from the King a banner bearing the royal arms. Then, with a blare of trumpets and the roll of drums, the ships weighed anchor and set out on the first strictly commercial voyage of the Portuguese to the Indies.

Taking advantage of the northeast trade winds, the fleet sailed past the Canaries and the Cape Verde Islands. On Monday, March 23, shortly beyond the Cape Verdes, lookouts noticed that the ship commanded by Vasco de Ataíde was missing. Apparently it had foundered in clear weather and sunk in the night, for it was never heard of again. The twelve remaining vessels took a wide swing to the west, perhaps in an effort to avoid the equatorial doldrums, and on April 22 sighted land.

By accident or design Cabral had reached a land later to be called Brazil. Like many other episodes in the early history of discovery in the New World, the question of priority among those who first sighted the Brazilian coast has aroused much controversy, and claims have been put forward for previous Portuguese, Spanish, and French sightings. Cabral, however, must be given the credit for making the first effective discovery and sending back word of the country.[2]

After lingering briefly on the unprotected coast that he first reached, Cabral sought a harbor safer from storms and brought the fleet to an anchorage behind a barrier reef on what is now the coast of Bahia; he called the harbor Porto Seguro, a name that it has retained. To this newly found land he gave the name Terra da Vera Cruz, soon changed to Santa Cruz. Only later did the

[2] *Ibid.*, pp. xlvi–lxvii.

country come to be known as Brazil, from brazil wood, a dye-wood that was to be the land's first important commodity for export.

The Portuguese had suspected that land might exist in the west, south of the equator, and it has been suggested that Cabral deliberately sought to make this discovery; but that seems doubt-ful. Since he had instructions to make all speed to India, it is un-likely that he took a whole commercial fleet on an exploring ex-pedition. Having found a hitherto unknown land, however, he dispatched a supply ship under the command of Gaspar de Lemos with letters to King Manuel telling of his good fortune. Cabral did not, of course, realize it, but he had found a country larger than the future continental United States, possessing un-told wealth in natural resources that would be worth more to Portugal than all the goods of the Indies.

Another letter to the King, written by Pedro Vaz de Caminha, an aristocrat who went along as an official writer ("escrivão", a sort of combination secretary-reporter), gives a vivid picture of events on the coast of Brazil in the spring of 1500. The Indians, who swarmed to the beach to see the visitors, had bows and ar-rows that they put down on a sign from the sailors. Good-naturedly they helped bring water and wood to the ships and were highly entertained by bagpipes that some of the seamen played. So impressed was Caminha by the apparent gentleness of the Indians that he was convinced they would soon become good Christians. Oddly enough, he placed his trust in the evangelizing ability of two convicts whom Cabral was planning to leave to learn the language and proselytize the Indians. "And therefore," wrote Caminha, "if the convicts who are to remain here will learn their language well and understand them, I do not doubt that they will become Christians, in accordance with the pious intent of Your Highness, and that they will believe in the Holy Faith, to which, may it please Our Lord to bring them." [3] Whether the convicts turned out to be good evangelists history does not reveal, but since some of these "gentle" Indians later

[3] *Ibid.*, p. 29.

proved to be ravenous cannibals, the convicts more likely became pièces de résistance of a barbecue.

On Sunday, April 26, Cabral, all his captains, and as many men as could be spared went ashore on an island in the harbor for the celebration of mass and a sermon. Since Cabral was a member of the Order of Christ, he carried that banner ashore and placed it on the Gospel side of the altar. Father Amrique, one of several priests in the expedition, "preached a solemn and profitable sermon on the history of the Gospel," Caminha reported, "and at the end of it he dealt with our coming and with the discovery of this land, and referred to the sign of the Cross in obedience to which we came: which was very fitting, and which inspired much devotion."[4] Whatever other motives might dominate them, the Portuguese continually reminded themselves that they had an obligation to convert the heathen and spread the influence of their own faith.

On Friday, May 1, Cabral and his men held a solemn religious procession and erected a cross on this new-found land. Caminha was vastly pleased that some fifty or sixty natives took part in this service, "all kneeling as we were, and when it came to the Gospel and we all rose to our feet with hands lifted, they rose with us and lifted their hands, remaining thus until it was over. And then they again sat down as we did. And at the elevation of the Host when we knelt, they placed themselves as we were, with hands uplifted, and so quietly that I assure your Highness that they gave us much edification. They stayed there with us until communion was over."[5] Impressed by these potential Christians, Nicolau Coelho brought out a box of tin crucifixes left over from a previous voyage, and Father Amrique hung one around the neck of each of the worshipful natives, first making him kiss it.

The day after this edifying experience, May 2, Cabral resumed his voyage toward the Cape of Good Hope. The fleet caught the prevailing southwesterlies and went bowling along. On May 12,

[4] *Ibid.*, p. 17.
[5] *Ibid.*, p. 29.

however, the superstitious sailors were frightened at the appearance of a comet "with a very long tail in the direction of Arabia," which remained visible for the next ten nights. The seamen, convinced that this was an omen of ill-fortune, had their fears confirmed on May 24 when a violent storm struck the fleet. For twenty days the wind raged so that they "had no desire to set sails to the wind." When it was over, four ships, including the one commanded by Bartholomeu Dias, were gone. Now only seven vessels of the thirteen that had sailed from the Tagus remained to round the Cape.

Scattered in the storm, the seven vessels made their several ways around the Cape of Good Hope. Six ships finally came together at Mozambique on July 20, but the seventh, commanded by Diogo Dias, was swept by the winds so far east that when it eventually turned north, it made a landfall upon a large island not hitherto visited by Europeans; this was Madagascar, another inadvertent discovery.

Some distance north of Sofala, an East African town already reported to be a source of gold, Cabral captured two ships, but, to his disappointment, they belonged to a cousin of the King of Malindi, who had befriended da Gama and whose help Cabral needed. They were conveying gold from Sofala, which made the restoration of ships and cargo to their owner all the more painful. When pursued, these ships had cast a portion of their gold into the sea, and the officers now asked Cabral if he had a magician who could recover it. "Our captain replied that we were Christians and that among us such things were not the custom," stated a reporter with the fleet, known to history simply as the author of "The Anonymous Narrative." [6] Cabral's instructions were to capture any Moslem ships that he encountered at sea, and he regretted that diplomacy required him to forgo this plunder.

On the way to Malindi, Cabral stopped at Kilwa, where, reported the Anonymous Narrative, the houses were like those of Spain and the rich merchants dressed in fine cottons, silk, and other finery. Unable to make a treaty of trade with the King of

[6] *Ibid.*, p. 62.

Kilwa, Cabral continued his voyage to Malindi, which he reached on August 2. To make amends for the shoddy presents that da Gama had brought, Cabral sent the King a silver-mounted saddle, silver spurs and stirrups, an enameled bridle, and other rich gifts, along with a letter of friendship from King Manuel. So pleased was the King of Malindi over Manuel's letter that he and his court, "all gathered in the middle of the room, uttered a cry rendering thanks to God that they had for a friend so great a king and lord as the King of Portugal." [7]

During the stay at Malindi the author of the Anonymous Narrative commented that "the King sent those to visit us with many sheep, hens, and geese, and lemons and oranges. In our ships there were some men sick with the scurvy whom the oranges made well." [8] If the surgeons in the fleet realized that this observation was the clue to a sure cure for a malady that frequently devastated crews on long voyages, they gave no indication of it. Not until Captain James Cook's time was lemon juice generally used as a preventive of scurvy, a disease that took a terrible toll of seamen in the Portuguese voyages to India.

Cabrel found a pilot at Malindi and continued his voyage to the coast of India. After careening and repairing his ships on Anjediva Island—and waiting hopefully but in vain for Moslem ships that he might capture—Cabral turned south and cast anchor off Calicut on September 13, 1500. He had brought six ships of his fleet of thirteen safely to India in six months and five days. Now it remained for him to open a profitable trade with the King of Calicut.

To that end, he had in his fleet trained factors and merchants. He had also brought trade goods more suitable for Indian tastes than da Gama had had in his ships. The Samorin of Calicut showed more interest in trade than he had displayed at the time of da Gama's visit. The Moslem merchants, who had previously enjoyed a monopoly in Calicut, had driven hard bargains, and the Samorin was not averse to encouraging competition. He

[7] *Ibid.*, p. 67, Anonymous Narrative.
[8] *Ibid.*, p. 65.

readily agreed to Cabral's demand for hostages to ensure the safety of his men ashore, and he assigned to the chief factor, Ayres Correia, and his assistants a residence with a fine garden and set aside a convenient warehouse for the display of their goods.

All went well for a time. At the Samorin's entreaty, Cabral even captured at sea an Indian vessel from Ceylon carrying a cargo of elephants, including a prized war elephant that the Samorin coveted. Since the ship also was reported to have spices aboard, the Samorin assured Cabral that he could have all of this booty. Though Cabral was successful in taking the ship and its elephants, it contained no spices, and the Portuguese had to be content with one elephant killed in the fray, which they ate. They evidently acquired a taste for elephant meat and later ate three elephants captured in another ship. After all, cows were sacred in India and Cabral's crews had been a long time without beef.

The smoldering hatred of the Arab merchants of Calicut blazed into fury on the night of December 16, when a mob of several thousand attacked and looted the warehouse and residence of the Portuguese. In the melee that followed, only thirty-six of Cabral's shore-based men survived to regain the ships, and twenty of these suffered serious injuries. Among the dead was Ayres Correia, the factor, but his eleven-year-old son was saved and became an important figure in the later development of trade with Asia.

Cabral was not one to endure this onslaught without revenge. Because the Samorin had done nothing to prevent the massacre and had not even sent a word of regret, the Portuguese burned ten Moslem ships anchored before Calicut and then bombarded the city. The Anonymous Narrative explains the action:

And when the chief captain [Cabral] saw this dissension and bad treatment, he ordered ten Moorish ships which were in the port to be taken, and all the people whom we found in the said ships to be killed. And thus we slew to the number of five hundred or six hundred men, and captured twenty or thirty who were hiding in the holds of the ships and also merchandise; and thus we robbed the ships, and took what they had within them. One had in it three elephants which we killed and ate; and we burned all nine of the unloaded ships; and the following day our ships drew nearer to land and bombarded the city, so that we slew an endless number of people and did much damage, and they fired from on shore with very weak bombards.[9]

Cabral's action was characteristic of Portuguese policy henceforth: When peaceful means did not suffice, they did not hesitate to use force to strike terror in recalcitrant rulers who refused offers of trade. They had come thousands of storm-tossed miles for spices and luxury goods, and they did not intend to be put off by the rivalry of Moslem merchants or the whims of local kings.

The Portuguese soon discovered that the rivalry of local potentates along the Malabar Coast made it easy to play one against another. After the massacre at Calicut, Cabral sailed south some thirty leagues to Cochin, whose ruler hated the Samorin of Calicut and was glad to make a treaty of friendship and commerce. On the way Cabral overhauled two Moslem ships and burned them. From now on no Moslem ship encountered at sea would be safe from Portuguese guns. The King of Cochin gave Cabral every assistance in finding cargoes of pepper, cinnamon, fine cottons, silks, drugs, and perfumes. The ships were loaded a short distance above Cochin at Cranganore, where Cabral was happy to find some Christians, two of whom asked for passage to Portugal because they wanted to go thence to Rome and Jerusalem.

After something over a fortnight of trade, the ships were laden and ready to sail. Cabral had succeeded beyond his expectation in obtaining spices and other products of the East. As he was departing, an armada of more than eighty sail appeared, sent by the Samorin of Calicut to avenge the bombardment of his city. Since the Portuguese knew they could outsail and outgun the Indian

[9] *Ibid.*, p. 85.

ships, Cabral was anxious to make contact, but the winds were unfavorable and he sailed away. On January 15, 1501, as the Portuguese were sailing past Cannanore, north of Calicut, the King of Cannanore sent a ship to beg Cabral to land for the purpose of trade. But with the ships already heavily loaded, the fleet could take on only a few bags of cinnamon, with the promise of trade with the next Portuguese fleet. Obviously, despite the hostility at Calicut, the commerce of India would be profitable.

After a voyage of many vicissitudes, Cabral's main fleet straggled into the port of Lisbon during the last week of July 1501. One ship, the *Anunciada*, owned by the Italian merchants and commanded by the veteran Nicoláu Coelho, had reached Lisbon on June 23. Of the thirteen vessels that Cabral took out, six got back. On the way home one heavily laden ship, commanded by Sancto di Tovar, ran aground off Malindi and had to be burned lest its cargo fall into the hands of Moslems. The other vessels were already so stuffed with freight that they could not accommodate Tovar's spices. After the loss of his ship, Tovar was given command of a caravel and ordered to put into Sofala to explore the possibility of the gold trade there. The surviving vessels from this voyage brought back such rich freight that the profits more than offset the losses. Cabral had proved that trade with India, for all of its hazards, held out the promise of great returns on the investment. He had also confirmed that India had some Christians, and as witnesses had brought back two pilgrims bound for Rome and Jerusalem.

King Manuel was so elated over the return of the ships that he hastened to get off a jubilant letter to his royal in-laws of Spain, Ferdinand and Isabella, a letter dated July 29, 1501. Evidently Sancto di Tovar had told some tall tales of his reconnaissance at Sofala and the quantity of gold available there, for Manuel reported to the Spanish sovereigns that Tovar's ship had just come in from Sofala and had brought him

> definite information of it and also concerning the trade and merchandise of the country and of the great quantity of gold which is there; and there he found news that among the men

who carry gold from there [the interior] to the coasts, they saw many who have four eyes, namely two in front and two behind. The men are small of body and strong, and it is said that they are cruel, and that they eat the men with whom they have war, and that the cows of the king wear collars of heavy gold around their necks. Near this mine there are two islands on which they gather much pearl and amber.[10]

Clearly, trade with East Africa as well as India would bring treasure to Portugal.

In addition to giving a brief account of Cabral's achievements and the prospects for further commercial developments, Manuel told Ferdinand and Isabella of the discovery of the grave of St. Thomas, and of Indian Christians who still lived in apostolic simplicity: "In that kingdom [Cochin]," he asserted,

there are many true Christians of the conversion of Saint Thomas, and their priests follow the manner of life of the apostles with much strictness. . . . And there he [Cabral] found definite information concerning where the body of Saint Thomas lies, which is 150 leagues from there, on the seacoast, in a city which is called Maliapor [Mylapore], of a small population; and he brought me earth from his tomb.[11]

This earth from St. Thomas' grave was supposed to have miraculous powers of healing.

King Manuel foresaw a new era of prosperity and glory opening to Portugal. Italian merchants and diplomats in Lisbon were also convinced that this new trade with the East by way of the Cape of Good Hope would have a profound influence on the Mediterranean commerce. The news of Cabral's return, immediately forwarded to Venice, created consternation there, because for centuries Venice had reaped immense profits from the spice

[10] *Ibid.*, p. 51.
[11] *Ibid.*, p. 49. A valuable account of the legends of St. Thomas and of Christians in the land of Prester John, India, and other parts of the East will be found in Francis M. Rogers, *The Quest for Eastern Christians* (Minneapolis, 1962).

trade based on Alexandria. Now Portugal threatened to interfere with this Venetian monopoly.

The letters and reports sent back to Venice after Cabral's return clearly indicate King Manuel's conviction that he was about to change the course of trade with the East. The Venetian observers in Lisbon also revealed their fears that Portuguese optimism was well founded. One of the first to report to Venice was Giovanni Camerino, sometimes called Giovanni Matteo Cretico, a Paduan Greek scholar who served as secretary to the Venetian ambassador to Spain and Portugal. Coelho, it will be remembered, had brought in the *Anunciada* on June 23, 1501, well ahead of the rest of Cabral's ships. On June 27, Il Cretico (as he was generally designated) got off a letter to the Doge of Venice telling him that the other ships were nearby and that the King of Portugal was elated at the outcome of the voyage. Lisbon henceforth, the King declared, would be the spice center of the world. "This one [Coelho's ship] arrived on the eve of St. John," Il Cretico wrote.

I was with the Most Serene King, who called me and told me that I might congratulate him because his ships had arrived from India, loaded with spices; and so I rejoiced in due form with him. He had a feast held in the palace that evening and a ringing of bells throughout the land and on the following day he had a solemn procession. . . . Afterward . . . he referred again to his ships and he told me that I should write to Your Serenity that from now on you should send your ships to carry spices from here. . . . He wishes to put forty ships in this trade, some going, some returning. In short he feels that he has India at his command.[12]

Other letters and reports conveyed similar information to Venice, some in greater detail. So great was the interest that printers rushed to publish accounts of the voyage, and soon merchants throughout Italy were speculating about the possibility of Portugal's taking over the spice trade.

[12] Greenlee, *Voyages*, p. 122.

A letter from Amerigo Vespucci to a Florentine merchant, Lorenzo de' Medici, a kinsman of the more famous Medicis, is of particular interest because Vespucci wrote from Cape Verde on the African coast after encountering two of Cabral's returning ships and gave an account of the rich cargoes headed for Lisbon. Vespucci had already gone on a voyage to the west with the Spaniard Alonso de Hojeda; later he made somewhat dubious claims to have visited at this time the coast of Brazil. At any rate, according to his own account, he had now been invited by King Manuel to go on a voyage to explore the lands in the west found by Cabral. Whether he commanded a ship or went along with some other commander as astronomer, cartographer, and geographer is a matter of controversy. At least the letter that he wrote to Lorenzo de' Medici is explicit about the products that the Portuguese had brought back from India. This news was of much concern in Florence, which had long exported fine woolens to the East by way of Alexandria.

What the said ships carried is as follows. They came loaded with an infinite amount of cinnamon, green and dry ginger, and much pepper, and cloves, nutmegs, mace, musk, *algabia*, *istorac*, benzoin, porcelain, cassia, mastic, incense, myrrh, rose and white sandalwood, aloe-wood, camphor, amber, *canne*, much lac, *mumia*, *anib* and *tuzia*, opium, *aloe patico*, *folio indico*, and many other drugs which you know it would be a long thing to relate. Of jewels I know only that I saw many diamonds and rubies and pearls, among which I saw a ruby of one piece, round, of the most beautiful color, which weighed seven and one-half carats. I do not wish to relate more because the ship . . . it does not allow me to write. From Portugal you can learn the news. In conclusion, the King of Portugal has in his hands a very great traffic and great riches. May God grant prosperity. I believe that the spices come from these parts to Alexandria and to Italy, according to quality and to demand. Thus goes the world.[13]

[13] *Ibid.*, pp. 160–161. The authenticity of Vespucci's letters and the number of voyages that he actually made have been the subject of much

Some of these products, given as Vespucci wrote them, remain unidentified. "Mumia," however, is mummy, for Egyptian mummies had long been an article of commerce. Mummy was used in the preparation of drugs, and powdered mummy (containing bitumen used in mummifying bodies) was a favored ingredient in cough syrups of the time.

Although King Manuel in 1501 dispatched an expedition, probably under the command of Gonçalvo Coelho, to investigate the country in the west discovered by Cabral (the expedition on which Vespucci went in some capacity), the chief excitement in Portugal was over the profits from spices brought back from India, not over the discovery of an outlandish country inhabited by naked savages and parrots. Manuel and the merchants turned their energies to the exploitation of the Indies. At once they began to organize a great fleet to return to the East.

Even before Cabral's ships got back, Manuel had sent four vessels out to India under the command of João de Nova. This small fleet included one vessel supplied by Florentine merchants in Lisbon. The Italians were determined not to be left out of the profits of Eastern commerce. If the ancient trade with Alexandria was over, they would reap such benefits as they could from the new source of spices. João de Nova brought his ships back in September 1502. On the return voyage he discovered the island of St. Helena off the coast of Africa.

For the fourth voyage King Manuel picked as commander Vasco da Gama, who, it will be remembered, as Admiral of India had been given the right to command any expedition to India that he chose to take. Having rested ashore long enough, he was now ready to sail again. Incensed over the massacre of the Portu-

---

debate. For a discussion of the problem see Frederick J. Pohl, *Amerigo Vespucci, Pilot Major* (New York, 1944; reprint, 1966). Pohl is pro-Vespucci. For an attack on Vespucci's claims see Sir Clements R. Markham, *The Letters of Amerigo Vespucci and Other Documents Illustrative of His Career* (London, Hakluyt Society, 1894). Further information will be found in Samuel Eliot Morison, *Portuguese Voyages to America in the Fifteenth Century* (Cambridge, Mass., 1940), pp. 92, 109–110.

guese at Calicut—and remembering his own sorry treatment at
the hands of the Samorin—da Gama was eager to wreak revenge
on that ruler and anyone else who interfered with the progress of
the Portuguese in developing their Eastern bases for trade. Da
Gama planned to demonstrate the power of his nation and to
cow any hostile forces into submission. With that intention he
prepared his fleet, added the necessary guns and armament, and
recruited manpower. If necessary, the Portuguese planned to
trade at the point of their naval guns, and they went out with
instructions to sweep the seas of Moslem ships they might encounter. If possible, they intended to ruin the seaborne traffic in
spices through the Red Sea and the Persian Gulf in order to create a monopoly centered in Lisbon.

Da Gama's fleet was organized in three squadrons. The first
group of ten ships was under the direct command of da Gama
himself. For the officer in charge of the second group of five
ships he chose his uncle, Vicente Sodré, and for the commander
of the third group, also of five ships, he appointed a nephew,
Estavão da Gama. With everything shipshape and under control
of his own family, Vasco da Gama prepared to sail for India in
February 1502. The first two squadrons departed from Lisbon
on February 10, but Estavão da Gama delayed until April 1 because his ships required further fitting-out, as they were to be
left on station in India to protect resident Portuguese factors and
merchants.

The fleet followed the customary route around the Cape of
Good Hope. Since da Gama conceived of his expedition as
punitive as well as commercial, he anchored off Kilwa on the east
coast of Africa and threatened to burn the town if the ruler did
not swear allegiance to King Manuel and pay a large sum in tribute. The King of Kilwa had been less than cordial to Cabral, had
refused Cabral's suggestion that he turn Christian, and had contemptuously disdained a treaty of friendship with the Portuguese. With da Gama's bombards pointed toward Kilwa, the
King had a change of heart; he took the oath and paid a large
sum in gold. From this gold King Manuel had a master goldsmith

create a monstrance for the church of the Jeronimos at Belém, a work of art that still survives. Thus did the King of Kilwa serve the God whom he had rejected.

On this crossing to India da Gama sailed north along the African coast almost to the Gulf of Aden and thence to India, which he reached somewhere north of Bombay. Turning south, he anchored for a short time off Goa, later to be the capital of the Portuguese empire in India, and from there sailed for Cannanore. On the way his caravels overhauled a heavily laden Arab ship returning to India with pilgrims who had been to Mecca. After looting the vessel of such treasure and goods as could be found, da Gama had passengers and crew shut up in the hold and then ordered the ship set on fire. The burning of so many infidels would make a sweet incense to his Jehovah. But, to da Gama's chagrin, the infidels broke out and fought both the fire and the Portuguese sailors sent to relight it. For four days, as his caravels stood by firing into the doomed vessel, it refused to sink or burn completely. Finally, with the aid of a renegade from the Arab vessel, who bought his life that way, da Gama's sailors got a line to the ship's rudder and towed it into a position where it could be destroyed. More than three hundred Mohammedan men, women, and children perished in this vessel, but da Gama contrived to save twenty or so boys to be taken to Portugal for instruction in Christianity. Ultimately some of them became monks in the monastery at Belém. Even in vengeful moments the Admiral of India did not forget that he also had an evangelical mission.

At Cannanore, da Gama was certain of a hearty welcome, for the King of Cannanore was eager to cement a pact with the Portuguese against his inveterate enemy, the Samorin of Calicut. After the ships had loaded a quantity of spices at Cannanore, they sailed on October 30, 1502, for Calicut, where da Gama intended to settle his score with the Samorin. Remembering Cabral's bombardment, that ruler was now thoroughly frightened, but da Gama intended to terrify him even more. To twenty messengers sent by the Samorin offering peace, da Gama replied that

114

he would consent to peace only if the Samorin exiled every Moslem in his domains, something that he obviously could not, or would not, do. To signify the terror that Calicut might expect if he were refused, da Gama captured a number of fishermen and hanged thirty-eight of them from his ships' rigging. Then he bombarded the city. To emphasize further his intended severity, da Gama had the hanged fishermen taken down and cut up. The torsos he flung overboard to wash ashore. But the heads, hands, and feet he piled on a boat with a sail set to take it to land. Stuck on this gruesome heap was a message to the Samorin written in Arabic suggesting that he boil the lot into a curry hash. After further bombardment of Calicut and the capture and looting of another Moslem ship, da Gama with a portion of his fleet sailed south to Cochin. One squadron he left on patrol off Calicut to prevent the entry of any ship. Since the Samorin had unfortunately neglected the opportunity of trade and friendship with Portugal, a blockade would prevent commerce with any other nation. This news would not be lost on other local rulers to whom the Portuguese might suggest treaties and trade.

After some further hostilities, including a brief naval encounter with a host of ships sent against him by the Samorin, da Gama concluded that he had driven home his lesson and prepared to sail for Portugal. His ships were heavily laden with goods taken on at Cochin and Cannanore; he had made treaties with the rulers of these cities; and he now stationed factors there to oversee the developing commerce. To protect them he left the patrol squadron under the command of his nephew, Estavão da Gama. With everything done to his liking, Vasco da Gama weighed anchor on February 20, 1503. On September 1 two of his fastest caravels reached Lisbon with news of the success of the voyage. The rest of the fleet reached Lisbon on October 11. Vasco da Gama had shown how ruthless Portuguese power could be in pursuit of its ends, but he had again proved that trade with the East could be immensely profitable. King Manuel immediately set about exploiting this trade.

It was obvious that, with thousands of hostile Moslems bent

upon maintaining their old monopoly of the spice trade, the Portuguese would have to establish powerful bases in India. Otherwise Portuguese traders left in India and Portuguese merchant ships would not be safe. Without adequate protection Portuguese commerce with India ultimately would be wiped out by Moslem competitors. Furthermore, the Malabar coast of India was not the source of most spices, which came from regions still farther east. With fortified bases in India, Portugal could send ships to these spice islands and reap even greater profits. From this time onward less and less was said about Christianizing the heathen, as greed overtook piety.

In the year of da Gama's return, 1503, King Manuel sent out three expeditions to India, and thereafter dozens of merchantmen made their way to the East. To ensure their protection, in 1505 the King appointed Francisco de Almeida to a new office, that of Viceroy of India, and sent him out with a fleet of twenty-two ships carrying, in addition to seamen, a complement of officers and 1,500 soldiers. He had orders to establish forts on the east African coast as well as in India. The first African base that he fortified was at Kilwa, whose ruler had no choice but to accept Portuguese occupation and nominal Christianity. In India, Almeida fortified the island of Anjediva, erected a fort at Cannanore, and fixed on Cochin as his capital, which he protected by a strong fortification. Under Almeida the Portuguese made their first trading voyage to Ceylon, whence they brought back a rich cargo of cinnamon.

So great was the Portuguese threat to the spice traffic which had traditionally funneled through Alexandria that the Sultan of Egypt decided the intruders had to be suppressed. He had already threatened to destroy the holy places of the Christians in Palestine if the Portuguese did not withdraw from India, but this had availed nothing. More vigorous action was required, and in March of 1508 a combined fleet supplied by Egypt, the sultanate of Gujerat in northwest India, and other Moslem principalities sailed against the Portuguese in India. Encountering a squadron commanded by the Viceroy's son Lourenço at Chaul, south of

Bombay, the Moslems attacked and, after a fierce fight, won the battle and managed to kill Lourenço.

This was the first naval defeat the Portuguese had suffered in the East, and it was imperative for them to prove that they could still command the seas. To achieve this purpose—and to avenge the death of his son—in February 1509 Almeida armed a fleet and went out to destroy the naval power of the enemy. The Portuguese met a Moslem armada of more than 100 ships at Diu, the principal port of Gujerat; and though they had only nineteen vessels, they won what an English historian has called "one of the decisive battles of Asiatic history" because "thenceforth for a century the dominion of the Indian Ocean remained in Portuguese hands." [14]

Even before he sailed against the Moslem armada, Almeida had been relieved by a new viceroy, Afonso d'Albuquerque, an aristocrat, cruel and ruthless, but competent as a soldier and as a diplomat when he chose to exercise diplomacy instead of the sword. Almeida, on receiving the news of his replacement, had refused to vacate the office and had even put Albuquerque under arrest until a new fleet from Portugal arrived and forced the change in command. On his way back to Portugal, Almeida was killed in a fray on the east coast of Africa.

To Albuquerque, more than to any other single individual, Portugal owed the creation of its Eastern empire. His policies and campaigns sought to transform the Indian Ocean, the Red Sea, and the Persian Gulf into Portuguese lakes, and he very nearly succeeded. Furthermore, he conceived of the plan to seize Malacca and control the approaches from the Far East. During his term as viceroy the main outlines of Portuguese policy for the next century were marked out and began to take shape.

Albuquerque's career as a conqueror in the East began in 1507, when he separated from the fleet of Tristão da Cunha and made a damaging raid on the Arabian coast that culminated in the capture of the rich Persian city of Hormuz at the mouth of the Persian Gulf. He had sailed from Portugal in March 1506 in

[14] Edgar Prestage, *The Portuguese Pioneers* (London, 1933), p. 297.

company with da Cunha, who had command of fourteen ships. While da Cunha was busy fortifying the island of Socotra near the entrance to the Gulf of Aden, Albuquerque with six ships had laid waste town after town in southern Arabia. Only those that swore to become vassals of Portugal escaped destruction. After sacking Muscat, he had "put all the Moors, with their women and children found in the houses, to the sword without giving any quarter" [15] and had then burned the town. At Kalhat, Albuquerque had "ordered them [his soldiers] to cut off the ears and noses of all the Moors whom they had captured and left them on the shore and went on board the boats and proceeded to the ships, giving many thanks to our Lord for the favor he had shown him in giving him such a city gained without danger to our men with so small a force." [16] With his usual ferocity, Albuquerque slaughtered hundreds of Moslems after the capture of Hormuz. His cannon had devastated the defending fleet, and as the Moslem seamen struggled in the water, the Portuguese went about in boats, lancing and stabbing them to death. One cabin boy was praised for thus killing eighty Moslems. Albuquerque's cruelty was part of a deliberate policy: He proposed to spread such terror that towns would hasten to capitulate without a fight. Even before he arrived in India his reputation for harsh dealings with the recalcitrant had preceded him, and native rulers heard with terror of his approach.

After assuming the viceroyship Albuquerque looked for a more suitable capital than Cochin and chose Goa, centrally located on the Malabar Coast, on an island surrounded by tidal streams and hence defensible by a fleet. In January 1510 Albuquerque led an expedition consisting of twenty-three vessels against Goa and captured it. Two months later he had to evacu-

[15] *The Commentaries of the Great Afonso Dalboquerque, Second Viceroy of India*, trans. and ed. Walter de Gray Birch (London, Hakluyt Society, 1875), p. 79. These *Commentaries*, written by Albuquerque's son, give a vast amount of detail about the Viceroy's activities. They are available in English translation in the Hakluyt Society Publications, in four volumes, for 1875, 1877, 1880, and 1884.

[16] *Ibid.* (1875), p. 221.

118

ate the city temporarily in the face of an overwhelming Moslem army, but he gave a demonstration of his severity by slaughtering all Goans suspected of treachery. Some of the more beautiful women he saved to become the brides of the Portuguese whom he intended to settle in India, and some children he saved to be taught the tenets of Christianity. When he recaptured the city in the autumn, he ordered every man, woman, and child of the Moslem faith, amounting to some 6,000 souls, to be killed on the spot. Henceforth the Cross predominated over the Crescent in Goa, and so firmly did Albuquerque establish his rule that the city remained a Portuguese possession until 1961, when India took it over.

With ruthless efficiency Albuquerque continued to expand Portugal's influence and power. In 1511 he captured Malacca on the Malaysian Peninsula, northwest of the present city of Singapore, and established a fortified base there. Two years earlier a Portuguese expedition under Diogo Lopes de Sequeira had visited Malacca, but had been driven off. To prove that Portuguese power had come to the East to stay, Albuquerque himself led the assault on Malacca and supervised the fortification of this strategic gateway to the Farther East. While at Malacca he sent a mission to Siam and opened friendly relations with that nation. A Portuguese squadron also went farther east to the Moluccas, known as the "Spice Islands," whence came cloves, and paved the way for bases there. Albuquerque's agents collected information about many islands of the region that we now know as Indonesia, particularly about Java and Sumatra. The whole East beckoned, and the day would soon come when the Portuguese would reach even China and Japan.

From the base at Malacca the Portuguese for years controlled trade in the Indies. As yet, however, they were unable to cut off all Moslem traffic through the Red Sea. In 1513 Albuquerque sought to plug that loophole by attempting to take Aden. Beaten off by well-armed Arabs, the Viceroy experienced his one defeat and had to content himself with cruising into the Red Sea and scaring the wits out of the Sultan of Egypt. He even considered digging a canal to drain the Nile's waters out of Egypt and thus ruin the hated sons of Islam who dwelt in its valley. Thwarted at Aden, Albuquerque returned to the Persian Gulf in 1515 and sacked Hormuz, which had defaulted on its promise of allegiance to Portugal made when Albuquerque had captured it on his way to India eight years before. This time he left nothing to chance, but took possession of the city, executed the most dangerous members of the ruling clique, and built a fortress and naval base to command the adjacent sea routes. Aden, however, was the key to Red Sea shipping, and Aden held out against the Portuguese. This was the only failure in the completion of Albuquerque's strategic chain of bases. Already, on the east coast of Africa at Kilwa and elsewhere, the Portuguese had established forts and naval stations designed to protect their commerce and keep marauders out of the Indian Ocean.

To perpetuate the Portuguese in their Eastern empire, Albuquerque contrived a plan that he thought would ensure a loyal population: He would marry Portuguese men to native women and hope that their offspring would be numerous. To achieve this, with characteristic efficiency he ordered men who were to remain in the East to marry, and he himself conducted some of the wedding ceremonies. Many of the brides were widows of Moslems whom his troops had slain. In this fashion did Albuquerque make amends for some of his cruelty.

The children of mixed blood multiplied, but they were not a vigorous stock and they proved less useful than Albuquerque had imagined. Family discipline was lax, and spoiled children frequently grew up into unruly adults who were problems for colonial authorities.

Indeed, the conditions of life in Goa and other cities occupied by the Portuguese caused a deterioration in the moral fiber of both Europeans and their offspring. The women of Goa were noted for their beauty and their easy morals. So lascivious—and irresistible—were they that Portuguese men fell easy victims and many collapsed into lives of amorous ease and ultimate exhaustion. Nearly a century after Albuquerque's time, in 1599, an Italian traveler, Francesco Carletti, visited Goa and described, not without a touch of envy, the lives of Portuguese who dawdled away their days in the company of the most beautiful and complaisant women the Italian had ever seen. These women, he declared, were "amorous, kind, attractive, and clean." They exceeded "all the women who have been or are endowed with similar graces, if not everywhere in the world, at least among those women whom I have seen and experienced in circumnavigating the world completely." [17] Too much ease and too many women helped to enervate the Portuguese whose task it was to rule the empire that the pioneers had established.

Albuquerque, like Almeida before him, had enemies at court, and schemers around King Manuel at length brought about his recall. While the Viceroy was raiding Moslem shipping and ports in the Persian Gulf in 1515, he got word that the King was sending out a successor to him, one Lope Soares de Albergaria. He wrote to his sovereign that all was in order in India, and sailed back from Hormuz to Goa. Albuquerque was already desperately ill, however, and just as his ship reached Goa he died.

As Albuquerque had reported to King Manuel, Portuguese affairs in India were in order. He had established the authority of his nation from the east coast of Africa to Malacca in Malaysia. He had terrorized the Moslems along the coast of Arabia and had made the Sultan of Egypt tremble at the threat of Portuguese invasion of the Red Sea. Although Albuquerque had come to India to make Portuguese trade with the Indies safe and profitable, he also conceived of himself as a crusader against the infidels of Islam; it happened that this zeal to destroy the enemies of Christendom coincided with the best commercial strategy. By the end of Albuquerque's regime no ship could travel in safety across the Indian Ocean without a Portuguese pass, but the Viceroy refused to give any ship a pass to carry goods into the Red Sea. Such vessels as entered the Red Sea did so at their peril. By

[17] *My Voyage Around the World, by Francesco Carletti, a 16th Century Florentine Merchant,* trans. Herbert Weinstock (New York, 1964), p. 211.

establishing a base at Malacca, Albuquerque's forces could control the narrow straits through which traffic from the farther Indies had to pass. Although he could be harsh and cruel when he deemed it essential, he could also employ the arts of diplomacy, and his negotiations with the Siamese and with Chinese merchants gave a favorable impression of the Portuguese and paved the way for further expansion of Portuguese trade and power in the Far East.

Unhappily, Albuquerque's successors for the next nine years were either incompetents or rascals, or both. The three viceroys who ruled in turn from 1515 to 1524 looked upon their appointments as opportunities for personal aggrandizement and the enrichment of their favorites. Rampant greed dictated every decision, and corruption spread from the top of the hierarchy to the lowest seaman able to embezzle valuables from a homeward-bound ship. Some commercial progress, however, was made, despite corruption and incompetence. For example, the Portuguese moved into the Moluccas and established factories in these rich spice-producing islands.

Although valuable cargoes continued to pour into Lisbon, transforming it into a vast emporium of Oriental goods, the authorities came to realize that reforms were needed to ensure the security of their developing Eastern empire. In 1521 King Manuel the Fortunate died and was succeeded by his son João III, a youth not yet twenty, who was to reign for the next thirty-six years. On the advice of his council, King João in 1524 called Vasco da Gama from retirement, made him Viceroy of India, and sent him to straighten out the troubled affairs at Goa. The stern old veteran immediately began to discipline the corrupt and the indolent. When his predecessor in office, Duarte de Menezes, sailed back to Cochin from a piratical voyage with a cargo of loot, da Gama ordered him arrested for malfeasance of office. To his amazement, da Gama found that officers under the previous viceroys had been selling to the natives cannon needed for defense. By threatening to hang these malefactors, he got back his guns. But da Gama had only a little time to work his reforms. He had arrived at Goa in September; by mid-December it was evident that he was a very sick man, and on Christmas Eve he died. In less than four months, however, he had scared or shamed officials into greater decency and order than they had shown in years.

Vasco da Gama was buried with great pomp in the monastery of St. Anthony in Goa, but the Admiral of India had left instructions that his body was to be sent back to his native land. Like Columbus, it was da Gama's fate to be disturbed in death. His body was shipped home in 1539 and buried in the Church of Our Lady of the Relics in Vidigueira. When the church was rebuilt in 1593, da Gama's body was moved to the new structure. This church was deconsecrated and abandoned in 1834, gravestones were tossed about, and some graves were plundered. Finally, in 1841, a benefactor bought the property and restored church and tombs. In the late nineteenth century the Portuguese government at long last decided to inter the bones of Vasco da Gama and Luis de Camões, the epic poet, in the church of the Jeronimos at Belém. This was done with great ceremony on June 8, 1880. Unhappily, a scholar discovered evidence that the authorities had dug up the wrong coffin in the church at Vidigueira. After much debate the bones believed to be the correct remains of da Gama were exhumed and transferred to Belém on May 9, 1898. There they rest—if they are indeed the true remains of the great explorer—in an ornate tomb that tourists dutifully visit.[18]

After da Gama's time the Portuguese continued to expand their empire in the East until in 1557 they gained a foothold at Macao in southern China, which they have managed to retain to this day. This Chinese base, for many generations the only one possessed by any European nation, gave Portugal access by sea to Chinese products that came to other nations over long caravan routes. Portuguese traders also made contact with Japan, and eventually Jesuits from Portugal sent missions to Japan.

But Portugal, with a population of less than a million and a

[18] See Henry H. Hart, *Sea Road to the Indies* (New York, 1950), pp. 259–265, for the bizarre story of da Gama's bones.

half, found that an empire stretching around half the earth was a burden that she carried with difficulty. Although merchants from many countries—especially from Italy and Germany—found trade with Lisbon profitable, the government itself was often hard pressed to finance an imperial establishment. Ships were expensive and losses heavy; the pay of troops and the salaries of officials were a constant drain on the exchequer; but in the end it was lack of trained manpower that ruined the Portuguese empire in the East.

Although Portugal learned to hire mercenary troops in India —at a price—to defend the establishment, she could not man her ships with hired seamen, for few or none could be found. The annual fleets that went to the Indies drained Portuguese farms of men needed at home, many of whom never returned. Shipwrecks took a heavy toll,[19] and some men elected to remain in India or the islands of the East. Tragic narratives of shipwrecks became a popular literary form in Lisbon in the sixteenth century, for nearly every Portuguese at home had known someone on the voyages to the East and many had lost kinsmen and friends in the frequent disasters of the sea. A notable collection describing eighteen famous wrecks of this period was edited by Bernardo Gomes de Brito in 1735–36 under the title *Historia Tragico-Maritima.*[20]

The Portuguese empire in Asia remained a continual embarrassment to the royal treasury. Although some Portuguese merchants and noblemen acquired great wealth from the importation of Asiatic products, the government itself could not obtain enough revenue from duties, taxes, and even monopolies to defray the enormous expense of maintaining an imperial establish-

[19] A detailed account of the impact of shipwrecks upon Portugal's economy will be found in James Duffy, *Shipwreck and Empire* (Cambridge, Mass., 1955).
[20] Translated versions of some of these narratives will be found in *The Tragic History of the Sea, 1589–1622*, trans. and ed. C. R. Boxer (Cambridge, Hakluyt Society, 1959), and *Further Selections from the Tragic History of the Sea, 1559–1565*, trans. and ed. C. R. Boxer (Cambridge, Hakluyt Society, 1968).

ment overseas. Many of those who prospered most from the trade of Asia were foreign importers in Lisbon. The money they earned did not stay in Portugal, but found its way to banks in Venice, Genoa, Florence, Antwerp, and other trading centers of Europe. Portugal itself lacked sufficient capital to finance the trading ventures of its fleets and the commercial activities of its empire and had to depend largely upon Italian, Flemish, and German financing. In the end Portugal lost most of its Eastern empire to enterprising and belligerent Dutch and English traders, but that development required a century. "The wonder is not that their eastern empire ultimately collapsed," remarks Charles R. Boxer, the distinguished historian of Portuguese expansion, "but that it flourished for exactly a century and lasted for as long as it did." [21]

The religious motivation of Prince Henry and João II lost much of its force during the reign of Manuel I, but under João III a renewed effort was made to convert the heathen. The King asked the Pope for Jesuit missionaries to go out to the Indies and had the good fortune to enlist Francisco de Xavier, a brilliant young priest burning with zeal. He reached Goa in 1542 with an appointment as papal nuncio and for the remainder of his life was instrumental in setting up missions from Hormuz to Japan. He died in 1552 on his way to China, but his body was returned to Goa, where it was buried in an ornate tomb. To St. Francis Xavier must be given the credit for such success as the missionary enterprise had in the Far East under the Portuguese.

Though St. Francis Xavier is said to have made many converts, the religious endeavor was a disappointment to the Portuguese. No vast hosts of Christians had been found in India, as had been expected, and many of those whom they did discover were of doubtful orthodoxy, having fallen into Nestorian and other heresies. The kingdom of Prester John was also a bitter disappointment, for Ethiopia proved less than promising as an ally against the Moslems or as an abode of Christians eager to follow

[21] Charles R. Boxer, *Four Centuries of Portuguese Expansion, 1415–1825: A Succinct Survey* (Johannesburg, 1965), p. 21.

125

the dictates of Rome. The dream of uniting Eastern and Western Christians into an alliance to crush the Moslems died as the Portuguese learned the realities of religious and political life in the Far East.

The hope of cutting off Moslem shipping through the Red Sea also failed. Afonso d'Albuquerque made valiant war on the Arabs and endeavored in vain to capture Aden, key to the Red Sea, but he failed, and no successor managed to surpass his efforts. Spices continued to move through the Red Sea and on to Alexandria, where Venetian merchants found enough cargo to maintain their merchant vessels.[22] The first country in modern Europe to create an empire, Portugal made a heroic effort to defend it, but at last she had to relinquish her power in the Indies to the Dutch and the English. When the crown of Portugal passed to Spain in 1580 for the long period known as the Babylonian Captivity, the imperial interests of Portugal were subordinated to those of Spain.

The achievements of Portugal during the great days of exploration and expansion were sufficient to inspire her greatest poet, Luis Vaz de Camões, to write an epic with Vasco da Gama as its central hero. The *Lusiads*, first published in 1572, sought, among other things, to stir the Portuguese during the reign of feckless King Sebastião to remember their heritage and defend it against the onslaughts of enemies of any nation. Near the end of the poem Camões thus addresses the King:

> *So do, my Lord, that never German, Gaul,*
> *Italian, Briton, though admired, can say*
> *That the Portuguese take orders from them all.*
> *Rather 'tis Portugal they must obey.*
> *To counsel only the experienced call,*
> *Who saw hard months and hard years in their day.*
> *For though of knowledge many can dispose,*
> *In things particular the expert knows.*[23]

[22] Frederic C. Lane, "Venetian Shipping During the Commercial Revolution," *American Historical Review*, XXXVIII (1932–33), 219–237.
[23] Canto X, 152; I have used the translation of Leonard Bacon, *The Lusiads of Luiz de Camões* (New York, 1950), p. 255.

Portugal had shown the way in creating an empire. In some "things particular" the English were later to follow Portuguese practice in India and elsewhere, as the Spaniards were to adopt some of Portugal's methods in creating their own empire. Portugal, small and proud, may have exhausted herself in the effort, but for a century she controlled a vast empire and became the tutor to more powerful nations.

Magellan's Feat: Spain's Westward Route to the Spice Islands

THE THREAT OF A PORTUGUESE MONOPOLY OF THE SPICE TRADE based on Lisbon depressed Spaniards who had hoped that Columbus' discoveries would guarantee them a profitable water route to the wealth of the Indies. Instead they found their way blocked by a land mass and a demarcation line around the globe that cut them off from the Cape of Good Hope passage to Asia. As Portugal was developing trade with India and farther Asia, Spain had to be content with frantic gold-mining on Hispaniola while her mariners probed in vain for a sea passage to Cathay. The letters of King Manuel of Portugal addressed dutifully to his royal in-laws of Spain, Ferdinand and Isabella, telling of the Portuguese success in India, did nothing to raise the spirits of Spaniards disappointed at the outcome of their own explorations.

Consequently, when an experienced Portuguese navigator appeared in Seville on October 20, 1517, with a plan to circumvent his own countrymen by sailing through a westward passage to the Indies, Spaniards were ready to listen. The Portuguese had a reputation for secrecy about their own explorations, and this navigator might indeed know a strait leading into the South Sea. His name was Fernão de Magalhães, better known outside Portugal as Ferdinand Magellan. Born of an aristocratic family in northern Portugal not far from Oporto, Magellan had served as a page in the court of King João II. Fired by ambition to see the Far East, he had gone in the fleet of Francisco de Almeida when that nobleman went out to India as viceroy, and he had seen service in both East Africa and India. A companion on the outward voyage was another former page, Francisco Serrão, who became his fast friend. That friendship would have an important impact upon Magellan's later career.

Both Magellan and Serrão in 1509 went in the fleet of Diogo Lopes de Sequeira to Malacca on the Malaysian peninsula (near modern Singapore), then an important center of the spice trade. Though the Malaysians attacked Sequeira's ships and forced him to sail away, the Portuguese had seen enough of the region to know that they must establish bases at Malacca and in the islands beyond. When the viceroy who succeeded Almeida, Afonso de Albuquerque, in 1511 sent a more powerful fleet to Malaysia, both Magellan and Serrão went along and took part in the six-week siege of Malacca that ended in victory. In the hands of the Portuguese, Malacca was made into a base controlling sea lanes whence passed native junks carrying cloves, cinnamon, nutmegs, mace, pepper, gold, porcelains, silks, and drugs from the Indonesian islands and the more distant Chinese mainland.

Since the most valuable spices, including cloves, came from the Molucca Islands (lying between the Celebes and New Guinea, southeast of the Philippines), the Portuguese were determined to reach them. In December 1511 Albuquerque ordered António de Abreu to explore the Moluccas, but the season was late and the threat of bad weather forced Abreu to turn back before he had completed his mission. He managed, however, to return to Malacca with a cargo of nutmegs and mace taken on at the Banda Islands south of the Molucca group. He had also seen the waters of the Pacific Ocean and had picked up information about the principal sources of spice.

Participating in this expedition as captain of one of Abreu's three ships was the ubiquitous Francisco Serrão, Magellan's friend. No clear evidence indicates that Magellan was along. When Serrão's ship foundered, he obtained a native craft, but that too wrecked, and Serrão with several companions managed to reach the island of Ternate in the Moluccas.

No sixteenth-century sailor could have found a more idyllic spot on which to be marooned. The island was fruitful, the climate benign, and the women beautiful. Furthermore, the ruler of the island, having heard about the enterprise of the Portuguese from Malaysian traders, welcomed Serrão and his fellow survivors. Soon Serrão made such a good impression on the Rajah that he found himself the ruler's chief counselor, provided with a whole harem of island beauties. The upshot was that Serrão could not be persuaded to abandon paradise, and he determined to live out his life on Ternate. But he did write Magellan about the riches of the Moluccas, and his letter influenced Magellan to undertake the voyage in search of a passage to the Pacific.

Magellan returned to Portugal from the Far East sometime before 1513, and the next year he enlisted in an expedition against the Moroccan city of Azemmour, which had rebelled against its Portuguese overlords. The campaign, successful against the Moroccans, was a personal disaster to Magellan. A leg wound that he received left him lame for life; he was unable to obtain compensation for a valuable horse lost in the fighting; he was accused of appropriating to his own use money from the sale of captured cattle; and when he left his command and went to Portugal to appeal to King Manuel, that monarch not only refused to increase his paltry compensation as requested but ordered Magellan back to Africa to clear up the cattle matter.

Nearly two years later, probably early in 1516, Magellan made another appeal to King Manuel, this time to be given command of an expedition to the Moluccas. We can be certain that he did not suggest to the Portuguese King a search for a westward passage to the Indies, for the discovery of a strait through the American land mass would have taken the voyager through Spanish territory and would have been to Spain's advantage, not Portugal's. Magellan's plea to King Manuel was clearly for command of a ship or ships to go to the Moluccas by the conventional Cape of Good Hope route. The letter from Serrão telling of the wealth to be obtained in the islands where cloves and other spices grew obviously gave Magellan an incentive to embroider his description of the profits that he would make for the King—and himself—by the hoped-for expedition. But King Manuel—perhaps remembering the earlier troubles of Magellan in Morocco or an unfavorable report from Albuquerque, the Viceroy of India, who also disliked Magellan—refused his request and dismissed him with scant courtesy. Furthermore, the King added that the would-be voyager was free to find service where he could.

Resentful of royal disfavor, Magellan determined to take his case to the Spanish court. But before he left Portugal, he set about collecting such information as he could obtain from friendly Portuguese pilots and from maps, charts, and globes in their possession. At this time the Portuguese had the best information in the world about routes into distant seas, and this intelligence they jealously guarded. Even so, Magellan had friends from whom he could learn. When he had acquired all the data available in Portugal, he set out for Spain in the autumn of 1517.

Seville was his natural objective, for that city was becoming the center for trade with the New World. Situated on the Guadalquivir River, which was navigable that far to ocean-going craft, Seville was an important port. Already its Casa de la Contratación, created by Ferdinand and Isabella to license shipping destined for the new Atlantic region, was expanding an authority that in time would cover much of Spain's overseas activities. Seville, with a useful out-port down the river at Sanlúcar de Barrameda, would soon dominate Spanish trade, and many Portuguese and other foreigners were finding employment in this thriving Spanish port. An experienced voyager like Magellan

131

was certain to find influential friends in Seville.

While in India Magellan had made friends with one Duarte Barbosa, an official secretary representing King Manuel. Barbosa had returned to Portugal and, like Magellan, had been rejected by the King. Without hope of preferment in Portugal, he made contact with Spanish authorities in Seville and was recruiting Portuguese pilots in Oporto when Magellan was contemplating his own journey to Spain. Before Magellan left Portugal, Barbosa may have arranged with Juan Fonseca, Bishop of Burgos, the head of the Casa de la Contratación, to offer the Portuguese navigator the command of an expedition to search for a westward passage to the Indies.[1] At any rate, it is certain that Barbosa gave Magellan an introduction to his uncle, Diogo Barbosa, a Portuguese who had already risen high in the Spanish service at Seville and was now commander of the castle and governor of the arsenal. He was also wealthy and the father of two daughters. Within a few weeks of his arrival in Seville, Magellan had married Beatriz Barbosa and had received a handsome dowry with his bride. He had also made a favorable impression upon Juan de Aranda, factor (executive officer) of the Casa de la Contratación, who investigated Magellan's background and satisfied himself that here was a reliable and competent person for the voyage that he was proposing.

Another disgruntled Portuguese had joined Magellan and associated himself with the proposed venture to seek a westward passage to Asia. He was Ruy Faleiro, a dyspeptic and embittered astrologer whom King Manuel had refused to appoint Astronomer Royal. Faleiro claimed to be able to make accurate calculations of longitude, something no one else at this time could do, and he asserted that the demarcation line around the globe estab-

---

[1] Biographical information in great detail will be found in the most recent full-length life of Magellan: Charles McKew Parr, *So Noble a Captain: The Life and Times of Ferdinand Magellan* (New York, 1953). More succinct information about Magellan will be found in the introduction to *Magellan's Voyage Around the World: Three Contemporary Accounts*, ed. with an Introduction by Charles E. Nowell (Evanston, Ill., 1962).

lished by the Treaty of Tordesillas placed the Molucca Islands, source of the best spices, inside the Spanish zone. He was wrong, for the line ran east of the Philippines and split Australia down the middle, but nobody had yet precisely located the line in the Pacific, and Spain hoped that she could claim the rich spice islands. The claim would be made practically effective if she could discover a westward route to the source of this wealth.

In late February 1518, under the auspices of Bishop Fonseca, other court dignitaries, and Aranda, Magellan and his astrologer colleague, Faleiro, journeyed to Valladolid for an audience with young King Charles I (soon to be the Emperor Charles V of the Holy Roman Empire). A memorandum skillfully drawn up by Magellan's sponsors had prepared the King for a favorable impression of Magellan by emphasizing his courage in fighting the Moslems, his dedication to the cause of Christ and eagerness to spread the Gospel, his knowledge of the secrets of the Orient, and his belief that he could find the elusive passage to the South Sea. At the audience Magellan explained his plan to reach Asia by a strait in the South Atlantic. He displayed a globe, probably one copied from that made by Martin Behaim, which indicated that the spice islands lay east of the line of demarcation in the Spanish portion of the world. Faleiro confirmed all this with a panoply of learned jargon.

The King was so impressed and excited that he approved Magellan's scheme; and on March 22, 1518, he signed capitulations (essentially a contract) guaranteeing to Magellan and Faleiro one twentieth part of the profits from the discoveries, as well as hereditary titles and various other privileges. He also undertook to provide and fit out five ships with adequate crews and supplies. These capitulations were followed by a series of decrees providing further authorizations for the expedition. Somewhat later, when private capital was needed to complete the funding of the voyage, several Spanish and a few foreign investors came forward, including Jacob Fugger of the famous Augsburg banking house, who subscribed surreptitiously lest he offend the Portuguese with whom his banking house had large interests. Another important investor was Cristóbal de Haro, a member of a rich merchant family of Antwerp, who had a business establishment in Lisbon and had invested heavily in both Portuguese and Spanish enterprises. He had reason to hold a grudge against King Manuel and was not averse to a venture that promised a personal profit and a blow to the arrogant Portuguese King's monopoly of the spice trade.

From March until September Magellan was busy organizing the expedition. His associate Faleiro proved contentious and testy and showed no capacity to command. Consequently, an order from the King forbade him to go in the fleet. Gossips reported, however, that Faleiro, having cast his own horoscope and discovered signs in the stars foretelling disaster to himself, had wanted to abandon the enterprise and remain at home. Could Magellan have looked into the future, even that stout-hearted man might have had qualms, but since he was not one to be put off by astrology, he hurried on with his preparations. Ships had to be found; ship's stores for a voyage that might last two years and more had to be collected; trade goods acceptable to all sorts of people, from savages to East Asian potentates, had to be selected with care; and crews had to be recruited.

By the late summer of 1519 five ships were tied up at the docks in Seville and were being loaded with cargo. The largest vessel, the *San Antonio*, was a craft of approximately 140 tons, according to modern methods of calculation.[2] The other vessels were smaller: the *Trinidad*, Magellan's flagship, was about 130 tons burden; the *Concepción*, 110 tons; the *Victoria*, 100 tons; and the *Santiago*, 90 tons. They were not the best ships afloat, to be sure, but they were the best that Juan de Aranda, the busy executive of the Casa de la Contratación, could come by with the funds available from the royal treasury. One of King Manuel's agents in Seville reported that he would not risk his neck on a voyage even to the Canaries in such rotten vessels.

Magellan insisted that food to last at least two years be stored

[2] See Nowell, *Magellan's Voyage*, pp. 59–60, for calculations of tonnage.

aboard, distributed so that the loss of no ship would leave the others without supplies. But during the bitter winter at Port San Julián on the coast of Patagonia, an inventory revealed that checkers in Seville had fraudulently receipted bills of the victualers and had allowed them to load only half enough foodstuffs. This shortage proved a disaster to starving sailors, but Magellan was unaware of the danger as preparations were being completed. The trade goods shipped aboard consisted of bars of copper and iron, flasks of mercury, mirrors, knives, cloth, both cheap and expensive fabrics, fishhooks, beads, glass, cheap jewelry as well as some expensive items for Eastern nobility, hawk bells (which had proved pleasing to Indians in the Caribbean), colored caps, cloaks, and even a few handsome throne-like chairs for presentation to Eastern princes. Magellan did not intend to repeat the mistake made by Vasco da Gama on his first voyage to India when he had no gifts suitable for the proud and disdainful rulers whom he encountered.

Recruiting a suitable crew for so long a voyage offered difficulties. Nobody in this age had heard of psychological tests, such as submariners undergo, to determine fitness for arduous duty. But Magellan knew many hardened Portuguese veterans of the Eastern voyages and sought to enlist them. The Spanish authorities, however, balked at taking on too many Portuguese. A rumor started that Magellan intended, once he was at sea, to take over the fleet with his fellow countrymen and sail to Portuguese India. A royal order forced him to dismiss some of the Portuguese whom he had already persuaded to join the expedition and to replace them with Spaniards. The King also ordered him to substitute in the place of Faleiro a certain Juan de Cartagena, said to have been a natural son of Bishop Fonseca. Cartagena came aboard with the ambiguous title of "conjuncta persona," which implied that he would have joint command with Magellan. But Magellan never admitted that Cartagena occupied such a position, distrusted him, refused to take him into his confidence, and made an enemy who later came near wrecking the expedition.[3]

[3] *Ibid.*, pp. 65–67.

Plagued though Magellan was with problems, by early August his ships were manned with a complement variously estimated at from 241 to 280 men.[4] Of these, 37 were Portuguese; 30 or more, Italian; 19, French; one, English; one, German; and the rest Spanish. Over this polyglot and often unruly group the Portuguese Captain-General would somehow have to maintain discipline.

Not only did Magellan have to contend with prejudices of Spaniards against Portuguese, but he also had to worry about the efforts of his own countrymen to sabotage the voyage. King Manuel's agents had kept him informed about the preparations for the expedition. So long as Magellan and Faleiro appeared to be two crack-brained visionaries, Manuel was unconcerned. But now that Magellan had convinced Spain that his scheme was worth the investment of five royal ships, the Portuguese King had some second thoughts. Perhaps the navigator whom he had dismissed so cavalierly knew a westward way to the Indies. That might spell misfortune for the Portuguese. So Manuel called a council to ponder the matter and did his best to recall Magellan to Portugal. When persuasion failed, he instructed his ambassador to Spain to thwart somehow the sailing of the fleet. But he stopped short of taking the advice of one of his councilors, a bishop, who urged that he have Magellan murdered.

Finally, in the second week of August 1519, preparations appeared to be complete. On August 10, after mass at the church of Santa María de la Victoria, Magellan took an oath of allegiance to the Spanish King, and his four captains swore to obey Magellan in everything and to follow the course set by him. With that the ships cast off their mooring lines, swung out into the current of the Guadalquivir, and drifted with the current downriver to Sanlúcar de Barrameda on the open sea.

[4] *Ibid.*, p. 67. Nowell cites the figure 241. James A. Robertson, *Magellan's Voyage Around the World by Antonio Pigafetta* (Cleveland, Ohio, 1906), I, 204, notes that "The exact number of men who accompanied Magalhães is a matter of doubt." He cites statements ranging from 235 to 280 and lists by name 265.

The voyage from Seville to Sanlúcar, serving as a sort of shakedown cruise, revealed many deficiencies. For nearly six weeks more the fleet was tied up at Sanlúcar while Magellan frantically sought additional equipment and supplies from Seville. At last, on September 20, 1519, the fleet weighed anchor and sailed out into the vast Atlantic on a voyage that was to be marked by disaster and tragedy, yet a voyage that would prove Asia could be reached from the Atlantic, the goal that Columbus had sought in vain.

Magellan as Captain-General was in supreme command, but from the start he had to face incipient rebellion from his Spanish captains, who hated to be subordinate to a foreigner. Columbus, as a Genoese, to a lesser degree had also been troubled by the prejudice and suspicion of the Spanish officers under him. Magellan himself commanded the flagship, the *Trinidad*. Juan de Cartagena, whom Bishop Fonseca wanted to take command, was captain of the *San Antonio;* Gaspar de Quesada, captain of the *Concepción;* Luis de Mendoza, captain of the *Victoria;* and Juan Rodriguez Serrano, captain of the *Santiago*. Some authorities describe Serrano as a Portuguese, the brother of Francisco Serrão, Magellan's friend then resident in the Moluccas, but that identification appears to be incorrect.[5] The Spanish priests, who went along as chaplains and as potential missionaries to the heathen, shared the views of the Spanish captains and were less than tolerant of the Portuguese Captain-General. Magellan, on his part, was not disposed to exert himself to win the friendship or confidence of his Spanish colleagues. Perhaps he realized that such efforts would be useless. Even so, at times his refusal to divulge his plans and his arrogance served only to exacerbate the pride of his colleagues.

One member of the complement, an Italian aristocrat from Vicenza, Antonio Pigafetta, would have an importance for the future greater than most, for Pigafetta survived to write a detailed and vivid account of the whole voyage. The precise reasons that induced Pigafetta to go on the voyage are not clear. He

[5] Nowell, *Magellan's Voyage*, pp. 67–68, 76n.

137

had been in Spain as a gentleman-in-waiting to the papal nuncio and had heard of the impending expedition. Perhaps a spirit of adventure made the young Italian seek permission from the Spanish King to go along; at any rate, he received the royal assent and Magellan took him aboard—a lucky thing, for Pigafetta quickly formed a high opinion of the Captain-General and remained loyal to him in life and to his memory. He was enrolled under the name of Antonio Lombardo. Later Pigafetta made a career of relating in person the story of the voyage. He reported first, as was proper, to the King of Spain, now the Emperor Charles V. From Spain he went to Lisbon to give an account to King João III, who had succeeded to the Portuguese throne on the death of Manuel. After that he visited the court of Maria Luisa of Savoy, mother of King Francis I of France; then Federico Gonzaga, Marquis of Mantua; the Doge and Council of Ten in Venice; and finally Pope Clement VII. As a Knight of Rhodes himself, he dedicated the published work to the Grand Master of that Order. So, whatever the hardships of the voyage, Pigafetta forgot the difficulties in the pleasure of repeating the tale of adventure.

The course set by Magellan took the fleet by the Canaries, where they stopped five or six days for fresh meat, wood, and water, and thence by the Cape Verdes along the African coast until they reached Sierra Leone. Portuguese pilots regarded this route as the best to follow before heading west toward Brazil. But Magellan's Spanish captains questioned his judgment in sailing so far south and began to murmur and complain. When Juan de Cartagena went so far as to refuse to give the courtesy signals prescribed in the royal orders, and again to complain about the route with an intention of stirring up disaffection among the other officers, Magellan personally arrested him and ordered Captain Luis de Mendoza to keep him in irons on board the *Victoria*. The command of the *San Antonio* Magellan gave to a Spanish nobleman serving as chief purser of the fleet, one Antonio de Coca. Though Cartagena was under arrest, Magellan was aware that trouble was brewing, but for the time being all

138

went well. The current gradually took the ships out of the doldrums on the coast of Africa and the easterly trades drove them toward Brazil.

Ten weeks after leaving Sanlúcar the fleet made a landfall on the hump of Brazil, somewhere in the vicinity of modern Pernambuco. But Magellan stood out to sea lest he fall into the hands of Portuguese ships now accustomed to trade with that portion of Brazil. Not until he was reasonably sure that he was too far south to encounter lurking Portuguese ships did he risk a landing. On December 13, 1519, sailing into a harbor that he called Santa Lucia in honor of the saint whose name day it was, Magellan cast anchor and his men looked out upon a pleasant and inviting land. Today we call the site Rio de Janeiro. The sea-weary sailors went ashore and supplied themselves, says Pigafetta, with "a plentiful refreshment of fowls, potatoes, many sweet pineapples (in truth the most delicious fruit that can be found), the flesh of the *anta* [tapir, or perhaps llama], which resembles beef, sugar cane, and innumerable other things which I shall not mention in order not to be prolix." [6] Among the "other things" that cheered the sailors were Indian maidens, some of whom, Pigafetta declares, were beautiful and wore not a shred of clothing to hide their charms.

Since the conversion of heathen was one of the declared objectives of the expedition, Pigafetta observed that the Indians appeared to him to be good prospects for Christianity, cannibals though they were. "Mass was said twice on shore, during which those people remained on their knees with so great contrition and with clasped hands raised aloft, that it was an exceeding great pleasure to behold them. . . . Those people could be converted easily to the faith of Jesus Christ." [7] The natives had never before seen white men or ships, and conceived the notion that the men came from the sky and had brought a hoped-for rain that broke a great drought.

After thirteen days in this pleasant port, the fleet sailed again

[6] Robertson, *Magellan's Voyage . . . by Pigafetta*, I, 37.
[7] *Ibid.*, I, 43–45.

in search of a strait to the South Sea. Reaching the Río de la Plata, which they called the Santa María, they searched the estuary for some forty days and then once more headed south. The Río de la Plata was also called the "River of Solís" after Juan Díaz de Solís, who before Magellan had been sent to search for a southwest passage. Unhappily, in the autumn of 1516 he landed on the upper Plata and he and some of his men were killed and eaten by the Charrua Indians. Pigafetta was aware of this episode and comments: "A Spanish captain called Johan de Solís and sixty men, who were going to discover lands like us, were formerly eaten at that river by those cannibals because of too great confidence." [8]

Magellan's next landing was at Port San Julían, some 49°20′ of south latitude, which the fleet reached on March 31, 1520. Here, on the bleak shores of Patagonia, Magellan planned to establish winter quarters, for the weather was growing cold and constant storms made the seas too rough for ships to risk a further search in the antarctic waters to the south.

The Spanish captains, fretting and stewing over what they claimed was Magellan's ill-treatment, were fomenting a mutiny. They were tired of a voyage that seemed endless. They complained that Magellan had no real knowledge of a strait to the South Sea and had fraudulently persuaded Charles V to support his vain pretensions. If they could carry out their plot successfully, they would arrest Magellan and take him home in chains. With the fleet in their power, Juan de Cartagena would assume command, continue to the Moluccas by way of the Cape of Good Hope, load cargoes of spices, and sail back to Seville with riches enough for everybody. So ran the argument whispered among the Spanish officers as they matured their plot.

Magellan, who suspected that something was afoot, did not have to wait long for the Spaniards to show their hands. On Palm Sunday, April 1, he called upon all the officers and pilots to dine with him on board the flagship *Trinidad* after hearing mass on shore. Only one officer, Alvaro de Mesquita, a Portuguese,

[8] *Ibid.*, I, 47.

showed up. Mesquita was now captain of the *San Antonio*, for Magellan had relieved Antonio de Coca of that command. The same night de Coca, Cartagena, and Gaspar de Quesada, with a crew of thirty men, rowed to the *San Antonio*, overpowered Mesquita, fatally stabbed the mate, and took possession of the ship. They ordered Juan Sebastián del Cano, who was later to perform the remarkable feat of sailing the *Victoria* back to Spain, to take charge of the *San Antonio*.[9]

The mutineers now controlled the *San Antonio* (the largest vessel), the *Concepción*, and the *Victoria*. Magellan, however, commanding the *Trinidad*, was anchored nearest the entrance to the harbor, a fact of some importance as events developed. Alongside the *Trinidad* lay the *Santiago*, smallest craft of the fleet, commanded by Juan Serrano, who had refused to go along with the rebels. Magellan now demonstrated his courage and audacity in a bold stroke that defeated the mutineers. They suggested a parley, which Magellan interpreted as a ruse to capture him, and promised obedience to the Captain-General if he would come to terms with them. During an interchange of messages between the flagship and the other vessels, Magellan sent six men commanded by the constable of the fleet, Gonzalo Gómez Espinosa, to the *Victoria* to carry a letter to the captain, Luís de Mendoza. Espinosa's crew kept their weapons carefully hidden as they clambered aboard. As Mendoza contemptuously read Magellan's letter, Espinosa stabbed him in the throat and another member of the boarding party crushed his skull. A second boat crew headed by Duarte Barbosa now swarmed aboard the *Victoria* and took charge of the vessel. Under Barbosa the *Victoria* upped anchor and moved over to the mouth of the harbor. With three loyal ships, Magellan now had the harbor fairly well blocked; even so, the *San Antonio* tried to run by the *Trinidad* in the night, but fouled the flagship, so that Magellan's men

[9] Pigafetta barely mentions the mutiny, for reasons best known to him. A succinct account is given by Nowell, *Magellan's Voyage*, pp. 110–113. A good summary of the facts will be found in Robertson, *Magellan's Voyage . . . by Pigafetta*, I, 230–234.

jumped to the rebel ship's deck and quickly captured it. Now only the *Concepción,* which Juan de Cartagena had taken over, remained in the hands of the mutineers. Cartagena knew that the jig was up and that he had no choice but to surrender.

Magellan had to punish the mutineers and make an example of the rebellious officers. Something over forty of the mutineers received sentences of death, but since he could not afford to execute so many of the sailors who were needed to work the ships, the Captain-General made a virtue of necessity and mercifully commuted the sentences of the seamen and junior officers to hard labor. The fate of the leaders, however, was another matter. He ordered that Mendoza, killed aboard the *Victoria,* should be proclaimed a traitor and that his body should be taken ashore, drawn and quartered, and hung upon a gibbet. He also had Quesada proclaimed a traitor and beheaded. To perform the execution, he gave Quesada's sub-lieutenant, Luís de Molino, the choice of death by hanging or severing the head of his master. Molino chose the latter alternative.

For some reason, Magellan hesitated to execute Cartagena, possibly because of his influence back in Spain. Nevertheless, he gave him perhaps a grimmer punishment. When the fleet sailed away, he left Cartagena and a rebellious priest marooned on the bitter shores of Patagonia. Nothing was ever heard of them again.

More than fifty years later, when Francis Drake was making his own circumnavigation of the world, he too put into the harbor at San Julián—by a curious coincidence, to execute a potential mutineer in his fleet, one Thomas Doughty. A contemporary account of Drake's voyage notes that he found the Spanish gibbet, "made of a spruce mast," on shore.

The fleet's stay at San Julián lasted nearly five months. The vessels had to be careened, the bottoms scraped, seams caulked, and braces strengthened against the beating waves of the Antarctic. While the larger ships were undergoing repairs, Magellan sent the *Santiago* under Juan Serrano to probe the coastline to the south in the hope of finding the elusive strait. After sixteen days of beating against the wind, Serrano found a protected bay, but when he attempted to put to sea again, his ship foundered and he beached it on a sandbank, saving the entire crew except his own body servant. Two of the sailors undertook to travel overland to San Julián to get aid while the remainder waited on the shores of the bay, which Serrano named Santa Cruz. Miraculously, after eleven days the two got through, and Magellan sent a rescue party to bring back Serrano and his men.

On August 24, 1520, Magellan took Serrano's advice and moved his winter quarters from San Julián to a better anchorage at Santa Cruz. For two months, while waiting for the storms to abate, the men hunted, fished, and trapped. While at San Julián, Magellan had discovered the shortage in his supplies, and he now did his best to smoke enough meat and fish to feed his men on the voyage across the South Sea, once they had found the strait. Some equipment they managed to salvage from the hulk of the *Santiago*, discovered where it was beached down the coast.

With the approach of the southern spring, on October 18, 1520, the fleet left its winter quarters and again turned south. Three days later they cast anchor under the lee of a headland that Magellan named the Cape of the Eleven Thousand Virgins, because October 21, the day of their arrival, memorializes a legend of the Huns' slaughter at Cologne of a host of virgins led by St. Ursula. Though Magellan did not know it, he had anchored near the approach to the long-sought strait.

The season of storms, however, was not over—if it ever is in that region—and a raging tempest blew the *San Antonio* and the *Concepción* into a bay to the west while the *Trinidad* and the *Victoria* rode out the storm in the open sea. All contact between the vessels was of course lost, but when the winds abated, Magellan sighted the *Victoria* on the horizon, and a few days later the *San Antonio* and *Concepción* miraculously came into view from the west with bunting and flags flying, indicative of good news. They reported that they had been blown into the strait. Though they had not traversed its entire length to the South Sea, all tests of currents, tides, and saltiness showed that it was not a river but a true strait between the oceans.

Even though they had found the strait, Magellan's captains all were ready to turn back now and make their way to the Moluccas by the known route around the Cape of Good Hope instead of attempting to cross the unknown reaches of the South Sea. The Captain-General overruled them and declared that they would go on. Supplies were short, to be sure, but they had already taken quantities of sardines while waiting for the *San Antonio* and *Concepción* to return. They had meat they had smoked at Santa Cruz and San Julián. They would go on if they had to eat the leather fittings on the rigging. So with some dismay the fleet prepared to make its way through the strait. But first Magellan sent his constable, Espinosa, in the longboat to explore the channel. After four days Espinosa returned with word that they had indeed reached the Great South Sea. The walls of the channel to the west were rocky and narrow, the way was tortuous, and the currents tricky, but ships could get through. Before attempting the passage, Magellan ordered fishing and hunting parties to catch and cure more sardines, sea birds, and small game for the long voyage ahead.

In the meantime the *San Antonio* had disappeared in the night. Believing that the vessel might have been blown out to sea, the three other ships searched the seas, but found no clue. Small wonder that they could not find her, for the crew had mutinied, put the captain, Mesquita, in chains, and sailed back to Spain to spread lies about Magellan's mismanagement of the expedition.

While the fleet was at anchor, a canoe of Indian men and women rowed to the ships and came aboard. The first humans encountered since the arrival in the strait, these were different from Indians met with at San Julián, who had astonished the voyagers because of their great size. Magellan evidently intended to take captive the new arrivals, as he had captured some of the Indians at San Julián, for his sailors pulled the canoe aboard and took their paddles. After feasting on fish, the savages stretched themselves naked on the bare deck, though it was sleeting, and went to sleep. Next morning the Indians and canoe were gone

144

from the deck, and none knew how they had escaped without being seen by the watch. Henceforth the crews were cautioned to guard against a return of more Indians for a night attack.

The Indians captured at San Julián were named Patagonians, or "men with big feet," by Magellan because of their awkward straw sandals. Described as "giants," they were being taken back to Spain as curiosities, but none survived. Pigafetta took a great interest in them and set about making a vocabulary of Patagonian words. Describing his efforts to Christianize one of the giants, christened Paulo, Pigafetta remarked: "Once I made the sign of the cross, and, showing it to him, kissed it. He immediately cried out 'Setebos,' and made me a sign that if I made the sign of the cross again, Setebos would enter into my body and cause it to burst." [10] Earlier Pigafetta had explained that Setebos was a Patagonian demon. Shakespeare evidently had read this passage in Richard Eden's translation of Pigafetta in *The Decades of the New World* when he had Caliban in *The Tempest* call upon his demon Setebos.

At last Magellan decided that he had taken on enough fish and smoked game to make the voyage across the South Sea possible; but before departing from the River of Sardines (the point where they had been fishing) he again called his officers into council. Again they expressed their opposition to an attempt to reach the Moluccas by sailing westward, and once again Magellan overruled them. On November 24 they weighed anchor, and on November 28 the fleet emerged into the South Sea, which seemed so benign that Magellan christened it the Pacific, a name that it retained. His designation of the sea passage as All Saints did not stick, for history has chosen to call it by the name of the captain-general who discovered it.[11]

On leaving the strait, Magellan set a northerly course up the coast of South America, then northwesterly until he reached Clipperton Island, far out to sea from the coast of Central Amer-

[10] Robertson, *Magellan's Voyage . . . by Pigafetta*, I, 83.
[11] See the excellent chapter by Parr, *So Noble a Captain*, pp. 307–321, for an account of Magellan's traversing the strait.

ica. After passing what was probably Clarion Island, a bit farther
to the north, he took a westerly course across a barren ocean in
which he made no landfall until the Marianas, after a voyage of
nearly four months.[12] With singular ill-luck, he managed to miss
islands in the central Pacific where he could have found fresh
food in plenty.

Scholars have wondered why the great mariner chose such a
northwesterly course, but Charles E. Nowell, in his edition of
Pigafetta, expresses the conviction that Magellan had a dream not
only of reaching the Moluccas but of discovering the lands of
Ophir and Tarshish, whence, according to II Chronicles, 9:21,
King Solomon obtained "gold, and silver, ivory, and apes, and
peacocks." The Biblical Ophir and Tarshish would be found,
Magellan believed, about where we now locate Formosa or the
Ryukyus.[13]

The endless days in the Pacific were a torment to hungry and
thirsty sailors suffering from scurvy, often prostrated by equatorial heat. They had long since eaten such of the slender stock of
fish and smoked meat that had not spoiled. Such water as they
had left was foul and nauseating. Pigafetta comments:

> We were three months and twenty days without getting any
> kind of fresh food. We ate biscuit, which was no longer
> biscuit, but powder of biscuits swarming with worms, for
> they had eaten the good. It stank strongly of the urine of
> rats. We drank yellow water that had been putrid for many
> days. We also ate some ox hides that covered the top of the
> mainyard to prevent the yard from chafing the shrouds, and
> which had become exceedingly hard because of the sun, rain,
> and wind. We left them in the sea for four or five days, and
> then placed them for a few moments on top of the embers,
> and so ate them; and often we ate sawdust from boards. Rats
> were sold for one-half ducado apiece, and even then we could
> not get them. . . . Had not God and His blessed mother
> given us so good weather we would all have died of hunger

[12] Nowell, *Magellan's Voyage*, pp. 124–125.
[13] *Ibid.*, pp. 20–22.

in that exceeding vast sea. Of a verity I believe no such voyage will ever be made [again].[14]

When his crews were almost dead from hunger, thirst, and scurvy, Magellan at last, on March 6, 1521, reached an island in the Pacific that we now know as Guam. As the ships came to anchor offshore, outrigger canoes put out from the beach, and soon the deck of the *Trinidad* was swarming with stout, brown-skinned warriors who appeared friendly at first but soon were pillaging the ship of everything movable and mistreating the sick and feeble sailors. In order to clear the ship of the marauders, crossbowmen sent a volley of arrows into them, killing several. Such weapons the natives had never seen, and those left un-wounded quickly abandoned the vessel and rowed ashore. The next morning, desperate for food and water, so near and yet so difficult to get, the Captain-General had all three ships bombard the seaside village; he then led a party of some forty of his ablest men ashore. Systematically they collected all the food left by the fleeing natives: pigs, chickens, coconuts, bananas (which Pigafetta called figs), rice, breadfruit, and fresh vegetables and fruits whose names they did not know. Water casks were filled, and the ships got under way once more. Magellan did not care to risk another encounter with the inhabitants of this island, one of a group that he named the Ladrones, or Islands of Thieves.

Sailing to a nearby island now called Rota, Magellan traded for more foodstuffs and again set sail for the southwest. His men were now nourished, and those sick with the scurvy were recov-ering. He was on his way to the Moluccas, or perhaps the lands of Ophir and Tarshish. He little knew it, but his next stop would be in islands that would later be christened the Philippines after a king of Spain.

Or March 16, 1521, the fleet reached the shores of a large island, which it skirted, and sailed into a bay that promised pro-tection against storms. The ships cast anchor off a small, unin-habited island, and the next day a party of men went ashore to

[14] Robertson, *Magellan's Voyage . . . by Pigafetta*, I, 83–85.

investigate. They found deserted fields containing banana and coconut-palm trees and other vegetables and fruits that a native of Guam, whom they had captured and brought along, pointed out as good to eat. Magellan set up a rest camp ashore for the recuperation of the sick and ordered the careening and repair of his battered craft. He learned from a native chief who rowed over from another island that this island was called Homonhon, a name it still bears. Magellan was anchored in Leyte Gulf, an area to be made famous more than four centuries later by an American encounter with a Japanese fleet. The island to the north was Samar, one of the largest in the Philippine archipelago.

The natives who visited the Spanish camp on Homonhon spoke no language that anyone in the party understood, neither the captive from Guam nor a Malay bondservant named Henrique whom Magellan had acquired years before in Malacca. But they wore gold armlets and bracelets, and carried shields and weapons adorned with gold—and gold carried a message that all understood. Magellan believed that he had indeed reached the lands of Ophir and Tarshish, and he determined to search for the source of the precious metal.

If the prospect of finding gold held the interest of Magellan at Homonhon, the utility of the coconut most interested Pigafetta. In describing the virtues of the coconut palm, which provides food, wine, milk, oil, vinegar, and cordage, Pigafetta grows ecstatic. Even the shell, when burned, makes an ash useful as a medicine. For the scurvy-ridden patients from the fleet, however, not coconut ashes but coconut milk proved a refreshing elixir, and with oranges and fresh vegetables they quickly recovered their health.

After a week of rest on Homonhon the seamen were ready to sail again, and on March 25 the fleet began to thread its way southwesterly through Surigao Strait. Three days later they anchored near a small island now called Limasaua, off northern Mindanao, and received aboard the flagship a friendly chieftain who, to Magellan's delight, spoke a Malaysian language that Henrique understood. More than that, he came bearing

148

gold, in which Magellan, to keep the basis of exchange low, pretended to have little interest; he finally established the rate of exchange at one pound of gold for one pound of iron, which the islanders prized more than gold. The friendly chief, Rajah Colambu, had a brother, the Rajah Siaui, who also came to visit Magellan. Pigafetta, impressed with the second Rajah's account of his riches, remarks: "Pieces of gold of the size of walnuts and eggs are found by sifting the earth in the island of that king [Siaui] who came to our ships. All the dishes of that king are of gold and also some portion of his house, as we were told by that king himself." [15]

To see what Rajah Colambu's island was like, Magellan got permission for Pigafetta and Henrique to accompany him home. The visit, which took place on Good Friday, was memorable; Colambu wined and dined his guests to the risk of their salvation, for they were forced to eat meat on this holy day, and the palm wine went to their heads. Pigafetta writes:

> The king had a plate of pork brought in and a large jar filled with wine. . . . Before the king took the cup to drink, he raised his clasped hands toward the sky, and then toward me; and when he was about to drink, he extended the fist of his left hand toward me (at first I thought that he was about to strike me) and then drank. I did the same toward the king. They all make those signs one toward another when they drink. We ate with such ceremonies and with other signs of friendship. I ate meat on holy Friday, for I could not help myself. . . . Two large porcelain dishes were brought in, one full of rice and the other of pork with its gravy. . . . My companion became intoxicated as a consequence of so much drinking and eating.[16]

Pigafetta does not confess to his own condition, but clearly he too was far gone in drink and sinful feasting.

On Easter Sunday, Magellan had a company go ashore in their

[15] *Ibid.*, I, 117–119.
[16] *Ibid.*, I, 115–117.

best clothes for a solemn mass. To the two Rajahs the priest explained the ceremonies and the significance of the cross, nails, and crown of thorns that were brought in. The Rajahs kissed the cross and gave evidence of a becoming piety, which pleased Magellan. In the afternoon he and his men erected a cross on the highest peak of the island and explained to the Rajahs that it would protect them against any Christians who might later land there—and against lightning and tempests. Second only to his search for gold was Magellan's concern for the salvation of these heathen. With fanatical zeal he set about evangelizing the natives whom he now encountered.

The time had come to continue his exploration, and he asked Colambu for pilots to take him to Cebu, an island that Colambu had described as the richest in the archipelago. After a brief visit there, he planned to push on to Ternate in the Moluccas. As soon as the rice harvest was over, Colambu offered to go himself with Magellan to Cebu. To hasten the harvest, the Captain-General ordered a party of seamen to assist. Never was a harvest completed more expeditiously, and rarely was a harvest festival more convivial—so convivial, in fact, that Magellan had to send details of marines to round up the revelers. At length, on April 3, the harvesters were sober enough to sail, and the fleet set out for Cebu, where after four days they anchored in the harbor of the same name.

The ruler of Cebu, the Rajah Humabon, a short fat little man, at first demanded tribute to allow the Spaniards to land. On the advice, however, of a Siamese trader in his court, who explained that people similar to these had conquered many cities of India and Malacca, he had a change of heart and made a pact of peace and friendship with Magellan. Indeed, impressed by the trade goods, he allowed the Spaniards to set up a shop on shore and gave the crews a hearty welcome. "Whenever any of our men went on shore, both by day and by night, everyone invited him to eat and to drink," Pigafetta remarks; and he adds a significant comment: "The women loved us very much more than their own men." [17] The women of Cebu were attractive and complai-

[17] *Ibid.*, I, 169.

sant, but Magellan decreed that his men could have nothing to do with them until they were baptized as Christians, a condition that made every young seaman an ardent missionary.

The Christianization of Cebu became Magellan's obsession, and he went about the undertaking with soldierly dispatch. The rewards of Christianity that he held out to Humabon increased that potentate's eagerness to embrace the new faith, for Magellan assured him that he could now conquer his enemies more easily. When some of Humabon's chiefs resisted the Rajah's orders to become Christian, Magellan called them together and announced that he would kill all who did not obey Humabon.

The priests worked overtime baptizing the new converts. Humabon was christened Don Carlo, after Charles V, and members of his family, including the Queen, received names of the Spanish royal family. "Counting men, women, and children," Pigafetta reports, "we baptized eight hundred souls. . . . Before that week had gone, all the persons of that island, and some from the other islands, were baptized. We burned one hamlet which was located in a neighboring island, because it refused to obey the king or us. We set up the cross there, for those people were heathen." [18] The fact that many of the natives had more than one wife caused some questioning, but Magellan and his priests decided not to raise that issue and to baptize all the multiple wives. It was enough that these heathen had agreed to burn their idols. Magellan himself took such an active part in the baptismal and other ceremonies that one would have thought he himself held some sacerdotal office. As part of the acceptance of the heathen into the Church, he had them all swear allegiance to the King of Spain. He was adding a new realm to the empire of Spain and new souls to the Kingdom of Christ.

Magellan's religious zeal and his desire to set up Rajah Humabon as the Christian king of the archipelago (which he had named the Islands of St. Lazarus) in the end proved his undoing. When word came that the chief of the island of Mactan, occupying one side of the harbor of Cebu, refused to obey the Christian king and his Spanish friends, Magellan determined to make an

[18] *Ibid.*, I, 155–157.

example of him. Furthermore, convinced that God would give him victory, he announced that he himself would lead a party of volunteers to Mactan and would accept no assistance from Humabon or any other chieftain. In fact, he invited Humabon to come along in one of his own boats, not as a combatant but as a spectator of the victory that the Christian God would vouchsafe them. Clearly, religious hysteria had usurped Magellan's judgment. His own captains attempted in vain to dissuade him from such a rash decision.

Shortly after midnight on Saturday, April 27, 1521, Magellan led a contingent of sixty men across the harbor to Mactan. Pigafetta was one of the group and gives an eyewitness account of the catastrophe. When Magellan offered peace if the rebel chief would recognize the Christian king and pay tribute, the only answer was a refusal accompanied by a request to hold off the attack until daylight while more men assembled. The wily chieftain hoped thereby to precipitate an immediate attack in the dark, for he had dug pits between the houses to entrap the Spaniards.

Magellan decided to wait until daylight, when forty-nine men splashed ashore, leaving eleven to guard the boats. Shooting from a distance, the crossbowmen and musketeers did little damage and soon exhausted their missiles. They managed to set fire to a few houses, which aroused the fury of the islanders, who swarmed upon the little band of Spaniards, hurling pointed stakes, rocks, and bamboo spears at them. The natives also shot poisoned arrows at the attackers' legs, which were bare of leg armor. After an arrow hit Magellan in the right leg, he ordered his men to retire slowly to the boats, but, says Pigafetta,

the men took flight, except six or eight of us who remained with the captain. . . . So we continued to retire for more than a good crossbow flight from the shore, always fighting up to our knees in the water. The natives continued to pursue us, and picking up the same spear four or six times, hurled it at us again and again. Recognizing the captain, so

152

many turned upon him that they knocked his helmet off his head twice, but he always stood firmly like a good knight, together with some others. Thus did we fight for more than an hour, refusing to retire farther. An Indian hurled a bamboo spear into the captain's face, but the latter immediately killed him with his lance, which he left in the Indian's body. Then, trying to lay hand on sword, he could draw it out but halfway because he had been wounded in the arm with a bamboo spear. When the natives saw that, they all hurled themselves upon him. One of them wounded him on the left leg with a large cutlass, which resembles a scimitar, only being larger. That caused the captain to fall face downward, when immediately they rushed upon him with iron and bamboo spears and with their cutlasses, until they killed our mirror, our light, our comfort, and our true guide.[19]

Thus died Magellan, the victim of his own overconfidence in the strength of European arms and the intercession of his God. He had reached a point in Southeast Asia not far from the area that he had penetrated earlier on the expedition to Malacca. Thus in the two expeditions, from opposite directions, he had virtually circled the globe. It was not given him to complete the circumnavigation that he had begun in 1519, but the feat that he did perform was one of the most remarkable in the annals of exploration. Those who state that Magellan was the first to circumnavigate the globe forget that he himself did not complete the voyage. Yet it was his courage and dogged persistence that prevented the expedition from turning back and ultimately resulted in a remnant finishing the task that he had set himself.

With their leader gone, the captains chose Duarte Barbosa to be captain-general. The choice was a poor one, for Barbosa quickly revealed that he lacked the judgment to lead. He immediately antagonized Magellan's Malaysian bondservant, who had worshipped his master and who lay wounded after the fight on

[19] *Ibid.*, I, 175–177.

Mactan. Despite his injuries, Barbosa ordered him to get up and carry a message to Rajah Humabon. More than that, he warned him that he was still a slave and would remain one; with that he kicked him and sent him on his way. The message that Henrique carried was not the one that Barbosa intended. In short, Henrique persuaded Humabon to join the Rajah of Mactan and crush the Spaniards.

The thought of the loot to be taken in the Spanish ships convinced Humabon that he should give up his pretense of being "the Christian king"; he would go back to his old gods and be rich. To set his plan in motion, he invited Barbosa and all the leaders to a banquet ashore; charmed with the women that the Rajah provided and flushed with many bowls of palm wine, the men had no thought of danger. But at a signal from the Rajah, his henchmen fell on the guests with their knives and murdered or took captive all except two of them. These two, who had remained more sober than the rest, had grown suspicious and escaped. They were the constable, Espinosa, and a pilot, Juan Lopes Carvalho. Running to the shore, they leaped into a boat and rowed back to the ships. Espinosa took over the *Trinidad*, and Carvalho took command of the *Victoria*. He gave the alarm to Juan Sebastián del Cano, in charge of the *Concepción*. All three ships cut their cables and got under way at once, moving inshore to bombard the town. Juan Serrano, wounded and bleeding, was brought to the beach by his captors; he called to his shipmates to quit firing their cannon and to ransom him. "We asked him whether all the others and the interpreter [Henrique] were dead," says Pigafetta, who had been too seriously injured to go ashore. "He said that they were all dead except the interpreter. He begged us earnestly to redeem him with some of the merchandise; but Johan Carvaio [Juan Carvalho], his boon companion, would not allow the boat to go ashore so that they might remain masters of the ships." [20] Whether Carvalho, who had taken command, would not rescue Serrano because Serrano might displace him or whether he was afraid the natives might

[20] *Ibid.*, I, 181–183.

154

swarm out and seize the ships is a moot question; at any rate, the ships sailed away, leaving the doomed and supplicating captain kneeling on the beach.

The later history of the voyage is a sequence of disasters. Throughout the summer and early autumn the fleet sailed aimlessly around islands of the southern Philippines and northern Indonesia, without, however, reaching their destination in the Moluccas. The *Concepción* had become so unseaworthy that her crew and supplies were transferred to the remaining two ships and she was burned. Carvalho, ignorant and incompetent, appeared to be more interested in piracy than in finding Ternate. He installed a harem of captured women in his quarters and lived like a Malay potentate. The crews at last mutinied and elected Espinosa captain-general in his place. On November 8, 1521, Espinosa managed to get the fleet to the Moluccas, but, to his consternation, found that Francisco Serrão as well as the King of Ternate had been poisoned and that the Portuguese were installed on that island. To avoid capture he took the two ships to Tidore, a neighboring island to the south, where he obtained the local ruler's oath of allegiance to the King of Spain, built a fort for him, took on a cargo of spices, and got ready to sail for home by way of the Cape of Good Hope.

With both ships heavily laden with cloves and other spices, the Spaniards planned to sail from Tidore on December 18, 1521. The *Victoria* got under way, but the *Trinidad* sprang a leak that proved difficult to find and repair. Lest both ships miss the monsoon that would take them back to the Cape of Good Hope, the *Victoria* sailed alone on December 21 with Juan Sebastián del Cano in command and a crew of forty-seven Europeans and thirteen islanders. Pigafetta was one of the ship's company and reported the hazards of the voyage. Left behind on the *Trinidad* were Espinosa and Carvalho (who apparently again took command, but temporarily) with fifty-three men. Since they gave up hope of making the voyage by the Cape, they planned to try for the American coast at Darien, roughly the route followed later by the annual Spanish galleon from Manila. Actually they got only as far as the Mariana Islands and were forced to turn back. Captured by the Portuguese, only five of the fifty-three ever got back to Spain. Espinosa survived and was released by the Portuguese in 1526. On his return to Spain the Emperor Charles V made him a noble and gave him a handsome pension. For his loyalty and courage, he deserved it.

The homeward voyage of the *Victoria* under del Cano, one of the erstwhile mutineers off San Julián, was troubled and painful. With pilots provided by the King of Tidore, they made their way slowly through the Indonesian Islands, around the tip of Malaysia at Singapore, and across the Indian Ocean to the coast of East Africa. Thence they followed the coast southward and eventually rounded the Cape. Pigafetta gives a vivid account of the difficulties of the passage:

> It is the largest and most dangerous cape in the world. Some of our men, both sick and well, wished to go to a Portuguese settlement called Mozanbich [Mozambique], because the ship was leaking badly, because of the severe cold, and especially because we had no other food than rice and water. . . . Finally by God's help, we doubled that cape on May six at a distance of five leguas. Had we not approached so closely we could never have doubled it. Then we sailed northwest for two months continually without taking on any fresh food or water. Twenty-one men died during that short time. When we cast them into the sea, the Christians went to the bottom face upward, while the Indians [natives of the Moluccas] always went down face downward. Had not God given us good weather we would all have perished of hunger. Finally, constrained by our great extremity, we went to the islands of Capo Verde.[21]

The date was July 9, 1522. Although they obtained a small quantity of food and water by telling a tale of being storm-beset in Spanish waters, the Portuguese grew suspicious and detained thirteen men and the ship's boat. Fearful of being captured, the

[21] *Ibid.*, II, 183–185.

Victoria sailed immediately.

To their amazement, the ship's company discovered that they had gained a day in crossing what we now call the International Date Line. Pigafetta explains:

> We charged our men when they went ashore in the boat to ask what day it was, and they told us that it was Thursday with the Portuguese. We were greatly surprised, for it was Wednesday with us, and we could not see how we had made a mistake; for as I had always kept well, I had set down every day without any interruption. However, as was told us later, it was no error, but as the voyage had been made continually toward the west and we had returned to the same place as does the sun, we had made that gain of twenty-four hours, as is clearly seen.[22]

The weary voyage finally ended on September 8, 1522, when the *Victoria* tied up in the harbor of Seville. Nineteen Europeans and four East Indians were alive when the ship docked. Mutineer though he might have been at San Julián, del Cano had achieved the incredible feat of bringing back a leaking ship loaded with enough spices to pay a profit on the whole expedition, including the loss of four ships. Pigafetta evidently did not like him or approve of him, for he does not mention him by name. Del Cano received a coat-of-arms and a pension from the Emperor, but did not live long enough to enjoy either, for he died at sea on August 4, 1526, while serving as chief pilot of an expedition trying to repeat Magellan's feat of going to the Moluccas via the strait.

Spain claimed that the Moluccas lay on its side of the line of demarcation as established by the Treaty of Tordesillas. Actually they did not, but since the line was vague, the question was a matter of contention between Spain and Portugal for several years. As, however, the Spaniards had not been able to capitalize successfully upon the route to Asia via the Strait of Magellan, and as the Emperor Charles V needed money, he agreed in 1529 to accept from King João III of Portugal the sum of 350,000

[22] *Ibid.,* II, 185.

ducats to renounce any Spanish claims to the Moluccas. Thereafter the Portuguese held the spice islands until the Dutch seized them in the seventeenth century.

If Magellan's great voyage did not create an immediate Spanish empire in the Pacific, it nevertheless pointed the way to future developments in that region. It also went down in history as one of the most heroic ventures of the sixteenth century.

Magellan's immediate reputation, however, suffered, for the mutineers who came home in the *San Antonio* spread lies to justify their defection. Even the return of the *Victoria* did not restore his reputation, for its captain, Juan Sebastián del Cano, for all of his prowess in bringing back a crippled ship, had been one of the mutineers at San Julián; furthermore, he was a Spaniard and, like most of the Spaniards on the voyage, he had bitterly resented the frequent high-handedness of the Portuguese Captain-General. Consequently, he merely confirmed the tales told by the crew of the *San Antonio*. In Portugal too the name of the great navigator was reviled, for the Portuguese felt that he had betrayed his own country in taking service with Spain, even though King Manuel had dismissed him and held out no hope for him in his native land.

Eventually, however, the account that Pigafetta delighted in relating in every European court where he found a reception had its effect. Europeans began to realize the heroic accomplishments of this dedicated man. His most recent biographer takes his title from Pigafetta's prayer that "the fame of so noble a captain will not be effaced in our time." [23] In fact his fame continued to grow through the centuries.

Magellan, like many of his contemporaries, had one foot in the medieval world of the Crusaders and the other foot in the new world of scientific investigation. He took pride in being a Knight of St. James, and wore into battle the Cross of St. James. Devoutly he believed in his mission to convert the heathen. On the bleak coast of Patagonia he took time to baptize such Indians as he could capture. In the Philippines he labored to convert the

[23] Parr, *So Noble a Captain*, p. 377.

natives and lost his life for his devotion to this cause. Careful to observe all holy days, he designated newly discovered places by the name of the saint on whose day he arrived. Hence he called the archipelago that we now know as the Philippines the St. Lazarus Islands, a name that, happily, did not survive. Like Columbus, Magellan always remembered that he was not only an explorer but also a latter-day apostle of Christ. To neither Magellan nor Columbus did the search for wealth in the Indies, even if that search included the enslavement of the heathen, seem incompatible with the Christian mission of first saving the souls of those same heathen. The humanitarianism of a later age had not yet been born.

Hernán Cortés, Greatest of the Conquistadors

ACROSS THE TABLELANDS OF ESTREMADURA IN SOUTHWESTERN Spain harsh winds blow in winter, and in the summer a brazen sun bakes the dusty earth. At the end of the fifteenth century, countless sheep wandered over the scrub-covered plains, while herds of swine rooted for nuts and acorns among the beech and oak forests of the hillsides. Gaunt cattle and wiry horses grazed in the better pastureland. Here and there in the lonely waste, shepherds and swineherds had their huts. Villages and towns, then as now, were few and far between, for this was a thinly populated region that offered little ease or comfort to its inhabitants. Its men, weatherbeaten and tough, rode like centaurs and knew well how to handle sword and lance. They and their ancestors had fought the Moors on these selfsame plains, and they had developed a dexterity at arms that exceeded any other skill or accomplishment.

If nature had failed to lavish the good things of the earth upon Estremadura, she had not been niggardly in providing courageous men. Hardened by the stubborn land, convinced by long

160

wars against the Moors that they were chosen soldiers of the Cross, nourished on romances of chivalry, and proud of their heritage, men of Estremadura in particular were ready and eager for fresh ventures when the opportunities of the New World opened before them. Since many of them had little besides a horse and a sword, they also desperately needed material resources. Consequently, Estremadura supplied many heroes of the Conquest overseas, as it had furnished warriors for the Re-Conquest of the homeland.

The greatest of the conquistadors was Hernán Cortés, an Estremaduran born in 1485 in the sleepy little town of Medellín, on the south side of the Guadiana River. Both his father and mother belonged to the minor aristocracy, people of "little wealth but much honor," [1] says Francisco López de Gómara, Cortés' chaplain and his first biographer. They were well enough off, however, to send young Cortés away for his education to Salamanca—not to the famous university, but to the house of a family connection where he was supposed to learn grammar and good manners. But schooling was not to the liking of this lad of fourteen, and after two years he returned home, a disappointment to his family, who had hoped he would study law and prosper.

The virus of adventure was already in the blood of the youth, who first thought of going away to Naples and joining the forces of the "Great Captain," Gonzalo Fernández de Córdoba, whose campaigns in Italy had made him famous. But after due reflection Cortés elected to cast his lot with the newly appointed governor of Hispaniola, Nicolás de Ovando. His choice was determined, says Gómara, by his opinion that the Indies appeared to be "the more promising because of the quantity of gold that was being brought from there."

The hot-blooded young Estremaduran, just short of eighteen years old, had romantic trysts to keep before sailing away with

---

[1] *Cortés: The Life of the Conqueror by His Secretary, Francisco López de Gómara*, trans. and ed. Lesley Byrd Simpson (Berkeley and Los Angeles, Calif., 1964), p. 7.

Ovando. A few nights prior to the fleet's departure, as he was attempting to reach the window of his lady-love, a wall gave way and dropped him in a pile of rubble with a damaged leg. Worse still, an angry husband rushed out with sword in hand. He was with difficulty restrained from putting an end to the intruder. It took some months for Cortés to recover, and he did not sail for the Indies until nearly a year later, in 1504.

Landing at Santo Domingo, capital of Hispaniola, then the center of Spanish activities in the New World, Cortés was offered a farm and some Indian laborers. He at first disdained them, declaring that he had come to mine gold. Governor Ovando, however, gave the youth of nineteen some sage advice, made him notary of the town council of Azúa, and assigned him land and enough Indians to enable him to prosper as rancher and trader.

The prosaic existence of a rancher made no appeal to Cortés, who yearned for more stirring activities. In 1509 he learned of an expedition about to set out under Diego de Nicuesa to explore and settle Veragua (now known as Panama), where gold was reported to be abundant. Cortés at once planned to go along, but again his amorous nature cost him the opportunity: promiscuous affairs with Indian women had left him with an unhealed venereal ailment, and he had to remain in Hispaniola, nursing himself back to health. For this he had reason to thank the fates, for Nicuesa's expedition met with complete disaster, and few lived to tell the tale of its misfortunes.[2] Providence, it seemed, was saving Cortés for greater things.

At this time Hispaniola was the staging area for explorations and conquests of other islands of the Caribbean and the mainland beyond—"A Nest of Hawks," as Salvador de Madariaga called it in a chapter heading of his biography, *Hernán Cortés, Conqueror of Mexico*. Would-be conquerors, landing on the island like hawks resting before further flight, soon winged their way to what they hoped would be some rich prey. Many returned

[2] The story of the unfortunate expedition is related in some detail by Sir Arthur Helps, *The Spanish Conquest in America* (4 vols., London, 1900–1904), I, 220–235.

poorer than they went; others never got back; but a few swooped down upon a valuable quarry. Like Hispaniola, Cuba would serve a few years later, as the same sort of eyrie for other hawks of the Conquest.

Typical of the adventurers who swarmed into Hispaniola was Alonso de Hojeda (sometimes spelled Ojeda), a wiry little man of infinite courage and poor judgment who had been one of Columbus' captains on the Second Voyage. Once he had demonstrated his daredeviltry in the presence of Queen Isabella, who had gone to visit the Cathedral of Seville. Hojeda ascended the Moorish tower, the famous Giralda, and ran out upon a plank extending from an opening more than two hundred feet above the ground. As he reached the end of the plank, he pirouetted on one foot, then danced back to the tower. The Queen was duly impressed. Whether this feat had anything to do with Hojeda's later career, history does not report, but he did gain the favor of Bishop Fonseca. In a succession of adventures, he continued to demonstrate more foolhardiness than wisdom.

In 1499, with a chart obtained surreptitiously from Columbus, and in company with Juan de la Cosa, map-maker, and Amerigo Vespucci, Florentine merchant and adventurer, Hojeda sailed on a voyage that led to the exploitation of the pearl fisheries on the coast of Venezuela west of the island of Margarita. Ten years later, with somewhat more experience and an unsatisfied appetite for treasure, he got himself named governor of the still unsubdued province of Urabá, which lay south of Veragua, in what is now Colombia. Several days before Nicuesa sailed on the ill-fated expedition that Cortés so narrowly missed, Hojeda set out with some three hundred men to take possession of this province. He, too, met with disaster. Landing with seventy or more men near the present site of Cartagena, he encountered Indians who attacked so effectively with poisoned arrows that only Hojeda and one other escaped.

Rescued by his ships, Hojeda made another landing farther north at a spot that he called San Sebastián. Wounded in the thigh by a poisoned arrow, he ordered the surgeon to burn out the wound with a red-hot iron and so managed to survive. Ho-

GOLD, GLORY, AND THE GOSPEL

jeda, like others of his kind, had begun his effort at establishing himself in the country by making war on the Indians. Thus, having cut themselves off from native food supplies, he and his men nearly starved. Leaving San Sebastián in the charge of a young Spaniard named Francisco Pizarro, who would be heard from later, Hojeda started back to Santo Domingo to seek supplies. Shipwrecked on the Cuban coast, he endured incredible hardships before finally reaching Hispaniola.

During a month-long trek through Cuban swamps Hojeda displayed a piety not usually expected from his type. He carried with him an image of the Virgin Mary given him by Bishop Fonseca, and he was accustomed to hang it on a tree limb and pray before it. And when he had failed to gain succor for his colony and in dire poverty came to die in Santo Domingo, he asked to be wrapped in a Franciscan's habit and thus breathed his last, "making a more praiseworthy end than other captains in these parts have done," says Gonzalo Fernandez de Oviedo in his *Historia General y Natural de las Indias*.[3] Though Hojeda may have given more visible evidence of his piety than some other conquistadors, as Oviedo implies, many shared his curious devotion to religion while manifesting incredible ferocity toward both the Indians and fellow Spaniards who might stand in their way.

While Cortés was rusticating in Hispaniola, waiting for the time when he could go on ventures farther afield, others were probing the mainland in search of gold. Hispaniola had already attracted hundreds of adventurers who possessed little besides their cloaks and swords and a burning desire to better their fortunes. They were also inordinately arrogant and proud, quick to take offense, quarrelsome, and envious. Madariaga remarks that a "German is usually afflicted by *Schadenfreude*, or joy at his neighbor's fall; the Spaniard suffers from sadness at his neighbor's rise."[4] Those Spaniards on Hispaniola who had found enough gold to rise above the common lot were envied by the less fortunate and were sometimes the victims of plots against

[3] Quoted by Helps, *ibid.*, I, 219.
[4] Salvador de Madariaga, *Hernán Cortés, Conqueror of Mexico* (London, 1942), p. 417.

them. Chicanery and treachery marred many of the expeditions that went out to seek new goldfields on the other islands and the mainland, as ambitious individuals tried to wrest advantages for themselves. A struggle for power and advantage would characterize much of the exploration and conquest, and Cortés himself was to suffer from this trait of the Spanish adventurers.

Among disgruntled residents of Hispaniola contemporary with Cortés was another Estremaduran, one Vasco Núñez de Balboa, from Jerez de los Caballeros, who had acquired a few Indians and was nursing his discontent on a farm, an occupation not to his taste. Like many of his kind, he was known more for his swordplay than for his prudence; at the moment he was in debt and in hazard of such law as existed on the island. He thus was more eager than most to join some expedition that might help him mend his fortunes. Consequently, when he heard in September 1510 that Martín Fernández de Enciso, a lawyer who had helped finance Hojeda, was taking supplies and reinforcements to Hojeda's luckless colonists at San Sebastián, he joined the expedition. Tradition reports that in order to avoid his creditors he had himself smuggled aboard in a barrel. At any rate, he wormed his way into the confidence of the group and persuaded them to move the colony farther along the coast to Darien. He then managed to seize the leadership from the lawyer Enciso, whom he shipped off to Spain. Balboa then persuaded Francisco Pizarro, erstwhile commander of the colony, a fellow Estremaduran, to serve as his subordinate. Balboa had good reason to detest lawyers like Enciso; he reflects this prejudice in a letter to the King of Spain in which he begs that "no bachelor of law or of anything else except medicine should be allowed to come to these parts . . . [for] not only are they bad themselves but they also make and contrive a thousand lawsuits and iniquities." [5]

Explorers were eagerly looking for a strait through the land barrier. Balboa had reports of the sea beyond a narrow neck of land; perhaps he could find a passage through. More than that, stories had come to him about a people on the other sea who possessed immense quantities of gold. The metal was so plentiful,

[5] Helps, *The Spanish Conquest*, I, 249, n.1.

165

reports said, that the natives gathered it in baskets and stored it in a kind of corncrib. In September of 1513 Balboa heard from Spain that Enciso had lodged damaging complaints against him. That made it necessary, he believed, to succeed in some great enterprise that would win the King's favor. The discovery of the rumored gold and an ocean route to Asia would clearly offset any charges brought by Enciso. In short, Balboa organized an expedition of some 190 Spaniards, with a number of ferocious bloodhounds, and on September 6 began cutting his way across the isthmus of Darien. Hostile Indians attacked them, but Balboa's men and dogs drove them off. Snakes, mosquitoes, and almost impenetrable vines hindered them, but they slogged on. At last at the end of nearly three weeks, on September 25, after climbing over a bony escarpment they came out upon a plain that Indians said led down to the sea. In order to be the first to sight this long-sought body of water, Balboa had his men wait while he climbed a hill that gave him a better view. Before him lay the illimitable expanse of the Pacific, or, as Balboa named it, "the South Sea."

Four days later on St. Michael's Day, Balboa, proud of being the first European to gaze upon the Pacific from American shores, marched boldly into the surf with drawn sword and claimed the great South Sea for the King of Spain. In honor of the saint he called the place the bay of San Miguel. No hero of chivalric romance could have made the ceremony more dramatic. It is one of the ironies of history that Cortés' reputation later so overshadowed Balboa's that John Keats in one of his finest poems, "On First Looking into Chapman's Homer," gave credit for the discovery to Cortés:

> Then felt I like some watcher of the skies
> When a new planet swims into his ken;
> Or like stout Cortez when with eagle eyes
> He star'd at the Pacific—and all his men
> Look'd at each other with a wild surmise—
> Silent, upon a peak in Darien.

Balboa and his men did not remain long silent in Darien; the discovery of the South Sea warranted a messenger to King Ferdinand. Furthermore, Balboa was eager to find the gold that Indians had reported in such quantities. Small amounts he did obtain, and he heard of more, somewhere down the coast of the South Sea. He also discovered an island where the natives dredged up lustrous pearls, an island that he called Isla Rica. To emphasize the richness of the South Sea, his messenger to King Ferdinand carried among his gifts to the sovereign two hundred of the finest pearls. Balboa now waited anxiously in the hope of receiving some royal commendation and reward.

But before his messenger arrived in Spain, King Ferdinand had already decided to send out as governor of Darien and Golden Castile (as the surrounding country had been named) an elderly and irascible aristocrat of Segovia, one Pedro Arias de Ávila, commonly called Pedrarias. He sailed from Sanlúcar in April 1514 with a notable company of more than fifteen hundred men, including a bishop for the new land, Juan de Quevedo; a historian who would write a useful account of Spanish activities, Gonzalo Fernández de Oviedo; an explorer who would push far into the interior of the country, Francisco Vásquez Coronado de Valdés; another explorer who would discover the Mississippi River and be buried beneath its waters, Hernando de Soto; and a common soldier who would write the most fascinating of all the accounts of Cortés' conquest of Mexico, Bernal Díaz del Castillo. Returning as chief constable was the lawyer Enciso whom Balboa had summarily replaced and shipped off to Spain.

Ferdinand provided Pedrarias with careful instructions for Christianizing the Indians, a policy laid down for all future conquerors and one that Cortés repeatedly exemplified. The most significant document that the King gave Pedrarias concerned making war on the natives. Used later by Cortés and others, it is called *El Requerimiento*, usually translated as "The Requisition." This statement, drawn up by a learned jurist, Dr. Palacios Rubios, is a notification that invading commanders were required to read to the Indians before making war upon them. It informs

167

Slavery in L.A.
better than annihilation
of USA.

investment, then
need to protect it.

them briefly about the principles of Christianity and the mystery of the Trinity. It then states that the Indians must acknowledge the supremacy of the Pope, accept the rulers of Spain as their overlords, and receive missionaries who will instruct them in Christian doctrine. If they refuse this,

> and maliciously make delay in it, I certify to you that, with the help of God, we shall powerfully enter into your country and shall make war against you in all ways and manners that we can, and shall subject you to the yoke and obedience of the Church and of Their Highnesses. We shall take you and your wives and your children, and shall make slaves of them, and as such shall sell and dispose of them as Their Highnesses may command. And we shall take your goods, and shall do you all the mischief and damage that we can, as to vassals who do not obey and refuse to receive their lord and resist and contradict him.[6]

The legalistic and theological Spaniards, having first given the Indians this information, were then free to attack if the natives were slow to capitulate.

Conquerors were warned not to make slaves of harmless and peaceable Indians. But cannibals might be enslaved without ceremony, for they were beyond the pale of human consideration. In practice, Indians usually proved sufficiently hostile to invite warfare, with a resultant supply of captives. When Indians of conquered territory were not actually enslaved, they might be parceled out to landholders under the system of encomiendas, which meant, in effect, land with serfs attached. An encomienda was an apportionment of land *and Indian workers* to a Spaniard who would benefit from the labor of his serfs; he was required "to teach them the things of our holy Catholic Faith." [7] This system was already in use in Hispaniola. Pedrarias merely brought royal sanctions in parchment for procedures that would be followed for long years to come.

[6] *Ibid.*, I, 264–267.
[7] *Ibid.*, I, 139.

Pedrarias' regime in Darien was ruthless, tyrannical, and at times incompetent. His greed was insatiable, and his captains tortured and slaughtered Indians without number in their search for gold. At first suspicious of the old Governor's intentions, Balboa at length patched up a peace with him and even was betrothed to Pedrarias' daughter safely distant in Spain. With brigantines built in parts on the east coast and transported over the mountains to the South Sea, Balboa planned to go in search of the wealth of Peru, but before he could accomplish his dream, Pedrarias lured him back to Acla (then his headquarters), accused him of treason, and ordered him beheaded at once in the town square. Balboa's "friend" who carried out the execution was Francisco Pizarro. Thus died in 1517 the discoverer of the South Sea, and thus Pizarro demonstrated a callousness that was to characterize his later career. Pedrarias lived on as Governor of Golden Castile and afterward as Governor of Nicaragua. At last he died in 1630. Oviedo is authority for the statement that he slaughtered or enslaved two million Indians. But it was under Pedrarias that the government of Spain first attempted to regularize the treatment of the Indians and provide for their methodical accession into the Christian fold.

While all of these events were transpiring on the mainland, Cortés was not twiddling his thumbs in Hispaniola. Diego Columbus, who had come out as Viceroy of the Indies, sent captains to conquer Puerto Rico and Cuba. The leader of the expedition to Cuba was one of the richest landholders on Hispaniola, Diego Velázquez. To help in the conquest he had as lieutenant Pánfilo de Narváez, who came from Jamaica with a company of bowmen. Another associate in the enterprise was Bartolomé de Las Casas, later Bishop of Chiapas, who became known as the Apostle to the Indians. He went along as one of Velázquez' secretaries. Another secretary, and treasurer to keep account of the King's fifth of the wealth captured, was Cortés, now twenty-six years old. A shrewd and worldly-wise young man, he made friends where he could and managed to rise to power by diplomacy rather than arms. Already he was demonstrating a

169

genius for tact and persuasion that would later serve him well in dealing with both Indians and Spaniards.

The conquest of Cuba offered no great difficulties, and though Diego Velázquez distributed profitable encomiendas to his friends, many adventurers yearned for something more. Always rumors of a richer land beyond the horizon stirred the restless. In February 1517 Velázquez authorized Hernández de Córdoba to take three ships from Cuba to explore the lands to the west. Bernal Díaz went along, and in *The True History of the Conquest of New Spain,* written in his old age to correct errors in other histories, he gives an account of this expedition, which made contact with the Mayas of Yucatán.

At one point a landing party observed a town of white-walled houses, so fine they named it Grand Cairo. Soon, however, the natives attacked, and the Spaniards had to retreat to their ships, but not before they had carried off a few idols, some gold, and two captives whom they hoped to make interpreters. Later, at another landing, they encountered such fierce resistance that they lost fifty men killed and many others were wounded, including the commander, Hernández de Córdoba, who later died of his injuries. Bernal Díaz himself received arrow wounds. The expedition returned to Cuba by way of Florida, which Ponce de León had earlier discovered.

The gold and the reports of fine cities on the mainland whetted the appetites of Cuban settlers for further investigation. Diego Velázquez, whose greed was exceeded only by his obesity, was eager to gain control of a land that might bring him both credit and riches. So in January 1518 he placed four ships under the command of a kinsman, Juan de Grijalva, and sent them to explore and trade with the mysterious people to the west. Bernal Díaz, a participant, wrote about the voyage. Grijalva sailed along the coast of Yucatán, touching land here and there with varying luck. In one of his first encounters the Indians fought so fiercely that Grijalva himself was hit in the mouth by an arrow and lost three teeth, an injury he attributed to the fact that he had cursed the chaplain for being slow in coming ashore. Elsewhere he bartered for gilded hatchets (that turned out to be copper), acquired some gold, and learned that farther inland (in Mexico) the precious metal abounded.

At a landing in northern Yucatán the Spaniards were astonished to receive a warm welcome by a delegation of Indians who made green bowers to protect the visitors from the sun, served excellent food, and displayed white cotton cloths bearing painted pictures. Grijalva did not realize that these were emissaries from Montezuma, ruler of Mexico, who had heard of strange white men from the sea. Their coming confirmed a belief that the god Quetzalcoatl would one day appear from this same sea. These newcomers, reasoned Montezuma, might be the forerunners of Quetzalcoatl's arrival. Cortés would profit from this myth, but Grijalva, intent upon bartering for gold, saw no significance in the welcome and the painted cloths.

Back in Cuba, Velázquez began to worry about Grijalva. Since Velázquez himself had usurped authority in Cuba that rightfully belonged to the Viceroy, he might well suspect that Grijalva, kinsman though he was, might be playing a similar game. So he ordered Cristóbal de Olid, an adventurer later to cause trouble for Cortés, to take a caravel and investigate Grijalva's doings. When neither came back soon enough to ease his anxiety, Velázquez set about preparing another expedition and gave the command to Cortés. Rarely in those days did one Spaniard trust another, and Velázquez, with an uneasy conscience, had greater reason than most to be suspicious.

Though Cristóbal and Grijalva at last returned to Cuba, they had conquered no new lands for Velázquez to report to the King of Spain. Perhaps Cortés would be more successful. Preparations for the new expedition therefore went on apace. Cortés, knowing the suspicious and changeable nature of the Governor, stuck by his side, says Bernal Díaz, "and always showed himself to be his zealous servant and kept on telling him that, God willing, he was going to make him a very illustrious and wealthy gentleman in a very short time." [8]

[8] *The True History of the Conquest of New Spain, by Bernal Díaz del Castillo,* trans. by Alfred P. Maudslay (5 vols., London, Hakluyt Society, 1908–1916), I, 75.

Despite Cortés' smooth assurances, envious enemies dropped hints that the new Captain-General was intending to run off with the fleet to serve his own ends. Realizing that Velázquez was nearly ready to cancel his commission, Cortés suddenly sailed from Santiago on the night of November 18, 1518. Accounts of his departure vary, but, clearly, he left as Velázquez was about to relieve him of his command. The fleet of eleven vessels made a rendezvous on the southern coast of Cuba and there finished fitting out and enlisting men for the venture. On February 10, 1519, Cortés at last sailed for the coast of Mexico. In the eleven ships he had 508 soldiers, 100 seamen, sixteen horses, ten bronze guns, four falconets, and thirteen blunderbuses.[9] His other armament consisted of crossbows, swords, and lances. This was no mighty host to conquer a nation of warriors numbering hundreds of thousands, but Cortés was to accomplish the miracle.

Although Velázquez had sent emissaries to stop Cortés and to arrest him, the soldier-diplomat won over the Governor's messengers and added them to his train. He even wrote placatingly to Velázquez, Bernal Díaz reports, "in the agreeable and complimentary terms which he knew so well how to use . . . that he remained his humble servant." [10] If Cortés' diplomacy could not win over the suspicious Velázquez, it proved highly successful with both Indians and Spaniards as problems increased during the Conquest.

Cortés' fleet made its first landing on the island of Cozumel off the east coast of Yucatán. There they got word of two Spaniards held captive by mainland Indians and succeeded in rescuing one, Jerónimo de Aguilar, who had been shipwrecked eight years before. The second Spaniard, married to an Indian woman and in high favor with the cacique, refused to be repatriated. Aguilar, who had learned to speak the Mayan language, proved invaluable as an interpreter.

At Cozumel, Cortés made his first effort to overthrow the

[9] Madariaga, *Hernán Cortés*, p. 102.
[10] *True History*, I, 89.

heathen idols and preach Christianity to the natives. To natives assembled at a shrine on the island Cortés announced, through an Indian interpreter who understood a little Spanish, that they must give up their idols, which would lead them to hell. "Then he spoke to them about good and holy things," Bernal Díaz asserts,

> and told them to set up in the place of their idols an image of Our Lady which he gave them, and a cross, which would always aid them and bring them good harvests and would save their souls, and he told them in a very excellent way other things about our holy faith. . . . Then Cortés ordered us to break the idols to pieces and roll them down the steps, and this we did. Then he ordered lime to be brought, of which there was a good store in the town, and Indian masons, and he set up a very fair altar on which he placed the figure of Our Lady. And he ordered two of our party . . . to make a cross of some rough timber . . . and it was placed in a small chapel near the altar and the priest named Juan Díaz said mass there, and the cacique and the heathen priest and all the Indians stood watching us with attention.[11]

Thus Cortés began a mission as preacher of Christian doctrine to the heathen. What the Indians made of Christian theology strained through the intelligence of an Indian interpreter who ill understood ordinary Spanish, much less the mysteries of doctrinal matters, one can only guess.

After rounding the Yucatán Peninsula the fleet anchored in the Gulf of Campeche at the mouth of the Tabasco River. Though Cortés found an army of Indians drawn up in battle array, he offered peace. He and his men only wanted "to land and take water and speak to them about God and about His Majesty." But the Tabascans, who showed no inclination to hear about God or His Majesty, answered with a shower of arrows and fire-hardened darts, so that the Spaniards had to attack and drive them from their town. Cortés then formally took posses-

[11] *Ibid.*, I, 97–98.

sion of the land in the name of the King of Spain by drawing his sword, making three slashes on the biggest tree in the town square, and offering to fight in single combat any person who raised objection. This ceremonial might have come straight out of one of the chivalric romances. The King's notary wrote it all down in his parchments to make it regular and legal, something that Cortés was always careful to insist upon. A few of Velázquez' partisans grumbled that Cortés had failed to name the Governor in his proclamation, as protocol of the day demanded. But Cortés was preparing for the day when he would declare himself free of Velázquez' jurisdiction.

When scouting parties sent to explore the country discovered Indians massing for war, Cortés decided the time had come to demonstrate the power of the Spaniards, and he laid plans for a pitched battle. To support his foot soldiers, Cortés mounted his best riders on the sixteen horses and personally led them. The Indians, who had never seen a horse, thought that beast and man were one creature and fled in terror before this fearful thing advancing with such speed to pierce their faces with lances. All through the Conquest Cortés was to find his horses more terrifying to the Indians than even artillery.

In this first full-scale battle between Spaniards and Indians, fought on March 25, 1519, the invaders killed more than eight hundred natives and lost only two of their own men. Several men and horses received wounds which the Spaniards sterilized by searing them with melted fat obtained by cutting open a fat Indian. Since Cortés had no other medicaments for dealing with wounds, this treatment became standard practice during the succeeding campaign. Many a fat Indian contributed to the healing process.

Bernal Díaz, writing about this first encounter many years later, expressed annoyance that the historian Gómara felt called upon to take some of the glory away from the soldiers and attribute victory to the intercession on the battlefield of St. James and St. Peter. Indeed, his own book was written in part because of his dissatisfaction with Gómara's narrative, and he is frequently at pains to correct its alleged errors.

It was on this occasion that Francisco López de Gómara says Francisco de Morla set out on a dapple gray horse before Cortés and the other horsemen arrived, and that the sainted Apostles, Señor Santiago and Señor San Pedro appeared. I say that all our doings and our victories are at the hands of our Lord Jesus Christ, and that in this battle there were so many Indians to every one of us that they could have blinded us with the dust they raised but for the pity of God who always helped us. It may be that as Gómara says the Glorious Apostles Señor Santiago and Señor San Pedro came to our aid and that I, being a sinner, was not worthy to behold them. . . . If it was as Gómara says, we must have all been very bad Christians, when our Lord God sent his holy Apostles to us, not to recognize the great favor that he was showing us.[12]

Almost as miraculous and of greater value to Cortés than any supposed appearance of St. James and St. Peter on the field of battle was the acquisition of a remarkable woman without whose linguistic ability, loyalty, and wisdom Cortés might not have succeeded in conquering Mexico. This woman was Marina, a Mexican princess, immediately recognized as both noble and beautiful by the Spaniards and henceforth called Doña Marina. When she was a child, her stepfather had given her to the Tabascans, and she had grown up in Tabasco and was fluent in that language as well as her own. Aguilar, the Spaniard rescued earlier, knew only Tabascan. Now Cortés had "tongues" to communicate with both Tabascans and the people on the high plains of Mexico. Doña Marina played a role somewhat similar but even more important than that of Sacajawea, the Indian girl who nearly three centuries later saved the Lewis-and-Clark expedition from disaster.

After the victory over the Tabascans Cortés began negotiations for peace with a skill that distinguished him from other Spanish conquerors. Within a few days, by a shrewd combination of terror and tact, he won over the hostile caciques, who

[12] *Ibid.*, I, 121.

were soon showing him every sign of respect and bringing gifts of food and gold. More pleasing to Cortés' officers was a gift of twenty Indian maidens, all comely. In the lot was Marina. Cortés had with him a nobleman from his own land of Estremadura, Alonzo Hernández Puertocarrero, whom he wished to favor especially. To him he awarded Marina, though when Puertocarrero later departed with a message for the Emperor in Spain, Cortés took Marina as his own mistress.

Writing sixty years later, Bernal Díaz still remembered vividly the impression Marina made upon him:

> One Indian lady who was given to us here was christened Doña Marina, and she was truly a great chieftainess and the daughter of great caciques and the mistress of vassals, and this her appearance clearly showed. . . . I do not remember the names of the other women, . . . the first women to become Christians in New Spain. Cortés allotted one of them to each of his captains, and Doña Marina, as she was good looking and intelligent and without embarrassment, he gave to Alonzo Hernández Puertocarrero, who . . . was a distinguished gentleman, cousin to the Count of Medellín. When Puertocarrero went to Spain, Doña Marina lived with Cortés, and bore him a son named Don Martín Cortés.[13]

The conversion of these first female captives was rapid. Each of the lucky captains who had been awarded a girl saw to it that she was immediately baptized and made Christian, for Cortés, ever meticulous in such matters, would not permit his men of any degree to cohabit with a heathen. Baptism invariably had to precede copulation. In subsequent encounters, when the Spaniards received large levies of women, the priests labored long and diligently baptizing, christening, instructing these hitherto lost ewe lambs. Thus many Christians were made and the foundation was laid of families who trace their lineage to the conquerors.

As at Cozumel, Cortés explained to the Indians the beauty of the Christian religion and demanded that they throw down their

[13] *Ibid.*, I, 128–129.

idols and abandon human sacrifice, a practice the Spaniards had discovered to their horror. With Aguilar as interpreter, Cortés "told them as well as he was able about matters concerning our holy faith, how we were Christians and worshipped one true and only God, and he showed them an image of Our Lady with her precious Son in her arms and explained to them that we paid the greatest reverence to it as it was the image of the Mother of our Lord God who was in heaven." [14] This message the caciques received gravely and replied that they liked the looks of the great lady of the Christians and asked to keep the image in their town, which Cortés had renamed Santa María de la Victoria. Pleased with the success of his instruction, Cortés ordered carpenters to build an altar for the Virgin and erect a cross. The next day, Palm Sunday, he had all the caciques with their women and children come to the altar to do homage and then to take part in a procession, followed by mass. With a final injunction to the chiefs to take care of the holy image and the cross and to keep the altar well swept so that they might enjoy good health and bountiful harvests, Cortés and his men went aboard their ships and prepared for the next stage of their journey. They had learned that gold came from a region toward the setting sun called Mexico, and it was this mysterious place that they now sought.

On the Thursday before Easter the whole fleet cast anchor at San Juan de Ulúa, a spot that would witness many dramatic events in the future. On Good Friday the men went ashore, built huts among the sand dunes, and placed their artillery at strategic points. Soon emissaries arrived bringing turkeys, maize cakes, plums, and gold jewelry intricately made. They came from their great prince, Montezuma, who sent to know whence they came and who they were. Aguilar did not understand their speech, but Marina could translate into Tabascan, which Aguilar in turn turned into Spanish. Thus communication was established, and for the remainder of the Conquest, Cortés used his two "tongues" in this fashion, to communicate with the Mexicans.

[14] *Ibid.*, I, 127.

Montezuma, he learned, was the ruler of the Aztecs, a people who had established an overlordship in the central valley of Mexico and dominated neighboring tribes as far as the coast. Theirs was no true kingdom or empire, for they made no effort to establish their law and rule among subject tribes; they merely sought to exact from vassal tribes a tribute of food and other goods—and a continuing supply of human sacrifices for their bloodthirsty gods.

Cortés received the ambassadors from Montezuma like a true diplomat. He explained that he came from the greatest ruler on earth, the Emperor Don Carlos, who had heard of the great Montezuma and had sent Cortés to visit him and to establish trade relations. To the ambassadors he gave gifts of glass beads and to Montezuma he sent a richly carved armchair inlaid with lapis-lazuli, a string of beads packed in sweet-scented cotton, and a crimson cap to which a medal of St. George slaying the dragon was attached. One of the messengers noticed a soldier wearing a rusty helmet something like the headpiece that adorned their war god, Huitzilopochtli. When he begged this helmet, Cortés suggested that he take it to Montezuma—and bring it back filled with grains of gold so that they might see whether the gold of Mexico was like that found in the rivers of their country.

The ambassadors from Montezuma had brought skilled painters who transferred to white cotton cloths pictures of the newcomers and all their works, including the mysterious horses, so that Montezuma might know with what beings he was dealing. For the ruler of Mexico was vastly puzzled and troubled in his mind. He had already sought wisdom from his soothsayers and magicians, and they had left him unsatisfied. He had sacrificed many young men to Huitzilopochtli and his other gods, but not all the blood and palpitating hearts torn from the living victims had brought a satisfactory answer. Perhaps these beings from the sea were gods and Quetzalcoatl had come to establish his rule over Mexico as had been foretold. It behooved Montezuma to act with circumspection. His bewilderment and uncertainty on this score would serve Cortés' purposes.

178

In due time the ambassadors returned with a retinue of servants bearing rich gifts of cotton cloth, featherwork, food, precious stones, gold, and two disks of gold and silver inscribed with signs of the calendar which impressed Bernal Díaz as they later astonished the court of Charles V:

> The first article presented was a wheel like a sun, as big as a cartwheel, with many sorts of pictures on it, the whole of fine gold, and a wonderful thing to behold, which those who afterward weighed it said was worth more than ten thousand dollars. Then another wheel was presented of greater size made of silver of great brilliancy in imitation of the moon with other figures shown on it, and this was of great value as it was very heavy. And the chief brought back the helmet full of fine grains of gold just as they got it from the mines.[15]

The ambassadors also brought twenty golden ducks, other golden animals, jewels, and much fine cotton and featherwork. But about the visit that the strangers wished to make to Montezuma the ambassadors were firm. Their ruler suggested that they stay in the port where they were; he would assist them in any way, but a visit to him was not to be thought of. This refusal of course did not please Cortés, and he sent the messengers back with more gifts and a further request for an invitation to court. For months to come the Mexican ruler would try to fend off the would-be visitors, while Cortés would continue tactful pressure to be asked to come to Montezuma's city.

In the meantime, however, the situation at San Juan de Ulúa was less than comfortable. The anchorage invited danger from northerly gales, and the mosquitoes that infested the sand dunes made life miserable. Consequently, Cortés moved up the coast a short distance to a more protected and fertile spot, where he made a landing. Previously a few of Velázquez' adherents had grumbled that the expedition had overstayed its time and should return to Cuba. Furthermore, they said, Cortés ought not permit

[15] *Ibid.*, I, 143–144. The term "dollar" was used to indicate a coin worth eight reals.

the common soldiers to barter for gold, which rightfully should be collected for the Governor of Cuba, who had sent out the expedition. Cortés pretended to agree that this view was doubtless correct, but he expressed indignation that anyone would want to rob the common soldiers of the little gold they had obtained after so much hardship. Having won the soldiers by this speech, he now secretly undertook another political maneuver which ended in his friends' demanding that he "settle" the country by founding a town. After giving the matter careful consideration, he agreed to establish on that site the town of Villa Rica de la Vera Cruz. Though the Rich Town of the True Cross was only a geographical expression, he invested it with all the trappings and traditions of a typical Spanish municipality, with a cabildo (governing council) and a full complement of municipal officers. The council then "demanded" that Cortés assume command of the expedition in the name of the King of Spain and thus free himself from the jurisdiction of the Governor of Cuba. With apparent reluctance he bowed to "the will of the people" and accepted the offices of captain-general and chief justice. When he conquered it, Mexico would be his and Velázquez could whistle for it.

Having freed himself from any pretense of recognizing the authority of Velázquez, Cortés could expect no further aid from Cuba unless he got it surreptitiously. Facing him and his little army lay an unknown and inhospitable terrain where untold hordes of warriors would dispute their passage. But, undaunted by inevitable dangers, Cortés and his men were ready to undertake the march over the mountains to Montezuma's stronghold. First, however, they had to establish stable relations with the coastal natives and leave a fortified base that would give them a gateway to the sea.

Already the invaders had organized a town, Villa Rica de la Vera Cruz, but it had yet to be given a physical habitation. Up the coast a few leagues from modern Vera Cruz Cortés laid out the town and set an example to his men by carrying stones and earth to help build its fortified walls. There they would leave a small garrison for safety's sake. He marched into the Indian town of Cempoala, a little farther to the north, and won an alliance with the head cacique of the Totonac tribe.

The discovery that the coastal tribes, recently conquered by the Aztecs, hated and feared Montezuma proved of immense value to Cortés. Henceforth he would follow a policy of "divide and rule." The cacique of Cempoala, believing the Spaniards to be gods of some kind, welcomed them and showered gifts and food upon them. He himself was too fat to travel to Cortés' camp, but he sent emissaries with flowers, turkeys, and eight daughters of chiefs whom he begged the newcomers to take as bed companions. Before this could happen, Cortés explained, the Cempoalans must give up their heathen gods and the girls must be baptized. At the risk of war with his new ally, he ordered idols thrown out of the temples, had the priests' hair, blood-matted from human sacrifices, shorn, and then set up a cross and an image of the Virgin. After the girls' baptism, he parceled them out to leaders of the army. To his friend Puertocarrero, to whom he had already given Marina, Cortés awarded the most beautiful of the maidens. He himself, out of policy, took the fat cacique's niece, whom he christened Doña Catalina, and "tried to look pleased" with her, though Bernal Díaz describes her as "very ugly." [16] Cortés always maintained a certain rationality toward women.

The Spaniards had now spent some three months on the coast of Mexico, and Cortés was eager to march into the interior. Some of the adherents of Velázquez, however, showed reluctance and plotted to steal a ship and return to Cuba. Discovering the conspiracy, Cortés hanged the ringleaders and then took a drastic step to prevent further defections. Calling his pilots together, he persuaded them to beach all except one ship. Ironware, cordage, and spars were salvaged and stored on shore. Some of this equipment would later serve to fit out brigantines on the lakes of Mexico.

Coincidental with the Spaniards' stay in Cempoala came a visit

[16] *True History*, I, 191.

of five tax collectors sent by Montezuma. Not only did they require the usual tribute, but they demanded twenty young men
and women to be sacrificed to the war god because the Cempoalans had received the bearded strangers. Bolstering the courage
of the Totonacs, Cortés ordered them to arrest the tax collectors
and turn them over to him. He then secretly sent them back to
Montezuma with a message that the Spaniards meant only
friendship to the great ruler in Mexico, that they wanted to visit
him, and that they had taken up quarters in Cempoala because
food supplies earlier promised by Montezuma had not been
forthcoming. Thus having ensured hostility between the Totonacs and the Aztecs, and having taken steps to maintain his own
peace, at least for the present, with Montezuma, Cortés prepared
for the next advance.

Before leaving the coast, however, he sent envoys to Spain in a
ship saved for the purpose. To carry letters to the court of Spain,
Cortés chose his friend Puertocarrero and Francisco de Montejo,
lately an adherent of Velázquez but now of a different frame of
mind, thanks to gold bestowed on him by Cortés. The
messengers to the King of Spain carried impressive quantities of
gold, including the two great wheels of precious metal, one of
gold and one silver; they also took four young Indian men and
two girls supplied by the fat cacique. The cabildo, or governing
council, of Villa Rica de la Vera Cruz drafted a letter praising
Cortés and begging the Emperor Charles V to confirm Cortés in
the offices of captain-general and chief justice to which the
cabildo had appointed him. Cortés too wrote to the Emperor, giving an account of his discoveries and hopes of conquest. Both
letters of course emphasized Cortés' loyalty and high purposes.

With Puertocarrero gone, Cortés took Marina into his own
bed; who got Puertocarrero's newly acquired Cempoalan damsel
is not clear. At any rate, Marina proved faithful to Cortés and
was of immense value to him as an interpreter and adviser, for
she was a woman of remarkable shrewdness.

The long march to the city of Mexico, a distance of more than
200 miles, took the Spaniards through rugged mountain country

at altitudes ranging from 4,000 to 8,000 feet. Montezuma was established in a city surrounded by lakes and marshes, for the whole area was ringed with mountains that drained down into a valley without an outlet. The altitude of the valley itself was something over 7,400 feet, with peaks towering in the distance. Toward this point Cortés now set his course.

Leaving a garrison of 150 men in Villa Rica de la Vera Cruz, Cortés departed from Cempoala on August 16, 1519. His "conquering army" consisted of not more than 400 soldiers, 15 horses, and about 1,000 Indian burden-bearers who carried six or seven small cannon and other equipment. For the next two weeks the Spaniards slogged through dusty valleys and over rough mountain passes, sometimes gasping under a burning sun and at other times freezing in bitter winds that swept down from snow-capped mountains.

By the end of August the Spaniards were in the territory of Tlaxcala, an independent city-state which stood in constant peril from the Mexicans. Knowing that the Tlaxcalans were enemies of the Aztecs, Cortés sent messengers offering peace and friendship, but received a defiant reply that the Tlaxcalans expected to kill and eat the invaders. A brief but bitter campaign followed in which the Spaniards, against heavy odds, won a victory over Tlaxcala. Once more Cortés offered peace and friendship, and at last the Tlaxcalans capitulated. In the meantime Cortés was entertaining messengers from Montezuma. With an adroitness characteristic of him at every stage, he played one against the other. What if the bearded white men joined the Mexicans? the Tlaxcalans reasoned. As they grew more anxious for an alliance with these new and powerful warriors, their chiefs came in a body to invite the Spaniards to Tlaxcala, where they would be welcome and would be supplied with food. Thus Cortés won a crucial alliance that remained firm in his later contests with the Aztecs.

On September 23, 1519, his army marched into Tlaxcala, a city, Cortés wrote to Emperor Charles V, larger, stronger, better housed, and more populous than Granada. He estimated that the city had 150,000 heads of families. The Tlaxcalan warriors were stout fighting men, as the Spaniards had learned to their sorrow, and they would prove to be excellent auxiliary troops in future wars.

In the meantime the Spaniards rested in Tlaxcala and recuperated from wounds and exhaustion after the long march over the mountains. They still had rough country to cross before reaching Mexico. To make amends for their previous hostility, the Tlaxcalans outdid themselves in hospitality. The chiefs brought their most beautiful daughters as gifts to the leaders and found concubines for the common soldiers. This generosity posed a problem for Cortés. The women first had to be made Christian. As a prelude he considered throwing down the heathen idols, whitewashing the temples, and setting up crosses, but his priests counseled patience. The women could be baptized and thus made acceptable, but a general attack on the gods of the Tlaxcalans at this moment seemed rash and might jeopardize a critical alliance. For once Cortés curbed his evangelical zeal in the interest of prudence, but he did insist upon freeing a group of prisoners whom the Tlaxcalans were fattening for a cannibal feast to follow the sacrifice of these plump prisoners to the war god.

After three weeks in Tlaxcala, Cortés on October 13 once more set his troops in motion. Against the advice of the Tlaxcalans, he decided to take the road to Cholula, a town confederated with Mexico and hostile to Tlaxcala. Although warned that Montezuma had sent 50,000 warriors to Cholula, he still chose that route because the town lay in a region well supplied with food and he believed that he could make peace with the Cholulans and prepare for an entry into Mexico itself without fighting. Cortés was ever sanguine about his diplomacy, and often he was right.

Cholulan delegations met the Spaniards on the road with gifts of food and with copal incense, with which, according to custom, they ceremonially fumigated the Spanish leaders. Cortés assured them that he came as a friend and asked peaceful passage to Mexico. He soon learned, however, that thousands of Montezuma's warriors were hidden in nearby ravines and that the Cho-

184

lulans were preparing to fall upon the Spaniards in the night. They had orders to send their prisoners bound to Mexico, though Montezuma conceded that they might retain twenty to sacrifice to their gods.

Faced with this conspiracy, Cortés ordered his men to remain on the alert, fully armed. He then called the Cholulan leaders to the enclosed courtyard where the Spaniards were quartered and addressed them from horseback. Bernal Díaz gives the substance of his speech: "So in return for our having come to treat them like brothers and to tell them what our Lord God and the King had ordained, they wished to kill us and eat our flesh, and had already prepared the pots with salt and peppers and tomatoes. If this was what they wanted, it would have been better for them to make war on us in the open fields like good and valiant warriors, as did their neighbors, the Tlaxcalans." [17] This clue to the recipe for cooking Spaniards reads uncannily like the modern recipe for chicken Mexicaine. But Cortés had no intention of becoming the pièce de résistance of a cannibal feast in Cholula. When he finished his speech, he ordered a musket fired as a signal for his troops to attack the Cholulans. Taking them unawares, the Spaniards slaughtered the leaders and some 3,000 others.

For this "massacre" Las Casas condemned his countryman, and some later writers have been equally critical. Realists, however, have pointed out that a handful of Spaniards found themselves vastly outnumbered by a force determined to wipe them out. Survival meant retaining the initiative and demoralizing their enemies. This tactic succeeded. As was his invariable custom, Cortés sought a faction willing to make peace, and in Cholula he found one. Shrewdly he pretended to Montezuma's ambassadors that the Cholulans had treacherously attempted to place the blame for their hostility on the great Montezuma. Knowing the magnanimity of this prince, he said, the Spaniards were more than ever eager to visit him and would soon be in Mexico. Thus Cortés continued his effort to reach Mexico without open warfare with Montezuma.

[17] *Ibid.*, II, 14.

To a present-day student of military strategy, Cortés' daring appears to be utterly foolhardy. With some 450 troops of his own and 4,000 Indian allies, he set out from Cholula on November 1, 1519, to conquer the capital of a ruler dreaded by all the surrounding country. The population of Mexico has been variously calculated, but Sir Arthur Helps asserts that "the very least number at which the population of Mexico can be estimated is three hundred thousand, and I conceive it to be much larger." [18] Furthermore, it was a warrior kingdom, and Montezuma could muster hordes of fighting men; not even the possession of firearms and a few horses that struck terror in the Indians would seem to give a handful of Spaniards sufficient advantage to keep from being crushed by the throngs of warriors that Montezuma could put in the field. Although a few Spaniards grumbled about the hazards, the little army marched undaunted toward its appointment with destiny.

Cortés chose a route that led along a mountainous trail between the two snow-capped volcanoes, Popocatepetl and Iztaccihuatl. Coming through a pass, the Spaniards saw for the first time the valley of Mexico spread out before them with Tenochtitlán (Mexico City) set like a glittering white jewel in the blue waters of surrounding lakes. Causeways connected the capital with the mainland, where other cities gleamed white against a dark background. They had looked down on the white houses of Moorish towns in Spain, but they had seen nothing quite so astonishing as the beauty and grandeur of Montezuma's capital with its satellite towns. Bernal Díaz comments that

> when we saw so many cities and villages built in the water and other great towns on dry land and that straight and level causeway going towards Mexico, we were amazed and said it was like the enchantments they tell of in the legend of Amadis, on account of the great towers and cues [temples] and buildings rising from the water, all built of masonry. And some of the soldiers even asked whether the things that we saw were not a dream.[19]

[18] Helps, *Spanish Conquest*, II, 223.
[19] *True History*, II, 37.

Emissaries from Montezuma came to greet the Spaniards, and to test them with various stratagems. Montezuma vacillated in his own thinking about the strangers. At one moment he appeared to believe that Cortés was the reincarnation of the god Quetzalcoatl; at other times he seemed ready to destroy the invaders by trickery or open onslaught. His tragedy was that he could not make up his mind, and in the end this vacillation was his ruin.

The Spaniards descended into the valley and marched across a causeway wide enough for eight horsemen to the town of Iztapalapa on a peninsula opposite Tenochtitlán. At Iztapalapa Montezuma's brother, Cuitlahuac, entertained the visitors graciously and presented them with gold, fine raiment, and beautiful women. After one night in Iztapalapa, however, the Spaniards were ready to move on to their final destination, and on November, 8, 1519, they marched across another causeway toward Tenochtitlán.

A little more than a mile from the city, a thousand of Mexico's nobility came to do homage to the visitors. By this time soothsayers had convinced Montezuma that the newcomers were gods. An hour later, as they entered the city on a broad avenue flanked by fine houses, a procession bearing a litter of the Great Montezuma (as Bernal Díaz invariably calls him) approached. When the litter, topped with green featherwork, reached Cortés astride his horse, courtiers swept the ground and put down cotton cloths upon which Montezuma stepped. He was wearing sandals with soles of solid gold, and gold and jewels hung from his neck. Cortés dismounted and went to meet the ruler of Mexico. At this moment two civilizations met as these "two men stood before each other, looking into each other's eyes. But the eyes of the Mexican were closed lakes, soon to dry up under the sun of another knowledge; while in the eyes of Cortés there lived the endless sea." [20]

Cortés with Spanish courtesy would have embraced Montezuma, but the latter's courtiers held him back; their ruler's person was too sacred to be touched. Montezuma made a grave and formal speech of welcome, which Doña Marina translated into

[20] Madariaga, *Hernán Cortés*, p. 239.

Tabascan and Aguilar turned into Spanish. Cortés replied by the same roundabout method and assured Montezuma that he came as a friend and that the Mexicans had nothing to fear. With that he threw around the Aztec's neck a string of colored glass beads perfumed with musk. Not to be outdone, Montezuma placed around Cortés' neck "two necklaces made of red shells which they hold in much estimation and from each necklace there hung eight golden shrimps of much perfection several inches long," symbols sacred to the god Quetzalcoatl.[21] With this ceremony over, the Mexicans led their guests to a vast palace, once the residence of Montezuma's father. A complex of buildings around an immense courtyard with gardens had been set aside for the Spaniards. So large was this establishment that all of the Spaniards and the women they had accumulated, as well as two thousand of their Indian allies, found quarters there without crowding.

As part of his official welcome, Montezuma made a ceremonial visit to Cortés which the Spanish leader immediately returned. The occasion gave Cortés an opportunity to deliver a sermon on the purpose of his expedition to Mexico. He had come on the command of the great King of the Spaniards to bring a message of salvation to Montezuma and his people. Bernal Díaz gives the substance of Cortés' address, which would have done credit to his chaplains:

> Then Cortés began to make an explanation through our interpreters Doña Marina and Aguilar. . . . [He explained] that we were Christians and worshipped one true and only God, named Jesus Christ, who suffered death and passion to save us . . . and that the death and passion which He suffered was for the salvation of the whole human race, which was lost, and that this our God rose on the third day and is now in heaven, and it is He who made the heavens and the earth, the sea and the sands, and created all things there are in the world, and He sends the rain and the dew, and nothing happens in the world without His holy will. That we believe

[21] *Ibid.*, p. 241.

in Him and worship Him, but that those whom they look upon as gods are not so, but are devils, which are evil things, and if their looks are bad, their deeds are worse. . . . Then he [Cortés] explained to him [Montezuma] very clearly about the creation . . . and how such a brother as our great Emperor, grieving for the perdition of so many souls such as those which their idols were leading to Hell where they burn in living flames, had sent us so that after what he [Montezuma] had now heard he would put a stop to it and they would no longer adore those Idols or sacrifice Indian men and women to them, for they were all brethren, nor should they commit sodomy or thefts. He also told them that in course of time our Lord and King would send some men who among us lead very holy lives much better than we do, who will explain to them all about it, for at present we merely came to give them due warning, and so he prayed him to do what was asked and carry it into effect.

Cortés then turned to his followers and said "with this we have done our duty considering it is the first attempt." Montezuma, however, had a word to say in reply.

Señor Malinche [a courtesy title given Cortés], I have understood your words and arguments very well before now, from what you said to my servants at the sand dunes, this about three Gods and the Cross, and all those things that you have preached in the towns through which you have come. We have not made answer to it because here throughout all time we have worshipped our own gods and thought they were good, as no doubt yours are, so do not trouble to speak to us any more about them at present. Regarding the creation of the world, we have held the same belief for ages past, and for this reason we take it for certain that you are those whom our ancestors predicted would come from the direction of the sunrise. As for your great King, I feel that I am indebted to him, and I will give him what I possess. . . .[22]

[22] *True History*, II, 56–58.

In this fashion the spokesmen of two civilizations expressed their views, views that would presently lead to mortal conflict.

Montezuma and his people were priest-ridden and superstitious. They were committed to a religion that demanded hordes of human sacrifices. Pyramid-like temples dotted the landscape of Tenochtitlán and other Mexican towns. Victims, driven up the steep steps, were stretched upon sacrificial stones, where their hearts were cut out of their living bodies with obsidian knives, and their bodies were then cast down the same steps to the multitude. Select portions were broiled and eaten and the rest thrown to jaguars and panthers kept in sacred menageries. The priests who performed these rites wore their hair long, hanging about their shoulders, matted with the blood of sacrificial victims. The blood-splashed temples reeked with the scent of death and the fumes of hearts burning before the images of the gods. The most demanding of all the gods was Huitzilopochtli, whom Bernal Díaz calls Huichilobos and Madariaga translates into Witchy-wolves.

These bloody rites made an amazing contrast with other aspects of Aztec life. The palaces of Montezuma and the houses of the upper class were spotlessly clean and fragrant with flowers. Officials and sometimes even warriors going into battle delighted in carrying roses in their hands. Courtyards were gay with flowering shrubs. Inside, the walls of houses were hung with fine cotton cloths, and on the floors were soft rugs of cotton or the skins of animals. Parrots and singing birds hung in cages. On cold days the rooms were warmed with braziers burning sweet-scented wood that gave off little smoke. Only the sleeping arrangements appeared to Bernal Díaz to be lacking in comfort, for the Aztecs lay on thin mats instead of beds.

The quantity and variety of food brought to Montezuma, seen in the markets, and served to the visitors, astonished Bernal Díaz. One haunting horror, however, bothered him and the other Spaniards: Montezuma was believed to feast on human flesh.

I have heard it said that they were wont to cook for him the flesh of young boys, but as he has such a variety of dishes, made of so many things, we could not succeed in seeing if they were of human flesh or of other things, for they daily cooked fowls, turkeys, pheasants, native partridges, quail, tame and wild ducks, venison, wild boar, reed birds, pigeons, hares and rabbits, and many sorts of birds and other things which are bred in this country, and they are so numerous that I cannot finish naming them in a hurry. So we had no insight into it, but I know for certain that after our Captain censured the sacrifice of human beings, and the eating of their flesh, he [Montezuma] ordered that such food should not be prepared for him henceforth.[23]

Of Montezuma's appearance Bernal Díaz provides a good account:

The Great Montezuma was about forty years old, of good height and well proportioned, slender and spare of flesh, not very swarthy, but of the natural color and shade of an Indian. He did not wear his hair long but so as just to cover his ears; his scanty black beard was well shaped and thin. His face was somewhat long, but cheerful, and showed in his appearance and manner both tenderness and, when necessary, gravity. He was very neat and clean, and bathed once every day in the afternoon. He had many women as mistresses, daughters of chieftains, and he had two great cacicas as his legitimate wives, and when he had intercourse with them it was so secretly that no one knew anything about it except some of his servants.[24]

The amenities of Cortés' palace were only a little less gorgeous than those of Montezuma's, and the example of dalliance that the Aztec ruler set was followed by the Spanish captains and their men, albeit with somewhat less privacy.

Montezuma heaped gifts upon the Spaniards: gold chains and other objects made of precious metal, gems, fine cotton cloth, raiment, and cloaks into which were woven the feathers of bril-

[23] *Ibid.*, II, 61–62.
[24] *Ibid.*, II, 60.

liantly colored birds. Cortés, with shrewd foresight, allowed his soldiers to accumulate gifts and did not attempt to confiscate the gold as had been the practice of other Spanish captains in Hispaniola and Cuba. In this way he retained the loyalty of his men despite the machinations of a few dissidents.

The peace and plenty of Tenochtitlán comforted the weary soldiers of Spain, but did not remove a gnawing worry that they too might be fattening for sacrifice to the bloodthirsty gods. A visit to the Great Teocalli, or principal temple of the capital, four days after their arrival did nothing to reassure the Spanish captains and the soldiers who accompanied them. Human hearts smoking in urns before the idols and the stench of blood, worse than the slaughterhouses of Castile, horrified them afresh. Furthermore, Tlaxcalan messengers brought word that one of Montezuma's chiefs, Quauhpopoca, had led an attack upon Spaniards left on the coast and had killed one of the captains, Juan de Escalante.

Convinced that Montezuma only waited for a favorable moment to fall upon him and his men, Cortés decided upon a daring move. With great courtesy, he placed the Aztec ruler under house arrest and moved him, his harem, and his retinue of servants to the palace occupied by the invaders. Montezuma was now a hostage held to ensure the safety of the Spaniards. After the initial shock, curiously, he submitted to this role and continued to order his people to supply food to his captors. Moreover, he concurred in the execution of Quauhpopoca. To make an example of the warriors who had slain Escalante and one other Spaniard on the coast, Cortés burned at the stake in the public square Quauhpopoca, his son, and fifteen prominent Indians who were his accomplices. After this show of authority Cortés could feel somewhat more secure.

In the meantime two soldiers had made an exciting discovery. Behind a secret door that had been plastered over, they found a vast amount of gold, silver, and jewels amassed by Montezuma's father. After the officers and soldiers had viewed slabs of precious metal and intricately wrought jewelry, they agreed to plaster up the door once more and keep the matter secret "until times should alter." This treasure trove they intended to convey to Spain when conditions were propitious. "When I saw it [the treasure]," Bernal Díaz comments, "I marvelled, and as at that time I was a youth and had never seen such riches as those in my life before, I took it for certain that there could not be another such store of wealth in the whole world." [25]

During the winter and early spring of 1519–20, Cortés and his men kept an uneasy peace at Tenochtitlán. Constantly on the alert, constantly expecting treachery, they nevertheless used their time profitably. Exploring parties went in search of the gold mines that supplied Montezuma with wealth. Probing the interior, they picked up information that would prove infinitely useful. Quantities of gold, obtained from Montezuma or collected as tribute by Spanish foragers, were melted down into convenient ingots against the time when this wealth could be transported to Spain. During the winter they also built two sloops to be used on the lakes.

Cortés also struck a blow for the True God by casting from the Great Teocalli the idols that Montezuma and his priests worshipped. In a letter to the Emperor Charles V he reports his missionary zeal: "The greatest of these idols and those in which they placed most faith and trust, I ordered to be dragged from their places and flung down the stairs, which done I had the temples which they occupy cleansed, for they were full of the blood of human victims who had been sacrificed, and [I] placed in them the images of Our Lady and other saints. . . ." He also gave orders that henceforth no human beings should be sacrificed, and his letter asserts that "during the whole time that I was in the city not a single living soul was known to be killed and sacrificed." [26] Bernal Díaz, writing much later, gives a different account, reporting an agreement with Montezuma whereby both Aztec and Christian shrines could be maintained on the Great Teocalli. If

[25] *Ibid.*, II, 85.
[26] *Hernando Cortés: Five Letters, 1519–1526*, trans. J. Bayard Morris (London, 1928), pp. 90–92. This quotation is from the "Second Letter."

Cortés really believed human sacrifices were ended, his men knew better.

Meanwhile Diego Velázquez, the Governor of Cuba, nursed his displeasure over Cortés' highhanded flouting of his authority. If Cortés hoped that Velázquez would forget him and allow him to carve out an empire for himself, he was doomed to disappointment. In May 1520 Cortés received a message from the coast that Pánfilo de Narváez had sailed into the port of San Juan de Ulúa with eighteen ships. Montezuma had also received from his intelligence the same news with more detail; he informed Cortés that 800 soldiers with 80 horses and 12 cannon had come ashore. And he suggested pointedly that, with shipping available, Cortés and his men could now depart.

Cortés' situation was critical. Surrounded by hostile warriors thirsting for his blood, he had now to face one of his own countrymen who had come with a strong force to arrest him and take him a prisoner back to Cuba. It would require all his skill in diplomacy and strategy to outwit both Montezuma and Narváez. To accomplish that, Cortés applied himself.

To Narváez' camp he sent messengers loaded with gold to prove how generous he was to his troops. Adroitly they insinuated that much profit might be gained by coming over to Cortés' command. After his emissaries had prepared the ground, Cortés placed Tenochtitlán under the command of a trusted captain, Pedro de Alvarado, and set out for the coast with seventy men. Alvarado had some eighty men to hold Tenochtitlán until Cortés' return. Before departing, Cortés took affectionate leave of Montezuma as if he were a trusted friend and instructed him, says Bernal Díaz, "to see that the image of Our Lady and the Cross should always be decked with garlands and that wax candles should always be kept burning there by day and by night." [27] Although Cortés knew that Montezuma was plotting his downfall, it was part of his strategy to pretend complete trust in the Mexican leader.

On the way to meet Narváez, Cortés added some 270 troops

[27] *True History*, II, 174.

called back from exploring parties in the country, but his total of 340 men did not equal Narváez' force of more than 800. Nevertheless, by tact, diplomacy, and the adroit distribution of gold, he won over some of Narváez' troops before the armies met, and he had weakened the resolution of the remainder of the enemy. When finally Cortés attacked, he won an easy victory and captured Narváez, who lost an eye in the fight. The defeated soldiers gladly enlisted under Cortés' banner. Not quite daring to trust all of his late enemies, he divided them and left some to garrison stations on the coast. The eighteen ships he partially dismantled and placed them under the command of a trusted officer who took an oath not to let any vessel return to Cuba.

Before Cortés could properly savor his victory, he received an urgent message from Alvarado that the Mexicans in Tenochtitlán were in revolt. In the name of God, Alvarado pleaded, hurry to the rescue. Alvarado had himself to blame for precipitating the revolt, for he had unwisely attempted to interfere with the annual spring religious festival of the Aztecs, probably to prevent the human sacrifices that were part of the ritual, and had slain at least 600 unarmed Mexicans.[28] Whipped to fury by their priests, the Mexicans laid siege to the Spaniards in their quarters.

With troops recruited from his recent opponents, Cortés hastened toward the Valley of Mexico. He had 1,300 soldiers, including 96 horsemen. On the day of John the Baptist, June 24, 1520, this army crossed the causeway into Tenochtitlán and reached in safety the besieged quarters of the Spanish troops.

The story of the ensuing struggle and the desperate evacuation of the Spaniards on the noche triste, the "sad night" of June 30–July 1, 1520, has been often told. Even with more than 1,300 men Cortés could not hope to hold back indefinitely the furious hordes of Mexican warriors. Though Spanish cannoneers blasted bloody gaps in the massed attackers, fresh warriors took the places of the fallen. No longer did gunfire or horses terrify the Indians. Masses of warriors swarmed to the attack. The Span-

[28] Helps, *Spanish Conquest*, II, 275. The estimates of the number of Mexicans killed vary from 400 to more than 3,000.

iards made movable sheds under which they could advance, protected from showers of stones, darts, and arrows hurled by the Mexicans. In a move to break the morale of the Indians, Cortés personally led an assault on the Great Teocalli, fighting inch by inch up the steps of the vast truncated pyramid until the Spaniards reached the summit and cast down the images of the heathen gods.

Courage and skill with swords and lances could do much, but the sheer weight of numbers told against the Spaniards. They agreed that the time had come to seek a truce with the Indians and to leave Tenochtitlán. Montezuma was induced to address his subjects from a rooftop in an effort to make peace, but his people would not listen. He had betrayed them. One hurled a lance, others stones that found their mark. Montezuma staggered back, badly wounded, and three days later he died. This strange ruler had somehow won the affection of the Spaniards around him, and they wept at his death. No longer was there any influence restraining the Indians. The Spaniards would have to fight their way out of the city.

The shortest causeway led to Tacuba on the mainland to the west. Eight gaps in the causeway, once covered by bridges, had to be crossed in some fashion. The Spaniards tried to fill the spaces with rubble from houses they had torn down along the way, and Cortés had a portable bridge built. About midnight on June 30, with a drizzling rain falling, the Spaniards made a dash for the causeway. They crossed the first gap, but by the time they reached the second, the Indians were swarming upon them in canoes and on foot along the roadway. In the stampede, horses, guns, burden-bearers, and soldiers fell into unbridged spaces in the causeway. The portable bridge jammed; in any case, it was useless without forty men to carry it. Some fugitives crossed on the bodies of their comrades. Others swam to safety. But many others, weighed down with gold that greed would not let them abandon, sank to the bottom of the lake, drowned by the treasure that they could not release.

What to do with Montezuma's treasure and the gold that the

men had accumulated had troubled Cortés. It would be difficult to save this wealth, he knew, but he turned over the King's fifth (the portion always legally required for the sovereign) to two officials and ordered it loaded upon eight lame and wounded horses and upon the backs of Tlaxcalan burden-bearers. The rest he allowed the soldiers to divide among themselves. It was this burden of gold that proved the undoing of many Spaniards. Montezuma's treasure did not survive the flight. Somewhere on the botton of the lagoon it rested, and there, for all that anyone knows, it still remains.

The battered remnant of Cortés' little army withdrew to a fortress-like teocalli at Tacuba. There they tended their wounds and braced for a further onslaught. "But as for anything to eat, there was no thought of it," Bernal Díaz comments. Hungry, thirsty, and suffering almost to a man from wounds, the soldiers expected the worst. Cortés himself was wounded in one arm, but he somehow managed to pull his men together and march on. On July 7 they reached the plains near Otumba to the northeast, where a vast host of warriors disputed their passage. The Mexican leader and his principal chieftains, resplendent with waving plumes and golden ornaments, made a brilliant display. Against them Cortés and several of his captains who still had horses charged and rode them down. Seeing their leaders dead or wounded and their banners captured, the Indians broke ranks and scattered. The Spaniards and their Tlaxcalan allies slaughtered hundreds of fleeing warriors to win a complete victory, for which, says Bernal Díaz, "we all gave many thanks to God for having escaped from such a great multitude of people, for there had never been seen or found throughout the Indies such a great number of warriors together in any battle that was fought." Nevertheless, the Spaniards had suffered heavy losses in running battles since the night of June 30, as Díaz explains:

I wish to give an account of how many of us they killed both in Mexico as well as on the bridges and causeways, and all the encounters including this one at Otumba, and those

197

that were killed on the road. I assert that within a matter of five days over eight hundred and sixty soldiers were killed and sacrificed, as well as seventy-two who were killed in a town named Tustepec, together with five Spanish women . . . and over a thousand Tlaxcalans were slain.[29]

The battle at Otumba proved so decisive that the Spaniards were able to continue their march toward Tlaxcala, which they reached on July 12, with only guerrilla action to hinder them. Based at last in Tlaxcala, they could nurse their wounds and think of recouping their losses. From the disaster Cortés had saved 440 men and 20 horses, approximately the number he had when he first entered Mexico.

Cortés had no intention of relinquishing the empire which he had so nearly won—which, indeed, for a time he had ruled with Montezuma as his puppet. Consequently, he immediately set about planning the recapture of Mexico. By October 1520 he had added recruits newly arrived from Vera Cruz and could muster 554 men. He also began building sloops at Tlaxcala which could be taken apart, carried overland, and reassembled on the Mexican lakes.

On December 28, 1520, he began a march for the second time against Mexico with a formidable Tlaxcalan army in support. He intended to ensure victory by first conquering the outlying towns. For the next four months the army invested these strategic towns in preparation for a grand assault on Tenochtitlán. But before beginning the siege Cortés exhausted every means of inducing the Mexicans to surrender peacefully.

On April 28, 1521, he launched on Lake Tezcuco thirteen vessels that he had brought in parts overland from Tlaxcala. He now had a navy as well as land forces, and his army of something less than 600 Spaniards was augmented by approximately 75,000 Tlaxcalan warriors. With this force he laid siege to Tenochtitlán, being careful to leave one causeway open so that the Mexicans, if they wished, could escape and leave their city to him.

[29] *True History*, II, 254–255.

This option they did not choose to take.

The battle for Tenochtitlán was long and bloody. Each side fought with a ferocity unusual even in this period. Day after day the Spaniards could hear the drum of the Aztecs sounding from the Great Teocalli as priests dragged prisoners up the pyramid steps to be sacrificed to the war god. The screams of victims having their chests cut open and their hearts torn out chilled the blood of every Spaniard, who feared that he himself might be the next one snatched to his death to appease Huitzilopochtli. To increase the terror, the Aztecs threw heads of dead captives back into the Spanish lines. The Indian allies of the Spaniards equaled the Aztecs in cruelty. They slaughtered captives indiscriminately and sent such as they needed to the cookpots. The cannibal feasts of the Tlaxcalans greatly simplified the problems of their commissary.

The battle for Tenochtitlán ended on August 13, 1521, when the Spaniards made a successful assault upon the last buildings still holding out. The city was in ruins. Montezuma's successor, Cuauhtemoc, attempting to flee his devastated capital, was captured and brought to Cortés, who treated him with the courtesy befitting a courageous soldier and the ruler of a kingdom. Try as he might, Cortés was unable to curb the blood lust of the Tlaxcalans, those allies who had assured his victory. In spite of orders to spare noncombatants, the Tlaxcalans slaughtered some 15,000. And the city that the Spaniards had first seen as a gleaming jewel in its setting of blue water, some enchanted thing from the legends of Amadis of Gaul, now lay a desolate waste. Such was the price of conquest.

The power of the native rulers was forever broken. Although sporadic warfare might break out here and there in the years to come, Cortés had gained another empire for Charles V. New Spain would become one of the Emperor's richest possessions. And missionaries would soon come to reap a harvest of souls to redound to the Emperor's glory.

Although he had destroyed to conquer, Cortés now vigorously turned to reconstruction. Surviving inhabitants of Te-

199

nochtitlán were encouraged to return, and some former officials were restored to authority and ordered to take charge of cleaning up the ruined city. Upon its site Cortés planned a Spanish city with churches to the Christian God on the spots where once heathen temples had stood.

Explorers continued their search for gold and silver mines, but other metals were needed: copper, tin, and iron for gun foundries, and sulfur for gunpowder. All of these Cortés' men discovered. Sulfur they obtained from the volcano Popocatepetl. The search for Montezuma's treasure also continued, and the greed of the soldiers for gold, as well as the zeal of the royal treasurer to see that the sovereign received his fifth, led to much unseemly squabbling. Enemies of Cortés accused him of hiding portions of the treasure that he had collected, and they demanded that Cuauhtemoc and the lord of Tacuba be put to the torture to reveal wealth they had sequestered. This was done, in an episode that left Cortés ashamed and disgraced in his own eyes, but the two potentates knew of little gold that they could reveal.

Cortés also had enemies in Spain, notably Bishop Fonseca, still a power in the Casa de la Contratación, who did his best to cheat the conqueror of all rewards. Fonseca was responsible for sending out a governor to New Spain to supplant Cortés, but the newcomer was induced to give up and return home. In the meantime Cortés had sent envoys to the Emperor with the wealth that he had been able to collect. Some of the gold that Cortés had sent by previous envoys had been intercepted by Fonseca. The latest treasure was captured by French corsairs and turned over to Francis I of France. The uproar that followed and the protests from the Emperor perhaps made this sovereign more conscious of the conqueror of New Spain than if the treasure had arrived safely. At any rate, on October 15, 1522, the Emperor named Cortés Governor and Captain-General of New Spain, thus conferring upon him legal titles for offices that he was already filling. Coincidentally, Bishop Fonseca was forced to retire from his office in the Casa de la Contratación.

An event close to Cortés' heart occurred on May 13, 1524, when twelve barefoot Franciscan friars arrived at San Juan de Ulúa to begin another conquest of New Spain, this time for the King of Kings. The symbolism of the arrival of the twelve, like the twelve apostles, was not lost upon the Spaniards in Mexico. When they came on foot to Mexico City, Cortés, his captains, and the Mexican officials, including Cuauhtemoc, all went out to meet them. Cortés knelt before the friars, as did all his officers, to the astonishment of the Mexicans, who received forthwith a lesson in pious devotion. These friars were the forerunners of others who in time established the authority of the Church throughout New Spain.

Although Cortés had achieved the seemingly impossible, he was not yet satisfied. He wanted to be named Viceroy of New Spain, an office more suitable, in his opinion, than that of governor. But the Emperor never conferred upon him that last honor, perhaps out of caution lest he raise up a man too ambitious for the good of the realm.

Cortés' rule in Mexico was not without its troubles that sometimes approached disaster. In October of 1524 he undertook an expedition to Honduras that resulted in usurpers taking over the government of New Spain. One of his old comrades-in-arms, Cristóbal de Olid, whom he had sent to conquer Honduras, had rebelled against his authority, and Cortés felt that he must bring him to justice. The expedition lasted nearly two years and ended with Cortés' virtual ruin. Lest Mexican leaders stir up trouble in his absence, he took with him to Honduras a number of chieftains, including Cuauhtemoc. When these chieftains conspired to revolt, Cortés hanged the leaders, Cuauhtemoc among them. While he was absent—and believed lost—enemies in Mexico and in Spain, envious of his previous successes, plotted against him.

In 1528 he went to Spain to plead his cause before the Emperor, and in the following year succeeded in being made Marquis of the Valley of Oaxaca. With gold enough to impress the grandees of Spain, Cortés was able to make a good match and succeeded in winning the hand of Doña Juana de Zúñiga, niece of the Duke of Béjar. Another lady of rank, Doña Francisca de Mendoza, young and beautiful—and the sister-in-law of Francisco de los Cobos, Emperor Charles V's Principal Secretary of State for Spanish foreign affairs—took a fancy to Cortés, but the conquistador had already plighted his troth to Juana, and Francisca was left forlorn. If Cortés had not felt obliged to reject Francisca, Madariaga, citing Bernal Díaz, thinks Cobos might have seen fit to persuade the Emperor to make him Viceroy of New Spain.[30]

In 1530, with his new wife and a retinue of retainers, Cortés, Marquis of the Valley of Oaxaca and Captain-General, returned to the land that he had conquered. In his absence the government had fallen into the hands of a group of rascals headed by one Nuño de Guzmán, who composed the Audiencia, the highest legal tribunal in the country. They had occupied Cortés' house in Mexico City and despoiled his property. They had also committed outrages against the Indians, contrary to Cortés' wishes. Thousands of Indians had been branded as slaves and many shipped away to labor in the Caribbean islands. At length Cortés induced the authorities in Spain to displace the tyrannical members of the Audiencia and to appoint honest men in their places.

For the next decade Cortés devoted his energies to further exploration and to the development of New Spain. He established his family at Cuernavaca, where he experimented in the production of cotton, silk, sugar, and wine; and he devoted much thought and energy to mining, particularly to silver mining. As a base for exploration into the Pacific, he developed a port at Tehuantepec and opened a shipyard. Long before this he had sent an expedition from Mexico to try to rescue some of Magellan's survivors in the Spice Islands; now once more he turned his eyes to the wide stretches of the Pacific. Might he not win new empires across the vast ocean? Though he made some efforts in this direction, Fate was not to grant him that favor. He did, however, explore Lower California, where an expedition that he led in 1535 nearly perished of hunger.

[30] Madariaga, *Hernán Cortés*, p. 453.

Fame and recognition meant more to Cortés even than wealth, but the ultimate in fame somehow eluded him. Enemies plagued and thwarted him, and his business enterprises in New Spain proved of little satisfaction. Finally, in 1540, weary with the struggle against greedy and envious rivals, he once more took ship for Spain. He was never again to see Mexico. In 1541 he went with the Emperor on the expedition against Algiers. That too turned out to be a disaster. Cortés asked to be allowed to lead an attack to retrieve defeat, but some of Charles V's captains laughed at his folly. They did not remember that he had won an empire with fewer than 500 men. Back in Spain, he trailed along after Emperor Charles V as that monarch moved from one Spanish city to another. Cortés was not born to be a suppliant courtier, and he was unhappy.

At the beginning of winter in 1547 he was in residence at the Castilleja de la Cuesta near Seville. There, on December 2, he died, exhausted and disappointed. Adequate recognition of his great feat in gaining New Spain for the Emperor had not come, for, as Madariaga comments, "seldom does a Spaniard attain recognition by his fellow men till he is dead." [31]

As Cortés realized that his end was near, he took thought of his children, not only those born in wedlock but also those born out of wedlock by adoring women, for he had had his share of feminine adulation and affection. He had two sons named Martín, one legitimate and one by Doña Marina, the Indian girl who had stood by him loyally throughout his campaign in Mexico. Martín the bastard, to whom Cortés gave his name, did well and became a grandee of Spain as Knight Commander of the Order of St. James.

Cortés' attitude toward women might puzzle Anglo-Saxons brought up in a romantic tradition. From early in his life he was a passionate lover of many women, but never when he could help it did he let romance interfere with matters more important to him. When he captured Doña Marina in Mexico, he willingly gave her to his friend Puertocarrero. When Puertocarrero went

[31] *Ibid.*, p. 477.

to Spain, he took Marina into his own bed. She apparently loved him devotedly and served him well. Without her ability to communicate with the Mexicans, Cortés could hardly have succeeded in his conquest. And though she had borne him a son, in 1523, during his campaign in Honduras, he gave her in marriage to a Spanish gentleman, Juan Jaramillo. Perhaps Cortés wanted to be sure that Doña Marina was safely provided for, but his action was not precisely that of the hero of romantic fiction. But whatever his attitude toward their mothers may have been, Cortés in his will generously provided for all of the children, legitimate and illegitimate.

In his will Cortés also remembered the Indians of New Spain and provided for the establishment of a hospital, a convent, and a college. He had fought to prevent the greed of those who came after him from enslaving the natives. He had always tried to see that the Indians who had fought hardest against him received fair treatment once they capitulated. Devoutly he encouraged the friars in their efforts to make Christians of the heathen. And despite his frustrations, he had come to love New Spain and specified that his bones should be given final rest in its soil. As Lesley Simpson points out in the introduction to his edition of Gómara's history, in 1946 someone claimed to have discovered "the bones of Cortés buried in the chapel wall of the Hospital de Jesús in Mexico City, where they had been hidden by Lucas Alamán during the War of Independence to secure them from desecration at the hands of the insurgents." This "occasion was seized upon by the pious to pronounce eulogies of Cortés, whom they hold to be the lay founder of the Mexican Church, and by professional patriots to denounce him for all the atrocities of the conquest, as, indeed, has been the fashion since 1810." [32] Today opinions of Cortés and the Conquest vary with the social views of the individual, but no one can deny the extraordinary accomplishments of the greatest of the conquistadors.

[32] *Cortés: The Life of the Conqueror*, p. xv.

Bartolomé de Las Casas and the "Black Legend"

T HE HIGH PURPOSES OF CHRISTIANIZING THE HEATHEN IN FOR-
eign lands, proclaimed by Pope Alexander VI, Queen
Isabella, Christopher Columbus, and the majority of the explorers and conquistadors, gave a noble and pious sound to official
utterances, but godly observers found the performance less than
satisfactory. Indeed, early in the Spanish occupation of America,
critics of the conquerors bombarded the sovereigns with complaints that greed promoted cruelty to native peoples and that
the wickedness of Spaniards in this respect was a scandal before
God and man. Among the critics, the most violent and persistent
was Bartolomé de Las Casas, named the first "Protector of the
Indians," a man who did more than any other to create and fix in
European consciousness the "black legend" of Spanish cruelty.
As is the case with other doctrinaire reformers, how much practical good he did by his zeal remains the subject of controversy
among scholars.[1] No doubt exists that he stirred the consciences

---

[1] Among the most useful treatments of various aspects of Las Casas'
career and influence are the following: Lewis Hanke, *Bartolomé de Las*

of the Emperor Charles V and other Spaniards in high place; but whether the laws that he promoted accomplished the ends that he sought may be questioned.

Las Casas and Cortés were both concerned about the treatment of the Indians and their salvation. These two better than any others represent the opposing views of men who had some of the same objectives. Las Casas, a firebrand who found no good to say about Cortés, condemned conquerors out of hand and declared that the Spanish occupiers of lands in the New World had no right to exploit Indians in any fashion; the conversion of the natives to the religion of the conquerors should proceed from love, not force. Obviously an idealistic doctrine, it did not comport with grim necessity. Cortés, who was eager to save the Indians from destruction—for economic reasons if no other—was sincerely concerned to carry out a mission of evangelization. He represented the realistic and practical point of view of the most enlightened conquerors. For him, conquest had to come before conversion, for without conquest the natives would remain sunk in idolatry.

The difference between the views of Las Casas and Cortés is emphasized by Gómara, Cortés' chaplain and biographer, in a passage explaining that the Indians had first to be defeated in battle:

Truth to tell, it is war and warriors that really persuade the Indians to give up their idols, their bestial rites, and their

Casas: *An Interpretation of His Life and Writings* (The Hague, 1951); *The Spanish Struggle for Justice in the Conquest of America* (Philadelphia, Pa., 1949); *The First Social Experiments in America* (Cambridge, Mass., 1935); and *Aristotle and the American Indians* (London, 1959); Lesley Byrd Simpson, *The Encomienda in New Spain* (Berkeley, Calif., 1950); Henry R. Wagner and Helen Rand, *The Life and Writings of Bartolomé de Las Casas* (Albuquerque, N.M., 1967). An excellent account of the activities of the Franciscans, Dominicans, and Augustinians in Mexico in the sixteenth century will be found in Robert Ricard, *The Spiritual Conquest of Mexico: An Essay on the Apostolate and the Evangelizing Methods of the Mendicant Orders in New Spain, 1523–1572*, trans. Lesley Byrd Simpson (Berkeley and Los Angeles, Calif., 1966).

206

abominable bloody sacrifices and the eating of men (which is
directly contrary to the law of God and nature), and it is
thus that of their own free will and consent they more
quickly receive, listen to, and believe our preachers, and accept the Gospel and baptism, which is what Christianity and
faith consist of.[2]

Views as contradictory as those of Las Casas and of Cortés
and his class could not be reconciled, and they resulted in controversy and debate that have not yet ended. They also posed a
problem for the sovereigns of Spain, who found themselves on
the horns of a moral dilemma. These rulers subscribed publicly
to the notion that their first obligation was to bring the heathen
to a knowledge of Christ and thus save their souls. But if Christians who went out to the New World mistreated the heathen,
enslaved them, and in the end annihilated them, missionaries
would find it hard to make the doctrines of Christianity convincing. Even so the sovereigns needed the labor of the heathen to
farm the lands pre-empted by emigrants from Spain, to mine the
gold and silver that enriched the royal coffers, and to dive for
pearls. The very survival of the empires won in America depended upon native labor, which had to be forced since Indians
could not be induced to provide an adequate supply without co-
ercion. Thus economic necessity interfered with the desirable
goal of saving souls. The colonists needed laborers and the sovereigns wanted revenue. The problem of the missionary priests was
to make salvation compatible with these demands.

Through a long life Bartolomé de Las Casas (who lived to be
ninety-two) continually dinned into the minds of Spanish authorities that their obligation to convert the heathen was being
thwarted by the wickedness and cruelties of the conquerors.
They were destroyers, he insisted, and laws were needed to curb
their rapacity and their tyrannies. Although he succeeded in having laws passed which were designed to protect the Indians, these

[2] *Cortés: The Life of the Conqueror by His Secretary, Francisco
López de Gómara*, ed. Lesley Byrd Simpson (Berkeley, Calif., 1964),
pp. xvi, 33.

laws often proved so impractical in application that they had to be modified or repealed; in some instances they were simply disregarded. Nevertheless, the knowledge that the central authority in Spain was concerned about justice to the Indians served in some measure to curb the worst excesses of local tyrants and exploiters.

Ironically, Cortés, one of the conquerors whom Las Casas condemned, appears to have won the love and loyalty of the Indians; after their capitulation, he did much to save them from the horrors described by Las Casas. As Lesley Byrd Simpson points out, "no other Spaniard among the conquerors ever commanded the love and respect of the Indians to an equal degree." A contemporary declared that this love resulted from the fact that he had "treated them better than any other." [3]

The rage expressed by Las Casas over the treatment of the Indians, a rage that remained undiminished for the duration of his long life, had its inception in his own observation of the cruelties and abominations perpetrated by settlers in Hispaniola and Cuba. His father, Pedro de Las Casas, had gone out to Hispaniola on Columbus' Second Voyage, and Bartolomé himself had come out with the new governor, Nicolás de Ovando, in 1502.

Ovando had received from Queen Isabella of Castile careful instructions about the treatment of the Indians. She solemnly announced that her "principal intention" in governing the islands and mainland of the Ocean Sea was "to procure, induce, bring, and convert their peoples to our Holy Catholic Faith," but she was also careful to give Ovando authority to force the Indians to work. She insisted that "the Indian inhabitants of the island of Española [Hispaniola] are free and not servile," but she had been informed that "because of the excessive liberty enjoyed by the said Indians, they avoid contact and community with the Spaniards to such an extent that they will not work even for wages but wander about idle and cannot be had by the Christians to convert to our Holy Catholic Faith." Since that was the case, she authorized Ovando to "compel and force" the Indians to live in

[3] Simpson, *The Encomienda*, p. 107.

community with the Christians and to work for them on their farms and in the mines to extract the gold to "bring profit to my kingdom and subjects." Albeit, the Indians were to perform all of this work "as free people, which they are, and not as slaves." [4] In effect, Ovando established the encomienda system, which Las Casas regarded as the chief instrument used to retain the Indians in servitude.

Columbus, one will recall, had observed that the gentle people of the islands he discovered were fit subjects for Christianity and for servitude. By laboring for Christians they would enjoy contacts that would ensure them salvation and bliss in the world to come. This concept suited the needs of Spanish colonists who were eager to receive an allotment of land with enough Indians to work it and, in return, would agree to see that their serfs had Christian instruction on feast days and other suitable occasions.

Few men in the sixteenth century questioned the justice of enslaving rebels and other prisoners captured in "just wars." Since a flagrant attack on Spanish explorers and settlers gave an excuse for a just war against the savages, the Spaniards had an opportunity to acquire a considerable labor force needed especially for the killing labor in the mines and as burden-bearers in a land yet lacking in pack animals.

Slaves could also be acquired by purchase from friendly Indians, for slave-holding was an ancient Indian practice. Since the warlike Caribs were cannibals and by their habits had given proof that they were children of the devil, their capture and enslavement could be considered a work of virtue. In practice, however, any Indians who might be provoked to attack Spaniards were liable to enslavement or capture. One had only to remember to read them the *Requerimiento*, that curious legal instrument drawn up by one of Queen Isabella's lawyers, which first explained the principles of Christianity, offered peace to the Indians if they heeded the doctrine, and then threatened their destruction if they resisted. The mere reading of the *Requerimiento*, a document carried by the notaries who accompanied

[4] *Ibid.*, pp. 12–14.

most expeditions, gave the Spaniards the right to attack uncomprehending Indians.

Queen Isabella was deeply concerned about her heathen subjects across the seas, even though she was also eager for the gold that they would produce. She was concerned to make them over into the image of Europeans. They were to be brought together to live in towns wherever possible. They were to be taught to wear clothes like "reasonable men," to be given religious instruction, taught to read and write, to make the sign of the Cross, and to recite the Paternoster, the Apostles' Creed, and the Salve Regina. Their instructors were also to warn them about all of their evil ways, including too frequent bathing, which, Queen Isabella had been informed, "does them much harm." [5]

After Queen Isabella's death in 1504, King Ferdinand became regent of the Indies. Isabella's piety had given her a genuine interest in the salvation and welfare of the Indians, even though she looked upon their labor as just compensation for the benefits derived from the Gospel Message. Ferdinand, however, one of the most cynical of rulers, was inspired by little zeal to save his heathen subjects, either for this world or the next; he connived at any expedient to stimulate the production of gold. Slaving expeditions against "cannibals" brought back workers for the mines, but Indians on Hispaniola died faster than replacements could be found. The King authorized the removal of whole tribes from the Bahamas to Hispaniola that they might hear words of Christian salvation and die in the mines. Starvation and disease took their toll until the island was almost depopulated.

In the meanwhile Bartolomé de Las Casas was observing conditions and undergoing a spiritual change in his own life. About 1510, apparently, he was ordained a priest, and in 1522 was admitted to the Dominican Order. Nevertheless, in 1512 he went to Cuba, where he participated in that island's conquest by Diego Velázquez. For a time Las Casas had an encomienda in Cuba and worked Indians like any other colonist, but by 1514 he had come to believe that holding Indians in virtual servitude, despite pre-

[5] *Ibid.*, p. 11.

tensions that they were free men, was iniquitous. Consequently, he gave up his encomienda and, in September of 1515, sailed for Spain to urge King Ferdinand to do something to save the Indians from destruction. Henceforth Las Casas was the fiery protagonist of the Indians. In particular he opposed the practice of keeping Indians in bondage; unremittingly he sought the abolition of encomiendas.

Accompanying Las Casas on this voyage was a Dominican, Antonio Montesinos, who in 1511 at Santo Domingo in Hispaniola had preached a sermon inveighing against the cruelties to the Indians. This was the first important attack by the Dominicans, though others had complained of conditions. In the year following his sermon, Montesinos had gone to Spain to appeal directly to King Ferdinand. Even this monarch was so stirred by the priest's description of the horrors perpetrated in the Indies that he called a council of theologians and scholars, who devised a code of laws, promulgated from Burgos in 1512 and hence known as the Laws of Burgos, a code that prevailed for the next three decades. Although one purpose was to provide protection for the Indians, the Laws of Burgos sanctioned encomiendas and in effect made forced labor legal.[6] The number of Indians whom one person could hold was limited, however, to not more than 150.

Now, in 1515, Las Casas and Montesinos were once more on their way to Spain to protest the continued ill-treatment of the Indians despite the humanitarian provisions in the Laws of Burgos. Laws that had seemed reasonable and just to the wise men in Spain proved either unworkable or undesirable to the exploiters in Hispaniola, Cuba, and the other regions across the seas. Montesinos and Las Casas, who had seen with their own eyes the afflictions of the Indians, burned with zeal to correct the mistakes and punish the iniquities of their fellow countrymen.

Precisely how to achieve the results that Montesinos and Las Casas desired proved less easily answered than they may have

[6] *Ibid.*, pp. 32–34. Simpson gives a brief synopsis of the chief provisions of the Laws of Burgos.

expected. When an advanced civilization, motivated by instincts for trade and commerce, comes in contact with a primitive civilization unaware of the benefits flowing from diligence and sobriety, stresses and strains are inevitable. The aborigines of the New World showed no natural inclination to work. That appeared to the Spaniards a sin so grievous that strong measures were required to redeem them from congenital laziness. For if the Indians would not work, how would Spanish hidalgos maintain the station to which they felt called? No Spaniard, however humble, wanted to labor with his own hands in the paradise to which he had come. When the supply of Indian labor in Hispaniola proved insufficient to grow corn to feed the populace, Spaniards chose to starve proudly rather than to toil in the fields. The primary reason for the Spaniards' harsh treatment of the Indians was the necessity of forcing them to work. Greed often made taskmasters drive them unmercifully, especially in washing the gold-bearing sands of the rivers and in mining gold. In these operations Indians died from overwork and malnutrition, for the food supply often failed.

Although the enemies of Spain liked to believe that sadistic cruelty accounted for the destruction of the Indians in the Caribbean Islands and on the mainland, many other factors were responsible. The mere contact of two differing civilizations, with the social upheavals that went with the confrontations, caused immense damage. The disruption of hunting and food-gathering practices brought on famine. The introduction of European diseases—influenza, measles, smallpox, and other ailments to which the Indians had no immunity—carried off thousands. As with natives of the South Sea islands later, contacts with Europeans proved a disaster. Even if the Spaniards had conducted themselves with exemplary charity toward the aborigines, they could not have prevented untold misery. As it was, they were anything but charitable, and Las Casas by his constant propaganda, which emphasized every shortcoming of the conquerors, convinced all Europe, then and ever since, that the black legend of Spanish cruelty and tyranny was true. The conquerors themselves had given sufficient proof to make the exaggerated descriptions of Las Casas sound like the whole truth.

On reaching Seville in November 1515, Las Casas immediately sought an audience with King Ferdinand, who received him on Christmas Eve. Las Casas was now convinced that the keeping of Indians in the bondage of the encomiendas was leading to their destruction, and he drove home this point in his remarks to the King. Impressed by the priest's earnestness, Ferdinand agreed to see him again after Christmas, but the King was already a sick man and died on January 25, 1516, without again hearing him.

Two officials in Spain at this time practically ruled the Indies: Juan de Fonseca, Bishop of Burgos and effective head of the Casa de la Contratación, and Lope de Conchillos, secretary of the Council of Castile. From these officials Las Casas could get no support for his proposals to eliminate the encomiendas, for they, like many other officials and courtiers, had received allotments of land and Indians which they held as absentee landlords. With the death of Ferdinand, however, the situation changed. Since the successor to the throne, Charles I (later the Emperor Charles V), was in Flanders at the time, he appointed as regents in Spain Cardinal Francisco Ximénes de Cisneros and Florenz Adrian of Utrecht, the King's preceptor (elected a cardinal in 1517). To these two regents Las Casas presented a written report on the state of the Indies which so shocked them that they called a council to consider what should be done. Las Casas urged upon the council the elimination of encomiendas, freedom for Indians, and supervision of Indian affairs by the clergy. Probably to the petitioner's own surprise, Cardinal Ximénes approved his plan and authorized him to select three members of the Order of St. Jerome to go out to the Indies as commissioners—in fact, to be governors. The Jeronymites were designated for the task in the belief that they would be neutral and not subject to the rivalry that existed between the Dominicans and Franciscans who were already in the field.

The three men chosen by Las Casas were Luis de Figueroa, Bernardino de Manzanedo, and Alonso de Santo Domingo; al-

2 1 3

most at once Las Casas realized that he had made a mistake, for these three refused to take his dictation. He claimed that Spaniards opposed to reform had influenced the three friars, but it is obvious that they quickly discerned that Las Casas was an impractical visionary. As Lesley Byrd Simpson observes in describing this strange episode in the administration of the Spanish domains overseas, "Their [the three friars'] experience with him was not unique. All his schemes met with the same fate. For some reason he rarely retained for long the confidence of his coworkers. He would tolerate no dissent or opposition. He was a prime example of what the Spaniards call an 'exclusivista.' " [7]

Before the friars' departure from Spain, Cardinal Ximénes conferred upon Las Casas the title of "Protector of the Indians" with only vaguely defined duties. He was to accompany the Jeronymites, consult with them, and later to report back to Spain on conditions. The three commissioners were already so tired of Las Casas' repeated admonitions that they refused to sail in the same ship with him; so he had to sail alone. The commissioners reached Hispaniola on December 20, 1516; Las Casas arrived thirteen days later.

If Cardinal Ximénes had been unwise in agreeing to Las Casas' suggested reforms and in appointing three clerics to implement them, he at least gave the commissioners wide latitude, a latitude that perforce they had to adopt. In the face of monolithic resistance to the elimination of encomiendas, they compromised. They had come with an elaborate plan for resettlement of the Indians in supervised villages near the mines or close to arable farmlands. Las Casas himself had designed the utopian scheme. Although they succeeded in taking encomiendas away from absentee landlords, they could accomplish little more. They wrote back to the Cardinal that they found actual conditions different from what had been reported to them.[8] In the meanwhile Las Casas was on his way back to Spain to complain because the Jeronymites had not carried out all of his reforms.

[7] *Ibid.*, p. 40.
[8] *Ibid.*, pp. 44–45.

The commissioners, distressed at the scarcity of labor and the diminished population, urged that Negro slaves be sent to the colonies and that farmers from Portugal and the Canaries be induced to migrate to Hispaniola and Cuba; for the food supply was short and the colonies desperately needed good farmers. Las Casas himself had declared that "if necessary white and black slaves can be brought from Castile to keep herds and build sugar mills, wash gold, and engage in other things which they understand or at which they can be occupied." [9] Several times in this early period Las Casas recommended the importation of Negro slaves from Africa to save the Indians, but he later expressed regret that he had been so benighted as to condone Negro slavery.

The three Jeronymite friars, surely the most unlikely governors any colonial territory could expect, labored earnestly to work reforms, but they accomplished little. By the beginning of 1519 they had erected thirty villages, but before Indians could occupy them, smallpox swept Hispaniola and wiped out a third of the population. Once more they begged that Negro slaves be sent to the island to relieve the labor shortage. Finally in August of 1519 they gave up their offices and were permitted to return to Spain, for, as one of them declared, "these are not things which we think are fitting to our cloth and our order." [10] When Charles V refused to receive a personal report from the friars, Las Casas rejoiced. They had not worked instant reforms, and he would not forgive them.

In Spain, Las Casas followed the court from place to place, gaining an audience with Charles V when he could to keep ever before the sovereign the need to give his Indian subjects their freedom. He finally laid before the Emperor a plan to establish a free commonwealth of Indians under the direction of Las Casas. To that end, he received the grant of a large territory on the coast of Venezuela and the right to recruit Spanish peasants and others to settle there. In theory, the Spaniards would live among the Indians and, by example, show them how to work. They

[9] Quoted in Wagner and Rand, *The Life and Writings*, p. 22.
[10] Quotation from Manzanedo by Simpson, *The Encomienda*, p. 52.

215

would in the meantime inculcate the Christian virtues in their
heathen neighbors and bring them to salvation. Like heroes in the
romances of chivalry—or in *Don Quixote*—the peasant settlers
would be known as Knights of the Golden Spur. Las Casas designed as a uniform for the settlers a white robe with a red cross
on the front, but he later admitted that he was the only one who
ever wore it.[11] It is hard not to believe that Charles V or his secretaries agreed to this madcap scheme in order to rid the court of a
ubiquitous petitioner, for no one except Las Casas could have
dreamed that it would succeed.

Las Casas did manage to recruit a few peasants, and in December 1520 sailed from Sanlúcar with a small group to build towns
and make settlements on the Pearl Coast. Nothing ever came of
this fantastic venture. On arrival in Puerto Rico in February
1521, he received news that the Indians on the coast where his
grant lay were in revolt and had killed two missionary friars.
Furthermore, he could not prevent a punitive expedition from
raiding the coast and enslaving such Indians as it could capture.
In the meantime his peasant Knights of the Golden Spur deserted
and joined other raiding parties themselves. Although in the late
summer of 1521 Las Casas contrived to reach the mainland,
where he built a storehouse and left a few followers, roistering
Spaniards engaged in pearl fishing on the offshore islands made
constant trouble. Early in 1522 he went to Hispaniola to complain of the conduct of his fellow countrymen. Shortly afterward the Indians destroyed the tiny foothold he had gained.
Thus ended an idealist's demonstration of the way to civilize the
Indians.

Heartsick and discouraged at the failure of his noble efforts,
Las Casas became a novitiate in the Dominican monastery at
Santo Domingo sometime in 1522, and in 1523 he took his final
vows. For almost a decade thereafter he virtually drops out of
sight, but we know that he began writing his voluminous *Historia general de las Indias* in this period.[12] And we know from his
later writings that he continued to brood over the mistreatment

[11] Wagner and Rand, *The Life and Writings*, pp. 58–69.
[12] *Ibid.*, pp. 70–72.

216

of the Indians and to plan a further attack on the problem.

From the monastery of Puerto la Plata in Hispaniola Las Casas drew up a memorial to the Council of the Indies dated January 20, 1531. In it he described with increasing emphasis the horrors visited upon the Indians. On Hispaniola alone, he asserted, more than a million men, women, and children had been slaughtered, some by burning, others by stabbing, while still others were thrown to the dogs. He recommended that the Emperor remember the duty to convert the aborigines imposed by Pope Alexander VI's Bull of Donation. To that end he advised that fortresses be built on the mainland to protect colonies which would be supervised by bishops and friars. Once more he urged that Negro slaves be sent to supply needed labor and that licenses to import Negroes be more freely issued. His repentance for this advice was still some distance in the future. His ten years of contemplation had not made him any more temperate in his attacks on his fellow Spaniards in America. In fact, so violent was one of his sermons against encomiendas, delivered while he was serving as prior of the monastery of Puerto la Plata, that the governing council of Hispaniola complained to the Council of the Indies and the Emperor rebuked him.[13] Once more the reformer was at war with the wicked.

For another decade Las Casas was busy with missionary activities that took him to Nicaragua, Guatemala, and Mexico. In 1537 he fearlessly led a small band of missionaries into an unconquered territory, then called "the Land of War," in what is now northeastern Guatemala. By shrewd gift-giving and the use of several Christian Indian merchants who had learned to sing narrative songs that captured the fancy of their listeners, the missionaries converted several caciques and their tribesmen, a feat that strengthened Las Casas' contention that the Indians were merely waiting for the Gospel message. In 1538 he went to Mexico City on an official mission for the Dominicans, and there he wrote *Del único modo*, a work that defended his thesis of the peaceful conversion of the Indians.

But Las Casas could not long remain free of controversy, for,

[13] *Ibid.*, pp. 73–74.

217

like many dedicated men, he was convinced that he alone was the custodian of truth. Unhappily for his later reputation, he fell afoul of a Franciscan who had great credit among the Indians, Toribio de Benavente, generally called Motolinía, one of the "Twelve Apostles" welcomed to New Spain by Cortés in 1524. Las Casas, drawing upon subtle theological reasoning, condemned Motolinía and others like him for indiscriminately baptizing Indian adults who had not been given adequate instructions in Christian doctrine. Many years later Motolinía wrote a bitter letter to Emperor Charles V describing Las Casas' rigid views and visionary fantasies.

After two years in Mexico, Las Casas received instructions to proceed to Spain in order to recruit more missionaries. He arrived sometime in 1540 and immediately set about enlisting both Franciscans and Dominicans. But recruiting friars for the mission field was not Las Casas' primary purpose in returning to Spain. He wanted to renew his struggle for the freedom of the Indians. A request to the Emperor that he be permitted to remain in Spain to further the cause of the Indians was granted, and in 1541 he began the most extensive propaganda campaign of his career. Memorials, reports, and tracts flowed from his pen. In 1542 he was at court reporting directly to the Emperor on the iniquitous treatment of the Indians. His vivid descriptions of the cruelties meted out to the Emperor's Indian subjects disturbed that monarch's conscience and paved the way for the famous New Laws of the Indies, approved by Charles V at Barcelona on November 20, 1542.[14] Las Casas' voice, of course, was not the only one raised in behalf of the Indians. For example, scholars can still argue as to whether Las Casas or Francisco de Vitoria, another reformer who questioned the right of the Spaniards to conquer the Indians, exerted the greater influence. But in the New World the colonists blamed Las Casas for the provisions in the New Laws forbidding Indian servitude.

[14] Hanke, *The Spanish Struggle for Justice*, pp. 91–95, and Simpson, *The Encomienda*, pp. 123–144. Simpson gives a brief summary of the provisions of the New Laws affecting the Indians, pp. 129–132.

Less than three weeks after the New Laws were signed, Las Casas completed a tract that was to have an enormous influence in persuading the world that Spanish misdeeds were as black as Spain's enemies painted them. This was the famous *Brevissima relación de la destruición de las Indias,* which Las Casas himself saw through the press ten years later in 1552. The printed version left out the names of "tyrants" that Las Casas had specifically named in reading to the Council of the Indies the detailed memorial that became the basis of the *Brevissima.* Among these tyrants was Cortés.

The New Laws ordered the reformation of administrative procedures throughout the Spanish territories and laid down new regulations for the treatment of the Indians. Henceforth no Indians were to be enslaved, even those captured in war. Efforts were to be made to free slaves already acquired after an investigation of the owners' titles to these human chattels. Indians were not to be used as burden-carriers except in exceptional circumstances, and then they were not to be overloaded and were to be paid adequately. No pearl divers were to be forced into this hazardous occupation against their wills. Encomiendas held by officials were to be immediately abolished, and these Indians were to be placed under the jurisdiction of Crown officials. No new encomiendas would be permitted, and private holdings of Indians would be liquidated gradually over a period of years. The Indians who survived in Hispaniola, Puerto Rico, and Cuba, where the death rate had been highest, were to be exempt from tribute and all personal service so that they might recuperate and multiply. The Laws included other regulations and spelled out in detail the proper treatment of the Indians. Even so, they were not as drastic as Las Casas had wished, for not all encomiendas were immediately wiped out, as he had demanded.

The promulgation of the New Laws created consternation throughout the Spanish possessions. The colonists maintained that they could not produce the gold and silver demanded by the Crown, or raise the crops required for subsistence of both Indians and Spaniards, under the new regulations. If Spanish America was to survive, forced labor was essential, they maintained. To enforce the New Laws, the Council of the Indies dispatched commissioners to Peru, New Spain, Central America, and the islands and the Pearl Coast, one to each region. So high was the feeling against the New Laws that the Peruvian commissioner was beheaded on arrival. The others had somewhat better luck. Tello de Sandoval, the commissioner to New Spain, indicated a willingness to listen to the complaints of the colonists; and after much persuasion from Antonio de Mendoza, the Viceroy, and Archbishop Juan de Zumárraga, he agreed to suspend the laws forbidding encomiendas until the colonists could make an appeal to the Council of the Indies. In this fashion Sandoval averted possible rebellion in Mexico.[15]

In the meantime Cortés wrote to the Council of the Indies that abandonment of the encomiendas would be a disaster to the imperial government. The very backbone of government in New Spain, he pointed out, depended upon those Spanish leaders, the encomenderos (the owners of encomiendas), who constituted an effective militia in case of an Indian uprising. Furthermore, as experience had shown, the Indians would not work even to support themselves unless directed by Spaniards. The encomienda was the best method yet devised to keep pressure upon the Indians to work, and it had proved useful to the Indians themselves. This argument, not too surprisingly, was also made by the Dominicans and the Franciscans of Mexico. The encomenderos petitioned the Council of the Indies to suspend the New Laws and to make encomiendas pass to the holders' heirs in perpetuity. The upshot was that the laws were modified, but the question of encomiendas in perpetuity continued to be a matter of persistent wrangling for some years to come.

Although Las Casas and the reformers did not get all they asked, particularly the abolition of encomiendas, they did succeed in giving the Crown a weapon to enforce better treatment of the Indians. Under the New Laws the Crown had an incentive: If the holder of an encomienda was found violating the

[15] Simpson, *The Encomienda*, pp. 132–133.

laws, his property might be escheated to the Crown. This possibility was a great inducement to a more rigid surveillance as well as a reason for obedience. Las Casas, however, was never satisfied with the laws or their enforcement. He continued to serve as a gadfly and to plague the Council and the Emperor with memorials and petitions.

In the spring of 1544 Las Casas, now seventy years of age, was consecrated Bishop of Chiapa, a see on the border between Mexico and Guatemala. Here presumably the Emperor and the Pope believed he would have an opportunity to exert those energies for the salvation of the Indians that he had so long displayed in debate. He planned to demonstrate his theories of the peaceful conversion of the Indians and at the same time punish Spaniards in his see who kept Indians in servitude.

Chiapa did not welcome its new Bishop with open arms. This prelate had been responsible for the New Laws, or at least he was an advocate for them, and Chiapa received the news of his appointment sullenly. Soon after his arrival in March 1545 he began to preach against Indian slavery and commanded his priests to withhold Christian rites from slaveholders. When the Dean of the new Cathedral, one Gil de Quintana, defied him and gave absolution to slave-owning Spaniards, Las Casas ordered him arrested. This was too much. The citizens rioted, released the Dean, stormed the Bishop's house, and threatened to kill him. Thanks to a few godly Spaniards with swords, Las Casas escaped with his life, but he had already discovered that peace would not reign in Chiapa while he remained Bishop.

This episode was merely the prelude for further dissension and riots. Finally in March 1546, after barely a year in office, Las Casas left Chiapa and went to Mexico, where he took part in councils discussing the New Laws and the problem of the Indians. Always he was a controversial figure. Finally, in the spring of 1547 he sailed from Vera Cruz for Spain, never to return to the New World, though it continued to be the focus of his attention. In 1550 he resigned the bishopric that had proved only a calamity.

If Spanish Americans thought they had heard the last of the tempestuous reformer, they were mistaken. He continued to write and argue about the treatment of the Indians, stubbornly retaining his original beliefs. At Valladolid in 1550–51 he took part in a famous debate with Juan Ginés de Sepúlveda, the scholarly translator of Aristotle's *Politics*, on the nature of the Indians and the treatment they deserved. The precise question, which Charles V proposed, was whether the Spanish sovereign had a right to conquer the Indians in war as a preliminary to Christianizing them. Sepúlveda had prepared a document proving to his satisfaction that wars with the Indians were necessary and just as a prelude to their evangelization. On the authority of Aristotle, he maintained that certain people were destined by their inferiority to be hewers of wood and drawers of water—or, in other words, slaves. The Indians, by their barbaric ways, the practice of cannibalism, and other uncivilized behavior, had demonstrated their natural inferiority and hence were subject to servitude while they underwent tutelage necessary to raise them to a higher status. To this argument Las Casas, of course, was violently opposed. To sit in judgment, the Emperor called in August 1550 a Council of Fourteen including theologians, lawyers, and officials of state. They listened to heated discussions as the two protagonists set forth their views. The debate carried over into the following year, and in the end the councilors were as confused as when they assembled.[16] Sepúlveda had made some telling points in stressing that the good of Spanish civilization outweighed the iniquities perpetrated by evil men. Las Casas had stung once more the consciences of men by describing the horrors that he had seen with his own eyes. All agreed that Spain had a duty to Christianize the heathen; the problem remained of how this was to be done and at the same time make a profit out of the empire.

The debate at Valladolid stirred the old reformer to publish more tracts on the Indians, and in 1552 he saw through the press

[16] Hanke, *Aristotle and the American Indians* gives a detailed account of the great debate, *passim*.

the book that scattered his propaganda through the world, the *Brevissima relación*. Almost to the day of his death on July 20, 1566, at the age of ninety-two, he was writing incessantly in behalf of the Indians and urging further councils to remedy their condition. The Emperor Charles V, whom he had so long badgered about the problem, was long since dead. He had given up the throne of Spain in 1556 and had died in 1558. Now Philip II ruled as King of Spain and the problem of the Indians was still vexing the sovereign. Furthermore, his enemies were blaming Spain and its rulers for condoning cruelty to the aborigines of America. For this Las Casas bore a heavy burden of responsibility.

Las Casas—an enthusiast, an idealist, and a dedicated reformer —would not concede one jot or tittle to the practical necessities of the Spanish conquest. That he was morally right in his arguments, no one can deny. Virtue was on his side. But that the Spanish sovereign, however much he might be troubled in his conscience, would renounce all right to the treasure of the New World; or that the conquerors themselves, in the face of poisoned arrows, sacrificial obsidian knives, and stone axes, would stop to preach a religion of love to their screaming opponents went beyond reason. Las Casas represented the tragedy of the virtuous idealist in conflict with the practical empire-builder. In the conflict of cultures, the one with the highest degree of economic sophistication and technology was determined to dominate.

With the intensification of the Protestant fear of Spain, Las Casas' *Brevissima relación* became a potent instrument of propaganda. In 1578 it had its first translation into Dutch, and in the following year Jacques de Miggrode made a translation into French which was published in Antwerp and retranslated into English in 1583. The title page of Miggrode's French version announced its intention: *"Pour servir d'exemple & advertisement aux XVII Provinces du pais bas."* The English version in the preface to the reader also declared that the book was designed "to serve as a President [precedent] and warning to the

223

xij. Provinces of the lowe Countries." Miggrode had given his French version the title *Tyrannies et Cruautez des Espagnols perpetrees e's Indies Occidentales, qu'on dit Le Nouveau monde.*[17] The English translator called his work *The Spanish Colonie, Or Briefe Chronicle of the Acts and gestes of the Spaniardes in the West Indies, called the newe World, for the space of xl. yeeres,* but he retained as a sort of subtitle under his preface "To the Reader" loaded words taken from Miggrode: "Spanish cruelties and tyrannies, perpetrated in the West Indies, commonly termed The newe founde worlde."

The anonymous English translator clearly wanted to make the most of the attack on the Spaniards, whom he was delighted to convict out of the writings of one of their own, a priest and a Dominican, who surely would not have told such horrible stories had they not been true.

Thou shalt, friendly reader, in this discourse behold so many millions of men put to death as hardly there have been so many Spaniards procreated into this world since their first fathers, the Goths, inhabited their country, either since their second progenitors, the Saracens, expelled and murdered the most part of the Goths, as it seemeth that the Spaniards have murdered and put to death in the Western Indies by all such means as barbarousness itself could imagine to forge upon the anvil of cruelty. They have destroyed thrice so much land as Christendom doth comprehend. Such torments have they invented, yea so great and excessive have their treachery been, that the posterity shall hardly think that ever so barbarous or cruel a nation have been in the world, if, as you would say, we had not with our eyes seen it, and with our hands felt it. I confess that I never loved that nation generally by reason of their intolerable pride, notwithstand-

[17] For a detailed bibliography of Las Casas, see Lewis Hanke and Manuel Giménez Fernández, *Bartolomé de Las Casas, 1474–1566: Bibliografía crítica y cuerpo de materiales para el estudio de su vida, escritos, actuación y polémicas que suscitaron durante cuatro siglos* (Santiago de Chile, 1954), *passim,* especially pp. 205–212.

ing I can not but commend and love sundry excellent persons that are among them. Howbeit, God is my witness, hatred procureth me not to write those things, as also the author of the book is by nation a Spaniard, and besides writeth far more bitterly than myself.[18]

Las Casas belonged to the "noble savage" school of thought, and he contrasted the gentle people of the New World (living, as it were, in the Golden Age) with the savagery of the Spaniards who came to conquer them. "Undoubtedly these folks [the Indians] should be the happiest in the world if only they knew God," he asserted, and he followed this observation with the statement:

Upon these lambs so meek, so qualified and endowed of their maker and creator, as hath been said, entered the Spanish incontinent . . . as wolves, as lions, and as tigers most cruel of long time famished. And have not done in those quarters these forty years be past, neither yet do at this present, ought else save tear them in pieces, kill them, martyr them, afflict them, torment them, and destroy them by strange sorts of cruelties never neither seen, nor read, nor heard of the like (of the which some shall be set down hereafter) so far forth that of above three millions of souls that were in the Isle of Hispaniola, and that we have seen, there are not now two hundred natives of the country.[19]

Region by region, Las Casas, extenuating nothing, detailed the cruelties and destruction wrought by his countrymen. Concerning Cortés' conquest of Mexico, he could find no circumstance to exonerate the leader from the charge of arrant cruelty and cold-blooded pleasure in the suffering of his victims. At the massacre at Cholula, he pictured Cortés taking a gay pleasure in the slaughter, and he cited a ballad that "their captain having his

[18] From the English edition of 1583, "To the Reader." Spelling has been modernized.
[19] *Ibid.*, sig. A$_1$ verso.

heart all in a jollity sang." [20]

The grim tale reached a climax in Las Casas' description of the slaughter of the Indians in Peru. The verifiable facts of this conquest were made to order for the propagandist, and Las Casas gave them verisimilitude by direct quotations from a priest who claimed to have witnessed untold cruelties: thousands burned, others cut down with swords, and many mutilated by having their hands, ears, and noses cut off. Women and children were slain, he declared, out of mere desire to annoy husbands and fathers; babies were snatched from their mothers' breasts and flung to their deaths, some to bloodthirsty mastiffs. Las Casas concluded:

> If it should be expedient to recount the particularities of the cruelties and slaughters that the Spanish have committed, and yet daily do commit, in Peru, without all doubt they should be so frightful and in so great number that all that we have hitherto said of other parts of the Indies would be but shadowed, and it would seem a small matter in the respect of the grievousness and great number thereof.[21]

Although Las Casas wrote many other diatribes against the cruelty and misgovernment of his countrymen in the New World, this tract served best the purposes of the enemies of Spain. It continued to be published for generations after its first appearance, and it fixed in the public consciousness the notion that the Spaniards were a greedy, cruel, and heartless people intent only upon the exploitation of the native peoples of the New World. The Protestants, particularly the Dutch and English, were glad to have documentation for a belief that they accepted without question. In their later efforts to wrest a portion of the New World from the Spaniards they would make good use of this tract, as they contended that they were doing God's work in punishing such sinful tyrants. In the meantime, the conquerors of Peru would give them further material for such propaganda.

[20] *Ibid.*, sig. D₃.
[21] *Ibid.*, sig. L₄ verso.

The Curse of the Incas and the Wealth of Potosí

T HE ENGLISH VERSION OF LAS CASAS EMPHASIZED AND EXAGER-
ated the Spaniards' cruelty and their slaughter of the Indians, especially in Peru. The invaders, the text asserts, "have with
less reverence of God or the King, and with less pity than before,
abolished a great part of the lineage of mankind. They have slain
unto this day in these same realms (and yet daily they do slay
them) more than four millions of souls." [1] Although all of this
slaughter could not have occurred in Peru, other contemporary
accounts provide grim narratives of the bloodshed that occurred
during the conquest of Peru, both among Indians and Spaniards.
The gold of the Incas proved a curse, and few survived to enjoy
the richest treasure trove discovered in the New World. The
gold amassed by the Incas and the silver later mined at Potosí
made Peru a modern Golconda, but this wealth had a malignancy
that carried beyond the country of its origin. Yet tales of untold
treasure to be found in Peru and other regions of South America

[1] English translation of Bartolomé de Las Casas, *Brevissima relación*
entitled *The Spanish Colonie* (1583), sig. L₁ verso.

227

acted like a virus in the blood of countless adventurers. From elsewhere in the "Indies" and eventually from various countries of Europe came gold-seekers. Their search took them on mad and frequently fatal expeditions to the freezing heights of the Andes and to the miasmic swamps of the Orinoco and the Amazon.

The first to get wind of the gold of Peru was Vasco Núñez de Balboa, beheaded in 1517 on a trumped-up charge of treason by his father-in-law, the implacable Pedrarias, then Governor of Darien. Ironically, as we have seen, the man sent to arrest Balboa was his friend Francisco Pizarro, later to be conqueror of Peru. Stories of the abundance of gold somewhere in the south continued to circulate, arousing the cupidity of Pizarro and his colleagues in Central America. They already had experience in searching for gold on the long sweep of the Central American coast, then called Castilla del Oro, but this region so swarmed with greedy and ruthless adventurers that the appeal of fresh fields was strong.

Francisco Pizarro, whose incredible feats of courage and endurance read like the doings of some knight in the chivalric romances, began life in Estremadura. He was the illegitimate son of an impecunious landowner and soldier from the little town of Trujillo. His mother abandoned him on the church steps; later legend reports that he was first suckled by a sow and that he became a swineherd on his father's farm, from which he fled after he had lost some pigs. If this Romulus-and-Remus type of beginning is myth, at least it is certain that Francisco had no formal education and never learned to read or sign his name. Illiterate and poverty-stricken, he nevertheless learned to use a sword and lance. Early in life he heard the call of adventure and joined the throng of emigrants from Estremadura who were determined to make their fortunes in the New World. One fellow Estremaduran who left about the same time was Balboa. As early as 1509 Pizarro had made an impression for courage upon Alonso de Hojeda, who took him on his ill-fated expedition to the coast of Colombia and left him in charge of a handful of men at San

228

Sebastián. Balboa soon turned up, and Pizarro joined him on the expedition that discovered the Pacific. By a chance of fate Pizarro had to preside at Balboa's beheading.

For his efforts in controlling the Indians in Golden Castile, Pedrarias granted Pizarro an encomienda, and for a time he conducted a cattle ranch and farm. If this life was too reminiscent of his early days in Estremadura, it did not last for long. In the meantime he had made friends with a certain Diego de Almagro, another illiterate foundling who had grown up to be a skilled swordsman. These two had found a mutual friend, a priest and schoolmaster, one Ferdinand de Luque, who had made money, was looked upon with favor by Pedrarias, and had an unsatisfied lust for greater wealth. These three, having listened to continued reports of the gold to be had on the southern coast of the great South Sea, made a compact to find it. While Pizarro and Almagro actually led expeditions, Luque stayed ashore to manage affairs, raise money for ships and supplies, and keep Pedrarias satisfied with promises of treasure to be found. He ultimately dropped from sight.

Although other conquerors might assert that they led expeditions to convert the heathen, Pizarro made no such pretense. These three partners were intent upon enriching themselves. Their days of poverty in Spain had left a mark that they intended to erase with gold. Later on, when Pizarro had achieved his ambition and a priest sought to induce him to do more to Christianize the Indians of Peru, he replied: "I have not come for any such reasons. I have come to take away from them their gold." [2] Nevertheless, as in the case of other conquistadors, even he had a streak of piety which he displayed on occasion. If he feared no man or devil, he was not willing to flout the Almighty and His saints.

Only a man of dogged persistence, endurance, and invincible courage could have struggled for the eight long years that it took Pizarro to accomplish his ends and gain the treasure of the Incas.

[2] Quoted by Lewis Hanke, *Bartolomé de Las Casas: An Interpretation of His Life and Writings* (The Hague, 1951), p. 8.

Although he first left Panama in November of 1524 with one ship and 100 men, he did not finally make decisive contact with the Incas until November 15, 1532. The preceding eight years were a period of trial, error, and frustration. Perhaps the delay was fortunate because the ruling house of Peru in the meantime engaged in a fratricidal civil war that divided the central authority and left the country weak enough for the Spaniards to conquer.

The difficulty that Pizarro and Almagro faced was total ignorance of the country to the south. Their information was based only upon rumors and vague stories. It is true that Pedrarias had sent out in 1522 a certain Pascual de Andagoya, who had sailed along the coast of western Colombia and had entered a region that he called Biru, a name later adapted and applied to the land of the Incas farther south. Andagoya was incapacitated in an accident, and nothing came of his explorations save the name and further stories of a gold-producing region beyond the point that he reached. His reports, however, encouraged Pedrarias to support Pizarro and his two partners in their venture.

For two years Pizarro and Almagro, setting out in separate ships, struggled to find a clue to the region of gold. Contrary winds off the coast of Colombia damaged their vessels and threatened total loss. When they succeeded in landing, hostile Indians, impenetrable swamps, and lack of food made progress impossible. Finally, in 1526, with supplies exhausted and many of their men dead, the two partners returned to Panama to seek fresh aid. With borrowed money they contrived to hire two small ships and recruit about 160 men, some of them rogues and rascals; once more they set forth down the Colombian coast. Capturing one Indian town, they obtained some corn and a little gold. Encouraged, Pizarro established a camp at the mouth of the San Juan River while Almagro returned to Panama to get more supplies and to recruit additional troops.

Pizarro, who had one ship left, sent out Bartolomé Ruiz, a skilled pilot, who reconnoitered the coast and brought back the most promising information the explorers had yet obtained. Ruiz had found evidence of a relatively civilized society on the coast near the Equator. He had seen Indians dressed in fine-spun garments of wool dyed in bright colors and often richly embroidered. Furthermore, they had gold ornaments, and he had observed other evidences of skilled craftmanship. The fields were laid out regularly and cultivated with care. A balsa raft that he overtook was occupied by merchants with goods that they reported came from Tumbes, a prosperous town farther south. All in all, Ruiz brought back news that encouraged Pizarro to believe he was at last on the way to the fabulous land of gold.[3]

Almagro returned with scanty supplies and a few more men, but they lacked sufficient men and equipment to launch an invasion. Once more Almagro undertook to return to Panama for additional help while Pizarro grudgingly agreed to remain behind with a handful of discontented men on the island of Gallo, a little more than two degrees north of the Equator. Tempers wore thin, and both the leaders and the men were ready to cut one another's throats.

In Panama, Almagro found in place of Pedrarias a new governor, Pedro de los Ríos, who had no sympathy with an exploring project that had already used up too many men without returning a profit. Instead of encouraging Almagro with further help, he dispatched a vessel to Gallo Island to bring back any of Pizarro's scanty band who had had enough of fruitless exploration. Beside himself with rage at this news, Pizarro drew a line in the sand with his dagger and called upon anyone who would go with him to find the riches of Peru to step across it. Only Bartolomé Ruiz, the pilot, and twelve men elected to stay. The rest re-

[3] A succinct account of Pizarro will be found in F. A. Kirkpatrick, *The Spanish Conquistadores* (London, 1934), pp. 138–216. A more recent and highly readable narrative is Jean Descola, *The Conquistadors* (New York, 1957), pp. 229–293. Useful still is Sir Arthur Helps, *The Spanish Conquest in America* (4 vols., London, 1900–04), III, 289ff. Of course W. H. Prescott, *The History of the Conquest of Peru* (2 vols., Boston, 1847) is a classic in this field and provides details of continuing interest. Useful information is given in Philip A. Means, *Fall of the Inca Empire and the Spanish Rule in Peru, 1530–1780* (New York, 1931; reprint, 1964).

turned to Panama. As it turned out, Ruiz had to pilot the ship back; so Pizarro was left with only twelve brave followers.

Pizarro and his companions, seeking less swampy quarters, moved from Gallo to Gorgone Island, a few miles away, but the improvement was slight. For seven months they fought off mosquitoes, vampire bats, snakes, and jaguars. Food gave out, and they lived on shellfish, turtle eggs, and anything else that was edible. At last Ruiz returned from Panama, but with a message that the Governor demanded their return in six months. Even so, perhaps that would give time enough to make some significant discovery. Instead of sailing back to Panama immediately, the band went aboard Ruiz' ship and sailed south.

On his first expedition Ruiz had crossed the Equator and had observed a goodly country below the Line. Now he took Pizarro and his group farther south to the Gulf of Guayaquil. There at the southern extremity of the gulf they discovered the city of Tumbes. As Cortés' men had looked down on the fairy city of Tenochtitlán, so Pizarro and his band gazed upon this town and found it good. If it was not the golden capital of Peru, it was at least pleasing to men who for many months had found no respite from torrential rains and the pests of tropical swamps.

The natives of Tumbes were as excited by the arrival of the Spaniards as Pizarro's men were at finding such a civilized place. To the Indians the newcomers appeared to be gods. Indeed, as in Mexico, the Peruvian Indians also had a legend of white gods who would arrive from the sea. At any rate, the Spaniards were hospitably received at Tumbes, a fortified town well supplied with soldiers. Realizing that he could not take the town with a handful of men, Pizarro contented himself with receiving gifts of woolen fabrics, emeralds, and golden ornaments. He also picked up something far more valuable: the most precise information yet obtained about Peru. Somewhere in the vast mountains visible from Tumbes lay the capital of the empire of Peru, ruled by the Incas. A civil war was raging between rival factions among the Incas. Surely with additional men, Pizarro reasoned, he could turn this civil war to his advantage.

So, having ingratiated himself to the best of his limited abilities with the inhabitants of Tumbes, he sailed away. After exploring the coastline still farther to the south, Pizarro at last turned his ship toward Panama. Taking several natives of Tumbes, a few llamas (which Spaniards had not previously known), and tangible gold to prove that more could be found in the mountains of Peru, he arrived in Panama in 1528, four years after he first started on his adventures. In that time he had suffered much, but he had not given up his dream of conquering a golden empire.

In Panama, opinion was not favorable to Pizarro's schemes. The Governor would not support another expedition, and the partners, unable to raise money in Central America, decided that they must appeal to the Emperor himself. To that end they chose Pizarro to carry their appeal to Spain. Bearing objects of gold, emeralds, and fine cloths woven by the Peruvians, and taking along a llama, Pizarro appeared before the Emperor at Toledo in the summer of 1528, but it was another year before the audience bore fruit. Finally, in July 1529 Charles V appointed Francisco Pizarro governor, chief justice, and captain-general of Peru when and if it should be conquered. His salary would come from the new state when and if it had any revenue. He was also named a Knight of the Order of Santiago. The Emperor's agreement for the conquest of Peru, known as the "Capitulation," was signed by the Queen Regent since the Emperor himself at this time was off in Italy.

The illiterate swordsman of Estremadura, elated over his honors and the princely favors shown him by the Emperor, hurried off to Trujillo to preen himself before his relatives and friends. So convincing were his stories of the prospect of wealth that he persuaded his one legitimate brother, Hernando Pizarro, and three other half-brothers—Juan and Gonzalo Pizarro, and Martín de Alcántara (son of his mother)—to return with him to Panama. This brood would prove a potent force in the future of South America. Another Pizarro also came along, a young cousin named Pedro, who had the advantage of literacy; he would later write an account of the deeds of his elders.

233

From the Emperor, Francisco Pizarro obtained an appointment for his partner Almagro as Governor of Tumbes. Since his
salary was fixed at half that promised Pizarro, he naturally felt
cheated and stirred up a row on Pizarro's return to Panama. Although they patched up the quarrel, the seeds of future dissension had been sown. The priestly member of the triumvirate,
Luque, was appointed Bishop of Tumbes and made no complaint
about his bishopric-to-be.

The twelve soldiers who had refused to desert Pizarro on
Gallo Island were not forgotten. The Emperor made them all
hidalgos with titles of nobility. Henceforth they would be
known as Knights of the Golden Sword. Ruiz was made Grand
Pilot of the Southern Sea. This episode might have been taken
from one of the chivalric romances that Charles V was addicted
to reading. If the ex-swineherd of Trujillo and his twelve cutthroats did not precisely fit the picture of Roland and the
Twelve Peers of France, the deeds of these Spaniards would
equal anything in the Song of Roland.

Pizarro also received from the Emperor a modest grant toward
equipping the expedition to conquer Peru, but the burden of rais-
ing the required sum fell on the Captain-General. Charles V
found it easier to dispense honors than to give cash. In some fashion Pizarro found three ships, rounded up a scanty stock of supplies, enlisted a few fellow adventurers in Estremadura and
Andalusia, and sailed from Sanlúcar for Panama in January 1530.

For the remainder of 1530 Pizarro labored in Panama to recruit a larger force. But by the end of the year the best he could
muster was 183 men with 27 horses; nevertheless, in January
1531 he set out in three ships for the coast of Peru. This was
Pizarro's third venture, but this time he had accurate knowledge
of where he was going. Almagro remained in Panama to try to
find reinforcements.

Although the destination of the little fleet was Tumbes, Pizarro was forced by bad weather to make a landing more than
two hundred miles north of the town. From there his army
marched slowly overland toward Tumbes. For six months they

plodded south, living off the land and plundering villages and towns of gold, emeralds, and any other objects of value they could discover. Many of the men were afflicted with dreadful ulcers, and all suffered from the burning sun beating down upon polished armor, the worst possible equipment for a tropical invasion. But their armor was necessary, for they had ceased to be peaceful and courteous hidalgos and were now hostile invaders. At the town of Coaque, for example, they rushed upon the inhabitants with swords in hand and occupied and plundered buildings deserted by their owners.

At Puerto Viejo they received a small increment of recruits from Panama led by Sebastián de Belalcázar. Although some of Pizarro's weary troops wanted to stop and make a settlement at this point, he pushed on to Puna Island in the Gulf of Guayaquil, where he decided to wait out the rainy season in the expectation of further reinforcements. Tumbes lay not far away, and he intended to take it. In the meantime, by the ship that had brought Belalcázar and his handful of men, he sent some of his treasure back to Panama to serve as visible evidence of the wealth awaiting conquerors and thus to encourage Almagro's recruiting.

Puna proved no peaceful rest camp, for the natives were a constant threat and at length several thousand of them attacked the Spaniards. Swords and lances, the thunder of guns, and terror inspired by the horses won the day, and the natives left hundreds of their dead on the field. It had not been an easy victory, however, and a priest declared that St. Michael had been seen high over the battlefield directing the Christians.

More tangible help soon arrived in two vessels from Panama, led this time by a gallant soldier, another impoverished gentleman from Estremadura, Hernando de Soto. He would prove invaluable to Pizarro in the conquest of Peru and would later die in the swamps of the Mississippi, seeking another golden empire of his own. He brought with him a hundred troopers, and with this company Pizarro felt strong enough to fall upon Tumbes, which yielded a quantity of treasure.

Pizarro was now ready to strike at the heart of the Inca empire. But first he established a base on the coast at the mouth of the Chira River. This camp, set up with all the formalities of a Spanish municipality, he named San Miguel.

The empire that Pizarro was determined to conquer with his handful of men was the strongest and most closely knit political organization developed by aborigines in the New World. In extent it stretched roughly from the Equator to the thirty-fifth degree of south latitude, or from Quito, Ecuador, to a point beyond Santiago, Chile—a distance of 2,700 miles. By the time the Spaniards arrived, the Incas had established their influence over large portions of the region now occupied by the modern states of Ecuador, Peru, Bolivia, Chile, and Argentina. Their realm was connected by a system of roads similar to those built by the Romans to link their empire together. Along these roads posthouses with relays of messengers enabled the central government of the Incas to maintain rapid communication with the far-flung parts of the empire. Unlike the Aztecs, the Incas had created a genuine empire and had imposed their laws and customs upon conquered tribes. They levied taxes and established such a complete welfare state that their subject people had lost all individual initiative. This condition may help to explain why the Indian population of Peru could so easily be induced to switch masters. Spanish or Inca rule made little difference to a conquered people.

The realm of the Incas appeared well-nigh impregnable. Most of their cities were situated on the high plateaus of the Andes. Mountain chains in a double and in places a triple line rose to immense heights along the spine of South America. The coastal region, sometimes less than a hundred miles in width, was frequently an arid desert. The mountain wall made a 14,000-foot barrier, with peaks rising to 22,000 feet and more. To the south of the empire lay a vast lake, Titicaca, at an elevation of 12,500 feet.

The dominant Incas called themselves "People of the Sun," and the royal family claimed direct descent from the sun. This sun worship distinguished the Peruvians from the Aztecs and other tribes to the north. They had no gods calling insatiably for human sacrifices, though on extraordinary occasions human sacrifices might be offered. Instead, their worship was normally characterized by festivals where plays were performed and bards gave recitations glorifying the deeds of folk heroes. In their principal cities they erected temples to the sun where beautiful maidens lived in convent-like buildings as Virgins of the Sun. At Tumbes Pedro de Candia, a Greek, one of the original Twelve Knights of the Golden Sword, managed to visit one of these convents and came back with an alluring account not only of the gold treasure that he had observed but of the beauty of the Virgins, who had looked with favor upon him. From this time onward, Pizarro's soldiers might slaughter the soldiers of the Inca, but they kept a sharp eye for enticing damsels who were equally tempted by the bearded strangers. In an astonishingly short time Peru had a number of young half-breeds who played a part in the future history of the land.

A tale soon got into circulation that when the Indians of Tumbes unleashed jaguars and set them upon Pedro de Candia, he merely stroked them as he would a cat and they lay down and rolled over. This Pedro, whom not even a jaguar dared attack, was in command of Pizarro's artillery and later proved a terror to the Peruvians.

The buildings of stone erected by the Incas astonished the Spaniards. Nowhere else in the New World had they seen stone so accurately cut and fitted or buildings and walls of such strength and size. The Peruvians had advanced further in architectural skill than any other natives on this continent. They also were expert farmers and had developed elaborate irrigation projects. Terraced fields climbed the hillsides where incredible human exertion had gone into the erection of retaining walls which held fertile soil that had been carried up in baskets. Some of these terraced fields extended over several acres where corn, beans, squash, and other food crops grew luxuriantly.

Yet despite their high degree of culture, the Peruvians had no written language. Nevertheless, they kept intricate records by

237

means of knotted strings called quipus. Primitive as this method was, no one dared dispute the records kept by the inexorable tax collectors.

The ruling Incas at the time of the arrival of the Spaniards were themselves conquistadors. They had extended their sway over numerous tribes and had created an empire kept in subjection by a highly organized central government supported by thousands of warriors. The ruler of this domain was the Inca Huayna Capac. His most recent conquest was the kingdom of Quito to the north, and he had spent much effort in pacifying the region and in integrating it into his empire.

Unfortunately for his people, Huayna Capac doted on one of his many illegitimate sons. According to the account written down later from hearsay by Garcilaso de la Vega in *The Royal Commentaries of the Inca*, Huayna Capac had two hundred sons —some said three hundred—by the numerous women whom he kept in his harem. But the son that he particularly favored was Atahualpa. As the old Inca approached his end, he persuaded Huascar, his legitimate heir, to make an unprecedented agreement to divide the empire. Huascar would retain the southern portion with Cuzco as his capital while Atahualpa would govern the north from Quito.

Not long after Huayna Capac's death in 1525, Atahualpa decided to seize the southern half of the Inca empire from his easygoing half-brother Huascar, who preferred to loll with his women in his palace at Cuzco rather than lead armies of warriors. Although Atahualpa also surrounded himself with the most beautiful women in his kingdom, he did not let uxoriousness stand between him and ambition. Pretending friendship at first, he moved south with his armies, captured Huascar, and led him captive to Cuzco. Even Huascar's favorite mistress, a girl of surpassing charm, deserted him and ran off with a soldier. Later captured by the Spaniards, these two were brought before de Soto, who heard their story, looked upon the girl with favor, and took her as his own.

In the meantime Atahualpa sought out all he could find of the descendants and loyal followers of Huayna Capac and slaughtered them without mercy. Using the cunning that Machiavelli prescribed in *The Prince*, he proposed to wipe out the entire brood of those who might dispute his authority. So the blood of Incas flowed like water. Even after his own capture by the Spaniards he contrived to send a message to Cuzco ordering Huascar's murder. The internecine warfare between Huascar and Atahualpa gave Pizarro the opportunity he needed.

Another circumstance aided Pizarro's conquest: a prediction, revealed by Huayna Capac before his death, that the strange white visitors to the shores of Peru would one day conquer the Incas, for, according to this prophecy, they were the sons of the white demigod Viracocha, who had long ago vanished into the sea.[4] As Cortés had exploited the belief in the return of Quetzalcoatl, so Pizarro encouraged the notion that the Spaniards were the sons of the great Viracocha. This belief may have helped to befuddle Atahualpa and his followers and to prevent more decisive action from a warrior who had a vast force at his command.

Early in October 1532 Pizarro started on his march from San Miguel to the interior—and to victory, as he hoped. His destination was Cajamarca, a watering place in a high valley of the Andes, where Atahualpa had taken up residence. First he had to cross the parched Sechura Desert between the sea and the mountains; then by slow degrees he and his men climbed the western escarpment to the snows of the first range of the cordillera. The little army consisted of only 106 foot soldiers and 62 cavalrymen. Of the infantrymen, 20 were equipped with crossbows and 3 with muskets. He also had a few small cannon. This was the force that went out to conquer the great empire of Peru. Facing them was a warrior hitherto invincible at the head of some 30,000 trained soldiers accustomed to fighting at high altitudes.

The western slope of the Andes is steep and rugged. Many of the defiles through which Pizarro and his men had to pass were

---

[4] Garcilaso de la Vega elaborates upon this legend. See *The Incas: The Royal Commentaries of the Inca, Garcilaso de la Vega, 1539–1616*, ed. Alain Gheerbrant (New York, 1961), pp. 287–289.

barely wide enough for the horses, and in several places fortresses overhung the passes. At a dozen points a few soldiers with
only stones to roll down upon the advancing Spaniards could
have blocked the invasion, but the Peruvians allowed the strangers to make their way over the peaks and down the slopes to the
valley beyond. On November 15, 1532, Pizarro and his men entered Cajamarca and found it deserted. The Peruvians had
moved to a camp on the hillside some three miles away, where
pennons from their tents could be seen fluttering in the wind.
With a comfortable town vacant before them, the Spaniards settled themselves in the best buildings, including Atahualpa's palace.

Both Spaniards and Peruvians were puzzled and uneasy. Some
30,000 warriors confronted the handful of invaders, but Atahualpa, like Montezuma in Mexico, was apparently confused by
the prophecy of the coming of a white god. At any rate, he took
no decisive action until it was too late. Pizarro, remembering
Cortés' strategy, decided to take the initiative and seize the Inca.
With the ruler in his power, he could make him serve Spanish
ends as a puppet.

Atahualpa had sent messengers to greet the Spaniards and to
pretend friendship. In the meantime, however, he had ordered
his general, Ruminagui, to block all the roads by which the Spaniards might escape. In good time he would capture these intruders.

Pizarro returned Atahualpa's courtesy by sending a mission of
twenty horsemen led by de Soto to the Peruvian camp to invite
the Inca to a meeting. Presently Hernando Pizarro with fifteen
more horsemen joined de Soto at the Peruvian camp. The Spaniards, in shining armor and mounted on creatures the Indians had
never seen, wanted to make a vivid impression. To show his skill,
de Soto galloped his horse, caused him to rear and curvet, and
then pulled him up short at the feet of Atahualpa, who looked on
impassively. When several of the Indians about him fled in
fright, the Inca ordered them beheaded for cowardice.

The upshot of the mission was a promise that Atahualpa

would visit Pizarro at Cajamarca. Pizarro at once set about preparing for Atahualpa's capture. The principal buildings of Cajamarca surrounded an open square where Atahualpa would be welcomed. In these buildings Pizarro concealed his troops and horsemen. At strategic points to sweep the open spaces, he mounted his small cannon. All was in readiness save an appeal to God for victory. Though Pizarro had shown little evidence as yet of a missionary spirit, he wanted to take no chances. He ordered his men to make confession and take communion. He himself preached them a sermon in which he pointed out the godliness of smiting idolators and bringing them to a knowledge of the Christian faith. That done, he gave instructions to his chaplain, Father Vicente de Valverde, to prepare on the morrow to read the "Requisition" to Atahualpa—that wondrous engine of legalism by which the Spaniards expounded the mysteries of the Trinity and Christian doctrine before demanding the hearer's submission to the Papacy and the Emperor Charles V. With these preparations made, Pizarro could wait for the appearance of the Inca and his train.

The day of the rendezvous dawned, but Atahualpa sent excuses. He found it inconvenient to make his visit that day; perhaps tomorrow would be better. In the meantime he was disposing his own army around the Spanish position at Cajamarca. Pizarro's situation was precarious. He must seize the Inca as quickly as possible. By Atahualpa's own messenger Pizarro replied, inviting the Emperor to dinner that evening.

The Emperor of the Inca realm arrived with a retinue of some five thousand unarmed followers, though the Spaniards claimed that they had darts and slings concealed under their garments. Borne on a golden throne atop a litter carried by his great nobles, Atahualpa advanced to the center of the town square. Servants swept the ground before the litter and others danced around it. Glittering with a necklace of emeralds and a breastplate of gold, Atahualpa surveyed the scene impassively as he waited for the strangers, who remained hidden within the buildings.

The first Spaniard to appear was Father Valverde, with crucifix and book, to read to Atahualpa the Requisition commanding his allegiance to Pope and Emperor. If he refused, the Spaniards were then legally free to make war upon him and utterly to destroy him and his people. The theology and the politics of the Requisition had to be translated by an Indian interpreter scarcely competent in elementary Spanish, much less in philosophic nuances, but Atahualpa at least understood the demand for submission to an alien power. When he scornfully asked Valverde for his authority for such arrogance, the priest handed him a breviary, which the Inca tossed to the earth. Scandalized, Valverde hastily reported to Pizarro. The time had come for action. The Spanish leader waved his scarf and a musketeer fired a shot, the signal for attack. Cannon roared, and horsemen, with sword and lance, dashed into the crowd of Indians. Pizarro himself had to rush to save Atahualpa from slaughter, and in so doing received a cut on his hand from one of his own men, the only Spanish casualty. Within half an hour the Spaniards slew some 2,000 Indians, perhaps more. The rest they took captive.

Atahualpa, though snatched ingloriously from his golden throne, was taken to Pizarro's quarters and treated with the respect due to royalty. Like Montezuma, he made the best of his captivity, sometimes dined with Pizarro, received messengers, and exercised the prerogatives of a ruler subject to the Spaniards' interests. Pizarro welcomed the Inca's harem and saw that they were available to the prisoner. Some of the more beautiful women quickly succumbed to the charms of the strangers, who found their new conjugal partners both pleasing and eager to please.

The Inca empire had fallen. As Cortés had won Mexico by the capture of Montezuma, so Pizarro, copying his strategy, brought down an even greater power by seizing the head of state. To the submissive subjects of the Inca, the change of masters was as yet scarcely known. Indeed, from his prison Atahualpa continued to rule after a fashion.

Spanish greed for gold so impressed Atahualpa that he conceived a plan for his own release. The room where he was confined was a space seventeen feet by twelve; he offered to fill it with the precious metal as high as he could reach, on condition that he would be freed. This he would do within two months. Pizarro agreed to the bargain, and messengers went out to the far corners of the kingdom. Soon carriers swarmed into Cajamarca bearing objects of gold: dishes, vases, figurines, masks, birds and animals wrought in gold, and sheets of pure gold. The treasure reached higher and higher, but not yet had it topped the seven-foot line marked around the wall. Pizarro agreed that silver might be added to the pile. At last the room was packed solid with gold and silver to the agreed line.

That many of these objects in gold and silver were works of art meant nothing to the Spaniards. They called in Indian gold-smiths to melt down the treasure into ingots of standard size. For more than a month they labored to reduce the treasure to a form that could be fairly divided and transported. When finally the ingots were weighed, the gold amounted to 13,265.4 pounds weight, and the silver to 26,000 pounds, surely treasure enough to satisfy the greediest conquistador.

But in the meantime Pizarro's erstwhile partner in the Peru-vian venture, Almagro, had turned up with reinforcements of 150 foot soldiers and 50 cavalrymen. When these demanded an equal share of the wealth, grudgingly Pizarro had to comply. After setting aside the Royal Fifth, the treasure was divided so that every man got enough to make him rich in Spain—if he could ever reach that land with his booty. Pizarro's own share was the largest after the King's, and his brothers and his other officers each received a fortune.

But what of Atahualpa and Pizarro's agreement to free him? Obviously that would be inconvenient and dangerous, for even with Almagro's reinforcements the Spanish forces numbered only 368 men. It was also inconvenient to deny that an honest bargain had been made which the Spaniards now wished to for-get. The simplest way out was to trump up a charge of treason against the Inca and execute him. All must be done with a show of legality. So Atahualpa was charged with attempting to rouse

243

his people to attack the Spaniards, but when de Soto went out on a reconnaissance, he reported that no armed men could be found anywhere. Nevertheless, Atahualpa was brought to trial, found guilty as expected, and sentenced to be burned to death in the town square. In consideration, however, of his accepting Christian baptism, the sentence was commuted to strangulation at the stake. The execution was duly carried out on August 29, 1533, a little more than ten months from the time that Pizarro entered Cajamarca. Father Valverde, who had baptized the victim and administered the last rites, had the satisfaction of sending to salvation a heathen soul previously deaf to his missionary message.

The death of Atahualpa, however, raised more problems than it solved. With a little more foresight, Pizarro might have realized that the living Inca serving him as a puppet would remain useful. Now he had no one to issue orders to the Peruvian subjects. Soon the Spanish leaders were blaming one another for this error in judgment. They tried to make some sort of amends by giving Atahualpa a fine funeral. Pizarro, with black crape draped over his breastplate and sword hilt, marched at the head of the funeral procession. Father Valverde, who had urged the execution of the Inca, intoned the solemn service for the dead. But after the Inca had been given Christian burial, some of his followers, it is reported, dug up the body and carried it to Quito for burial. Contemporary reports of the incident do not all agree. Some say the body was burned.[5]

To remedy the mistake of eliminating the Inca, Pizarro sought out a new puppet, a certain Toparca, one of the many sons of the Inca Huayna Capac. He proclaimed Toparca reigning Inca and added him to his own entourage. This subterfuge, however, brought little satisfaction, for Toparca died within less than two months and Pizarro had to look for another puppet.

With further reinforcements from Panama, Pizarro now had an army of some 600. After leaving a garrison force of 150 men at San Miguel under a loyal Estremaduran, Sebastián de Belalcá-

[5] See the account given in Kirkpatrick, *The Spanish Conquistadores,* pp. 165–167, and in Descola, *The Conquistadors,* p. 276.

244

zar, Pizarro set out for Cuzco, ancient capital of Peru, where additional gold could be expected. A year to the day after he arrived at Cajamarca, he entered Cuzco, on November 15, 1533. The army, which had captured some loot on the journey, now began pillaging Cuzco systematically. Not even the graves of the dead were respected, and from mummies the looters stripped golden masks, rings, jewels, and ornaments. One report describes the discovery of ten planks of silver, each twenty feet long, a foot wide, and three inches thick.[6] Once more the Indian goldsmiths were ordered to melt down the treasure, and once more Pizarro divided the wealth so that every common soldier received a handsome reward while the officers added substantially to fortunes already acquired. No other conquerors in the New World had obtained such wealth.

The seizure of wealth, however, had not solved the problem of governing the territory that had fallen so easily into Spanish hands. Pizarro had reason to regret bitterly the execution of Atahualpa. But as he approached Cuzco he had an unexpected piece of luck. A visitor to his camp announced that he was Manco, the oldest legitimate son of Huayna Capac, and the heir to the throne after Huascar. In the name of the Emperor Charles V, Pizarro eagerly proclaimed Manco the true Inca and ruler of Peru. Since Atahualpa had been a rebel, albeit a successful rebel, against the legitimate line, Pizarro now declared himself the defender of Huascar's rightful heir. Thus opportunely finding himself the defender of legitimacy, Pizarro made the most of an alliance with Manco. Together they wiped out a pocket of resistance to the Spaniards led by one of Atahualpa's generals with the implausible name of Quizquiz.

In addition to recalcitrant Peruvians Pizarro soon had other troubles to worry him. News reached him that Pedro de Alvarado, a veteran of the Mexican campaign and Governor of Guatemala, was leading a force from Guatemala to capture Quito. To prevent this disaster, Almagro hurried north. He found on reaching San Miguel that Belalcázar had already marched on

[6] Kirkpatrick, *The Spanish Conquistadores*, p. 170.

245

Quito to meet a rebel Peruvian, Atahualpa's general Ruminagui. Reaching Quito as Belalcázar was making a final victorious attack on Ruminagui, Almagro seized part of the spoils and returned to Cuzco, leaving Belalcázar in control of the northern territory. They had been unable to locate Alvarado.

No sooner had Almagro reached Cuzco, however, than he heard that Alvarado had climbed the dizzy cordilleras and was camped in the valley of Riobamba, some sixty miles from Quito. Again he made a forced march north; meanwhile Belalcázar had also received the news and was marching to meet Alvarado. The three Spanish captains, each at the head of a column of men, met in the Riobamba. After some negotiation, they decided not to fight. Almagro offered Alvarado 100,000 pesos, to be delivered to him by Pizarro, if he would return to Guatemala. Since he had already taken a fair amount of loot on his march to the Riobamba, Alvarado agreed to this bargain. At Pachácamac on the coast they met Pizarro, who paid over the pesos and bade God's speed to Alvarado as he set out for Guatemala. A generous bribe had averted a crisis, but the virus of gold was in the blood of Spanish captains who would not willingly leave the Pizarros in undisturbed possession of vast wealth when they might have some of it for the taking. Furthermore, many gentlemen of good birth who had accompanied Alvarado to Peru elected to remain there. They would become adventurers on their own and would make trouble for Pizarro.

In the meantime Hernando Pizarro, the one legitimate—and literate—Pizarro, had returned to Spain with the Royal Fifth, which he duly delivered to Charles V, most of it in ingots but a small portion in objects of art for the Emperor's amusement and interest. Charles, more concerned with ingots than with art, was impressed by the wealth that Peru offered, and rewarded the conquerors with titles and grants of territory. Francisco Pizarro, erstwhile swineherd of Trujillo in Estremadura, was created Marquis d'Altabillos and appointed Governor of Peru, which was given the name of New Castile. Almagro was appointed Governor of a nebulous territory south of New Castile, which

246

was named New Toledo. The boundaries between the territories were undefined since neither Charles V nor anyone else knew the terrain. This vagueness became the source of deadly enmity between the two former partners, Francisco Pizarro and Almagro, for each wanted and claimed the rich city of Cuzco, which lay in disputed territory. Charles also made Hernando a Knight of Santiago; and the Dominican chaplain, Valverde, he made Bishop of Cuzco.

Pizarro, believing that neither Cuzco nor Quito was suitably situated for the capital of his domain, decided to lay out a new city. After considering several sites, he chose a spot on the Rimac River, six miles from the sea. The river would open a route to the interior, while the capital would have a port on the sea at Callao, which was soon established. With pomp and ceremony, on January 18, 1535, the new Marquis (as Pizarro preferred henceforth to be called), founded his capital and gave it the name of Ciudad de los Reyes (the City of Kings), but it quickly came to be called Lima. Secure in his own fortune, he busied himself with creating a Spanish city. Indians by the hundreds were drafted to lay out streets, haul stone, build walls, and erect buildings. For himself he chose a square on the north side of the large central plaza. On another side of the plaza he set aside ground for a church and ecclesiastical buildings. To worthy Spaniards he awarded town lots and land in the suburbs. He also established the encomienda system, with Indians assigned to work the land for their Spanish overlords.

Back in Cuzco, the Marquis' two brothers Juan and Gonzalo Pizarro were in command for a time. Satisfied at first with his own honors and territory, the Marquis decided to let Almagro have control of Cuzco, but shortly afterward changed his mind and ordered Juan and Gonzalo to repossess the city in his name. This move enraged Almagro and brought the two factions to the verge of civil war. The Marquis, however, journeyed to Cuzco in June 1535 and made peace with his old comrade. The two drew up a solemn compact, witnessed by a notary, in which they swore by the Holy Apostles and the Trinity to keep peace and

247

not to malign each other in reports to His Majesty the King of Spain. The compact, however, did not solve any territorial questions, even the possession of Cuzco. Almagro, biding his time, went on an expedition to the south to see what New Toledo offered; he hoped to discover more hoards of gold that would make Cuzco of no moment.

The news of Peru's wealth already had brought many Spaniards to the land, and Cuzco had drawn a large share of the adventurers. Almagro was therefore able to muster an army of more than 550 men, later augmented by additional recruits. He also drafted thousands of Indians as carriers. This contingent marched out of Cuzco in July 1535. For nearly two years Almagro explored what is now Bolivia, Chile, and part of Argentina. From the basin of Lake Titicaca he led his horde through southwestern Bolivia to Tupiza, something over a hundred miles from the northern border of Argentina. Thence the army scaled the snowy heights of the Andes and marched south as far as Santiago, Chile. This journey entailed hardships to daunt even veterans of the first expedition over the Andes. Indian carriers, sweating under the burden of baggage or of Spanish soldiers carried in hammocks, died by the score, but Almagro filled their places with fresh captives. He was a man without mercy, and he drove his carriers to the limit of their strength. If there was wealth in New Toledo, he meant to find it. New Toledo, alas, was a disappointment: freezing mountain passes, burning deserts, barren plains, but little or no treasure. The tattered army returned to Cuzco in March 1537. After spending much of his own wealth on the expedition, Almagro was determined to recoup his losses by holding Cuzco.

While Almagro was away in Chile, the Marquis had placed his brother Hernando in command at Cuzco. Hernando's greed for gold was equaled only by the lust of the Spaniards under him for Indian women. Not even high-caste wives of the Inca's court were respected in the Spanish search for female beauty. That many of these women showed an alacrity for liaisons with the strangers did nothing to improve relations with Indian men. Tak-

248

ing advantage of the smoldering fury of the Indians, the Inca puppet Manco mounted a revolt in February 1536 that nearly succeeded. Secretly fleeing from Cuzco, he took command of thousands of Indians flocking to his banner. He laid siege to Cuzco, Lima, and other Spanish settlements and cut communications between the beleaguered Spaniards.

The three Pizarro brothers, Juan, Gonzalo, and Hernando, with such Spaniards as had not gone on exploring expeditions, defended Cuzco from March 1536 to April 1537 against an enveloping army of Indians amounting at times to perhaps 100,-000.[7] The Indians bombarded the town with stones and flaming arrows until they burned the thatched roofs of houses and drove the Spaniards to the central plaza. Juan Pizarro was killed by a stone as he was fighting by Hernando's side. In March 1537 Almagro, returning from the south, came to the rescue of the city. Attacked from the rear, Manco raised the siege and fled northward. Henceforth his guerrillas could harass the Spaniards, but he would no longer be a power in the land.

Almagro's arrival dispersed the Peruvians, but his presence did not please the Pizarros. When Hernando declined to turn over the city to him, Almagro arrested him and Gonzalo and proclaimed himself governor. Knowing, however, that the implacable Marquis would not tolerate this action, he decided to march on Lima with his hardened troops. They would be able to clinch any argument. He took Hernando with him, perhaps to act as intermediary, but Gonzalo he left in a Cuzco jail.

When Almagro was on the approaches to Lima, before a battle could be joined, a Spanish priest arranged a meeting between the old partners. As before, they agreed to settle their affairs peaceably, and the Marquis invited Almagro to dinner. As they were seated, Almagro received a message reporting that Gonzalo had escaped and was plotting his assassination. Leaving his meal unfinished, Almagro mounted his horse and rode away to rouse his followers. Obviously peace with the Pizarros was out of the question.

[7] Means, *Fall of the Inca Empire*, p. 61.

On his part, the Marquis ordered Hernando to raise an army of 800 men and to follow Almagro to Cuzco. The two forces met on April 6, 1538, at Las Salinas (The Salt Pits), near Cuzco. Almagro had 600 hardened veterans. Both sides fought with a ferocity that only Spaniards enraged at each other could exhibit. Many a cavalier died that day, slain by swords and lances previously reserved for Indians. When the dust of conflict settled, Hernando's troops commanded the field and Almagro and his men were his prisoners. Like Cortés, Hernando tried to win over his surviving opponents by diplomacy and kind words.

But Almagro himself he kept a prisoner. The old conquistador had caused too much trouble for the Pizarros. Hernando determined to make an end of him, but, as always, it must be done according to law, with a notary to write it all down. So Almagro was tried for treason and sentenced to death. Though he fell at Hernando's feet and begged for his life, the executioner strangled him with a rope and dragged him to the marketplace of Cuzco, where he cut off his head. The next day, like Atahualpa, he was given an impressive funeral at which Hernando Pizarro wore crape and mourned his late opponent's death.

By an Indian woman, Almagro had a son, a youth named Diego, whom Hernando placed under the protection of his brother the Marquis. Diego received kind treatment in Lima and developed into a shrewd and cunning young man who gathered about him partisans of his late father.

The Pizarros had settled their score with Almagro, their most persistent rival for power and wealth. Though Peru teemed with other ambitious captains, they for a time were content with distant explorations and adventures. Thus the Marquis reigned in reasonable peace at Lima as governor of a princely domain. His palace was sumptuous, and he lived like an Eastern potentate, with Indian women always ready to do his bidding. The sister of the Inca Atahualpa was one of his favorite concubines. She bore him a daughter of singular beauty whom his brother Hernando, disregarding consanguinity, later married. If the Marquis felt alone because of the absence of his brothers, he never showed it.

Juan had died in the siege of Cuzco. Hernando had gone back to Spain to take additional treasure to Charles V—and to combat at court the Pizarros' enemies, who were numerous and venomous. Gonzalo was leading an expedition to the northeast, to the Land of Cinnamon and to the country of El Dorado (the fabled king who was reported to cover his body with gold dust), a venture of incredible hardship in which many Spaniards and 4,000 Indian carriers perished. Only one half-brother, Francisco Martín de Alcántara, was with the Marquis at Lima.

Perhaps the old man—he was now sixty-six—had grown careless or felt too secure, for though he had received whispered warnings of a plot against him, he refused to believe that he was in danger. On Sunday, June 26, 1541, he heard mass in his house, dined with a few friends, and was sitting at ease when the noise of a tumult in the streets reached his ears. Voices were shouting, "Death to the tyrant!" Soon a mob of Almagro's partisans burst in at the door. Most of the Marquis' companions fled, but the old man tried to defend himself and his brother. Grabbing a shield and his sword, he fought to the end. Stabbed in a dozen places, he fell with his throat cut. Marking the sign of the cross in his own blood on the floor, he kissed it and died. Alcántara fell by his side. Thus ended the regime of the swineherd from Estremadura who had gained vast wealth for himself and for his sovereign, who had given another empire to Charles V.

The gold won by the Peruvian conquistadors carried with it a curse and brought little happiness to the conquerors. For few lived to enjoy their gains, either in Peru or in Spain. After the Marquis' death Peru was racked by civil wars. Old comrades turned against each other and fought savagely for power or treasure.

Young Diego Almagro fought to retain power that he seized after the Marquis' assassination, but royalist leaders rallied to defeat him. Vaca de Castro, a lawyer sent out by the Emperor to make an investigation and to assume the governorship of Peru, consolidated the enemies of young Almagro and defeated him on September 18, 1542, in a bloody battle in the Chupas Mountains

251

where nearly one fifth of the combatants in both armies perished, for the wounded, left on the field in the bitter cold, died of exposure. As an example of justice, Vaca de Castro executed some fifty rebels. Young Almagro, captured later in Cuzco, was beheaded on the spot where his father had suffered.

Vaca de Castro, a stern man, might have brought peace to Peru, but he was replaced by a successor who came with instructions to work reforms. Charles V sent out as viceroy Blasco Nuñez de la Vela to proclaim the New Laws of the Indies and to bring peace to Peru, a feat that he was unable to accomplish. Gonzalo Pizarro, who had returned to Quito in August 1542 from his disastrous search for cinnamon and the gilded king, raised a faction and quickly won recruits among Spanish settlers who had no intention of obeying the New Laws and releasing their Indian serfs.

With the help of a ferocious old man of nearly eighty, Francisco de Carbajal, Gonzalo contrived for a time to rule Peru, or New Castile, and even to extend his sway to Panama, where he could control the route to Spain and the whole South Sea area. By judicious hangings Carbajal kept Peru in subjection to Gonzalo, whom he counseled to proclaim himself king. Gonzalo's lieutenants mercilessly put down revolts. On January 16, 1546, Gonzalo himself routed the forces of the Viceroy, captured that unfortunate individual, and beheaded him on the spot.

While Gonzalo was fighting in the north, Carbajal went south to put down a rebellion in the province of Charcas. When he finished, all rebels unhanged had fled to the hills. He left enough bodies swinging from trees to serve as a warning to any who might object to his and Gonzalo's authority.

Carbajal's expedition to the Charcas had an important and unforeseen result for the future of Peru. One of his Indian servants, following the trail of a missing llama up a hill, pulled up a shrub and found bits of silver twined in the roots. The hill was Potosí, the richest silver mine ever discovered, and the source of infinite wealth for two centuries to come. Carbajal himself recognized its value and happily set about mining the treasure.

Gonzalo Pizarro's days as dictator of Peru, however, were numbered. Charles V could not tolerate the flouting of his authority and the execution of a viceroy. To settle affairs in Peru he picked an unlikely man, a quiet unsoldier-like cleric, one Pedro de La Gasca, who asked for and received from the Emperor unlimited authority. With the royal seal on his documents, he landed in what is now Colombia in the summer of 1546. Shrewd and wise, this gray eminence studied the problem, consulted with those able to give advice, and won the confidence of men who had been Gonzalo's deputies. By November he had succeeded in taking over from Gonzalo's commander a fleet of twenty-two ships at Panama. In February 1547 he sent messengers to Lima offering Gonzalo pardon if he would submit peacefully. The dictator chose to resist, though he must have sensed ultimate defeat, for he was conscious that some of his leaders were already deserting and going over to La Gasca. Nevertheless he marched out of Lima at the head of an army of 1,000 well-equipped Spaniards. He planned to head south and make a stand at Cuzco. The men around Gonzalo, however, perceived that the end had come. They melted away and joined the forces of the Emperor's envoy, now recognized as governor.

Finally, on April 9, 1548, La Gasca met the remnant of Gonzalo's army in a valley about fifteen miles from Cuzco. Although Gonzalo put on a brave front and was determined to fight, his men continued to desert before his eyes. Some cannon were fired from each side, but they were too far away to have any effect. Gonzalo and his captains killed several deserters attempting to flee; in all, fourteen of his men lost their lives. La Gasca lost only one man. Such was the "battle" that Gonzalo and Carbajal lost by defection. They had no choice but to surrender, defeated but still defiant.

The very next day both Gonzalo Pizarro and Carbajal were tried for treason and other crimes. Gonzalo was immediately beheaded; Carbajal was hanged, drawn, and quartered, and the four quarters were sent to four Peruvian cities. By sentence of the court, the houses of both Gonzalo and Carbajal were torn down and the sites sown with salt. Several of their confederates were also executed. In this fashion did the cleric La Gasca restore the authority of the Emperor in Peru.

No longer did any Pizarro disturb the peace of the country. Away in Spain, Hernando Pizarro languished in prison, for his enemies had convinced the authorities that he too was an enemy of the state. For twenty years he remained a prisoner, and was at last released to linger out his days and reach the age of a hundred years.

La Gasca's firm rule brought peace to Peru. Although some further disturbances occurred, the chaos brought by civil war was ended. He commemorated the coming of peace by founding the city of La Paz, which in time became the capital of Bolivia, and at the end of 1549 he returned to Spain to serve out his life as a bishop. In 1551 Antonio de Mendoza, who had made a distinguished Viceroy of New Spain, arrived to serve as Viceroy of Peru. Old and in ill-health, Mendoza was plagued by the efforts of Las Casas to have the New Laws enforced in Peru and to free all Indians from servitude. After the Viceroy's death in July 1552, discontented landowners in danger of losing their encomiendas rose in rebellion, but his successor put it down with severity. The story of Peru's settlement is grim and bloody. Las Casas maintained that the land was cursed because of the iniquity of the conquistadors and their lack of care for God's kingdom.

Human greed, however, is sufficient to account for Peru's afflictions in the early years of exploitation. The vast stores of treasure actually found in Peru, greater even than those in Mexico—and wild reports carried back to Europe—attracted every type of adventurer, from noblemen to Spain's lowest thugs and cutthroats. They swarmed to Peru, determined to make their fortunes with their swords, and they little cared whether Indians or rival Spaniards died at their hands. No land in previous recorded history had seen such a gold rush.

The discovery of silver at Potosí precipitated another stampede to exploit treasure, and the slopes of Potosí saw the mushroom growth of the first boom town in the New World. This mountain of silver in the inaccessible Andes, in what is now southwestern Bolivia, also had a profound influence on the economic and political history of western Europe; for the silver that came from its mines helped to bolster the power of Spain, stirred the envy of Spain's enemies, particularly Holland and England, and continued to fuel an inflation that the advent of bullion from America had already stimulated.[8]

To the high reaches of Potosí, where it was bitter cold much of the time, adventurers from all of Spanish America, from Spain, and from foreign countries swarmed to stake claims and make their fortunes. Fifteen years before Walter Raleigh sent his first explorers to Virginia, Potosí had a population of 120,000, and by the mid-seventeenth century its population numbered 160,000.

Most of the grueling labor in the mines was performed by Indians who were brought by the thousands from all over the viceroyalty of Peru to drudge and die in the mines. Some Negro slaves also labored in the mines, but Negro slaves were not sufficiently numerous in the early days to play much part, and they could not endure the cold of Potosí as well as the native Indians. In 1559 the Viceroy decreed that any Indian condemned to death or exile should be sent to Potosí; most of the Indian laborers, however, came under the system of forced labor known as the mita, which the government condoned in spite of the opposition of the clergy, for upon the production of silver, one fifth of which was reserved for the Crown of Spain, the stability of Spanish finance depended. So important was Potosí to the Crown that Charles V named it an "Imperial City." A shield that he sent the city bore the legend, "I am rich Potosí, the treasure of the world and the envy of kings." Charles's successor as King of Spain, Philip II, also sent a shield to Potosí, with a legend that boasted, "For the powerful emperor, for the wise king, this lofty mountain of silver could conquer the whole world."[9] For two centuries after the beginning of exploitation in 1545 Potosí re-

[8] Lewis Hanke, *The Imperial City of Potosí: An Unwritten Chapter in the History of Spanish America* (The Hague, 1956) gives some provocative facts about this episode in the history of colonial Peru.
[9] *Ibid.*, p. 30.

mained a vital source of treasure, the largest city in the New World, and a byword in various languages for wealth.

As a boom town, Potosí also was a wild town, wilder than anything that California's later gold rush could show. "By the end of the sixteenth century," Lewis Hanke has written, "miners in search of recreation could choose among the fourteen dance halls, the thirty-six gambling houses, and the one theater, the price of admission to which ranged from forty to fifty pesos. . . . At one time, in the early part of the seventeenth century, there were some 700 or 800 professional gamblers in the city and 120 prostitutes, among them the redoubtable courtesan Doña Clara, whose wealth and beauty, the chroniclers assure us, were unrivalled." [10] Fighting between rivals for the favors of women or for disputed claims was an everyday occurrence, and assassination became routine. Even officials of the city government came armed and dressed in coats of mail to council meetings. Although missionaries might lament the "accursed hill of Potosí," officers of the royal government blessed it as the principal support of the realm. Some of the wicked sought to atone for their sins by generosity to the Church, always a salve to uneasy consciences, and in time the city boasted eighty churches, most of them established by wealthy miners in need of salvation.

Foreigners who flocked to Potisí in spite of efforts to discourage them were a source of worry to Spanish authorities, who suspected them of fomenting trouble. In 1599 English miners, described as "pirates," helped to stir up a rebellion. The stories that foreigners carried home about the riches of Potosí and the treasure that Spain was reaping in South America encouraged corsairs to watch for the treasure fleets and stimulated envious governments to plan ways of breaking the Spanish monopoly of the wealth of the New World. Riches that came from Peru had a significant role in stirring other nations to demand and to seize a portion of the New World.

[10] *Ibid.*, pp. 2–3.

Competition for El Dorado

WHILE THE PIZARROS WERE CONQUERING THE INCA EMPIRE in Peru, other adventurers were probing the vast interior of South America in search of riches. The chaos in Peru that followed the assassination of Francisco Pizarro caused only a lull in the activities of explorers. If Peru at the moment offered fewer opportunities for gain or glory, other regions beckoned, though often their promises were illusory, and many a foolhardy cavalier followed some will-o'-the-wisp to his death. Rumors of rich kingdoms in the highlands of Colombia, the freezing heights of the Andes, the unknown reaches of southern Chile, or the fever-ridden swamps of the Orinoco and the Amazon spread like a prairie fire throughout Spanish America and the countries of western Europe. Bands of men, both Spanish and foreign, swarmed to South America. With a few scanty supplies, they were always ready to mount their horses and set out on expeditions so dangerous and desperate that seemingly only madmen would undertake them. Success rewarded a few, but more often than not death took its toll, and hundreds of would-be conquistadors left their bones to bleach in the wilderness.

Even though many failed, an occasional success kept

excitement high. For example, in April 1536 Gonzalo Jiménez de Quesada, an honest, careful, and prudent lawyer, organized an expedition at Santa Marta on the Atlantic coast of Colombia, with the intention of finding a kingdom of great riches rumored to be somewhere in the mountains of the interior. With some 900 men, a portion of whom were embarked in brigantines on the Magdalena River while others rode horses along the banks, he set forth. The only clue to his destination, a contemporary asserted, was "blind report and the echo of an ill-formed rumor." [1] Yet after eleven months of toil and suffering. Quesada and a remnant of his army climbed from the swamps of the Magdalena and its tributaries to a pleasant upland country inhabited by a less war-like people than the river Indians who had harassed them with poisoned arrows for the length of their journey. Of his original 900 men, he could now muster only 166 with 62 horses. Besides poisoned arrows, a chronicler of the expedition declared that Quesada's troops were "diminished by fever and sores from the plagues of travel, ticks, bats, mosquitoes, serpents, crocodiles, tigers [jaguars], hunger, calamities and miseries with other ills which pass description." [2] The survivors had reached the country of the Chibchas, who were rich in gold and gentle in manner, though their own borders were beset with a fierce cannibal tribe called Panches.

The Chibchas had quantities of gold and emeralds, which Quesada's men soon sequestered, being careful to preserve the Royal Fifth for Charles V. The treasure garnered in Colombia was sufficient to remind veterans of the wealth of the Incas. Some reparation came to the Chibchas when the Spaniards made an onslaught on their cannibal enemies, the Panches, who had the disconcerting habit of devouring their captives on the battlefield. To establish a center of Spanish authority, Quesada on August 5, 1538, laid out the town of Santa Fe de Bogotá and named the whole country New Granada after his own native city.

[1] F. A. Kirkpatrick, *The Spanish Conquistadores* (London, 1934), p. 314, quoting Juan de Castellanos.
[2] *Ibid.*, p. 315.

258

One of the fairest and most honorable of the conquerors, Quesada was not destined to remain in undisturbed control of his new land. In February 1539 a troop of 160 ragged men with a few rawboned horses swarmed down the eastern mountains and drifted into Bogotá. They were led by Nicolas Federman, a German, who for three years had wandered with the remnant of an army of 500 men through the swamps of the Orinoco River in an effort to reach the fabled land of gold.

Federman was one of several Germans sent out by the banking house of the Welsers of Augsburg, under a capitulation of Charles V, to conquer what is now Venezuela. Hardly had Federman's tattered band reached Bogotá when Quesada got word that another troop of 163 men had come over the mountains from the direction of Quito and had camped in a valley something over a hundred miles from Bogotá. These turned out to be a well-equipped army led by Sebastián de Belalcázar, whose commissary consisted of a great herd of swine which his soldiers drove before them.

After a certain amount of bluster from both Belalcázar and Federman, Quesada made a peaceable agreement that they would all three go to Spain and let the Emperor settle matters in dispute between them. He sweetened the agreement with gifts to each captain of gold and emeralds and thus avoided the kind of bloodshed that had occurred in Peru. Quesada's own men relished the pork supplied by Belalcázar's swine.

One discovery that Quesada made in the valley of Bogotá was worth more than all the gold, though he did not realize it at the time. The Chibchas cultivated a nourishing tuber "of pleasant flavor much prized by the Indians and a delicacy even to the Spaniards," which Quesada himself called a "trufle." [3] This was the potato, a crop destined to transform the eating habits of Europe.

A different sort of conquest was made in the far south by Pedro de Valdivia, who found a little gold but established a farming community destined to be more important. The land was

[3] *Ibid.*, p. 311, quoting Castellanos.

first explored by Pizarro's old partner and later rival Diego de Almagro, whose cruelty to the Indians left a heritage of hatred that would plague his countrymen later; on one occasion he burned alive thirty Indian chiefs in retaliation for the slaying of three Spaniards. Although Almagro had discovered no hoards of gold in Chile, the hope of another Peru persisted, and in 1540 Francisco Pizarro appointed Valdivia, a veteran soldier, as his lieutenant to conquer the country. At the beginning of that year Valdivia left Cuzco with a troop of 150 Spanish soldiers and a woman, Inés de Saurez, his mistress. She would play an important part in the conquest. After a long and weary march down the coast Valdivia reached a fertile valley, where in 1541 he founded the city of Santiago, the future capital of the country. He parceled out captive Indians to his men in encomiendas and explained to the natives that they were now subjects of the great Emperor overseas. In return for Christian salvation, which the Spaniards would bring them, they would work diligently to build houses and till the fields. With that, he marked out sites for a church, a town hall, and a jail. After the erection of a gallows in the plaza, Santiago was declared a full-fledged municipality.

The Indians of Chile were far from docile, however, and Valdivia found himself constantly involved in warfare. Worse still, factions among his own men led to threatened revolt, and he had to hang five ringleaders as a warning to others. Six months after the founding of Santiago, while he himself was away fighting Indians, the natives besieged the town. But thanks to the courage of a fighting priest and Inés de Saurez, the little garrison held out. Wielding a machete herself, Inés helped behead seven Indian chiefs being held as hostages and tossed their heads into the Indian camp to discourage the attackers. In reward for her services Valdivia drew up a document praising his mistress and assigning to her an encomienda.

Though the Indians had not succeeded in killing off the garrison, they did burn the Spaniards' houses with their contents. When Valdivia returned, he found all of the survivors wounded, the horses dead, and his supplies, even to the last shreds of clothing, destroyed. To start again, he reported that he had only "a little maize, two handfuls of wheat, two little sows and a boar and one cock and hen. . . . We rebuilt the city and I set to work to sow and breed . . . and in the first year we reaped eighteen bushels of wheat." [4] Valdivia proved more provident than many settlers both before and after his time, including those at Jamestown many years later. Four years after the disaster he asserted that grain and pigs were abundant and chickens were as plentiful as grass. Evidently he had obtained some fresh breeding stock.

Though competent, Valdivia was not a beloved governor. His men grumbled that they had to appeal to his hard-bitten mistress, Inés, if they expected a favor from him. After La Gasca came to Peru to settle the troubles, he heard a complaint from some of the Chileans and summoned Valdivia to answer the charges. The Chilean leader got off with a reprimand and instructions to pay his debts, to be observant of justice, and to allow any discontented Spaniard to leave Chile. As for Inés, she was sentenced to exile if she did not marry. Since Valdivia had a wife, who presently came out from Spain to join him, he married off Inés to Rodrigo de Quiroga, who, a quarter of a century later (when Inés had been gathered to her reward), himself became Governor of Chile.

Whatever his shortcomings, Valdivia proved an able and intelligent conqueror of the Chilean country. His task was not easy, for, though he found some gold and silver, he himself had to be content with settling land that later proved a granary for Spanish America. Moreover, he was constantly at war with the Indians and in the end lost his life fighting the fierce Araucanas. The story of his deeds was told in verse by Alonso de Ercilla in Part One of a rambling epic, *La Araucana* (1569). Ercilla himself had come to Chile, fought the Indians in 1558, and picked up stories of Valdivia and his times which he incorporated in his narrative poem.

Explorers continued to hope for the discovery of another

[4] *Ibid.*, p. 278.

Peru, and their search concentrated upon a mysterious land in the central river valley east of the Andes, for there, it was reported, lived the Gilded King, El Dorado, proprietor of a region of infinite riches. The legend gained circulation after 1535 when an Indian from the plateau of Bogotá told Spaniards from Quito about the rites of an upland chieftain who was accustomed once a year to anoint himself with rosin and then roll in gold dust before jumping into a sacred lake to bathe.[5] The story of the Gilded King spread rapidly and grew with the telling; before long his habitat was reported in various places east of the Andes. In time the name of the Gilded King was transferred to the realm over which he was supposed to rule, and El Dorado became a synonym for the Land of Gold which every explorer hoped to find. From 1535, for two centuries afterward, the enticement of El Dorado seduced hundreds of men to destruction.

One of the objectives of Gonzalo Pizarro's expedition of 1539 –42 to the Land of Cinnamon was the discovery of El Dorado. In an effort to extract information about the mysterious king, he tortured Indians captured on the east slope of the Andes by turning his ferocious dogs upon them and by burning some alive. Terrified, surviving Indians invented tales of the Gilded King and of the rich city where he dwelt, a mythical city later given the name of Manoa. Always the country of El Dorado was a great distance from the spot where the Indians were captured, sometimes three days' journey, sometimes more—anything to send the hated Spaniards on their way. So it was that cruelty led to infinite wandering in trackless forests and swamps. At last Gonzalo's men, having eaten the swine that they drove before them and even their dogs, were on the verge of starvation when they reached the upper tributaries of the Amazon. There they built a brigantine and dispatched Francisco de Orellana with sixty-four soldiers[6] in search of food that they had heard could

[5] The most concise description of the lure of El Dorado will be found in the introduction to *The Discoverie of the large and bewtiful Empire of Guiana By Sir Walter Ralegh*, ed. V. T. Harlow (London, 1928). See pp. i–iv ff.

[6] The number of men in Orellana's party varies in different accounts. Sixty-four is the best estimate that I have been able to make.

be found ten days' journey downstream. Orellana was to load supplies and return to rescue the main body of troops.

Orellana found an inhabited village of friendly Indians who supplied him with food, but he never returned. Instead he built a second brigantine and continued his journey downstream. At the mouth of the Trombetas River he encountered a tribe whose women fought beside the men, a circumstance that he expanded into a marvelous analogy with the ancient legend of the Amazons, a wonder sufficient to provide a name for the river on which he continued to travel. After many perils, in late August 1542 the leader with fifty-three survivors reached the open sea and a month later made port at Cubagua off the Venezuelan coast. These argonauts had made an incredible journey from the Andes to the sea; they had observed the country and obtained some gold from the Indians; but they had not found El Dorado. Nevertheless the tales they told fired others to continue the search. Orellana himself went to Spain, explained that the river current was too strong to permit a return upstream to rescue Gonzalo Pizarro, and received a commission as governor of the Amazon country. On returning to conquer his principality, he and most of his men died at the mouth of the great river. In the meantime, as we have seen, Gonzalo Pizarro and his tattered remnant had made their way back over the mountains to Quito.

An expedition led by a German, Philip von Hutten (called by the Spaniards Felipe de Urre), made its way in 1541 from Coro in Venezuela to the highlands on the upper tributaries of the Orinoco; they brought back tales of a powerful nation called the Omaguas, possessed of much gold, dwelling in a vast city with straight streets and a temple at the center filled with idols of pure gold. Driven off by an Indian army of 15,000, von Hutten's expedition could only report the wonders of this city in the wilderness, assumed to be Manoa. Von Hutten himself, on returning to Coro, found that city in possession of a usurper, who ordered him beheaded with a blunt machete. The dream of the golden city of Manoa served as a lure for many years to come. Indeed, the viceroys of Peru were not above encouraging troublemaking adventurers within their borders to go in search of it.

263

Most of them would not come back to Peru to stir up factions. An expedition that would remain a byword for sensational horror began in 1559 when Pedro de Urzúa built a fleet of brigantines on a tributary of the Amazon and attempted to explore the river basin from the Andes to the sea. Stories told by Orellana and his men of the Gilded King somewhere in the interior excited Urzúa, a dashing knight of Navarre with more gallantry than wisdom. Against the advice of shrewder heads, he insisted upon taking along a beautiful and spirited widow, one Inés de Atienza. He also showed poor judgment in the selection of his men, for among them were many rebels and malcontents who enlisted to escape the justice of the Viceroy. Two of these, Fernando de Guzmán, a young man of twenty-six, and Lope de Aguirre, a hardened veteran, early began to plot against Urzúa, but found no suitable occasion for revolt until the party reached the mouth of the Río Putumayo, where during the Christmas holidays of 1560 the expedition made a base camp while parties explored the outlying country. On New Year's Day rebels stabbed Urzúa to death in his hut and proclaimed Guzmán governor and Aguirre campmaster. The actual leader was the seasoned Aguirre, and before long he was ruling with the tyranny of a madman.

Intending ultimately to return to Peru and seize the government, he forced the men to renounce King Philip II of Spain and swear allegiance to Guzmán as Prince of Peru. Any who refused he had strangled or stabbed to death. From this time onward Aguirre's career was a long sequence of murders as captains, priests, and women all fell in turn to his vindictive mood. The lady Inés had been given to some of the men following Urzúa's death. In a fit of rage Aguirre had her barbarously murdered after quarreling with her protector of the moment, whom he also murdered, because her mattress took too much room in the boat. To help carry out his executions, "he had in his train, day and night, more than sixty men well-armed and ready to commit any crime," the seventeenth-century chronicler Fray Pedro Simon asserts.[7] Concluding that he no longer needed Guzmán, his nom-

[7] *The Expedition of Pedro de Ursua and Lope de Aguirre . . . from*

264

inal "Prince of Peru," Aguirre next murdered him, along with a priest and others of his friends. The excuse was that Guzmán did not know how to rule and that all would perish because of his mistakes if he were not removed.

This bloodthirsty gang continued their way toward the coast, murdering and torturing Indians in their path as well as Spaniards who opposed Aguirre. Some doubt exists about their precise route, but it appears that they left the Amazon and went upstream on the Río Negro until they reached a natural cut called the Cassaquiari Canal, which led them to a tributary of the Orinoco River.[8] At any rate, in July 1561 they reached the mouth of that river and sailed up the coast to the island of Margarita. Falling on the Spanish inhabitants, they murdered the officials, raped their wives and daughters, pillaged and burned houses, stole the royal treasure ready for shipment to Seville, and wrote a defiant letter to Philip II himself.

No pirates who infested the Caribbean before or since proved more rapacious and merciless. For the rest of the summer of 1561 they terrorized the coast of Venezuela with robbery, murder, arson, and rape. Aguirre's mad rage prompted innumerable murders, not only of the unfortunate inhabitants of the towns and villages but of his own followers as well.

At last a loyal Spanish force overtook the band and captured Aguirre. His final act was to stab to death his daughter, who had accompanied him all the way from Peru. "The devil instigated Aguirre to kill his daughter," Fray Pedro Simon wrote, "so as to crown all his cruel acts with this most bloody and unnatural one, that of the destruction of his own flesh and blood. He said to her, 'Commend thyself to God, my daughter, for I am about to kill thee; that thou mayest not be pointed at with scorn, nor be in the power of anyone who may call thee the daughter of a traitor.' "[9] Aguirre's captors made short work of him. Two of

---

Fray Pedro Simon's "Sixth Historical Notice of the Conquest of Tierra Firme," ed. William Bollaert with an Introduction by Clements R. Markham (London, Hakluyt Society, 1861), p. 89.

[8] Harlow, *Discoverie*, pp. lxii–lxiii.

[9] Pedro Simon, *Expedition*, p. 227.

his own men shot him down, and one immediately cut off his head, which they placed in an iron cage to be exhibited in the town of Tocuyo as a warning to other evil-doers. Because of the tyrant's wickedness, says Fray Pedro Simon, the governor "ordered Aguirre's daughter to be buried in the church and the father to be quartered and thrown out in the road." [10]

Of the many desperate expeditions into the rain-soaked interior of South America in search of El Dorado, Aguirre's remains the one most notorious for its atrocities. For nearly three centuries he was remembered on the island of Margarita as "El Tirano," and V. T. Harlow comments that "the natives of Barquicimeto [in Venezuela] believe that the will-o'-the-wisp is the tyrant's soul wandering in the savannahs, like a flame fleeing the approach of man." [11]

Fray Pedro Simon declared that Aguirre, a Basque of good birth,

was the enemy of good men and good actions, particularly of praying, and he would allow no one to pray in his presence; so when he saw any of his soldiers with rosaries in their hands, he took them away, breaking them up, and saying that he did not want Christian soldiers, nor praying ones, that such occupations were only fit for monks and nuns, who understood such things; but that if necessary his men should play at dice for their souls. He sometimes told his men that God had heaven for those who chose to serve him, but that the earth was for the strongest arm; that he knew for certain there was no salvation, and that being in life was to be in hell; and that as he could not be blacker than the crow, he would commit every species of wickedness and cruelty, so that his name might ring throughout the earth, and even to the ninth heaven; that he would not spare his prisoners for fear of hell, but that he would commit all the cruelties he had the appetite for; that belief in God alone

[10] Ibid., p. 229.
[11] Harlow, Discoverie, p. lxiv.

would take anyone to heaven; that he would show Adam's will to the King of Castile to see if he had left him his heir to the Indies.[12]

Such a one was this child of the devil, Lope de Aguirre, who sought a reverse type of fame, that of being a man of utter wickedness, a man such as Christopher Marlowe might have put into a play had he known about his career. Yet so strong was the Catholic tradition that this demon once murdered a man merely for calling him a Lutheran. The pious were certain that the wickedness of types like Aguirre kept them from finding the land of El Dorado.

Lope de Aguirre's murderous journey down the Amazon and the Orinoco served only to excite further interest in El Dorado as expedition after expedition floundered through jungles or scrambled over mountain trails, always hearing of the Golden City somewhere beyond. One of the most intensive searches was made by a veteran Spanish soldier, Antonio de Berrio, who had married a niece of Quesada, the founder of Bogotá. When Quesada died, he bequeathed to this niece and her husband enormous properties in New Granada; a provision of the will enjoined them to use their energies and resources in seeking El Dorado, an injunction that did not displease Berrio, who was ever ready for adventure. Between January 1584 and September 1591 he was continuously engaged in efforts to find El Dorado. On his third and last expedition, he, with a handful of survivors, made his way down the Orinoco to the sea and landed on the island of Trinidad, which he described to Philip II as an ideal base for the exploitation of El Dorado. Although he had not found the fabulous kingdom, he had picked up evidence which made him believe that it lay in the highlands of Guiana; this mountainous region he had skirted, but he had found no pass through which he could gain access.

Berrio spent the rest of his life trying to establish his authority over land that he had explored. As always, envy and greed

[12] Pedro Simon, *Expedition*, p. 231.

caused dissension, and instead of helping him, authorities in the Venezuelan coastal settlements took information obtained from him and sent out expeditions of their own in the hope of reaping the rich rewards of discovering another Peru. At length, with the aid of a visionary lieutenant, Domingo de Vera, he managed to persuade the Governor of Venezuela to lend him a few troops to establish a base on Trinidad; but no sooner had Vera settled there than another claimant arrived from Spain with a royal commission giving him the governorship of the lower Orinoco region, including Trinidad. Disappointment and disaster dogged Berrio's footsteps. Though he was convinced that the golden city of Manoa, or perhaps many golden cities, lay in the mountains of Guiana, at every turn misfortune overtook him while rivals plunged feverishly into the jungle.

On April 4, 1595, an unexpected calamity overtook Berrio when Sir Walter Raleigh, with four ships and several light craft, anchored at Port of Spain in Trinidad, where Berrio was still retaining a precarious foothold in spite of rival claimants. Unfortunately, he did not have a sufficient force to keep Raleigh from making him a prisoner. Raleigh drained Berrio of information about El Dorado and finally released him. After Raleigh's own abortive search for the golden kingdom, Berrio continued to assert his claims to the region of the lower Orinoco. So persuasive was his lieutenant, Vera, on a trip back to Spain that he recruited some 1,500 emigrants, including many women and children, to settle at San Thomé, at the mouth of the Río Caroní, a tributary of the Orinoco, and in adjacent regions. There most of them died miserably, and there Berrio himself, his hopes gone, also died in 1597. He had not found El Dorado, but he had made the most intelligent and most extensive exploration of the Orinoco basin, and it was from him that Raleigh got the information that he used on his own ventures in that region.

Although seamen from England and from other rival nations had visited the Guiana coast before, Raleigh's expedition of 1595 marked a fresh effort to seize control of resources that enabled

Spain to keep great armies in the field and to threaten Protestant Europe. Raleigh was one of the leaders of a growing political faction in England who believed that Spain must be throttled by cutting off her supply of gold and silver from the New World. This belief had become a cardinal point of doctrine with many Protestants not only in England but on the Continent. They pointed out that the endless supply of bullion from mines in New Spain and Peru gave Philip II an immense advantage over other countries, for that wealth furnished his sinews of war. If this treasure could be intercepted at the source, or if new sources of wealth could be found, other countries could compete with Spain on equal terms.

Not only the Protestant countries of England and the Netherlands were concerned about Spain's monopoly of American wealth; France too would have been glad to cripple Spain by capturing her mines. The rebel tyrant Aguirre, who boasted that he would show King Philip the will of Adam to prove that he did not have sole right to the Indies, echoed Francis I of France, who had disdainfully observed that he would like to see the will of Father Adam to learn how he had disposed of his patrimony. French Huguenot corsairs, like English buccaneers, had long preyed on Spanish shipping and from time to time took galleons laden with treasure. Catholic Frenchmen were no more squeamish about despoiling Spain than their Huguenot countrymen.

Raleigh argued that raids on the coastal towns of Spanish America—objectives of men like Francis Drake, as we shall see in a later chapter—were not enough to damage Spain irreparably. He had earlier sought to found English colonies in the New World as a counterweight to the colonies of New Spain. Now, from freshly gathered information, he was convinced that it was possible to reach mines in Guiana richer than any Spain had found in Peru, mines that might give England financial superiority over Spain.

Raleigh's ambition in his venture to Guiana was to strike a decisive blow at Spain and to strengthen England. If incidentally he improved his own fortune, he, like every Elizabethan, would welcome that, too, but he was deeply imbued with a statesman-like zeal for his country. "His Spanish predecessors in the quest had been valiant adventurers," Harlow points out,

> but they had been solely bent upon plunder. Ralegh, on the other hand, undertook the search from the point of view of a statesman. If the monopoly of Spain was to be broken, she must be beaten on her own ground. In "yet unspoiled Guiana" a heaven-sent opportunity seemed to offer. Assuming . . . that it was inhabited by a civilized race and ruled by fugitive Incas, the obvious policy for England was to enter into possession, to gain the loyalty of the Guianians, and then with the aid of their vast numbers to drive the Spaniards from Peru. . . . Waiving the fallacious assumption, the scheme was flawless. It would appeal to every aspect of public opinion—religious, commercial, and political. Heathen souls would be saved from Catholicism; the resulting trade would be enormous; and Spain would be quickly superseded by her rival as the first power of Europe.[13]

Raleigh foresaw London as another Lisbon or Seville, with an English equivalent of the Casa de la Contratación controlling more trade from Guiana alone after a year or two than Seville received from all the Indies.

Raleigh gave proof of the sincerity of his convictions by investing his own fortune in the venture to Guiana. Indeed, for the rest of his life Guiana became an obsession that in the end wrecked his own and his wife's fortunes. Before he went out to Guiana himself, he sent one of his loyal privateering captains, Jacob Whiddon, in 1594, on a voyage of reconnaissance. This officer landed on Trinidad and lost eight men slaughtered by Berrio's soldiers. Although Whiddon had little useful information about El Dorado to report when he came home, Raleigh nevertheless set out in February 1595 to make a personal search. As we have seen, he captured Berrio, learned all he could from him, explored the Orinoco as far as the falls of the Río Caroní,

[13] Harlow, *Discoverie*, p. xcvii.

left two hostages among friendly Indians to learn the language (and to find a way to Manoa), pillaged the Spanish Main, and returned home in late August. Because Raleigh's enemies scornfully charged that he had been hiding in Devon and had never been across the Atlantic, he wrote *The Discoverie of the large and bewtiful Empire of Guiana* (1596) in his own defense—and as propaganda for further forays against the Spanish empire and its replacement with one ruled by England.

This narrative, dedicated to the High Admiral, Lord Charles Howard, and Sir Robert Cecil, provided a colorful account of land that Raleigh had explored only in part. For much of his material he drew upon rumor, reports of others, folklore, legend —and his poetic imagination. Yet this narrative had such a literary appeal that at least three London editions were required in the year of its publication, and Richard Hakluyt deemed it a significant tract for inclusion in his compilation of travels. It had a great influence on the Continent. In 1599 Levinus Hulsius published an abridged and illustrated Latin translation at Nuremburg. Theodor de Bry in the same year included a version in his own collection of voyages. Before 1602 three additional German editions were required. In the Netherlands it was even more popular, with editions in Dutch in 1598, 1605, and 1617, followed by several Dutch editions in the eighteenth century.[14] This narrative served to keep the interest of Englishmen focused on this tropical region for years to come. More than a half-century later Oliver Cromwell, an admirer of Raleigh, sought to translate the Elizabethan's propaganda into action by attempting to establish an empire in South America.[15]

Although Raleigh was only one of many Englishmen who dreamed of circumventing Spain by breaking her monopoly of American treasure and trade, his exploits in Guiana, which were to end in tragedy, had a dramatic impact upon England and western Europe. Although many of his contemporaries hated him for his arrogance and his efforts at personal aggrandizement,

[14] *Ibid.*, xcix.
[15] *Ibid.*, p. xxxix.

his reputation in the next generation grew larger; the Puritans in particular made him a hero because of his stalwart defense of Protestantism and the injustice that he received from a Stuart king.

In his dedication Raleigh emphasized that the way to hurt the Spanish king was not merely to raid seaside towns of the Spanish Main but to seize some of the gold-producing regions, where, he claimed, the natives were eager to welcome Englishmen. "After I had displanted Don Antonio Berrio . . . I wandered 400 miles into the said country [of Guiana] by land and river," he explained.

> The country hath more quantity of gold by manifold than the best parts of the Indies or Peru. All the most of the kings of the borders are already become her Majesty's vassals and seem to desire nothing more than her Majesty's protection and the return of the English nation. . . . The King of Spain is not so impoverished by taking three or four port towns in America as we suppose. . . . The port towns are few and poor in respect of the rest within the land, . . . and are only rich when the fleets are to receive the treasure for Spain.

In his opinion, he had found "a better Indies for her Majesty than the King of Spain hath any, which if it shall please her highness to undertake, I shall most willingly end the rest of my days in following the same." [16]

An eloquent appeal to the business interests of England and to the patriotism of all Englishmen was made in Raleigh's epistle "To the Reader," as he stressed the Spanish threat to Protestant Europe made acute by the wealth that Philip II drew from American sources. He rebuked Englishmen of little faith who doubted the value of his discoveries in Guiana, and then added:

> If the Spanish nation had been of like belief to these detractors, we should little have feared or doubted their attempts

[16] *Ibid.*, p. 5. I have modernized spelling and punctuation and normalized proper names to conform to general usage.

wherewith we now are daily threatened. But if we now consider of the actions both of Charles V, who had the maidenhead of Peru and the abundant treasures of Atahualpa, together with the affairs of the Spanish king now living, what territories he hath purchased [procured], what he hath added to the acts of his predecessors, how many kingdoms he hath endangered, how many armies, garrisons, and navies he hath and doth maintain, the great losses which he hath repaired, as in '88 above 100 sail of great ships with their artillery [the disaster to the Spanish Armada], and that no year is less unfortunate but that many vessels, treasures, and people are devoured, and yet notwithstanding he beginneth again like a storm to threaten shipwreck to us all. We shall find that these abilities rise not from the trades of sacks [sherry wines] and Seville oranges, nor from ought else that either Spain, Portugal, or any of his other provinces produce. It is his Indian gold that endangereth and disturbeth all the nations of Europe. It purchaseth intelligence, creepeth into councils, and setteth bound loyalty at liberty in the greatest monarchies of Europe. If the Spanish king can keep us from foreign enterprises and from the impeachment of his trades, either by offer of invasion or by besieging us in Britain, Ireland, or elsewhere, he hath then brought the work of our peril in great forwardness.[17]

Modern economic historians do not agree that American bullion was the mainstay of Spain's finances; they point out that other commodities brought from the New World and the market for Spanish goods in her overseas colonies made a more substantial basis for prosperity in the Iberian peninsula. Raleigh also realized that Spanish trade to the New World was essential to that country's well-being, and he thought English colonies in Guiana would help to "impeach" that trade. Because the areas from which Spain drew her sustenance were scattered and far apart, Raleigh thought war against the outlying regions would

[17] *Ibid.*, p. 9.

be easy and by this sort of conflict Philip II could be "brought from his powerfulness." This doctrine gained wide currency among Protestant opponents of Spain during the next two decades as they continued to lay plans to cut the stream of treasure, curtail Spain's American trade, seize portions of the New World, and establish colonies of their own.

One of Raleigh's most important contributions was the idea that England had a destiny to create an empire in tropical America by winning the friendship of the natives, already disgruntled because of Spanish injustice and cruelty. These natives, led by Englishmen, might spearhead an attack on the Spanish possessions, drive the Spaniards into the sea, and eventually capture Peru. Thus England would have an empire that stretched from the Atlantic to the Pacific and would possess mines richer than any the Spaniards had yet discovered. This was Raleigh's dream, which he never gave up during the rest of his life. Furthermore, it was a dream that he transmitted to others; even foreigners were convinced of the possibilities of gain in this region as Dutch, French, and Swedish adventurers contemplated Raleigh's arguments.

In a memorandum entitled "Of the Voyage for Guiana," drawn up by or for Raleigh, perhaps for the eyes of the Queen and her ministers but not published, the reasons for a further attempt to annex Guiana are clearly set forth. "It is honorable," the document states as its first premise,

both for that by this means infinite numbers of souls may be brought from their idolatry, bloody sacrifices, ignorance, and incivility to the worshiping of the true God aright to civil conversation, and also their bodies freed from the intolerable tyranny of the Spaniards whereunto they are already, or likely in short space to be subjected, unless her excellent Majesty or some other Christian prince do speedily assist and afterward protect them in their just defensive wars against the violence of usurpers. Which if it please her highness to undertake, besides that presently it will stop the

274

mouths of the Romish Catholics, who vaunt their great adventures for the propagation of the gospel, it will add great increase of honor to the memory of her Majesty's name upon earth to all posterity and in the end be rewarded with an excellent starlike splendency in the heavens, which is reserved for them that turn many unto righteousness, as the Prophet speaketh.[18]

The ideas in this passage, which sounds like the sermon of a Protestant preacher, become almost a refrain with propagandists against Spain. Religion, which had been a powerful motivation in the early days of Portuguese and Spanish conquest and remained an important factor in their colonization schemes, became an equally important motive of the Protestants. But with them it was a profound desire to prevent the whole world from being Romanized by Catholic missionaries from the Iberian peninsula. Protestant partisans were fired with as much zeal against the Catholics as the Spanish and Portuguese had ever shown against Moslems or bloody heathen in Aztec Mexico.

After this assertion of the religious reasons for an attempt on Guiana, the memorandum itemizes more mundane values: "Likewise it is profitable, for hereby the Queen's dominions may be exceedingly enlarged and this realm inestimably enriched with precious stones, gold, silver, pearl, and other commodities which those countries yield." If God should give good success to the seizure of Guiana, perhaps the capture of Peru would follow.

Even if no immediate profit would redound to the English or the Indian inhabitants of Guiana, the memorandum continues, "the necessity of attempting Guiana in regard to our own security . . . ought greatly to weigh with us. For if the Spaniards, by the treasure of those kingdoms which he hath already, be able to trouble the better part of Christendom, what would he do if he were once established in Guiana, which is thought to be more rich than all other lands which he enjoyeth either in the East or West Indies." The memorandum then shows how easy it will be

[18] *Ibid.*, p. 138.

to enlist the Indians in the English interest (since they already hate the Spaniards), to reach Guiana by sea, and to fortify it against attack.

As a further reason for taking over Guiana, it emphasizes, in words that not even Las Casas could equal, the cruelty of the Spaniards toward the natives. Englishmen would be performing a holy duty in saving the Guianians from the tyrants of Spain.

> Who would not be persuaded that now at length the great judge of the world hath heard the sighs, groans, lamentations, tears, and blood of so many millions of innocent men, women, and children afflicted, robbed, reviled, branded with hot irons, roasted, dismembered, mangled, stabbed, whipped, racked, scalded with hot oil, suet and hogs' grease, put to the strapado, ripped alive, beheaded in sport, drowned, dashed against the rocks, famished, devoured by mastiffs, burned, and by infinite cruelties consumed? [19]

Since God himself must now abhor the Spaniards, this document contends, surely Providence will grant success to the power that will succor the victims of these oppressors.

The fact that Guiana did not contain another rich Inca empire ready to rebel against Spain did not nullify the logic of Raleigh's arguments, for nobody at this time knew that no mountains of gold lay beyond the swamps of the Orinoco or that Manoa was a myth. In speaking of this memorandum and Raleigh's narrative of his voyage to Guiana, one of the great authorities on colonial expansion, David B. Quinn, remarks:

> This document, together with the *Discoverie*, presents for the first time a sketch of an English colonial policy for a tropical colony, concerned primarily with using native peoples, rather than English settlers, though they too would be needed for the benefit of the imperialist country. It is not very important that no semi-civilized empire of Guiana existed on which it might be tried, or that Elizabeth had no

[19] *Ibid.*, pp. 139–140.

276

intention of attempting it. The idea of a colonial empire, utilizing a self-interested benevolence towards native peoples, was one of Raleigh's important contributions to English colonial ideas. His was the positive aspect of his country's adoption of the "black legend" of Spain's cruelty to the colonial societies they subjugated.[20]

This black legend, which Las Casas did so much to create and to which the Pizarros and men like Lope de Aguirre gave substantiation, proved of infinite value to Protestant propagandists in their attacks on Spain.

If the English had been able to find an organized Indian civilization in Guiana, they might indeed have made a formidable alliance against the Spaniards, for Raleigh practiced what he preached in his own dealings with tribesmen whom he encountered in Guiana in 1595. He sternly commanded his men not to pilfer from the Indians or molest their women; he refused to sack any Indian villages of gold; and he tried to keep the Indians from realizing that they, like the Spaniards, were gold-hungry. "I would rather have lost the sack of one or two towns, although they might have been very profitable," he wrote, "than to have defaced or endangered the future hope of so many millions and the great good and rich trade which England may be possessed of thereby. I am assured now that they [the Indian tribesmen] will all die even to the last man against the Spaniards in hope of our succor and return." [21]

Near the confluence of the Río Caroni and the Orinoco, Raleigh found an old Indian chief named Topiawari who had suffered much from the Spaniards. He supplied the Englishmen with food, told Raleigh all he knew about the inhabitants of the interior, and allowed him to take his son back to England. As hostages Raleigh left two of his own party, Francis Sparrey and a boy named Hugh Goodwin. Sparrey was instructed to go on trading expeditions into the back country to search for Manoa,

[20] David B. Quinn, *Raleigh and the British Empire* (New York, 1962), p. 160.
[21] Harlow, *Discoverie*, pp. 62–63.

believed to exist somewhere across a great inland lake. Both hostages were to learn the Indian language so that they could interpret on the return of English explorers, which Raleigh told Topiawari would be soon.

Raleigh's narrative description of Guiana made thrilling reading for his contemporaries. A few modern scholars have observed that it was too "literary" to be believed. Certainly the author left himself open to criticism by appearing to believe stories of inhabitants in the back country of Guiana who had eyes in their shoulders and mouths in their chests.

> It was not my chance to hear of them till I was come away, and if I had but spoken one word of it while I was there, I might have brought one of them with me to put the matter out of doubt. Such a nation was written of by Mandeville, whose reports were held for fables many years and yet since the East Indies were discovered we find his relations true of such things as heretofore were held incredible.

Of the monsters reported in Guiana, Raleigh admits that he did not see them, "but I am resolved that so many people did not all combine or forethink to make the report." [22]

The swamps, the endlessly winding rivers, the snakes, the mosquitoes, and other miseries of the terrain found no emphasis in Raleigh's narrative. Instead, he lapsed into lyrical raptures about the beauties of the land and its promises, as, for example, in describing the savannahs near the falls of the Río Caroni.

> I never saw a more beautiful country nor more lively prospects; hills so raised here and there over the valleys, the river winding into divers branches, the plains adjoining without bush or stubble, all fair green grass, the ground of hard sand easy to march on, either for horse or foot, the deer crossing in every path, the birds towards the evening singing on every tree with a thousand several tunes, cranes and herons of white, crimson, and carnation perching on the river's side,

[22] *Ibid.*, pp. 56–57.

the air fresh with a gentle easterly wind, and every stone that we stooped to take up promised either gold or silver by his complexion.[23]

Perhaps Raleigh promised too much to be convincing. After all, Queen Elizabeth and her counselors had heard many brave assurances of the wealth that her seamen would bring back from expeditions to the New World. Too frequently they had invested and lost. With nagging doubts about Raleigh's reliability as a witness and as a leader, the Queen understandably did not risk the nation's ships and treasure in a venture merely on the strength of her sometime favorite's assertions. Nevertheless, his narrative could not be dismissed out of hand.

Those commanders and chieftains that shoot at honor and abundance shall find there more rich and beautiful cities, more temples adorned with golden images, more sepulchres filled with treasure, than either Cortés found in Mexico or Pizarro in Peru. And the shining glory of this conquest will eclipse all those so-far-extended beams of the Spanish nation. There is no country which yieldeth more pleasure to the inhabitants, either for these common delights of hunting, hawking, fishing, fowling, and the rest than Guiana doth. It hath so many plains, clear rivers, abundance of pheasants, partridges, quails, rails, cranes, herons, and all other fowl, deer of all sorts, porks, hares, lions, tigers, leopards, and divers other sorts of beasts, either for chase or food. It hath a kind of beast called *cama* or *anta* [tapir], as big as an English beef and in great plenty.[24]

What could an Englishman want more? To be rich in an earthly paradise where one could hunt or fish and find half the creatures that Noah took into the ark was what Raleigh promised his countrymen. Maybe it was all true. That was the thought that not even the Queen and the dourest of her councilors, Sir Robert

[23] *Ibid.*, pp. 54–55.
[24] *Ibid.*, pp. 71–72.

Cecil, could put out of their minds.

"To conclude, Guiana is a country that hath yet her maiden-head," the author declared, "never sacked, turned, nor wrought; the face of the earth hath not been torn, nor the virtue and salt of the soil spent by manurage; the graves have not been opened for gold; the mines not broken with sledges; nor their images pulled down out of their temples. It hath never been entered by an army of strength and never conquered or possessed by any Christian prince." [25] As he built up his final peroration, he made a rousing plea to the Queen to support the conquest of Guiana:

The West Indies were first offered to her Majesty's grand-father by Columbus, a stranger, in whom there might be doubt of deceit. . . . This empire is made known to her Majesty by her own vassal, and by him that oweth to her more duty than an ordinary subject. . . . The country is already discovered, many nations won to her Majesty's love and obedience, and those Spaniards, which have latest and longest labored about the conquest, beaten out, discouraged, and disgraced, which among these nations [the Indians of Guiana] were thought invincible. . . . And I hope, as we with these few hands have displanted the first garrison and driven them out of the said country, so her Majesty will give order for the rest, and either defend it and hold it as tributary, or conquer and keep it as empress of the same. For whatsoever prince shall possess it, shall be greatest, and if the King of Spain enjoy it, he will become unresistable. . . . To speak more at this time, I fear, would be but trou-blesome. I trust in God, this being true will suffice, and that He which is King of all kings and Lord of all lords will put it into her heart which is Lady of ladies to possess it. If not, I will judge those men worthy to be kings thereof that by her grace and leave will undertake it of themselves.[26]

[25] *Ibid.,* p. 73.
[26] *Ibid.,* pp. 74–76.

Though the Queen did not rush to order ships and men to Guiana, canny Sir Robert Cecil and even cannier Lord Burghley, his father, made modest investments in a voyage that Raleigh sent out in the autumn after his return. The complement consisted of a ship and a pinnace commanded by Lawrence Keymis, who was instructed to examine the country from the mouth of the Amazon to the Orinoco. He went up the Río Essequibo, found evidence of a great lake, at least during flood times, near its headwaters, and came back convinced that the golden city of Manoa lay somewhere beyond the lake on the Essequibo. He also discovered that the old chief Topiawari was dead and that Berrio had stationed a garrison at San Thomé, near the mouth of the Río Caroní. If he had waited a little longer, he would have heard about Berrio's efforts to colonize that region.

Raleigh's faith in Guiana never diminished. Though he himself was too busy with affairs nearer home to take personal command of another expedition to Guiana, at the end of December 1596 he sent Captain Leonard Berry to explore the Essequibo basin. Berry brought back more erroneous information about gold in the interior, and Raleigh continued his efforts. Since Queen Elizabeth would not send out a fleet to conquer the land, in 1598 he appealed to a Swedish duke (later King Charles IX). Rumors flew that a great expedition was fitting out, but nothing came of it. The reports at least aroused uneasiness in Spain, which had shown increasing concern since Raleigh's voyage to the Orinoco and the publication of his treatise. If Raleigh did not convince Queen Elizabeth of the strategic value of Guiana, he at least had persuaded Philip II that he must hold the region, and thereafter Spanish authorities became more vigilant.

The death of Queen Elizabeth in March 1603 and the accession of James VI of Scotland as James I of England brought disaster to Raleigh. In the devious game of politics, Sir Robert Cecil had poisoned the mind of the new sovereign against Raleigh so that he was easily suspected of complicity in plots against the King. In July 1603 he was indicted for treason and committed to the Tower, and in November of the same year he was tried, convicted, and sentenced to death. Until March 1616 he remained a prisoner in the Tower, at which time he was released, though not pardoned, to prepare another expedition to Guiana. He had convinced the avaricious King that he could find a gold mine that would make the monarch rich.

During his imprisonment Raleigh had retained his interest in Guiana, which in the meantime had also attracted the attention of Dutch, French, and English adventurers. Dutch traders had made contacts with the natives in the Amazon valley, and English colonists had attempted settlements there.[27] Though a prisoner, Raleigh had managed to invest £600 in an unsuccessful expedition to Guiana in 1610 commanded by Sir Thomas Roe. Despite continued failures, the English concluded that they had a destiny in tropical America.

Though James I had made peace with Spain, he was careful not to admit Spanish sovereignty over the New World. So far as he was concerned, the bulls of Alexander VI and the Treaty of Tordesillas were as if they had never existed. He held the view that Englishmen had the right to settle upon any land not already "occupied by any Christian prince," as the phrase ran. If they found territory in the Amazon or Orinoco basin not already settled by Spaniards or Portuguese (who were now subjects of Spain), they could legally take possession of it. But he was careful to insist that they avoid conflicts with the Spaniards.

By early June 1617 Raleigh had equipped a fleet of fourteen vessels with nearly 1,000 men to make his last attempt on Guiana. He had raised £30,000 toward defraying the expenses of the expedition, approximately half from funds that he and his wife put up. Clearly, he was willing to risk all in his effort to succeed. The captain who had made a reconnaissance of Guiana in 1596, Lawrence Keymis, went along as second in command. Also in the company were Raleigh's son Walter, called "Wat,"

[27] Details of English and Dutch efforts in the Amazon and Orinoco basins in this period will be found in James A. Williamson, *English Colonies in Guiana and on the Amazon*, 1604-1668 (Oxford, 1923), *passim*.

and his nephew George Raleigh.

If he could come home with a cargo of gold, or even gold ore from a proven mine, Raleigh believed that his fortune would be made. With the armament that his fourteen ships gave him, he was strong enough to prevent attack from freebooters or Spaniards who might dispute his passage. He must have remembered that when Drake returned from his voyage around the world with the *Golden Hind* laden with wealth, Queen Elizabeth forgave him, even though at the moment she was not at war with Spain. Surely James I would do the same if the voyage was successful.

Misfortunes plagued the expedition from the outset. Heavy weather prevented the ships from getting out of British waters until August 19, and by the time they reached the South American coast in November four vessels had deserted and many in the crews, including Raleigh himself, were ill with fever. In fact, Raleigh was too sick to lead a party up the Orinoco and had to entrust the command to Keymis while he remained off Trinidad with a portion of the fleet to guard against a surprise attack by Spaniards.

With 400 men and five light craft Keymis ascended the Orinoco toward the Río Caroni at the end of December. On New Year's Day of 1618 he was surprised to find a garrison of Spaniards blocking his way at a newly located San Thomé, about fifty miles downstream from the former site. When the Spaniards fired upon the English boats, Keymis ordered a landing party to take San Thomé, which they did, but in the attack young Walter Raleigh was killed. Tragedy was thus compounded, for King James had assured the Spanish ambassador, later known as Count Gondomar, that Raleigh's expedition would commit no depredations on Spanish territory or attack Spaniards. It made little difference that the Spaniards had fired first; the English had attacked and taken a Spanish fortified place. Worse still, Keymis could not find his way to any mine. Perhaps the mine had always been a figment of his and Raleigh's imaginations. At any rate, confused and conscience-stricken, he had to return to the ships at Trinidad and report to Raleigh that he had fought a Spanish garrison at San Thomé, that Raleigh's beloved son was dead, and that he could not find his way to the mine. The whole mission was a tragic failure. Keymis, realizing this, shot himself to death in his cabin. Raleigh, grief-stricken and bewildered, had to return to face the wrath of a small-souled sovereign. James was under the influence of a Spanish ambassador clamoring for the blood of an Englishman who had been the inveterate enemy of Spain throughout his career.

Dissension now ruined any chances of a concerted plan of action by Raleigh's fleet. Neither he nor his captains could agree on an objective. Soon one by one the ships departed, some to go on piratical cruises, others to head for home ports. Raleigh was left with the *Destiny*, and surely no vessel ever bore a more significant name. But even his own crew proved mutinous and threatened to take the vessel in search of prizes. After making a deal that he would put the mutineers ashore in Ireland without bringing charges against them, Raleigh was allowed to proceed and finally reached Plymouth in late June 1618. Why he deliberately returned to face King James has puzzled biographers. He could have gone to a French port or some other place of refuge, but decided against it. A concern for his honor required him to come back to England, whatever his fate.

Though King James might curry favor with the Spanish ambassador, a strong anti-Spanish sentiment still smoldered in England, and the King did not want to increase it by making a martyr of Raleigh. But Gondomar pressed for justice against a man who had dared attack a Spanish outpost in time of peace. James himself was not averse to being rid of Raleigh if the matter could be handled without arousing popular feeling. For fear of this, he dared not bring Raleigh to trial again, nor was it necessary, for his previous sentence of death for treason still hung over him. After a report from a commission of Privy Councilors assigned to look into the Guiana affair, Raleigh was taken before the Court of King's Bench, which confirmed his earlier sentence and ordered his immediate execution. The King signed the death warrant, and Raleigh was beheaded the next day, October 29, 1618, in Old Palace Yard, Westminster.

This man who had dreamed of a British empire in America, who had taught his countrymen that Spain was an enemy that must be thwarted overseas, met his death with dignity and cool courage. "Show me the axe," he said to the executioner. Feeling the blade to test its keenness, he commented: "This gives me no fear. It is a sharp and fair medicine to cure me of all my diseases." [28] When he prostrated himself with his head upon the block, someone said he ought to face the east. "So the heart be right, it is no matter which way the head lieth." He had previously declared: "I die in the faith professed by the Church of England. I hope to be saved and to have my sins washed away by the precious blood and merits of our Savior Christ." When the executioner struck off his head and held it up, someone in the crowd exclaimed, "We have not such another head to be cut off." The body was given to Lady Raleigh, who had it buried in St. Margaret's, Westminster. The head she had embalmed and kept it in a red leather bag as long as she lived. What became of it nobody knows with certainty.

Raleigh's reputation grew after his death. Interest in Guiana and the tropical portions of America continued to lure Englishmen as men recalled Raleigh's concern for that portion of the New World. England retained a foothold at Surinam until 1668, when she ceded that colony to the Dutch, and she gradually added profitable West Indian islands to her growing empire. Raleigh's dream was never entirely dissipated, even though no mountains of pure gold were ever found in Guiana and Manoa vanished in the mists. "The story of Raleigh in Guiana is as essentially a part of the history of British expansion as that of Raleigh in Virginia," V. T. Harlow remarks: "In both cases he worked for the commercial and political aggrandizement of his country.

---

[28] Edward Edwards, *The Life of Sir Walter Ralegh* (2 vols., London, 1868), I, 704–705. Slight variations occur in the wording of his last comments as reported by contemporaries, but they agree as to the substance of his remarks.

One side of his mind was capable of accepting such fantasies as El Dorado; another side viewed the matter as a shrewd and far-seeing statesman. He is the link between the Elizabethan pioneer and the sober hewers of wood and drawers of water of the seventeenth century who built where others had led." [29]

[29] Harlow, *Discoverie*, p. cvi.

The Long Struggle *Against* the Iberian Colossus

S IR WALTER RALEIGH'S PERSISTENT EFFORTS TO CHECKMATE Spain and to found a Protestant English empire in the New World reflected a concern that many Englishmen had felt long before his time. The notion that England had negligently slept over her rights while other nations were carving out rich domains overseas is an oversimplification of the facts and a failure to recognize the realities of politics. Though Henry VII had turned down overtures from Columbus, the news of a successful crossing of the great Ocean Sea so stirred him to action that he quickly sent out John Cabot to make further discoveries. Even before Cabot—and, indeed, before Columbus—daring fishermen from Bristol may have sailed past Iceland to misty lands beyond. Certainly from Cabot's time onward, Englishmen began a probing of seas and continents that would never end until England had an empire upon which the sun never set.

During the first half of the sixteenth century England and Spain were on friendly terms, even allies against a common enemy, France, and English rulers could not countenance—

openly—any encroachment upon Spanish claims in the New World. Only with the polarization of Catholic and Protestant sentiment, the recurrent unofficial raids on Spanish shipping, and finally the break with Spain after Elizabeth in 1585 sent the Earl of Leicester to help the Dutch rebels against Philip II did English animosity toward Spain escalate into a hot war. After that time, until the death of Queen Elizabeth and James I's peace with Spain in 1604, Englishmen were free to attack Spanish interests wherever they could. For a long time a few propagandists had been urging such action, and for an even longer time individual Englishmen—freebooters, smugglers, and privateers—had been carrying on private forays into Spanish territory overseas.

With the stability that Tudor rule brought to England, commerce and trade developed apace. Although disruptions and fluctuations occurred at intervals, the general trend of business was upward from the time of Henry VII to the death of Elizabeth. London became one of the important trading centers of Europe, and the cloth trade brought prosperity to countless merchants. As the merchant class grew in strength and importance, they sought outlets for their capital, new markets, and fresh sources of raw materials. The vitality of the merchants and their concern with seaborne shipping resulted in many voyages of discovery and the organization of trading companies for overseas commerce.

Despite the bulls of Alexander VI and the Treaty of Tordesillas, the English claimed portions of North America, citing discoveries made by John Cabot. A Genoese like Columbus but naturalized in Venice, Cabot had been engaged in the spice trade and knew that every trading country of western Europe was eager to find a short route to the riches of the East. In 1496 he came to Bristol, then one of the most enterprising ports in England, and offered his services to Henry VII. The King granted letters patent to him and his sons and authorized them to take as many as five ships to search west, north, or east, and to claim lands not previously explored by any Christian prince. Thrifty Henry VII did not provide the five ships; Cabot was expected to

288

find them for himself.

Since he was a poor man, Cabot had to persuade Bristol merchants to finance him. They came forward with one little vessel bearing the name of an Apostle, the *Matthew*, and in that, with a crew of eighteen, Cabot set out in the spring of 1496 upon a voyage that would enable England ultimately to argue her legitimate right to an empire in North America. By August, Cabot was back in Bristol with tall stories of coasting along the shores of a strange land that he had claimed for the King of England. Henry VII gave him a reward of £10 and a life pension of £20 per year, no mere trifle in the values of that time. The King, encouraged by information brought back by Cabot, authorized a second voyage for the following year.

News of Cabot's voyage spread quickly. In December the Milanese ambassador in London sent to his master, Ludovico Sforza, Duke of Milan, a report of the stir that Cabot had made in England. He was now called Admiral, stood in high favor with the King, and had a following eager to go on the next expedition.

Before very long they say that his Majesty will equip some ships, and in addition he will give them all the malefactors, and they will go to that country and form a colony. By means of this they hope to make London a more important mart for spices than Alexandria. . . . I have also spoken with a Burgundian, one of Messer Zoane's [John Cabot's] companions, who corroborates everything. He wants to go back because the Admiral . . . has given him an island. He has also given another to his barber, a Genoese by birth, and both consider themselves counts, while my lord the Admiral esteems himself at least a prince. I also believe that some poor Italian friars will go on this voyage, who have the promise of bishoprics.[1]

[1] *Calendar of State Papers, Milan* (London, 1912), I, No. 52; quoted in Louis B. Wright and Elaine W. Fowler, *English Colonization of North America* (London, 1968), p. 14.

The writer implied that Cabot thought he had touched the outskirts of Asia and could find his way to Japan and the rest of Asia.

If he had not actually discovered a route to the Spice Islands and the riches of the East, he had found something almost as valuable: the fisheries off Newfoundland. "These same English, his companions, say that they could bring so many fish that this kingdom would have no further need of Iceland, from which place there comes a very great quantity of the fish called stockfish [dried cod]," the Milanese ambassador reported. Within a few years Newfoundland would swarm with fishermen of many nationalities, but England would eventually claim it as her own.

On July 25, 1598, a Spanish agent in London, one López de Ayala, wrote a report to his sovereigns, Ferdinand and Isabella, that the King of England had equipped a fleet "to discover certain islands and mainland which he was informed some people from Bristol, who manned a few ships for the same purpose last year, had found. I have seen the map which the discoverer has made, who is another Genoese like Columbus." [2] The agent further added that he believed the new discoveries were within the territory allotted to Spain by the treaty with Portugal. "I told him [Henry VII] that in my opinion the land was already in the possession of your Majesties; but, though I gave him my reasons, he did not like it." Henry VII might marry his heir to the daughter of the Spanish sovereigns, and he might regard Spain as his ally, but he was not willing to admit that the Treaty of Tordesillas excluded England from all hope of profit by new discoveries. That would remain the view of other rulers whom the Iberians sought to eliminate from the prosperity promised by seaborne enterprise.

Little is recorded of Cabot's second voyage, which sailed from Bristol in 1498. Cabot himself apparently died before any ships returned, but some evidence points to contacts with the mainland of North America, perhaps as far south as the Carolinas. Spain was so concerned that in 1501 Ferdinand and Isabella ordered

[2] *Ibid.*, p. 15.

Alonso de Hojeda to sail from the South American coast northward "towards the region where it has been learned that the English were making discoveries." [3] Hojeda had instructions to intercept any English voyagers that he might encounter. The long contest with Spain for possessions in the New World had begun.

English hope centered upon the discovery of a northwest passage to Asia. This had been John Cabot's objective, and his son Sebastian continued the search in 1509. Other shipmasters probed the North Atlantic, and one brought back three Eskimos, whom he took to court to show Henry VII. If we do not know much about the activities of English seamen in the reign of Henry VII, it argues a loss of records rather than lack of enterprise. The English, especially the merchants of Bristol, were deeply concerned and were laying a foundation for later ventures. The search for the Northwest Passage would go on unrelentingly for three centuries. English merchants were determined to find a way to the wealth of Asia.

By the reign of Henry VIII, England was already well on the way to becoming the "nation of shopkeepers" that Napoleon so scorned. Its merchants were enterprising and were watching for opportunities to seize some of the trade that Spain and Portugal were gaining from the Far East and the New World. They had developed a prosperous business with the Iberian peninsula, and many had taken up residence in Spain and Portugal, where they served as middlemen in the distribution of luxury products to England and other markets in Europe.

Two influential English merchants in Seville, Roger Barlow and Robert Thorne, realizing from personal observation the wealth that access to the Indies would give England, became ardent advocates of further search. In fact, Thorne, whose father had made a voyage to the west before the turn of the sixteenth century, proposed to outfit a ship himself for discoveries in the Pacific but died in 1532 before he could put his plans into effect.

[3] James A. Williamson, *A Short History of British Expansion* (London, 1947), p. 71.

Six years before, in 1526, he had induced Sebastian Cabot, then in the service of Spain, to take along Thorne's friend Barlow on a voyage that ostensibly would follow Magellan's track and make further explorations in the Pacific. Instead Cabot spent four years exploring the Plata river basin, secretly hoping that he could find a way to the rumored wealth of the Incas which Pizarro was trying to reach from the other side of the Andes. On Barlow's return to England in 1530, he and Thorne wrote a report to Henry VIII emphasizing the great benefits that would redound if England discovered the unknown lands believed to exist in the Pacific. They proposed to reach the Pacific by a polar passage and then follow the American coastline southward until they reached Terra Australis Incognita, a vast region believed to exist in the South Sea. From their measurements on the globe, this route would be shorter than the long haul around the Cape of Good Hope or through the Strait of Magellan.[4] They argued that since boiling seas had not been found in the tropics, frozen waters in the arctic would not impede them, a logic that transcended experience. For many long years this dream of a safe and open waterway across the Pole lured English and French explorers who believed that they could easily reach the Indies by such a passage if only they could find it.

Although Henry VIII laid great store by ships and seamen, he was too concerned with high politics nearer home to play an important part in explorations. Nevertheless, he gave his tacit blessing, if nothing else, to adventurers who carried his flag to foreign seas. Evidence points to much more activity than the records show, a condition that led Richard Hakluyt in 1589 to comment on one expedition of this period: "And thus much by reason of the great negligence of the writers of those times, who should have used more care in preserving the memories of the worthy acts of our nation, is all that hitherto I can learn or find out of this voyage." [5]

[4] Ibid., p. 76.
[5] Richard Hakluyt, The Principal Navigations, Voyages, and Discoveries of the English Nation (London, 1589), p. 517.

Stories of the explorations of the Portuguese and the Spaniards, sent home by Englishmen resident in those countries, created so much excitement that even amateurs undertook voyages to see the wonders of the new-found lands—and perhaps come upon vast fortunes waiting to be taken. For example, in 1536 a young lawyer, a certain Master Hore of London, described by Hakluyt as "a man of goodly stature and of great courage and given to the study of cosmography," organized a party of gentlemen to go exploring into the north. He procured two ships and enlisted "within [a] short space many gentlemen of the Inns of Court and of Chancery, and divers other[s] of good worship desirous to see the strange things of the world." [6] They reached the coast of Labrador, touched at Cape Breton, anchored in some Newfoundland port, and ran out of food. Why they could not catch fish is not recorded, but it was probably because of ignorance or lack of equipment. At any rate, the ravages of hunger drove seamen who had gone ashore to turn cannibal.

When a search party came across a man broiling meat and reproached him for not sharing his feast, the cook replied: " 'If thou wouldest needs know, the broiled meat that I had was a piece of such a man's buttock.' The report of this brought to the ship, the captain found what became of those that were missing." The captain thereupon called all hands before the mast and delivered a sermon pointing out that they stood in danger of hellfire; instead of eating their fellows, they ought to pray. Whereupon they fell on their knees and miraculously succor appeared in the shape of a French ship, which they captured. "And such was the mercy of God that the same night [after the captain's sermon], there arrived a French ship in that port, well furnished with victual, and such was the policy of the English that they became masters of the same, and, changing ships and victualing them, they set sail to come into England," Hakluyt recorded. The morality of robbing Frenchmen and leaving them with a leaking craft and no victuals did not appear to bother the prayerful Englishmen. They always believed that God had a special regard for

[6] *Ibid.*, pp. 517–518.

them. Later the French sailors got to England and complained to Henry VIII, who, out of distress over the suffering of his own people, "was so moved with pity that he punished not his subjects but of his own purse made full and royal recompense unto the French." Hakluyt was so fascinated by this story that he rode two hundred miles to interview a survivor "to learn the whole truth of this voyage from his own mouth, as being the only man now alive that was in this discovery."

During the reign of Henry VIII trade with the Iberian peninsula continued to increase. English merchants in Seville, Lisbon, Malaga, and Sanlúcar contrived to get a share of the business that Spain and Portugal had opened with Africa, Asia, and the New World. They discovered that they could make immense profits by distributing to the Low Countries and to England exotic products—pepper and ivory from Africa; sugar, salt, cochineal, rare woods, indigo, tobacco, medicinal herbs, hides, and furs from the New World; spices, pepper, currants, raisins, dates, figs, perfumes, medicines, jewels, cotton goods, silks, and rugs from Asia. Enterprising Englishmen were frequently able to participate in Spanish and Portuguese trading voyages to the Atlantic islands, Africa, and America and were thus able to buy foreign commodities at the source at low prices. Since they made a great profit on the sale of these foreign products, they could afford to sell English cloth, demand for which was increasing, at a low profit margin. Thus the English merchants in Spain and Portugal found themselves in a favorable trading position and jealously guarded their privileges.

Englishmen engaged in this commerce were of two minds about voyages of discovery. They wanted to gain a larger share of the trade with the East and the New World, to be sure, but they did not want to antagonize their Iberian hosts to a point where they would be thrown out of Spain and Portugal. To make themselves acceptable, many of them adopted Spanish and Portuguese customs; after the spread of Protestantism, they found it expedient to conform to the Catholic faith as they tried to keep clear of the Inquisition. In England itself, many merchants were opposed to actions by English seamen which would rock the boat of amity with Spain. That concern explains a later division of opinion among Queen Elizabeth's counselors about reprisals against Spanish shipping in the period before open hostilities had begun.

Because the English government officially disapproved of incursions upon the Iberian monopoly during the first half of the sixteenth century, English seamen had to exercise restraint and be careful about seizing Spanish or Portuguese ships. But no such restrictions hampered the French, who for part of the time were at war with Spain. French corsairs from Normandy and Brittany regularly preyed on Spanish shipping and made attacks on Spanish settlements in the West Indies. They also sailed to the coasts of Africa and Brazil on trading expeditions. As the demand increased for brazilwood, which provided a dye highly valued by the cloth-makers of Europe, the French founded trading posts on the Brazilian coast and made friends with the Indians. Between 1516 and 1530 the Portuguese sent at least three expeditions to dislodge the French from their possessions, but they had only temporary success. In 1555 Admiral Nicholas Durand de Villegagnon established a French colony near the site of Rio de Janeiro, and it was not until the early seventeenth century that the Portuguese finally dislodged the French from Brazil.

During the mid-sixteenth century many French corsairs were Huguenots from La Rochelle and other Protestant centers. Some of these willingly shared information with English seamen setting out upon ventures against the Spaniards, whom the Huguenots hated. English captains could occasionally employ a French pilot who knew the way to Africa or to the Spanish possessions in America. At other times Englishmen hired renegade Portuguese or Spanish pilots who were ready to sell their knowledge and skill to the highest bidder.

Even though the government did not condone open attacks on Iberian interests, Henry VIII was not overly squeamish about the audacity of his merchantmen in developing markets overseas. For example, a Plymouth merchant and seaman known to history as "Old" William Hawkins made many voyages to the coast of Guinea and Brazil in the 1530s and '40s and brought back "elephant's teeth" (ivory), gold, sugar, brazilwood, and other commodities. Though Hawkins was not the only Englishman engaged in what were actually smuggling operations, he was a leader in these enterprises and he set a pattern of trade followed by his son John, later to be knighted by Queen Elizabeth. Hakluyt, in recounting William Hawkins' exploits, describes him as "a man for his wisdom, valor, experience, and skill in sea causes much esteemed and beloved by King Henry VIII." Because he was "not contented with the short voyages commonly then made only to the known coasts of Europe, [he] armed out a tall and goodly ship of his own, of the burden of 250 tons, called the *Paul of Plymouth*, wherewith he made three long and famous voyages unto the coast of Brazil, a thing in those days rare, especially to our nation." [7]

Hawkins in his second voyage to Africa and Brazil in 1531 left one of his seamen, Martin Cockeram of Plymouth, with the Brazilian Indians and brought back one of their "kings" who expressed a desire to see the world. "This Brazilian king being arrived was brought up to London and presented to King Henry VIII . . . at the sight of whom the King and all the nobility did not a little marvel," Hakluyt remarks. On his third voyage Hawkins undertook to return the king to his people, but the poor chieftain died on the voyage.

Customs records at Plymouth for the three early voyages do not exist, but in 1540 the *Paul of Plymouth* took as cargo on an outward-bound voyage to Africa and Brazil hatchets, combs, knives, copper, lead, woolen cloth, and "nineteen dozen night caps." Evidently, nightcaps passed current in Guinea or Brazil as decorative dress. On the return voyage the *Paul* was listed as

[7] Hakluyt, *Principal Navigations*, p. 520. The known facts about William Hawkins will be found in James A. Williamson, *Hawkins of Plymouth* (London, 1949), pp. 18–37. For information on the background of some of these enterprises, see K. R. Andrews, *Elizabethan Privateering During the Spanish War*, 1585–1603 (Cambridge, 1964), pp. 1–22.

bringing in one dozen ivory tusks and ninety-two tons of brazil-wood, but doubtless she also had malagueta pepper, a product of Guinea then much in demand, and other commodities which the skipper managed to get past customs without listing.[8]

The tradition of illicit trade begun by William Hawkins was continued by his son John, whose later exploits had a serious impact upon Anglo-Spanish relations. In the meantime, however, other Englishmen were making a breach in the Portuguese monopoly of the African trade. Since voyages by Englishmen to the African coast were of doubtful legality, they were organized furtively by syndicates of merchants, sometimes with the participation of Privy Councilors and other officials of the government. Nobody objected to trespassing upon Portugal's preserves if it could be done quietly without scandal—or trouble with the Portuguese government.

A group of highly respectable London merchants backed a voyage in 1551 by Captain Thomas Wyndham in the ship *Lion* to Morocco, in which he brought back a profitable cargo of dates, almonds, sugar, and molasses. So pleased was the syndicate with this expedition that they sent him on other forays to Africa, including one in 1553 in which he had two Navy ships under his command. As pilot he had a Portuguese named Antonio Pinteado. Pilots in the sixteenth century were a kind of seagoing condottieri, ready to serve any master whose pay was sufficient. Pinteado promised to lead the expedition to secret trading places in Africa where they could obtain gold, pepper, and other commodities. With magnificent audacity Wyndham sailed to sites on either side of the Portuguese base at São Jorge da Mina and bought gold from the natives. Then he browbeat Pinteado into guiding his ships to Benin to bargain for pepper.[9]

Because of the lateness of the season, Pinteado cautioned against the continuation of the voyage, but, according to an account by Richard Eden reprinted in Hakluyt, Wyndham "fell

[8] Williamson, *Hawkins of Plymouth*, pp. 32–33.
[9] Williamson, *Short History*, pp. 82–86, gives an account of Wyndham's voyages and others that followed.

into a sudden rage, reviling the said Pinteado, calling him Jew, with other opprobrious words, saying 'This whoreson Jew hath promised to bring us to such places as are not, or as he cannot bring us unto; but if he do not, I will cut off his ears and nail them to the mast.' " [10] Thus threatened, Pinteado led them to Benin, where fever carried off many of the party, including the evil-tempered captain. The rest panicked and sailed for home after sinking one vessel and abandoning some of their party who were upriver trading for pepper. Pinteado died on the homeward voyage. But when the one surviving ship, the *Primrose*, reached home, with a skeleton crew of 40 out of 140 men who had gone out, she had in her cargo 150 pounds of gold—enough to show a profit and to induce the London merchants to send out further expeditions.

Some of these voyages paid off handsomely. One in 1554–55, led by Captain John Lok, brought back 400 pounds of gold, a valuable cargo of pepper, and 250 elephant tusks. J. A. Williamson, who has investigated these expeditions, thinks Lok's voyage returned at least 1,000 percent profit to the investors. So great were the rewards that English officials only reluctantly sought to curb the traffic after the Portuguese government complained. Even during the reign of Mary Tudor, when Philip, heir to the Spanish throne, was her consort, the English authorities only halfheartedly enforced regulations against contraband traffic in the Iberian sphere. Furthermore, French corsairs were increasing in number, and between French and English smugglers, the Iberian monopoly slowly began to disintegrate. At first the interlopers in Africa and America were concerned merely with profits. As religious tensions developed, however, English Protestants and French Huguenots equated attacks on the commerce of Spain and Portugal with religion and patriotism. Smuggling thus became a work of virtue that paid dividends.

If trade with the Iberian possessions was technically off limits to English merchants, another possibility for profit occurred to them. Nothing prevented their search for a northeast passage to

[10] Hakluyt, *Principal Navigations*, p. 86.

298

Cathay, which possibly might provide a new route to riches. During the reign of Edward VI, a group including several noblemen and such magnates as Sir Thomas Gresham organized "The Merchant Adventurers of England for the Discovery of Lands, Territories, Isles, Dominions, and Seignories Unknown," which under its second charter came to be known as the Muscovy Company. Sebastian Cabot, who had returned to England after rising to pilot-major in the Spanish service, was made governor of the company.

In the spring of 1553 the company sent out an expedition of three ships under the command of Sir Hugh Willoughby, with Richard Chancellor as second in command. The captain of each ship carried a letter from King Edward VI, written in Latin, Greek, "and divers other languages," says Hakluyt, requesting aid from any kings and princes encountered in the unknown lands which the adventurers might discover. The little fleet separated in a storm. Willoughby with two vessels drove northeast until he reached the ice-ringed island of Novaya Zemlya; when he could not round it because of bad weather, he sought an anchorage at the mouth of a river on the Russian coast near Murmansk and attempted to wait out the winter. There he and his men froze to death. When the ice melted in the following summer, Russian fishermen found both ships and saved Willoughby's brief journal, which Hakluyt published.

Chancellor had better luck. After rounding the North Cape, he followed the coastline and sailed into the White Sea, which he hoped might be the desired passage to Asia. Natives whom he encountered in a boat led him to a village not far from Archangel. To his amazement, Chancellor learned that he was in Russia, then known as Muscovy, ruled by the Czar Ivan IV, later called the Terrible. Unlike Willoughby, who could find no inhabitants in the barren area where he anchored, Chancellor did not settle down to freeze, but set out by sledge to visit the Czar at Moscow. There his letter from Edward VI proved useful. Ivan welcomed him as an ambassador from a foreign prince, and Chancellor forthwith made a trade agreement with the Russians. The speed of his negotiations would be the envy of any modern mission to Moscow.

When Chancellor got back to England in 1554, he found that Edward VI had died and Mary, Henry VIII's elder daughter, now ruled. Her husband, Philip, was pleased to encourage English trade with Russia, for that would divert would-be trespassers from Spanish possessions. The London promoters of the expedition were also pleased, for this overseas route to Russia was their own discovery. Soon the Muscovy Company was making a profit from the sale of woolens to the Russians in exchange for beeswax, tallow, honey, tar, cordage, and ship stores of various sorts. If they found no northeast passage to Asia, they had discovered in Russia the next best thing: new markets.

From information that Chancellor had picked up in Moscow, English promoters were encouraged to believe that they might exploit an overland trade through Russia to the East. When Chancellor was lost at sea in 1556, the Muscovy Company appointed Anthony Jenkinson as its representative at the court of Ivan IV. Jenkinson had traveled as a merchant in the Near East and had even gained the favor of the Sultan of Turkey. He was an ideal choice to explore the possibilities of further trade in regions beyond Russia. He must have been a man of infinite tact, for he also found favor with Ivan. In 1558 he obtained passes from the Czar to lead a small overland expedition to India and China. Jenkinson and two English companions followed the Volga River to its mouth in the Caspian Sea, where they procured a craft that took them to the east side, whence they crossed the steppes to Bokhara. When they learned from native merchants that hostile tribesmen would make a continuance of their journey impossible, they returned to Moscow. Jenkinson had discovered that a profitable trade might be developed with Persia. On a second trip southward, in 1562, he visited the Shah of Persia, but failed to make a favorable trade agreement. Nevertheless, for more than another decade Englishmen continued efforts to develop an overland trade with the East, but gave up this route when the Levant Company gained ascendancy in the Near East.

Jenkinson's account of the Russians must have fascinated his contemporaries, who knew little about Russia but had heard vague stories of the country and its people. Jenkinson gave interesting sidelights on their customs. For example, he remarked that "they have many sorts of meats and drinks when they banquet, and delight in eating of gross meats and stinking fish. Before they drink, they use to blow in the cup. Their friendship is in drinking. They are great talkers and liars without any faith or trust in their words, flatterers and dissemblers. The women be there very obedient to their husbands and are kept in straitly from going abroad but at some seasons." [11]

The new interest in Russia and the overland route to Asia did not curb the activities of English merchantmen interested in the African and Brazilian trade. Voyages to those regions continued, even though Portugal made more vigorous efforts to stop them. A state of unofficial warfare existed at sea, and English vessels, which the Portuguese described as pirates, attacked any Portuguese ship that looked possible of capture.

During the early years of Queen Elizabeth's reign, when there was hope of rapprochement with Spain, a curious trade developed with the Spanish colonies which was technically illegal but was winked at both by Spanish colonial officials and by Queen Elizabeth and her councilors. The leader of this trade was John Hawkins (knighted in 1588), who followed his father's track to Africa and America. Hawkins had legal trading connections in the Canaries, where Spain admitted English merchants, and there he picked up useful information about the Spanish colonies. He learned, for example, that Negro slaves were in great demand since the supply of Indian labor in many places was exhausted. Spain made a practice of licensing traders to take African slaves to the colonies, and Hawkins apparently hoped to obtain a license and perhaps a monopoly of the slave trade. In the meantime he would demonstrate his ability to conduct such a trade successfully, and perhaps his success would induce the authorities in Seville to give him the necessary license. At this time Span-

[11] *Ibid.*, p. 337.

ish ships were under frequent attack from French corsairs, and
the ability to stay afloat uncaptured by Frenchmen might prove
a persuasive argument. As partner in the enterprise, Hawkins
took in a Spanish merchant in the Canaries, one Pedro de Ponte,
and sailed in October of 1562 with four ships for the African
coast. Touching at Cape Verde and Sierra Leone, he loaded pepper, ivory, and some 400 slaves bought from Portuguese traders,
and added a Portuguese ship to his fleet.[12] Sailing to Hispaniola,
he quickly disposed of his slaves and English wares after the
colonial authorities had made a pretense of resistance to comply
with the law. He chartered a Spanish vessel and loaded his fleet
with sugar and cowhides. He also acquired some gold and pearls.
One vessel he sent to Lisbon and the other to Seville; the rest
returned to England.

Even though the Lisbon and Seville cargoes were confiscated,
Hawkins made such a substantial profit that he immediately set
about organizing another expedition. This time the Queen herself
was one of the investors, along with Sir William Cecil (afterward Lord Burghley), the Earl of Leicester, the Earl of Pembroke, the Lord Admiral and other Navy officials, and prominent London merchants. In October of 1564 he sailed again from
Plymouth for the African coast, where he bought Negro slaves
from the Portuguese. This time he took his slaves to the Spanish
Main (the coast of Colombia and Venezuela), where eager pur-
chasers paid a handsome profit for both slaves and English goods.

Hawkins boasted on this voyage that he was commander of
the Queen's own squadron, and the expedition took on the air of
an official enterprise sponsored by the English government. The
Queen had supplied a large vessel, the *Jesus of Lübeck*, and
Hawkins had also the *Solomon*, the *Tiger*, and the *Swallow*. A
short distance out from Plymouth they encountered the *John
the Baptist*, also bound for Guinea in search of slaves, and it
joined Hawkins' fleet. After reaching Africa and loading a great
company of slaves, the fleet sailed from the coast of Sierra Leone

[12] Williamson, *Short History*, pp. 100ff., on which I have based my
account.

in January, but was becalmed for twenty-eight days, so that many thought they would never reach the Indies "without great death of Negroes and of themselves," wrote one of the crew, John Sparke. "But Almighty God, who never suffereth his elect to perish sent us the sixteen of February the ordinary breeze, which is the northwest wind, which never left us till we came to an island of the cannibals called Santa Dominica." [13] Disposing of his slaves at various ports where he met with little genuine resistance, Hawkins returned by way of the Florida coast, where he observed the use of tobacco by the Indians: "The Floridians when they travel have a kind of herb dried, who, with a cane and an earthen cup in the end, with fire and the dried herbs put together, do suck through the cane the smoke thereof, which smoke satisfieth their hunger, and therewith they live four or five days without meat or drink," Sparke wrote.[14] Other writers made even more extravagant claims for tobacco as a cure for most of the diseases of man. Hawkins was also impressed by Florida as a potential source for cattle-raising, an early recognition that gold and silver were not the only commodities that would bring a profit to settlers.

After Hawkins' return to England, he made efforts through the Spanish ambassador in London to obtain official permission to trade legally with the Spanish colonies, but Philip II turned him down. The King of Spain did not intend to let a foreigner break into the royal monopoly if he could help it, even if that foreigner could supply the colonies with much-needed English manufactured goods and slaves that were essential to the development of the new land. Even though he could not obtain a trading license, Hawkins fitted out yet another slaving expedition, and once more the Queen and her officials participated. Again he had the *Jesus of Lübeck* as his flagship and another naval vessel, the *Minion*, with four other craft. Among his officers was young Francis Drake.

This voyage, which began in 1567, promised to duplicate the

[13] Hakluyt, *Principal Navigations*, p. 529.
[14] *Ibid.*, p. 541.

previous expeditions. Hawkins loaded slaves at Sierra Leone, sailed to the Spanish Main, where he disposed of them after some scattered resistance from Spanish officials, and prepared to sail for home. Unfortunately, a storm damaged the old *Jesus* and on September 16, 1568, he had to put into San Juan de Ulúa (approximately the site of modern Vera Cruz) for repairs. To ensure his safety, he manned batteries ashore and prepared to defend the harbor. He also sent messengers to the authorities in Mexico City to report that he had landed out of necessity and his intentions were peaceful. Hawkins had learned that the Spanish plate fleet was momentarily expected and he wanted to avoid any appearance of hostility.

The very next day the Spanish fleet of thirteen sail appeared at the mouth of the harbor. Hawkins with his shore batteries could easily have kept them from entering, but he negotiated a promise that they would not attack and allowed them to anchor inside the harbor. On board was a new Viceroy of Mexico, who agreed to the conditions. In spite of solemn promises, the Viceroy himself on September 23 ordered a treacherous attack on Hawkins' little fleet. Only the *Minion*, with Hawkins in command, and the *Judith*, commanded by Drake, managed to escape. The Spaniards, Hawkins reported, "slew all our men ashore without mercy." [15] Drake sailed away without waiting for Hawkins and headed for England, an act that has never been explained satisfactorily. The *Minion*, with some 200 men aboard, could not start home with so large a number, for the ship was virtually without victuals. Since half the men chose to go ashore and take their chances with Indians or Spaniards, Hawkins on October 8 landed them and prepared to sail for England. By this time, he reported, he had wandered on the sea "until hunger enforced us to seek the land, for hides were thought very good meat, rats, cats, mice, and dogs, none escaped that might be gotten, parrots and monkeys, that were had in great price, were thought very profitable if they served the turn of one dinner." [16] After a peril-

[15] *Ibid.,* p. 555.
[16] *Ibid.,* p. 556.

ous voyage, some fifteen men survived to reach Mounts Bay in Cornwall on January 25, 1569. Five days earlier Drake had sailed into Plymouth harbor in the *Judith* with the half-starved remnant of his crew. "If all the miseries and troublesome affairs of this sorrowful voyage should be perfectly and thoroughly written," Hawkins himself wrote, "there should need a painful man with his pen, and as great a time as he had that wrote the lives and deaths of the martyrs" (a reference to John Foxe, the martyrologist).[17]

Of the men marooned in Mexico, twenty-three elected to head north into the unknown and take their chances. Of these only three survived to reach England. They claimed to have walked all the way to Cape Breton, where a French fishing vessel rescued them. An account of their wanderings was printed by Hakluyt in the 1589 edition of *The Principal Navigations*, but was omitted from later editions because, says Samuel Purchas, of "certain incredibilities." [18] Of the remainder of the crew who made for the Spanish settlements, most found employment with the Spaniards and some married and established themselves in New Spain. Eventually, however, all were examined by the Inquisition, and the older men received severe sentences for heresy: some to be burned at the stake after being first strangled, others to be whipped with two to three hundred lashes and then sentenced to the galleys for terms of six to ten years. Records of the testimony before the Inquisition of many of these men survive and provide a valuable clue to the thinking of English seamen in this period.[19]

The treacherous attack by the Spaniards on Hawkins and Drake at San Juan de Ulúa had profound repercussions on the English public. Though Queen Elizabeth might continue to

---

[17] *Ibid.*, p. 557.
[18] See Louis B. Wright, *The Elizabethans' America* (London, 1965), pp. 54–62.
[19] G. R. G. Conway, *An Englishman in the Mexican Inquisition* (Mexico City, 1927), *passim*. See also Frank Aydelotte, "Elizabethan Seamen in Mexico and Ports of the Spanish Main," *American Historical Review*, XLVIII (1942), 1–19.

hope for peace with Spain, her seamen from this time onward took a hard line and looked upon Spain as a deadly enemy.

Furthermore, the religious issue was intensified. In February of 1570 the Pope issued a bull of excommunication against Elizabeth, declaring her illegitimate and a usurper and absolving her subjects from their allegiance. Since even most English Catholics found the bull obnoxious, it had little influence in England except to arouse Protestant antagonism to Catholic powers. In 1571 English feelings against Catholics and Spaniards were further exacerbated when details of a plot cooked up by a Florentine banker in London, Roberto Ridolfi, came to light. It was to Ridolfi that the Pope had secretly sent copies of the bull of excommunication to be distributed. The scheme that Ridolfi now proposed, in connivance with the Spanish ambassador in London, was to support an English insurrection with from 7,000 to 10,000 Spanish troops that the Duke of Alva would send over from the Low Countries. They would depose Elizabeth, put Mary Stuart on the English throne, and restore the ancient Catholic religion. When news of the plot leaked out, feeling ran high against both Spaniards and Catholics. Finally, the Massacre of St. Bartholomew's Day (August 24, 1572), in which many Huguenot leaders in France were slain, along with hundreds of other less eminent Protestants, came as a warning of what could happen in London if pro-Spanish plotters had the opportunity. Sir Francis Walsingham, English ambassador in Paris and an eyewitness of the slaughter, had his own Protestant prejudices sharpened by this experience, and for the rest of his life was one of the leaders of an anti-Spanish, anti-Catholic faction among Elizabeth's councilors.

From 1568 onward, English sea rovers, Francis Drake being one of the most notable, carried on an incessant war against Spanish shipping. No longer did they have any illusions about amity with Spain. For them it was war, and whenever they could take a Spanish or Portuguese vessel, or sack a Spanish town in America, they regarded the act as a stroke for the Protestant Jehovah. Once more religion and patriotism united with greed to motivate the daring adventures of conquerors.

Protestant doctrine came easily to Drake, for his father was a sort of lay preacher of violent Protestant leanings, given to preaching to the dockyard workers at Chatham, where he lived with his family in an old hulk. Young Drake inherited a vigorous Protestant intensity and on occasion could deliver a rousing sermon to his seamen to remind them of their duties and responsibilities. Like most Elizabethan captains, he liked to take along a chaplain, and he insisted upon religious observances aboard ship—always good insurance, the Elizabethans believed.

Still burning with rage against the Spaniards for their treachery at San Juan de Ulúa, Drake returned to the Caribbean in 1571 with one small ship to take such loot as he could, but more particularly to collect information about the treasure route across the Isthmus of Panama which brought the gold and silver of Peru to Nombre de Dios for storage while waiting for the plate fleet to collect it. From a French corsair who had captured a fugitive Negro slave, Drake learned that the wilderness of Panama already had a sizable contingent of escaped Negro slaves who had taken Indian wives and were conducting an intermittent guerrilla warfare against the Spanish settlements. As Raleigh later sought to make allies of the Indians in Guiana, so Drake now conceived the plan of winning these fugitives, called Cimaroons, to an alliance with the English. Perhaps together they could seize the Isthmus and cut off Spain from its Peruvian treasure. Evidence suggests that Drake was acting under instructions from John Hawkins and Sir William Winter, both now officials of the Navy.[20] While Elizabeth was nominally at peace with Spain, her seamen could nevertheless sail as privateers on voyages of reprisal, and if they hampered Spanish shipping, that was unfortunate for Spain but of no official concern to the English government. The Queen could even denounce these freebooters, and she could claim an inability to control them. In this devious fashion the war at sea against Spain gained momentum, and Drake was one of its willing and eager instruments.

[20] James A. Williamson, *The Age of Drake* (New York, 1965), p. 118.

During the next few years Drake and others constantly raided Spanish shipping in the Caribbean and along the Spanish Main. In late May of 1572 Drake sailed on an expedition whose objective was the capture of Nombre de Dios. In a brilliant attack he took the town, but a wound in the leg kept him from leading his men to follow up their success and prevented his capture of the treasure from Peru. Remaining on the coast for more than a year and making sporadic raids on coastal shipping, he gradually accumulated a quantity of gold and silver. With reinforcements provided by a French corsair, Drake finally captured a pack train loaded with gold moving from Panama City to Nombre de Dios and sailed for Plymouth, which he reached in August 1573. He brought better than £20,000 in treasure. In 1576 John Oxenham led an expedition to the Isthmus of Panama, enlisted some Cimaroons, surprised Spanish treasure ships at the Pearl Islands on the Pacific side, but was at last defeated and taken prisoner to Lima, where he was eventually executed. His efforts were audacious, but he was no Drake, even though Charles Kingsley in *Westward Ho!* made him out a romantic hero, albeit on a Victorian model. Expeditions led by other English seamen were more successful, and a trickle of gold and silver filched from the Spaniards gradually found its way into English coffers.

These raids, however, were hardly more than pinpricks to the Spaniards, as Raleigh later pointed out. Something on a larger scale was needed, and Drake and other members of the anti-Spanish faction were already discussing more far-reaching plans to damage Spain and aggrandize England.

The cosmographers of the day were convinced that in the South Pacific lay a great unexplored continent which they designated Terra Australis Incognita. The atlas published in 1570 by Abraham Ortelius showed this land, and since it was widely used, the notion of new lands to be explored, possibly with outlying islands like those off the American coast, seized English imaginations. Magellan had discovered the strait that led to this region, and Englishmen in the 1570s began to urge exploitation of this southern route. The cosmographers were also convinced that in the north a passage similar to the Strait of Magellan would lead to the Pacific and thence to Asia. This supposed waterway came to be designated as the Straits of Anian, and later was the object of prolonged search from the Pacific side. The Northwest Passage from the Atlantic would presumably lead to the Straits of Anian, the immediate outlet to the Pacific. English seamen therefore had two routes that they might explore, both of which they believed would lead ultimately to new lands and a route to the East, one in the south and the other in the north.

In 1577 a syndicate that included such influential figures as Sir Francis Walsingham, the Earl of Leicester, Sir Christopher Hatton, the Earl of Lincoln (then Lord Admiral), Sir William Winter, John Hawkins, and other naval officials decided to fit out an expedition to explore the southern route through the Strait of Magellan. Drake himself was one of the investors. This scheme had been earlier proposed by Richard Grenville, but Grenville himself was not a member of the syndicate. The proposal was to pass the Strait and claim any land in Terra Australis Incognita not occupied by any Christian prince. The expedition was also to search for treasure and other valuable commodities, to make friends with the natives, and to discover markets for English products. So far so good.

The plan, however, soon took a different turn. Drake claimed afterward that the Queen herself called him into her presence and said that she "would be gladly revenged on the King of Spain for divers injuries that I have received." Drake himself then proposed an attack on the Spanish possessions on the undefended Pacific coast, to which the Queen agreed but declared "that of all men my Lord Treasurer [Lord Burghley] should not know it." [21] Burghley at the time was perfectly willing to seek lands not occupied by any Christian prince, but he wanted to avoid risking the loss of English trade with Spain by precipitating hostilities.

During the autumn of 1577 Drake organized a fleet consisting of the *Pelican* (renamed later the *Golden Hind*), the *Elizabeth*,

[21] *Ibid.*, p. 172.

the *Marigold*, the *Benedict* (a pinnace suitable for navigating rivers and shallow bays), and the *Swan* (a small vessel for extra supplies). In the holds of these ships he also carried four pinnaces knocked down, which could be put together at need. He was preparing for both exploration and offense. He had found in the West Indies that pinnaces could be rowed to attack ships that were becalmed and dead in the water.

After some damage to his ships in an autumn storm, Drake finally sailed from Plymouth on December 13, 1577, and made the long crossing to San Julián, some distance north of the Strait of Magellan, by June 18, 1578. On the coast of Morocco he had traded the *Benedict* for a Portuguese craft, and in the Cape Verde Islands he seized another Portuguese vessel loaded with wine. More important than the wine, however, was a Portuguese pilot, Nuño da Silva, whom he captured along with the ship. The long months at sea had been contentious and at times close to mutinous. When they sailed, the men forward of the mast thought they had shipped for a trading voyage to Alexandria; the principal officers believed that they were going in search of Terra Australis Incognita, beyond the Strait of Magellan; perhaps only two or three besides Drake knew that they were heading for an attack on the Spanish possessions, although Drake may have informed his officers of the real purpose of the voyage after leaving the Cape Verde Islands.[22]

A mysterious character who probably knew all along of Drake's goal was Thomas Doughty, a gentleman-officer of somewhat dubious reputation, who began to stir up trouble soon after the fleet passed the Cape Verde Islands. He openly advocated mutiny, made disparaging speeches about Drake, and gave evidence of wanting to take over the command himself. Since the danger of mutiny and desertion was ever present, Drake placed Doughty under arrest, and when the fleet finally reached San Julián, he brought him to trial. Convicted of sedition, Doughty was given the choice of being executed, being marooned on the mainland, or being sent home for re-trial there. He

[22] *Ibid.*, p. 177.

confessed his guilt and chose immediate execution, requesting only that he and Drake first take communion together. An account put together by Drake's nephew of the same name and published in 1628 as *The World Encompassed* asserts that after communion Drake and Doughty "dined also at the same table together as cheerfully in sobriety as ever in their lives they had done aforetime, each cheering up the other, and taking their leave by drinking each to the other as if some journey only had been in hand." [23] After this, Doughty laid his head on the block and bade the executioner do his work. San Julián was a place of ill-omen, for there Magellan had also executed mutineers, and there Drake's men found the fallen gibbet and the dead men's bones.

Despite the testimony concerning Doughty's mutinous action, Drake's decision to execute him has always posed something of a mystery. J. A. Williamson, after weighing all the evidence, concludes that Doughty had betrayed to Lord Burghley Drake's and the Queen's plan to raid the Spanish coast of the Pacific, that he had stirred up discontent in the fleet, and that he had tried to frustrate Drake's plans. But Williamson does not concede that any of this proves that Burghley had instructed Doughty to sabotage the venture. He may merely have told him to do what he could to keep Drake from attacking the Spaniards. [24] Whatever the real motives back of Doughty's execution, it exemplifies Drake's firmness of command.

Lest any malcontent thereafter call in question his discipline, Drake assembled all his crews on shore on Sunday, August 11, for further indoctrination. When the chaplain, Francis Fletcher, rose to give the sermon, Drake interrupted, as reported by John Cooke, one of the mariners.

"Nay, soft, Master Fletcher," quoth he, "I must preach this day myself, although I have small skill in preaching. Well, be all the company here, yea or not?" Answer was made that

[23] *The World Encompassed by Sir Francis Drake* (1628), edited by W. S. W. Vaux (London, Hakluyt Society, 1854), p. 67.
[24] Williamson, *The Age of Drake*, pp. 178–179.

they were all there. Then commanded he every ship's company severally to stand together, which was also done. Then said he, "My masters, I am a very bad orator, for my bringing up hath not been in learning, but what so I shall here speak, let any man take good notice of what I shall say, and let him write it down, for I will speak nothing but I will answer it in England, yea and before her Majesty, and I have it here already set down. . . . Thus it is, my masters, that we are very far from our country and friends. We are compassed in on every side with our enemies, wherefore we are not to make small reckoning of a man, for we cannot have a man if we would give for him ten thousand pounds. Wherefore we must have these mutinies and discords that are grown among us redressed, for by the life of God, it doth even take my wits from me to think on it. Here is such controversy between the sailors and the gentlemen, and such stomaching between the gentlemen and sailors, that it doth even make me mad to hear it. But, my masters, I must have it left, for I must have the gentleman to haul and draw with the mariner and the mariner with the gentleman. What, let us show ourselves all to be of a company, and let us not give occasion to the enemy to rejoice at our decay and overthrow. I would know him that would refuse to set his hand to a rope, but I know there is not any such here. And as gentlemen are very necessary for government's sake in the voyage, so have I shipped them for that, and to some farther intent; and yet though I know sailors to be the most envious people of the world and so unruly, without government, yet may not I be without them. Also if there be any here willing to return home, let me understand of them, and here is the *Marigold*, a ship that I can very well spare. I will furnish her to such as will return with the most credit I can give them, either to my letters or any way else. But let them take heed that they go homeward, for if I find them in my way, I will surely sink them. Therefore you shall have time to consider hereof until tomorrow, for by my troth I must needs be plain with you. I have taken that in hand that I know not in the world how to go through with all; it passeth my capacity; it hath even bereaved me of my wits to think on it." [25]

After this speech none of the men elected to go home in the *Marigold*. Drake further symbolized his authority by discharging all of his captains, who meekly submitted to their demotion, and, this being achieved, Drake reappointed them. He had demonstrated that he was master.

Not even the chaplain escaped his censure. Later in the voyage Fletcher offended in some fashion, perhaps in preaching a sermon tending to lower rather than raise morale. Whereupon Drake called all hands on deck and had the poor parson brought manacled before him. An eyewitness made notes of the scene:

Drake, sitting cross-legged on a chest, and a pair of pantoffles [slippers] in his hand, he said: "Francis Fletcher, I do here excommunicate thee out of the Church of God, and from all the benefits and graces thereof, and I denounce thee to the devil and all his angels." And then he charged him upon pain of death not once to come before the mast, for if he did, he sware he should be hanged. And Drake caused a posy to be written and bound about Fletcher's arm with charge that if he took it off he should then be hanged. The posy was, "Francis Fletcher, the falsest knave that liveth." [26]

On August 22, 1578, Drake entered the Strait of Magellan with three ships, the *Golden Hind* (now renamed from the *Pelican*), the *Elizabeth*, commanded by John Winter, and the *Marigold*. From his other vessels he had taken needed supplies, cannibalized useful equipment, and had then sunk them. Sixteen days later, on September 6, he entered the broad Pacific—which belied its name, for he encountered a storm that blew unabated for more than thirty days. The *Marigold* foundered and sank with all hands. The *Elizabeth* beat back into the Strait, and even-

[25] *The World Encompassed*, pp. 213–214.
[26] *Ibid.*, p. 176.

tually the crew forced Winter to sail for home. Meanwhile Drake in the *Golden Hind* was driven south and landed on a bit of land that may have been Cape Horn or some adjacent island. Not until November did he find winds that took him again north to the coast of Chile. On December 5 he encountered his first treasure ship in the harbor of Valparaiso and took from it 25,000 pesos in gold. This, with some badly needed victuals, cheered his crew and gave them heart.

From this time on, fortune favored Drake. Being a careful seaman, he careened and repaired the *Golden Hind* when opportunity offered and kept the vessel in fighting trim. As he passed up the coast of South America he pillaged Spanish towns and captured several small ships laden with victuals, wine, and some treasure. At the pillage of Santiago he graciously presented to Francis Fletcher, the parson (not yet disgraced), the spoil from a sacked chapel consisting of a silver chalice, two cruets, and an altar cloth. At Callao, the port of Lima, he found twelve merchantmen—unarmed, of course, and anchored. After ransacking them, he cut their cables and let them drift ashore or out to sea. Here he got wind of a ship heavily laden with silver that had just sailed for Panama. This was the *Nuestra Señora de la Concepción*, inelegantly nicknamed the *Cacafuego*. Drake put on all sail and went in hot pursuit. He took time out, however, to overhaul a small vessel loaded with ship stores and cordage, which he pillaged, and to his pleasure found also "80 pound weight of gold and a crucifix of gold with goodly great emeralds set in it, which he took." [27]

All eyes searched the sea as the *Golden Hind* rushed along with a favoring wind, for Drake had promised a golden chain to the first man who sighted the *Cacafuego*. About three o'clock on March 1, 1579, John Drake shouted the good news, and three hours later Drake's sailors swarmed aboard her. Her cargo alone would have justified the voyage, for, says the chronicler, "we found in her great riches, as jewels and precious stones, thirteen chests full of royals of plate, four score pound weight of gold,

[27] *Ibid.*, p. 241.

and six and twenty ton of silver. The place where we took this prize was called Cape de San Francisco, about one hundred and fifty leagues from Panama." One of the Spanish ship's boys told Drake: " 'Captain, our ship shall be called no more *Cacafuego* but the *Cacaplata*,' . . . which pretty speech . . . ministered matter of laughter to us both then and long after." [28]

Avoiding Panama and sailing toward the coast of Nicaragua, where he careened and repaired the *Golden Hind*, Drake overhauled a Spanish vessel that had as passengers two pilots headed for Panama to take a ship to the Philippines. Although he tried to get the pilots to take service with him, they refused, and he contented himself with keeping their charts for the Pacific crossing, a useful acquisition. After repairing his ship once more, Drake sailed for the north, intending to search for the western approaches of the Northwest Passage, the elusive Straits of Anian. The accounts of this portion of the voyage are so vague that we do not know precisely where he went. But he did not find the Straits.

After exploring for two months, from April 16 to June 17, Drake cast anchor in a harbor on the coast of California, which he claimed for the Queen and christened Nova Albion. The Indians showed no signs of hostility, but proved something of a nuisance as they swarmed around the mariners trying to careen the ship. Drake ordered the ship's company to prayers in the Indians' presence and tried to show by signs that they ought to worship the true God. "In the time of which prayers, singing of Psalms, and reading of certain chapters in the Bible, they sat very attentively," the chronicler of *The World Encompassed* reported. ". . . Yea, they took such pleasure in our singing of Psalms that whensoever they resorted to us their first request was commonly this '*Gnaáh*,' by which they entreated that we would sing." [29]

Before the English left the California coast, Drake erected "a monument of our being there, as also her Majesty's and her suc-

[28] *Ibid.*, p. 242.
[29] *Ibid.*, p. 124.

cessors' right and title to that kingdom, namely a plate of brass, fast nailed to a great and firm post, whereupon is engraven her grace's name, and the day and year of our arrival there . . . together with her highness' picture and arms in a piece of sixpence current English money showing itself by a hole made of purpose through the plate. Underneath was likewise engraven the name of our general." [30] A brass plate discovered in 1936 by a traveling salesman on a beach not far from San Francisco was declared genuine by enthusiastic Californians eager to believe in it, but skeptical scholars think it a forgery.

The voyage across the Pacific, which began on July 23, 1579, took the expedition to Ternate in the Moluccas, one of the fabled Spice Islands, where Drake anchored on November 5 and presently made a treaty with the Sultan giving the English the exclusive right to trade there. To his already heavily laden vessel he now added six tons of cloves, and on November 9 sailed on the homeward voyage. First, however, he had to find an uninhabited island where he could careen the ship to scrape and tallow its bottom. Drake's care for his ship undoubtedly accounts for his safety at sea and the confidence his mariners had in his seamanship. With all of the commander's care, however, the expedition nearly came to grief on January 9, 1580, when the *Golden Hind* grounded on a rock somewhere in the Java Sea. The situation looked desperate, but after some cannon and part of the cloves had been jettisoned, the lightened ship floated free undamaged. The rest of the voyage around the Cape of Good Hope, up the coast of Africa, and thence to England was made without serious mishap, and the *Golden Hind* sailed into Plymouth Harbor on September 26, 1580.

This first English circumnavigation of the world was more than a mere nautical feat. It stirred English imaginations as had no other expedition, and it stimulated other Englishmen to look to the East for trade or loot. It also signalized to Spain the determination of the English to break the Iberian monopoly in American and Eastern waters. In the very year of Drake's return, Spain took over the government of Portugal. Drake's expedition

[30] *Ibid.*, p. 132.

showed Spain that she would have to fight to protect the Portuguese and Spanish interests in the Far East. Though Lord Burghley might try to placate the Spanish ambassador for the raid on Spanish shipping, Queen Elizabeth herself finally let Spain know her sentiments when, on April 4, 1581, she knighted Drake on the deck of the *Golden Hind,* which she ordered him to bring up the Thames and anchor at Deptford. She had good cause to honor him, for her investment in the voyage returned a rich profit, equal to the total revenue of the English Crown for a year. The Queen permitted Drake to keep a fortune for himself and saw that members of the crew and the officers were well rewarded. The *Golden Hind* she ordered preserved at Deptford as a monument to English maritime prowess.

Drake's circumnavigation and raid on the west coast of America was the prelude to the final break with Spain, which came in 1585 when the Queen sent the Earl of Leicester to the Netherlands to aid the rebels against Philip II. From 1580 onward, Elizabeth's seamen preyed on Spanish shipping wherever they could find it. The experience thus gained provided Elizabeth with mariners equipped to circumvent Philip's "Enterprise of England" when in 1588 he sent his vast Armada against the island kingdom with such tragic results for Spain.

A group headed by Sir Francis Walsingham, Sir Humphrey Gilbert, the Earl of Leicester, Sir Walter Raleigh, Dr. John Dee, and other like-minded Englishmen in the 1570s and '80s kept up a constant demand for England to claim a part of the New World and establish colonies. Richard Hakluyt, the preacher and compiler of voyages, was their chief propagandist. They were convinced that in this fashion England must prevent Spain from preempting all of new-found lands and creating an unconquerable Catholic empire. The strength that this empire would give Spain would enable her to dominate all of Europe, including the British Isles, and to fasten the dreaded Inquisition upon Protestant countries, where she would try to root out heresy and reestablish the ancient Catholic faith. This was the threat that the propagandist constantly reiterated, as we have seen in the case of Raleigh's tract on Guiana.

More than a decade before Drake set out on his voyage around the world, French Huguenots had attempted to establish a Protestant colony just north of Spanish territory in Florida, and their efforts had repercussions in England. In 1562 the Huguenot leader, Admiral Gaspard Coligny, sent out two ships with colonists under the command of Jean Ribaut. He sailed into the St. Johns River, but finally settled his people at Port Royal in South Carolina and returned to France for reinforcements. Discouraged and desperate, the colonists revolted against their local governor and put to sea in a leaky craft, from which an English vessel rescued them. In the meantime Ribaut in 1563 went to England, where a translation of his account of the country was published and attracted immediate attention. Encouraged by John Hawkins, Ribaut hoped to enlist English Protestants to join their French brethren in South Carolina, but the scheme fell through. A second colony, sent out by Coligny in 1564 under René de Laudonnière, settled at Fort Caroline on the St. Johns River.

News of this colony of heretics on the fringes of Spanish possessions moved Philip II to order Pedro Menéndez de Avilés to take out a Spanish colony to the same region and to wipe out the French. By chance Avilés arrived at the site of St. Augustine on August 28, 1565, the very day that Jean Ribaut reached the destitute French colony on the St. Johns, some thirty-five miles to the north. In the subsequent fighting Ribaut was killed and most of the French colony were slaughtered. Laudonnière was one of the few who escaped to get back to France. Over the gibbet where he hanged some of his victims, Avilés put an inscription that read: "I do this not to Frenchmen but to Lutherans." A French Huguenot, however, had the last word. In April of 1568, Dominique de Gourgues, who had been a galley slave of the Spaniards and hated them with venom, sailed into the St. Johns River and slaughtered the Spanish usurpers, leaving this inscription: "I do this not to Spaniards . . . but as to traitors, robbers, and murderers." [31]

[31] See the brief introduction to *A Notable History Containing Four Voyages Made by Certain French Captains unto Florida*, by René Laudonnière, ed. Thomas R. Adams (London, 1964), pp. v–ix.

English propagandists for colonization and expansion made good use of the tracts by Ribaut and Laudonnière. News of events in Carolina and Florida incensed English Protestants and stirred them to activity. One of the earliest and most active of the Elizabethan advocates of expansion was Sir Humphrey Gilbert, half-brother of Sir Walter Raleigh, with a considerable following in the seaports of his native Devonshire. It is supposed that he may have derived information from Ribaut and wished to imitate the activities of the French Huguenot seamen who preyed constantly on Spanish shipping.[32]

As early as 1566 Gilbert prepared a tract advocating search for the Northwest Passage to Asia; this was published ten years later as *A Discourse of a Discovery for a New Passage to Cathay* (1576) at a time when the learned geographer and necromancer Dr. John Dee and many others were enthusiastic about such a discovery. In 1577 Gilbert drew up two memoranda for the Queen with the provocative title, "A Discourse How Her Majesty May Annoy the King of Spain." Since the Queen was willing to sabotage the King of Spain secretly but did not want publicly to "annoy" him, this may not have been the most tactful approach to Her Majesty.

In one of these memoranda Gilbert began with a damning indictment of the King of Spain as the "chief maintainer of the Romish religion" and the "enemy to all others that be not of the same religion." Queen Elizabeth, Gilbert also pointed out, was "the chief head of the Church of Christ and so an enemy to the Church of Rome, whereby it is certain that the King of Spain with all those of his affinity must needs be enemies to the Queen's Majesty and the realm of England." [33] Gilbert plainly saw that the religious differences between England and Spain made war

[32] The best account of Gilbert will be found in the introduction by David B. Quinn to *The Voyages and Colonizing Enterprises of Sir Humphrey Gilbert*, ed. David B. Quinn (2 vols., London, Hakluyt Society, 1940).

[33] *Ibid.*, I, 176–177. The second of the two memoranda, from which this quotation is taken, has a slight variation in the title: "A Discourse How Her Majesty May Meet with and Annoy the King of Spain." By "meet with" Gilbert means to confront the Spanish forces in the West Indies with English sea power.

inevitable and that Spain eventually would attempt to conquer England and impose Catholicism again upon the country. To prevent this, he urged the Queen to take the initiative, perhaps surreptitiously but at least actively, to cripple Spain in the New World by seizing Hispaniola and Cuba, which he believed could be easily accomplished by preying on the treasure fleets, by capturing the Iberian fishing fleets that went to Newfoundland, and by establishing colonies in the north, perhaps in the St. Lawrence region. He suggested that if the Queen believed the time unpropitious for an open affront to Spain, she could secretly send out fleets in the guise of freebooters, whom she could disavow if necessary. Gilbert himself offered to fit out such an expedition. Others besides Gilbert held these views, which became a drumbeat of propaganda in the next decade.

Gilbert's proposals evidently did not displease the Queen, who, as we have seen, in the next year sent Drake on an expedition destined to annoy grievously the King of Spain. Furthermore in 1578 she issued a patent to Gilbert to colonize lands in the New World not actually in the possession of any Christian prince. During the next five years Gilbert made efforts to send out colonizers, and on August 5, 1583, he landed in Newfoundland and claimed it for the Queen. With a motley crowd of fishermen of various nations looking on, he declared himself governor of the territory, parceled out land to prospective planters, and sailed for the mainland of North America, where he planned to make an immediate settlement, perhaps in Nova Scotia or New England. Unfortunately, his crews were discouraged and mutinous and the voyage proved disastrous. After one of his three vessels foundered and sank, Gilbert turned homeward. When the two surviving ships were off the Azores they encountered a storm, and the smallest of the two ships, the *Squirrel*, in which Gilbert himself had chosen to come home, sank with all hands. The afternoon before, Gilbert had called out to the captain of the other ship when it came within hailing distance, "We are as near to heaven by sea as by land." [34]

[34] Williamson, *A Short History*, p. 129.

Although Gilbert's own colonial ventures withered, he had sown seeds that might lie dormant but would not die. He had even encouraged a colonial refuge for English Catholics, which he believed might drain off a group of troublemakers at home. The concept of America as a refuge for dissident religious groups would influence later English colonial schemes. And Gilbert's colonial charter, in effect, was reissued to his half-brother Walter Raleigh and became the basis of the latter's attempts, beginning in 1585, to found a colony at Roanoke in what he called Virginia. The story of Raleigh's ill-fated colony has been so often told that its repetition is unnecessary. These schemes did not result in successful settlements, but they kept alive the notion of colonization as a means of counteracting Spanish influence and power.

While Gilbert and Raleigh were trying to establish colonial bases in America, others were seeking the Northwest Passage. In 1576 Martin Frobisher, a Yorkshireman who had gained experience in voyages to Africa and perhaps in piratical enterprises, interested Michael Lok, a London merchant, in undertaking a voyage to the Northwest. Lok became his strongest supporter and put up a fortune to underwrite three voyages that took Frobisher to the arctic waters of Canada. In the first voyage of 1576 he sailed into a gulf now named after him, Frobisher's Bay, which he believed to be the entrance to the Passage. Forced to return home because of the loss of men in a fight with Eskimos, he came back without exploring the bay, but nevertheless announced the discovery of the Passage. This so excited his backers that Lok organized the Company of Cathay and fitted out a second expedition in which the Queen supplied one of the three ships.

A sailor in the first voyage had found a piece of iron pyrites that an alchemist pronounced rich in gold. This announcement led to further excitement, though some London goldsmiths were skeptical about the quality of the piece of "ore." The second expedition sailed in 1577 to Baffin Island, but by this time search for gold had superseded exploration of the Northwest Passage that Frobisher thought he had found. Instead of probing the coast, he followed instructions of the promoters to load ore, and he came home with 200 tons of black earth. This "ore" was stored under strict guard in the Tower of London while the goldsmiths tried to smelt it. One complained that he could not get a furnace hot enough to melt out the gold; small wonder, as the dirt was worthless. That fact was not yet known, and the rumors about the gold ore stored in the Tower excited a wave of speculation. Lok himself, convinced that Frobisher had found a rich mine, held to that belief long after others had grown skeptical. Investors flocked to buy shares in the third voyage, which sailed with fifteen ships in May 1578. Frobisher had instructions this time to leave a garrison of 100 men to guard the mine. While trying to find the bay in which he had first landed, and the source of the original piece of pyrites that had started the gold mania, Frobisher this time stumbled on Hudson's Strait, but was unable to explore it. He came home again with 1,200 tons of ore that proved to have no value whatever. The Company of Cathay went bankrupt and Lok wound up in prison for debt. He accused Frobisher of building up false hopes of the discovery of gold to gain support for his voyages. The first serious attempt to find the Northwest Passage ended in recrimination, with seamen unpaid and investors fuming over losses.

The Northwest Passage continued to be a will-o'-the-wisp that lured navigators to the frozen north for generations to come, but none found it. John Davis, most scientific of the Elizabethan navigators, made three voyages to these northern waters between 1585 and 1587, and sailed up Davis Strait to 73 degrees north latitude. He believed that he had found an open waterway around North America, but the coming of the Spanish Armada kept him from following up his discovery. English, French, and Dutch explorers continued to look for the elusive waterway, but their explorations extend beyond the scope of this narrative. The lure of the Northwest Passage has continued to the present day, with efforts now being made to send ice-breaking oil tankers on the route that Roald Amundsen discovered in 1903–04. Oil from the Arctic is black gold about which Frobisher and Michael Lok did not know.

If the Northwest Passage eluded explorers, the routes to the East by the Strait of Magellan and the Cape of Good Hope still beckoned to mariners willing to hazard the enmity of Spain, which now also controlled Portuguese interests in the East. During the last decade of the sixteenth century the enterprise of both the English and the Dutch showed that the Iberians would not much longer enjoy a monopoly of the Eastern trade.

Drake's feat in breaching the Spanish bastion in the Pacific soon had others attempting the voyage through the Strait of Magellan. In 1586–88 Thomas Cavendish led a successful expedition around the world. He did not capture as much Spanish gold and silver in Chile and Peru as did Drake, but off the California coast he took a galleon bound from Manila loaded with Chinese goods and 122,000 gold pesos. On board were two Japanese and three Filipinos, whom Cavendish took back to England for such information as they could relate about the East. He also acquired a useful map of China. Cavendish got back to England in September 1588 while some of the vessels in the Armada were still trying to make their way back to Spain.[35] The details that he picked up about commerce with Eastern countries stimulated English merchants to continue their efforts to capture a share of this trade. Other English attempts in the sixteenth century to use the Strait of Magellan were less successful than Cavendish's, but they all showed a determination to break the Iberian hold on the East.

Interest in the Near East also increased in the last two decades of the sixteenth century as English merchants sought to open friendly relations with the Turks. Although Queen Elizabeth had once denied a willingness to deal with infidels, by 1583 she was sending William Harborne, a shrewd merchant, to Constantinople with the authority of an ambassador to negotiate a trade treaty with the Sublime Porte. Two years earlier she had granted a patent to a company of merchants to trade in Turkey for seven

[35] Williamson, *The Age of Drake*, pp. 337–339.

years, with Sir Richard Osborne, a wealthy merchant, as governor. Harborne had served as Osborne's factor in earlier trading
ventures in the Near East. Harborne served the Queen and the
merchants so well as ambassador, and proved so competent as a
publicity agent, that a contemporary observed satirically that
"Mr. Harborne . . . hath noised the name of our island and of
Yarmouth [his home town] so tritonly that not an infant of the
cur-tailed pagans but talk of London as frequently as of their
prophet's tomb at Mecca." [36]

The Turkey Company, as Osborne's group was called, was
reorganized in 1592 and amalgamated with the Venice Company, which had for a brief term the monopoly of trade with
ports controlled by Venice. The new grouping under the name
of the Levant Company pushed trade with Mediterranean and
Near Eastern markets. Though Spain sent warships to block the
Strait of Gibraltar, the company's ships got through. The Levant
Company established numerous trading posts in the Mediterranean and Near East, but its most important base was Aleppo in
Syria, where it developed a flourishing commerce that persisted
for two centuries. Curiously, however, one of the company's
most lucrative imports came not from the Turkish dominions but
from the islands of Zante and Cephalonia, then controlled by
Venice, which supplied great cargoes of currants. The English
appetite for what Sir Thomas Roe called "trash berries" was so
great that the Levant Company annually imported more than
2,000 tons of currants. Among valuable imports from the East
were indigo, raw silk, mohair, cotton—both raw cotton and cotton yarn—drugs, spices, and carpets. To offset these imports, the
company shipped out large quantities of cloth and some tin from
Cornwall.

The rebellious Dutch were another Protestant enemy of
Spain's that would soon help to destroy the Iberian monopoly
in the East. The Dutch began a new commercial era in the East
under the auspices of the Levant Company, which granted protection to ships from Amsterdam—and collected a "consulage

[36] Alfred C. Wood, *A History of the Levant Company* (New York,
1964), pp. 13–14.

fee" for the grant of this privilege. Before many years the Dutch would be serious competitors of the English throughout the East and would virtually eliminate the Portuguese from the spice trade.

A book published in 1595 by Jan van Linschoten, a Dutch traveler and observer in the East, profoundly influenced English and Dutch promoters of trade with Asia. This was the *Reysge-schrift* (*Pilot's Guide*), which contained remarkably accurate sailing charts for the route to India and the East Indies. The next year, 1596, Linschoten published his complete *Itinerario*, which reprinted the *Reysgeschrift* and included thirty-six engravings from drawings made by the author, many fine maps, and a vast amount of information that Linschoten had amassed at first hand.

For Jan van Linschoten was no ordinary traveler. He had left Holland in 1579 to join two half-brothers who were in business in Seville. Thence he went to Lisbon, where in 1583, as a sort of secretary, he joined the entourage of an archbishop going out to Goa in India. In 1589 he came back from Goa to the Azores, where he remained until 1592, when he at last returned to Holland. In his luggage he carried charts that the Portuguese for a century had jealously guarded. How he came by them remains a mystery.[37]

In the preparation of the *Itinerario* he had the help of a learned physician, Dr. Bernard Paludanus, who was convinced that spices would cure most diseases. Dr. Paludanus' commendation and his prescriptions helped to increase the demand for spices and thus multiplied the profits of the merchants.

Recognizing the value of the *Itinerario* for English commerce, Richard Hakluyt managed to get it translated into English and published in 1598 as . . . *Linschoten His Discourse of Voyages into the East and West Indies. Divided into Four Books.* The work was also translated into Latin, German, and French, and had several subsequent Dutch editions. Its factual information, its air of common sense, its pictures, and its maps and charts all

---

[37] An excellent account of Linschoten, his world, and his influence is Charles McKew Parr, *Jan van Linschoten: The Dutch Marco Polo* (New York, 1964).

had an enormous impact upon English and Dutch businessmen and politicians. With Linschoten to guide them, they did not see how they could fail to make profitable voyages to the East.

Two other events helped to stimulate English appetites for Eastern profits. In June of 1587 Francis Drake captured off the Azores a great Portuguese carrack, the *San Felipe*, stuffed to the gunwales with the produce of India and the East. The value of the loot was more than twice the cost of Drake's whole expedition, which had previously pillaged the coasts of Spain and Portugal. Five years later, in 1592, a syndicate of corsairs in which Sir Walter Raleigh was one of the principal investors captured another Portuguese prize, the *Madre de Dios*, a 1,600-ton carrack with the richest cargo of Eastern commodities ever yet brought into an English port. These two captures gave tangible proof of the wealth that Spain was now drawing from Portuguese bases in Asia and further excited Englishmen to cut in on that source of wealth.

By the end of the century both the English and the Dutch had begun seriously to exploit the Eastern trade around the Cape of Good Hope. Some of the early expeditions ended in disaster, but the survivors brought back enough information to encourage merchants and mariners to persevere. For example, James Lancaster barely survived a disastrous voyage that began in 1591 and ended in 1594 when he was rescued by French privateers, but he was ready to try again. In 1601, now knighted, Sir James Lancaster led the first expedition for the newly organized East India Company. This voyage was such a success that he returned to England in 1603 with a million pounds' worth of pepper and other cargo. A voyage sent out by the Dutch in 1595 with Cornelis Houtman as one of the chief officers met with many calamities, but three ships got back after two and a half years with 89 survivors of the 248 men who had originally sailed. Though this voyage showed a financial loss, Houtman pointed the way to the Indies and opened the spice trade for the Dutch.[38] By 1601 the

[38] See George Masselman, *The Cradle of Colonialism* (New Haven, Conn., 1963), pp. 91–97.

Dutch had sent fifteen expeditions to the Indies, and in 1602 they fused several trading groups into the Dutch East India Company.

The organization of the English East India Company, which received its charter from Queen Elizabeth on December 31, 1600, marks the beginning of a new epoch in English commerce. By 1612 the company had sent to the Indies a total of twenty-six large ships. The average profit throughout this period was about twenty percent on the investment. The Dutch were even more successful, as they crusaded in the East Indies as the saviors of the natives from the oppression of the Portuguese. They established a base on Amboina in the heart of the Spice Islands and drove the Portuguese from the vicinity. By the second decade of the seventeenth century the English and the Dutch were virtually at war in the Spice Islands as they competed for trade. On February 27, 1623, the Dutch governor of Amboina executed ten English merchants after torture on a trumped-up charge that they had conspired to take the Dutch fort. The news of this massacre created widespread indignation in England, and henceforth English traders in the East hated their former friends, the Dutch, with a venom previously reserved for Spaniards. The wheel had now gone full circle, and English and Dutch commercial interests had begun the course of empire that would establish both countries in Asia for three and a half centuries. They had successfully displaced the dominant Iberians.

Both the English and the Dutch continued to gnaw at the edges of the Spanish empire in America. Drake and other English seamen kept up successful raids on the Spanish coasts. Drake in 1585–86 began a voyage with the sacking of Vigo on the coast of Spain and then went on to ravage the Spanish Main. On his way home he picked up the discouraged remnants of one of Raleigh's settlements at Roanoke. Drake's reputation by this time was such that the Spaniards spoke of him in terror and mothers frightened their children with stories of "El Draque." Ironically, however, both Drake and Hawkins died in 1596 on a last fling at the Spanish West Indian empire.

English mariners had dreamed of a capture of the treasure

fleets that transported the silver and gold of American mines to Spain, but none ever achieved it. It remained for a Dutch admiral, Piet Heyn, sailing for the Dutch West India Company, to accomplish this feat. On the night of September 7, 1628, he bottled up the entire silver fleet in the Cuban port of Matanzas. With only a few shots he forced the surrender of all the ships and took the treasure home to Holland. An inventory listed 177,000 pounds of silver, 66 pounds of gold, 1,000 fine pearls, 2,000,000 hides, and miscellaneous cargo including perfumes, silk, medical herbs, dyestuffs, and other commodities.[39] The seizure bankrupted Spain, ruined the nation's credit, and paralyzed Spanish communications with the American empire so that other seamen made damaging raids on coastal towns. Small wonder that the Dutch acclaimed Piet Heyn a hero and that he lies buried in the Oude Kerk in Delft in a resplendent tomb.

The English and the Dutch had not toppled the Iberian colossus, but they had badly shaken it, and it would no longer cast a sinister shadow across the Protestant world. The Spanish empire would continue to survive for better than two centuries to come, but it would cease to cause the fear that it had inspired in Europe in the sixteenth century. Englishmen, Dutchmen, and other Protestants could sleep without nightmares of the Inquisition being imposed in their midst. They now had a free hand to make such converts of the heathen as they could. Their worry lest Spain make a Catholic dependency of the whole New World was ended.

[39] C. R. Boxer, *The Dutch in Brazil, 1624–1654* (Oxford, 1957), pp. 29–30.

The "Elect of God"

I N THE LONG STRUGGLE AGAINST THE DOMINATION OF CATHOLIC
Spain, English Protestants came to believe that they were the
elect of God, destined to lead their fellow religionists in a crusade
against what the propagandists liked to call anti-Christ. The notion of "manifest destiny" which Americans invoked when they
wanted to seize desirable portions of the North American continent in the nineteenth century was not an original idea. The
English had long before concluded that they had a manifest destiny to circumvent Spain and to create an empire of their own
overseas. This empire would spread the true Gospel as interpreted by English parsons and bring prosperity to God's chosen
people resident in that happy isle, England. Old John of Gaunt's
speech in Shakespeare's *Richard II* aptly reflected the concept
that Englishmen by the end of the sixteenth century had come to
have of themselves and of their land:

> *This royal throne of kings, this scept'red isle,*
> *This earth of majesty, this seat of Mars,*
> *This other Eden, demi-paradise,*
> *This fortress built by Nature for herself*

Against infection and the hand of war,
This happy breed of men, this little world,
This precious stone set in the silver sea,

. . .

This blessed plot, this earth, this realm, this England,
This nurse, this teeming womb of royal kings,
Feared by their breed and famous by their birth,
Renowned for their deeds as far from home,
For Christian service and true chivalry . . .

[II, 1]

At the zenith of Elizabeth's reign, Englishmen were concerned not merely with their only little island, demi-paradise though they might think it, but with a great world beyond. They had developed a sense of mission that would ultimately make them the bearer of "the white man's burden" with all that it entailed. Sir Humphrey Gilbert had reminded Queen Elizabeth of her mission to lead the Protestant cause overseas, and many others would echo that refrain. If some pragmatic Englishmen like Lord Burghley cautioned against crusading zealots, others like Sir Francis Walsingham were activists eager to push efforts against Spain wherever the campaign might take them. In the long run, pragmatists and activists found that their goals were similar, as merchants and mariners gradually spread English influence and power to the far corners of the earth without causing the skies to fall.

The idea of mission that dominated British imperialists in a later age had its beginning in the reign of Elizabeth with Protestant preachers and writers who kept up a drumfire of propaganda against the dangers, as they saw it, of Catholic domination. The most influential single religious writer was John Foxe, who published in 1563 an enormous work, *Acts and Monuments of These Latter and Perilous Days Touching Matters of the Church. Wherein Are Comprehended and Described the Great Persecutions and Horrible Troubles That Have Been Wrought and Practiced by the Romish Prelates, Specially in This Realm of*

330

England and Scotland, from the Year of Our Lord a Thousand unto the Time Now Present. This folio volume of nearly 1,500 pages, with fearsome woodcuts of victims burning at the stake, is commonly called *The Book of Martyrs.* It was expanded in the second edition of 1570 to 2,314 pages; seven other editions were required before the end of the seventeenth century. Second only to the Bible in its influence, Foxe's work frequently stood beside the Bible on pulpits and in libraries. Francis Drake carried a copy with him on his circumnavigation of the world and liked to open the volume and point out to captured Spaniards the iniquity of their persecuting confreres. The East India Company required *The Book of Martyrs* to be carried in its ships, along with copies of Hakluyt's *Principal Navigations,* that other work demonstrating to the English their imperial mission.

Foxe did more than merely chronicle English martyrologies. As Professor William Haller has brilliantly demonstrated in *Foxe's Book of Martyrs and the Elect Nation,*[1] this writer searched English history to show how the Creator chose England to lead the faithful in conflicts with the powers of darkness. England, as Foxe constantly reiterated, had had a divine mission conferred upon it, for this was a nation elected of God to be the spearhead of the Protestant cause throughout the world. Protestants by the thousands read Foxe and believed his message. More than that, they were terrified by the woodcuts of the tortures suffered by Protestant martyrs at the hands of Popish persecutors. Foxe's *Book of Martyrs* probably did more to keep England Protestant than all the sermons thundered from the pulpits. Furthermore, if Englishmen needed documentation for a congenial belief that God looked with especial favor upon them, they could find it in Foxe. To merchants venturing fortunes in voyages overseas and to seamen risking their lives upon the great waters, religion became a sort of insurance, and it was comforting to have the assurances that Foxe vouchsafed them.

In our cynical age we are prone to dismiss as self-serving hy-

[1] William Haller, *Foxe's Book of Martyrs and the Elect Nation* (London, 1963).

331

pocrisy the professions of faith in religion so frequently uttered by all types of men in the sixteenth and seventeenth centuries. It is difficult for us to conceive of the sincerity of hard-bitten corsairs who claimed the spread of the Gospel as one of their objectives. Yet we should remember that this was still an age of faith when men were ready to die for their religious beliefs. Tolerance of diversity in religion was still far in the future. Catholics and Protestants were equally convinced that they had the only true faith, which they ought to propagate and maintain, even by the sword and faggot if necessary.

The English, of course, were not the only Protestants who believed that they had a mission to combat the spread of the Catholic faith abroad. The Dutch Calvinists and the French Huguenots were also convinced that they had an obligation to spread Protestant doctrines. But the French Huguenots were prevented by the wars of religion at home, and by the time the Dutch were strong enough to be effective the English had taken the lead in establishing Protestant bases overseas. A Flemish Calvinist from Antwerp, however, Willem Usselincx, early in the seventeenth century became one of the most ardent advocates of Dutch colonization in the New World as a means of curbing Spanish power and bringing prosperity to the Netherlands.

The conviction that God would shower blessings upon the faithful was deep-seated in sixteenth-century thought, among both Catholics and Protestants. As we have seen, the Spanish conquistadors believed they had a responsibility to take the message of Christ to the heathen. If the heathen sacrificed their lives in hard labor for their masters, it was enough that they had been saved for eternity by the message that the conquerors brought. The treasure that the Spaniards discovered was the reward that the Lord bestowed upon them for bringing the Cross to heathen lands. The Protestants had similar beliefs, though they showed somewhat less zeal in preaching to the Indians. If they were faithful to their religious beliefs and piously invoked the aid of the Almighty, they were convinced that He would hear their petitions and grant them prosperity.

332

The value of religious faith and observance as a means of ensuring prosperity was ever-present in the thinking of English promoters and adventurers in this period as they convinced themselves that they were especially called of God to establish His Gospel—according to the Protestant dispensation—beyond the seas. As early as John Hawkins' voyages we find religious commentary from the most unlikely sources. Hawkins himself could mouth Scripture like a parson—to the annoyance of Queen Elizabeth, who on one occasion sharply exclaimed of him, "This fool went out a soldier and is come home a divine." [2]

Soldier, buccaneer, or divine, Hawkins understood and used the idiom of the church; a poem attributed to him, in praise of Sir Humphrey Gilbert's expedition to North America in 1583, asserts that zeal for religion, the country's welfare, and material profit all combine to urge support of colonization.[3]

Richard Hawkins, son of John Hawkins, inherited something of his father's belief in the practical value of piety. His rambling treatise entitled *Observations . . . in His Voyage into the South Sea, Anno Domini 1593* attributes to God his escapes from danger. The reason the Spaniards have been especially blessed in their overseas endeavors, Hawkins points out, may be found in the Almighty's desire to reward them for their noteworthy obedience to His commands. To secure the divine blessing upon his own enterprise, Hawkins provided that the Sabbath should be "reserved for God alone." But there were limits to his godliness. For instance, he objected without avail when his mother-in-law christened his ship the *Repentance*. Though the good woman asserted that "repentance was the safest ship we could sail in to purchase the haven of Heaven," Hawkins thought it an "un-

[2] Clements R. Markham (ed.), *The Hawkins' Voyages During the Reigns of Henry VIII, Queen Elizabeth, and James I* (London: Hakluyt Society, 1878), p. xv. Portions of this chapter have been adapted from material in Louis B. Wright, *Religion and Empire: The Alliance Between Piety and Commerce in English Expansion, 1558–1625* (Chapel Hill, N.C., 1943; reprint edition, New York, 1965).

[3] Prefatory poem signed John Hawkins to G.P., *A True Report of the Late Discovery . . . by . . . Sir Humphrey Gilbert, Knight* (1583).

couth name" and was pleased when the Queen also "disliked" it and rechristened the vessel the *Dainty*.

From the first voyage of Martin Frobisher in 1576 onward, the conversion of the heathen became an increasingly prominent motive in the discussions of westward expansion. Merchants, seamen, and preachers all joined in emphasizing the worthiness of missionary endeavors. Preachers eagerly joined the exploring expeditions, but they showed little desire to remain among the Indians and Eskimos. Instead, they returned to describe the wonders of the New World and to add their voices to the growing chorus urging colonial settlement.

No clergyman, however, could sound more like a missionary than Captain George Best, who went with Frobisher on his voyages in search of the Northwest Passage and wrote an account of their adventures. "By our Englishmen's industries and these late voyages," he observes in the dedication of his work to Sir Christopher Hatton, "the world is grown to a more fullness and perfection; many unknown lands and islands (not so much as thought upon before) made known unto us; Christ's name spread; the gospel preached; infidels like to be converted to Christianity in places where before the name of God had not once been heard of." [4] Every event of the voyages, in Best's opinion, was the result of God's direct intervention.

The discovery of the piece of iron pyrites believed to be gold ore, Best sanctimoniously concluded, was a miracle in that God had directed an Englishman to the only rich stone on the island because His "divine will and pleasure is to have our commonwealth increased with no less abundance of His hidden treasures and gold mines than any other nation." As an afterthought he added the wish that "the faith of His Gospel and holy name should be published and enlarged through all those corners of the earth, amongst these idolatrous infidels." [5]

On Frobisher's third voyage to the northwest in 1578 Lord

[4] Richard Collinson (ed.), *The Three Voyages of Martin Frobisher* . . . (London, Hakluyt Society, 1867), p. 20.
[5] *Ibid.*, p. 128.

Burghley himself gave special instructions that there should be a minister to conduct divine services "according to the Church of England," [6] and the Privy Council wrote to the Bishop of Bath asking that a parson named Wolfall be encouraged to go with the expedition "in respect of the necessity that such a company should be exercised in religion." [7] Frobisher received written instructions to banish from the fleet swearing, dice and card-playing, and filthy communication, and to "serve God twice a day, with the ordinary service usual in churches of England." [8] In times of danger and after miraculous escapes, special prayers were said on the ships, with the whole company gathered about the mainmast. Even the watchword sounded like a Biblical paraphrase from a sermon. The fleet received orders that any vessel approaching in the night should be hailed with the words, "Before the world was God," and if the challenged vessel belonged to their company, the watch was to reply, "After God came Christ His Son." [9]

Wolfall, the chaplain, proved himself worthy of his trust and won high praise from the chronicler of the voyage. He diligently preached to the mariners, visiting the ships by turn, and would have remained a year among the Eskimos "if occasion had served, being in every necessary action as forward as the resolutest men of all." [10]

Though simple piety and a zeal for Christianity inspired chaplains like Wolfall, these things alone do not account for the interest in religion displayed by some of the seagoing adventurers. Matters of state and religion were inextricably mixed in the politics that determined the nature of many important voyages. In the voyages of Sir Francis Drake, most famous of Queen Elizabeth's seamen and inveterate enemy of Spain, not much was said about the conversion of the infidels, but there was more than a

[6] *Ibid.,* p. 217.
[7] James R. Dasent (ed.), *Acts of the Privy Council,* . . . *1577–78* (London, 1895), p. 213.
[8] Collinson, *Three Voyages,* p. 229.
[9] *Ibid.,* p. 230; see also pp. 272–273.
[10] *Ibid.,* p. 252.

little talk of religion. Among the buccaneers who preyed on Spanish shipping, Drake was the best hater of papists. In his opinion, an attack on Spain was a blow for the true faith and a stroke against anti-Christ. Drake's voyages therefore became crusades against the powers of darkness, and he became the hero of countless English parsons who forgot the pirate in the glorification of Christ's emissary.

From boyhood Drake himself had experienced the combined influences of Protestant religion and the sea. Like other west-country Protestants, Drake's father was bitterly hostile to Catholics, and he must have imbued his sons with his own faith—as well as a hatred of the great Catholic sea power which the sailors who came into Plymouth harbor described in many a tale of horror. In his will the father commended the beginning of the Book of Romans and urged his sons to make much of the Bible. What fanatical purpose and inner strength Francis Drake's religious background gave him we can only guess, but it was no inconsequential factor in making him a successful foe of Spain.

When Drake set sail from Plymouth on the voyage that was to take him around the world, he carried for the instruction of his men Bibles, prayerbooks, and Foxe's *Book of Martyrs*, and had as chaplain Francis Fletcher, a parson whose energy in preaching and praying sometimes outran his discretion. Routine religious duties were as rigorously enforced as any other discipline of the ship, and in times of crisis the commander prescribed special religious exercises. Sermons were frequent on this voyage, and no event of importance passed without pious commentary.

Drake's piety was so deeply ingrained that in the face of imminent disaster he took time to implore divine help. His narrowest escape came in January 1579 when the *Golden Hind* ran aground on a shoal in the South Pacific. As the ship seemed about to split, he gave orders for prayers and made some "comfortable speeches of the joys of that other life," not neglecting, however, to man the pumps and to set an example of diligence to the crew. To strengthen their faith, Drake ordered the chaplain to administer the Sacrament and to preach a sermon. Then they lightened the ship and miraculously floated free.

Drake fared well at the hands of the preachers, who trumpeted his fame long after his death. Their praise was well merited, for he devoted his life to warring against the arch-enemy of all Protestant powers, and in their eyes was an appointed instrument of God's vengeance. True, he had often robbed and pillaged peaceful towns and ships, but in a conflict with the Amalekites a leader of Israel could do no wrong. Drake's apotheosis as a national hero owed much to the clergy, who were ever ready to glorify a seaman if he smote the Spanish papists hip and thigh. If he also had breath for a prayer and a word of Scripture, he was only little lower than the angels. In the next generation Philip Nichols, chaplain of the expedition against the Spanish coast in 1587, wrote an account of Drake's voyage to the West Indies in 1572–73 and the capture of Nombre de Dios. The very title, *Sir Francis Drake Revived: Calling Upon This Dull or Effeminate Age to Follow His Noble Steps for Gold and Silver . . .* (1626), was intended to magnify the deeds of the godly buccaneer and rebuke sluggards of a more peaceful day.

Chaplains in some of the voyages exerted an influence in excess of their normal duties as pastors of their seagoing flocks. The most conspicuous example of the power of seafaring preachers occurred in an expedition that set out from Southampton in May 1582 under the leadership of Captain Edward Fenton. Its main object was trade. The Privy Council instructed Fenton to go to the East Indies and Cathay by way of the Cape of Good Hope and on the return to seek the Northwest Passage from the Pacific side. These instructions specified that he was to have an executive committee composed of eight men besides himself, who would determine all "weighty causes." Two of the eight were ministers: the Reverend Richard Madox, fellow of All Souls College in Oxford, and the Reverend John Walker. Both preachers were of the Puritan group and both were protégés of the Earl of Leicester, who had a great interest in the voyage.

The Privy Council's instructions were more than usually specific, particularly concerning the responsibilities and privileges of the preachers. Madox, the senior chaplain, was to serve as secretary and keep for the Council a secret record of every happening. Walker likewise, in another ship, was to keep a careful record. Madox also carried one of the three keys to the two caskets containing wax balls in which had been sealed Her Majesty's orders concerning the command in case of Fenton's death. At all deliberations of the ships' officers Madox had to be present. The two ministers were advised to take up their quarters by turns in each of the four ships. Finally, Fenton's instructions read, "to the end God may bless this voyage with happy and prosperous success, you shall have an especial care to see that reverence and respect be had to the ministers." Furthermore, the commander was required to see that such rules as the preachers devised for the godly reformation of the crews should be enforced strictly and any "transgressors and contemners" should be severely punished.[11]

Madox took a high view of his duties and considered himself an apostolic missionary as well as the vicar of a floating parish. Before leaving Oxford he petitioned convocation to grant him a faculty "to preach the Word of God throughout the whole world." Perhaps the Earl of Leicester, who as chancellor of the University had procured Madox' leave from All Souls, looked upon him as a pioneer who would pave the way for the establishment of a Protestant bulwark against the Catholics beyond the seas. Clearly, Leicester had some great purpose in mind when he dictated the appointment of both Madox and Walker. They were no ordinary ship's chaplains. They enjoyed the favor of their bishops and received gifts from Sir Francis Drake. Before sailing they both had an audience with the Queen. Leicester and Drake probably hoped that the ministers would return and preach a Protestant crusade to save the heathen world from the Catholics.

From the start, the voyage took on the air of a conventicle. On the day of sailing, Madox preached an eloquent sermon, on the

[11] Richard Hakluyt, *The Principal Navigations*, XI (Glasgow, 1904), pp. 170–171.

deck of the flagship *Leicester*, before Henry Ughtrede, Mayor of Southampton, and other dignitaries who had come to see the expedition off. The chaplain brought credit to his patron, the Mayor wrote to the Earl of Leicester, who must have been equally pleased at the Mayor's added hope for the ships in this fleet: "I wish all the King of Spain, his gold, in their bellies to temper the pride of such a tyrant." [12] In their own way, the two parsons were also determined to humble the pride of His Catholic Majesty. At sea a religious atmosphere hovered over the ships. As in Frobisher's fleet, the watchword was a pious phrase: The challenging ship signaled, "If God be for us," and the other replied, "Who can be against us." Each day began and ended with prayer. Dice and card-playing, swearing, and even vain talk were strictly forbidden. To supply the place of these idle iniquities, common to seamen, Walker instituted religious discussion groups —a practice beloved of the Puritans—and is reported to have brought many souls to salvation.

After so much had been done to ensure the blessings of Providence, the Earl of Leicester must have been grievously puzzled at the results of the voyage, which proved one of the most miserable failures of the century. The fleet got no farther than the coast of Brazil, where quarrels between the captains and the appearance of a Spanish force led to the separation of the vessels, which then turned back to England. Before the fleet scattered they captured one prize, a small Spanish ship—manned by eighteen friars. Not even hatred of papists could give them an excuse to keep this peaceful vessel; so, after robbing the friars of sugar and ginger, they let them go.

That God had especially reserved certain portions of North America for the English, and hence had thwarted the Spanish and French in their efforts to push northward, was a belief fostered by Sir Humphrey Gilbert and his colleagues. Preachers were later to use this belief as an argument proving the manifest destiny of Englishmen to settle in the New World. Gilbert had a

[12] George Walker, *Puritan Salt: The Story of Richard Madox, Elizabethan Venturer* (London, 1935), p. 165.

bold dream of neutralizing Spanish commercial and colonial power by opening up a Northwest Passage and establishing English colonies in the adjacent lands of the North American continent.

Edward Hayes, captain of the one ship that survived Gilbert's ill-fated voyage to colonize Newfoundland and the mainland, wrote a narrative of the expedition, notable for the ingenious way in which he set out to prove the benevolent hand of God in English enterprise in the northern latitudes, and at the same time tried to excuse the disasters that overtook Gilbert. His narrative displays the language and the sanctimonious quality of a sermon. The first portion is a demonstration of England's claims to the north part of America, with an assertion of God's obvious intention that the English were to colonize and Christianize it. Success, Hayes pointed out emphatically, is dependent upon the purity of the motives of the adventurers, who must be stirred by a zeal to save "poor infidels captived by the devil," as well as by a desire to relieve the poor of England and advance the interest of the nation.[18] The time is now ripe to garner the infidels to God and to bring that vast realm under the banners of Christ and Queen Elizabeth. Divine Providence is ready to bestow a blessing upon any Englishman of "a virtuous and heroical mind" who undertakes this patriotic and godly adventure.

After such an assertion of God's interest in English colonization, Hayes had to account for Gilbert's misfortunes, because Gilbert was known for his personal piety and the missionary motive in his expedition had been prominently set forth. Although we must "leave unto God" the complete understanding of the mystery, Hayes implied that "many ill-disposed people" in the fleet—including a villainous crew of cutthroat pirates—had much to do with the disaster. Furthermore, the leader lacked seamanship and common sense—qualities that even the Almighty recognized as necessary in a North Atlantic voyage. Thus the expedition had within itself the seeds of ruin, and Hayes warns his readers not to jump to any unwarranted conclusions and "misdeem that God

---

[18] Hakluyt, *Principal Navigations*, VIII, 36.

doth resist all attempts intended that way." Richard Hakluyt, as a shrewd propagandist, knew the value of emphasizing the religious aspects of colonization, and perhaps his revision is responsible for the tone of Captain Hayes's relation, which he published in *The Principal Navigations*.

A harvest of heathen souls was not the only reward of colonization held out by Edward Hayes. He adroitly suggested that rich mines might also be found—and fat lands that would bring wealth to their owners. The happy union of material prosperity and spiritual benefits made an argument believed to be irresistible; at any rate, this idea was set forth with even greater cogency by a second apology for Gilbert's voyage, G.P.'s *A True Report of the Late Discoveries and Possession Taken . . . of the Newfound Lands by . . . Sir Humfrey Gilbert, Knight*, first published in 1583. The author pictures the poor pagans thirsting after salvation, "as well grateful to the savages, as gainful to the Christians." [14] Smugly he reasons that the infidels' deliverances from Satan will be sufficient recompense for the loss of their tribal lands to godly Englishmen. Moreover, when the heathen have been taught to dress in Christian apparel, English clothiers will find in America a great vent for their goods, to the immense profit of artisans and merchants alike. Thus the labor of civilizing the Indians will not be lost, and all classes will share in a divine prosperity. The hope of profits so obsessed G.P. that he conveys the impression that Christianity is a merchantable commodity in great demand on the coast of Nova Scotia; his tract had the essential outlines of an argument that was to be further developed and often used by merchants and missionaries for generations to come.

That the discovery of a Northwest Passage to the Pacific would have an immense spiritual value was the belief earnestly held by Captain John Davis of Sandridge, an explorer of much experience and the author of works on geography and navigation. Like Drake and other west-country seamen, Davis had a genuine piety that manifested itself in both practice and theory.

[14] Edition of 1583, sig. B₃ verso.

He believed that he owed to a fervent prayer his rescue from destruction during an October storm encountered in 1591, in Thomas Cavendish's second voyage to the South Seas. Captain Davis and his men had yielded themselves to death, but as a last comfort Davis took a stiff drink of brandy and made a long prayer, concluding with a supplication to Christ to "show us some merciful sign of thy love and our preservation." Whereupon reported one John Jane, his companion on the voyage, "before I went from him the sun shined clear." [15]

Because he attributed all the voyage's troubles to "our own offences against the divine Majesty," Davis exhorted his men to forget the vanities of this life so that they might find favor with God. Later, when he came to write *The World's Hydrographical Description* (1595), which had for its chief purpose proof of the existence of a northerly passage to the East Indies, he laid great stress on the religious aspects of the anticipated discovery. In a chapter enumerating advantages of that route to the Indies, he declared that "the benefits which may grow by this discovery are copious, and of two sorts—a benefit spiritual and a benefit corporal." Concerning the first, he quoted at length from Holy Writ to show the blessings to be derived from carrying out the Scriptural injunction to spread the message of Christianity and "to multiply and increase the flock of the faithful." Davis suggested that material success is dependent upon the sincere pursuance of missionary endeavor, and he concluded his treatise with the assertion that "it is impossible that any true English heart should be stayed from willing contribution to the performance of this so excellent a discovery, the Lords and subjects spiritual for the sole publication of God's glorious gospel. And the Lords and subjects temporal, for the renown of their prince and glory of their nation."

Practical Elizabethan seamen who by word and by deed emphasized their belief that they were the elect destined to carry out a mission for Protestant Christianity had this truth con-

[15] Albert H. Markham (ed.), *The Voyages and Works of John B. Davis, the Navigator* (London: Hakluyt Society, 1880), pp. 114-115.

stantly held up before them by Richard Hakluyt, who successfully merged geography, English expansion overseas, and religion.
Hakluyt, an active minister of God all his life, nevertheless found
time to become the chief propagandist for the expansionist group
in English politics headed by the Earl of Leicester and Sir Francis Walsingham. His great compilation of voyages was designed
to provide useful information and to give inspiration to English
explorers.

In one of the earliest pieces to survive from Hakluyt's pen, "A
Discourse of the Commodity of the Taking of the Strait of
Magellanus," dated 1580 and preserved in manuscript among the
state papers, he argues the grave peril to Europe if Spain is permitted to control Portugal and take over all of the East and West
Indies.[16] To prevent such a catastrophe, he urges three measures:
fortification and garrisoning of each end of the Strait of Magellan, capture and fortification of Cape St. Vincent in Brazil, and
the development of the northeastern trade routes to Russia and,
it was hoped, to Cathay. To prevent immediate trouble with
Spain, Hakluyt suggests, with shrewd cunning, that one Clerke,
a pirate, might be induced to establish a stronghold at the Strait
as if for himself, without the countenance of the English nation.
Garrisoning the forts might also become a Christian and humanitarian enterprise if Indians enslaved by the Spaniards could be
rescued and sent to people that region, along with a few English
convicts, men and women, who could win their freedom by emi-
grating. Nothing came of this bold scheme, but Hakluyt's arguments that permanent English colonies and adequate naval bases
were essential for protection against Spain demonstrated his developing sense of geopolitics.

Contacts with French Huguenots during his service as chaplain to the English ambassador to France accentuated an innate
suspicion of Catholics in general. The memory of the Massacre

[16] E. G. R. Taylor, *The Original Writings and Correspondence of the
Two Richard Hakluyts* (London, Hakluyt Society, 1935), I, 139–146.
For a full discussion of Hakluyt, see George B. Parks, *Richard Hakluyt
and the English Voyages* (New York, 1928).

of St. Bartholomew's Day was still bitter in the minds of French Protestants, and Hakluyt listened sympathetically to their stories of persecution. As he talked with his co-religionists and with geographers, the impression grew that the time had come for Protestantism to build an empire beyond the seas. England as the greatest Protestant power had an obligation to take the leadership. Already, prominent Puritans at home were urging such action upon the government, and Hakluyt quickly became a zealot for this cause.

The choice of Sir Philip Sidney—one of the noblest protagonists of the reformed religion—as the patron of Hakluyt's first compilation, *Divers Voyages* (1582), was significant of the editor's purpose. The opening sentence of the dedication is a tactful rebuke to Englishmen for allowing Spain and Portugal to gobble up the New World, but the compiler found consolation in Portugal's downfall and the weaknesses that Drake and others had discovered in Spain's defenses. He pointed out that a vast region northward from Florida now lay open, "unplanted by Christians." By citing the example of a noble Portuguese who wished to use all his substance in sending settlers "for the inhabiting of those countries, and reducing those gentile people to Christianity," the editor tried to shame his countrymen into recognizing their own duty. Here, again, Hakluyt urged the humanitarian value of colonization: English prisons were crowded with men and women, convicted of petty offenses, who asked only an opportunity to become honest and useful citizens in a new land. Failure of the English to establish a foothold abroad, the editor insisted, had come from "a preposterous desire of seeking rather gain than God's glory." Actually, material rewards would come incidentally when men began to put God first, said Hakluyt the preacher. Previously "we forgot that Godliness is great riches, and that if we first seek the kingdom of God, all other things will be given unto us." With earnest sincerity the parson urged the advancement of Christianity as a necessary policy in statecraft; neglect to spread the Gospel would result in the failure of English enterprise, as the Spaniards had already failed

344

in many ventures because their efforts at converting the infidels had been hollow pretenses.

The beliefs expressed by Hakluyt in his dedication to Sidney were reiterated and elaborated at every opportunity during the rest of his career. These ideas, common enough in the religious thinking of the day, gained new force by reason of Hakluyt's advocacy and helped a little later to influence the directors of the East India and Virginia companies.

A state paper, prepared by Hakluyt and presented in person to the Queen in 1584, set forth with great detail his views on the colonial enterprise then being pushed by Walter Raleigh. The document, conventionally abbreviated in title to the *Discourse of Western Planting*,[17] was prepared at the request of Raleigh himself and was designed to offer convincing reasons to Her Majesty for royal support of colonies in America, and in particular of Raleigh's infant colony just planted on the coast of North Carolina. Already Hakluyt had the confidence of Walsingham as well as of Raleigh, and the two hoped to use the geographer's knowledge and reasoning, both religious and secular, in persuading the Queen of the soundness of this oblique attack on Spain. Seven years earlier Sir Humphrey Gilbert had presented the Queen with his paper describing "How Her Majesty May Annoy the King of Spain," but no notice had been taken of his plan. Now Hakluyt, with the encouragement of influential men in the government, outlined a scheme by which Elizabeth might not only "annoy" but "bring King Philip from his high throne, and make him equal to the princes his neighbors."

In essence, the scheme provided for the fortification of bases to threaten the West Indies, the planting of colonies on the American coast north of Florida, and the securing of the Northwest Passage to the Far East. Much of the argument is based on religious grounds, with careful emphasis upon the dangers of popery and a description of the cruelties of the Spanish churchmen in the New World. By striking a blow for Protestantism and for England, the Queen would incidentally win the sources of the vast

[17] Taylor, *Original Writings*, II, 211–326.

wealth in gold and silver which had previously gone to enrich the coffers of His Majesty of Spain.

The *Discourse of Western Planting* begins like a sermon, and throughout its twenty-one chapters the author never forgets his holy vocation, albeit his advice could not have been more practical had it come from the most calculating worldling. One argument that Hakluyt used must have appealed to the shrewd Queen. Because preachers at home have not enough to do and are prone to idleness, they stir up strife, grow contentious about ceremonies, and are "always coining of new opinions." But if they were sent abroad with colonists, they would be too busy about the Lord's work to worry over trifling matters and would be content with established authority.

To the end of his days, Hakluyt as editor, geographer, and preacher continued his campaign to stir the English public to a realization of the necessity of expansion overseas as a counter-weight to the Spanish empire. He was instrumental in having works published that would influence public opinion, and his own great compilation of voyages long served its propagandic purpose.

As England began to expand its commerce overseas through the trading companies, religious matters were not forgotten. For example, the East India Company saw to it that ships were amply provided with edifying reading matter. In a commission to John Saris and Gabriel Towerson in 1611, the company provided the writings of Foxe, Hakluyt, and Perkins and enjoined the factors to read good books and observe the Sabbath. The tradition of pious reading by merchants in India apparently persisted, for in 1666 a group of factors requested a long list of the works of the church fathers, desired for their library. Richard Cocks, an English factor in Japan, noted in his journal for March 9, 1616, that he had lent from his library St. Augustine's *City of God*, "the Turkish History and a book of form of debitor and creditor" [18]

[18] Edward Maunde Thompson (ed.), *Diary of Richard Cocks, Cape-Merchant in the English Factory in Japan, 1615–1622* (London, Hakluyt Society, 1883), I, 118.

—a mixture of the pious and the practical that was characteristic of the little collections of books taken out by merchants.

Although the chaplains had to be orthodox Anglicans in good standing, the official point of view concerning morals and the actual behavior of the majority of the company agents was extremely puritanical, and their very language smacks of the canting vocabulary ridiculed by Ben Jonson and other satirists. It was conventional for their business letters to begin with some pious invocation like "Jesus," or "Emanuel," or "Laus Deo," and to end with a dedication to God. Although religious formulas were common enough in the early seventeenth century, the correspondence of the East India Company is noteworthy for evidences of a belief that God was a silent, though decisive, partner in their undertakings. Undoubtedly the piety of the factors in authority sometimes irked less godly Englishmen, who found difficulty in tolerating an atmosphere of persistent sanctimony.

An example of godliness was set by Sir Thomas Roe, sent out in 1616 at the behest of the East India Company, as royal ambassador to the court of the Great Mogul. Sir Thomas would not stir without a preacher in his train. When his chaplain died, he sadly observed that "thus it pleased God to lay a great affliction on me and my family for our sins," and wrote posthaste to Surat for another preacher, for he could not "live the life of an atheist." [19] The chaplain sent was Edward Terry, whose account of Roe's mission gives the writer a permanent place in the annals of eastward expansion. Since Roe's duties at the court at Agra included circumvention of the Jesuits, who were believed to be plotting against the English merchants, he needed all the ecclesiastical help he could get.

The piety of the Englishmen who were the spearhead of commercial expansion to the East in the early seventeenth century was an asset worth maintaining by all the powers of persuasion and authority that the East India Company and the government

[19] William Foster (ed.), *The Embassy of Sir Thomas Roe to the Court of the Great Mogul, 1615–1619* (London, Hakluyt Society, 1899), pp. 245–246.

could muster. Since communication was slow and difficult, company factors and even subordinate agents had to be entrusted with far more responsibility than would be necessary today. Peculiarly important, therefore, was a strict regard for the prudential virtues of frugality, sobriety, diligence, and honesty. Hence these virtues received especial emphasis in religious teachings. It was the pious hope that in every voyage God would go along as a sort of spiritual supercargo, and that, abroad, He would preside as a censor of morals and auditor invisible.

The record of the East India Company's preachers was high. Only once in a great while did one fail in his duty. One notable scandal occurred when a minister took to drink and the frequenting of brothels, but what bothered the company most was that he damaged its credit by paying the prostitutes in counterfeit coins.

The English colonial enterprises of the early seventeenth century, under the Stuarts, emphasized religious motivations and religious concern with the same vigor that Hakluyt and his colleagues had used in the previous reign. The Virginia Company of London employed preachers as publicists, and no less a cleric than John Donne advocated from his pulpit at St. Paul's the goodness of the Virginia enterprise.

The notion that God had especially reserved certain areas for English settlement, repeated so often in connection with Virginia, was advanced by both laymen and clergymen in recommendation of other regions as well. A little later, of course, it became a cardinal belief of the Puritans of New England. But in the period we are considering, advocates of Guiana and Bermuda maintained the theory of providential care for English settlements.

The promoter Robert Harcourt, for example, asserted in 1613 that the "rich and mighty empire of Guiana" had remained unconquered by the Spaniards because "the powerful hand of God doth work for us in this behalf and hath reserved the execution of this action for the honor of our nation." [20] The welfare of the

[20] Sir C. Alexander Harris (ed.), *A Relation of a Voyage to Guiana, by Robert Harcourt, 1613* (London, Hakluyt Society, 1928), pp. 55, 61.

nation and the glory of God dictate that Englishmen establish a nation there in opposition to Spain, Harcourt added.

Another emphatic assertion of divine intercession to preserve land in the Western Hemisphere for the English came from the Reverend Lewis Hughes, one of the first two ministers sent to the Bermudas, or the Somers Islands. Hughes evidently had instructions to write about the excellent qualities of that tropical paradise, and in 1615 appeared *A Letter, Sent into England from the Summer* [Somers] *Islands. Written by Mr. Lewis Hughes, Preacher of God's Word.* The author, who had attained some notoriety in 1602 for exorcising witches, was careful to point out that the previous bad reputation of these islands for enchantment and devils was merely part of the divine plan. As cherubim had been placed to watch the Garden of Eden, so "God had terrified and kept all people of the world from coming into these islands to inhabit them." In gratitude for "the goodness of Almighty God in keeping these islands secret . . . till now that it hath pleased His holy Majesty to discover and bestow them upon his people of England," Hughes believed only pious settlers should come to the new Eden. In a second pamphlet, *A Plain and True Relation of the Goodness of God towards the Somers Islands* (1621), the preacher further emphasized "the goodness of God, in reserving and keeping these islands ever since the beginning of the world for the English nation and in not discovering them to any to inhabit but to the English."

Throughout the reign of James I the clergy, with scarcely a dissenting voice, furthered the propaganda for expansion into the New World. Upon that topic Protestants of whatever sects could agree. The unanimous hatred of Catholic Spain, which came to a climax in 1623 with an outburst from the clergy over the marriage alliance planned for Prince Charles with the Spanish Infanta, gave a particular point to their consistent arguments for Protestant colonies overseas. Virginia was the first answer to their prayers. The clergy, with the horror of domination by the Spanish Catholic empire ever present in their minds, perceived more clearly than others the significance of that beginning of a counter-empire. Englishmen would presently wax strong and

349

smite the hosts of popery entrenched to the south. With such conviction did they preach this doctrine that Englishmen at length accepted it as their imperial destiny.

Long before the swarming from the hive that spread the English to the ends of the earth, Richard Hakluyt, the consummate propagandist for expansion, had foreseen the achievements of his nation. In the dedication of the 1589 edition of *The Principal Navigations* to Sir Francis Walsingham he paid an eloquent tribute to the prowess of a people who had begun a work that he believed would be for the benefit and glory of his country and the advancement of the Gospel:

To harp no longer upon this string, and to speak a word of that just commendation which our nation do indeed deserve: it cannot be denied but, as in all former ages they have been men full of activity, stirrers abroad, and searchers of the remote parts of the world, so in this most famous and peerless government of her most excellent Majesty her subjects, through the special assistance and blessing of God in searching the most opposite corners and quarters of the world and, to speak plainly, in compassing the vast globe of the earth more than once, have excelled all the nations and people of the earth.

For, which of the kings of this land before Her Majesty had their banners ever seen in the Caspian Sea? Which of them hath ever dealt with the Emperor of Persia, as Her Majesty hath done, and obtained for her merchants large and loving privileges? Who ever saw before this regiment [regime] an English Ligier [citizen] in the stately porch of the Grand Signor at Constantinople? Who ever found English consuls and agents at Tripolis in Syria, at Aleppo, at Babylon, at Balsara, and, which is more, who ever heard of [an] Englishman at Goa before now? What English ships did heretofore ever anchor in the mighty river of Plate, pass and repass the unpassable (in former opinion) Strait of Magellan, range along the coast of Chile, Peru, and all the backside of Nova Hispania further than any Christian ever passed; traverse the mighty breadth of the South Sea, land upon the Luzons in despite of the enemy, enter into alliance, amity, and traffic with the princes of the Moluccas and the Isle of Java, double the famous Cape of Bona Speranza [Good Hope], arrive at the Isle of Santa Helena, and last of all return home most richly laden with the commodities of China, as the subjects of this now flourishing monarchy have done? . . .

And have not we as good cause to admire that the kings of the Moluccas, and Java major, have desired the favor of Her Majesty and the commerce and traffic of her people? Is it not as strange that the born naturals [natives] of Japan and the Philippines are here to be seen, agreeing with our climate, speaking our language, and informing us of the state of their Eastern habitations? For mine own part I take it as a pledge of God's further favor both unto us and them; to them especially unto whose doors I doubt not in time shall be by us carried the incomparable treasure of the truth of Christianity and of the Gospel, while we use and exercise common trade with their merchants.

More than any other Englishman of his age, except perhaps Raleigh, Hakluyt had a vision of empire and of England's imperial destiny. He sincerely believed that it was God's own command that English Protestants should go forth and people the earth wherever they could, especially in those regions "not occupied by any Christian prince." The undeveloped areas of the world inhabited by backward people who had not yet had the benefits of Western civilization, who knew not the taboos of the Protestant Jehovah and His promises, offered godly Englishmen an opportunity to spread the message of salvation and reap a profit besides. Surely no patriotic Englishman could boggle over such a bargain: glory and gold in this world and the hope of a heavenly reward hereafter. So sensible and convincing were the arguments of Hakluyt and of others who shared his views that apprentices, merchants, plain citizens, speculators, noblemen, ecclesiastics, and great statesmen were converted to this doctrine.

From Hakluyt's time onward it was easier to persuade Englishmen of their destiny outside the little island girt by its silver sea. In our time imperialism has become an opprobrious word, and Great Britain has been damned for holding peoples of Africa and Asia in its eagle talons. But a question for students of society to ponder is what would have happened to those peoples if British imperialists had not imposed upon areas without political or philosophical cohesion Western ideas of law and justice, even the inhibitions and the decorum of religious faith.

If Western civilization has desirable values, it is a nice question how those values could have been transmitted to peoples who lacked them except for the labors of the imperialists, even if they made a profit in the process. Pure altruism is not a normal characteristic of any nation yet established.

INDEX

Abreu, António de, 129–30
Adrian of Utrecht, Florenz, 213
Afonso V, King of Portugal, 20–21, 46–47
  African commerce and, 49–51
Aguirre, Lope de, 264–67
Albergaria, Lope Soares de, 121
Albuquerque, Afonso d', 86
  Portugal's Eastern empire and, 117–121, 126
Alcántara, Francisco Martín de, 233, 251
Alcácer Ceguer (Alcazar), 47
Alenquer, Pero d', 57, 85
Alexander VI, Pope, 78
  bulls of, *see* Treaty of Tordesillas
Alexandria, spice trade and, 110, 116
Algarve, 13, 20
Algeciras, 7
Aljubarrota, battle of, 4
Almagro, Diego de
  cruelty of, 260
  death of, 250
  in New Toledo, 248
  Pizarro and, 229–31, 234–35, 243, 245–47
Almagro, Diego de (son), 250–52
Almeida, Francisco de, Viceroy of India, 116–17
Almeida, Lourenço de, 116–17
Alvarado, Pedro de, 194–95, 245
Álvares, Father Francisco, 56
Álvares, Gonçalo, 85
Amadis de Gaul, 5
Amazon, origin of name of, 263
Amrique, Father, 103
Andagoya, Pascual de, 230
Angola discovered by Portuguese, 53
Anonymous Narrative (of Cabral's voyage), 104, 106–7
Arabs
  East African trade of, 89–90
  traditional slave trade of, 30–31, 40, 90
  See also Moors; Moslems; Taureg
Aragon, 6
Aranda, Juan de, 132–34
Araucana, La (Ercilla), 261
Arguin as Portuguese base, 26–27, 29–30, 37
Arias de Ávila, Pedro, *see* Pedrarias
Armada, Spanish, 317
Atahualpa, 238–41
  capture of, 242–43
  death of, 244
Ataíde, Vasco de, 101
Atienza, Inés de, 264
Atlantic, medieval fear of, 15–16
Avis, House of, 4
Ayala, López de, 290
Azambuja, Diogo d', 51
Azevedo, Antão Lopes d', 25
Azores taken by Portugal, 18–19
Aztecs
  coastal tribes of Mexico and, 181–82
  Cortés and, 182–200
  religion of, 190
Azurara, Gomes Eannes de, 8
  on building of Sagres, 19–20
  on early Portuguese slave trade, 25, 28, 31
  on Prince Henry's explorations, 16–17, 22

Bajazet I, Sultan, 13
Bahamas explored by Columbus, 74
Balboa, Vasco Nuñez de, *see* Nuñez Balboa, Vasco
Baldaya, Afonso Gonçalves, 21–22
Barbosa, Beatriz, 132
Barbosa, Diogo, 132
Barbosa, Duarte, 132, 141, 153–54
Barlow, Roger, 291–92
Barros, João de, 50, 51
Bartholomew's Day Massacre, 306
Behaim, Martin, 133
Belalcázar, Sebastián de, 235, 244–46, 259
Benavente, Toribio de, 218
Berrio, Antonio de, 267–68
Berry, Leonard, 281
Best, George, 334
Béthencourt, Jean de, 16
Bobadilla, Francisco de, 80

Bogotá, foundation of, 259
Bojador, Cape, 15–16, 17
    rounded by Gil Eannes, 21
Book of Martyrs, The (Foxe), 330–31,
    336
Book of Roger (El-Edrisi), 16
Brazil
    Portugal's claim to, 78–79
    reached by Cabral, 59, 101–3
*Brevissima relación de la destruición
    de las Indias* (Las Casas), 219,
    223–26
    English translation of, 223–27
    French translation of, 223–24
Brito, Bernardo Gomes de, 124
Bry, Theodor de, 271
Burghley, Lord, 300, 302, 311, 317, 330,
    334–35
    Raleigh and, 281
Byzantine Empire, capitulation of, 13–
    14

Cabot, John, 287–89
Cabot, Sebastian, 292, 299
Cabral, Gonçalo Velho, 18–19
Cabral, Pedro Álvares, 59
    Indian voyage of, 101–8
        discovery of Brazil, 101–3
        East Africa, 104–5
Cadamosto, Alvise da, 19
    on African customs, 40–42
    on African fauna, 42, 45
    voyages of, 37–45
Cajamarca, Peru, 240–44
Calicut, Samorin of
    Cabral and, 105–8
    da Gama and, 92–93, 114–15
California, Drake in, 315–16
Camerino, Giovanni, 110
Caminha, Pedro Vaz de, 102, 103
Camõens, Luis de, 98, 123, 126
Canaries
    annexed by Spain, 18
    early voyages to, 16
Candia, Pedro de, 237
Cannanore, 108, 114
Cano, Juan Sebastian del, 141, 154–57,
    158
Cao, Diogo, discovery of Congo and
    Angola by, 53
Cape of Good Hope rounded by Dias,
    58–59
Cape Verde Islands, possession of, by
    Portugal, 18–19
Cape Verde rounded, 35
Carbajal, Francisco de, 252–53
Caribs, 73
    cannibalism of, 79
Carletti, Francesco, 121

Cartagena, Juan de, 135, 137, 138, 140–
    142
Carvalho, Juan Lopes, 154–55
Castile, 6
Castro, Vaca de, 251–52
Cavendish, Thomas, 323
Cecil, Sir Robert, 271, 279–80
Cecil, Sir William, *see* Burghley, Lord
Ceuta
    captured by Portuguese, 5–11
    decline of commerce in, 22–23
    importance of, 8–9
    Moorish counterattack on, 10–11
Ceylon, 116
Chancellor, Richard, 299–300
Charles I, King of Spain
    support for Magellan from, 133
    See also Charles V, Holy Roman
        Emperor
Charles V, Holy Roman Emperor, 33,
    157, 215
    Cortés and, 180, 193, 201–3
Charles VIII, King of France, and Co-
    lumbus, 65
Chaul, battle of, 116
Chiapa, 221
Chibchas, country of, discovered by
    Quesada, 258–59
Chile explored and settled, 260–61
China, Portuguese in, 123
Cholulans defeated by Cortés, 184–85
Christians, Eastern
    Hindus taken for, by da Gama, 94
    Portuguese search for, 17, 54–55
    supposed, in Cochin, 109
Cimaroons, 307, 308
Coca, Antonio de, 138, 141
Cochin, 107, 116, 118
    "Christians" of, 109
Cockeram, Martin, 296
Cocks, Richard, 346
Coelho, Gonçalvo, 112
Coelho, Nicolau, 85, 88, 103, 108
Coimbra, João de, 85
Colambu, Rajah, 148–49
Coligny, Gaspard, 318
Columbus, Bartholomew, 61, 65–66, 80
Columbus, Christopher, 51, 59
    attitude to slavery of, 73, 75, 82, 209
    burial place of, 81–82
    death of, 81
    early life and voyages of, 61–62
    England and France reject proposal
        of, 65–66
    failure of, as administrator, 80, 81
    First Voyage of, 69–76
        preparations, 68–69
    Fourth Voyage of, 80–81
    marriage of, 62
    motives of, 62, 69–70

Columbus, Christopher (*continued*)
  rejected by Portugal, 60–63
  Second Voyage of, 79–80
  Spanish support for, 63–68
  theories of, 64–65
  Third Voyage of, 80
Columbus, Diego (brother of Christopher), 80, 169
Columbus, Diego (son of Christopher), 63, 66
Columbus, Ferdinand, 62, 63, 64
Company of Cathay, 321–22
Conchillos, Lope de, 213
Congo discovered by Portuguese, 53
Constantinople, 13
Cook, James, 105
Cooke, John, 311
Córdoba, Hernández de, 170
Correia, Ayres, 106
Cortés, Hernán
  Charles V and, 180, 193, 201–3
  Christianization policy of, 76–77
  conquest of Mexico by, 171–205
    alliance with Tlaxcalans, 183–84
    contact made with Montezuma, 177–79
    "divide and rule" policy, 181–82, 183
    evacuation of Spanish from Tenochtitlán, 195–97
    march on Tenochtitlán, 182–87
    Tabascans defeated, 173–75
    Tenochtitlán recaptured, 199–200
    Vera Cruz founded, 180–81
  death of, 203
  Diego Velazquez and, 171–72, 179–180, 194–95
  early career of, 161–62, 169–70
  Honduran expedition of, 201
  Las Casas and, 185, 206–8, 219, 220, 225
  later career of, 201–4
  women and, 201–4
Cortés, Martín, 176
Costa, Jorge da, Cardinal Protector of Portugal, 97–98
Costa, Sueiro da, Mayor of Lagos, 35
Covilha, Pero da, 55–57
Cresques, Abraham, 33
Cretico, Giovanni Matteo (Il Cretico), *see* Camerino, Giovanni
Cromwell, Oliver, and South America, 271
Cuauhtemoc, 199, 200
  hanged, 201
Cuba
  reached by Columbus, 74
  conquered by Spanish, 169–70
Cuitlahuac, 187

Cunha, Tristão da, 117–18
Cuzco, Peru, 245–50

Darien, 165
  Pedrarias' régime in, 169
Davis, John, 322, 341–42
Dee, Dr. John, 317
Demarcation line, papal, *see* Treaty of Tordesillas
Dias, Bartolomeu, 51, 54–55, 84–85, 88, 101
  Africa rounded by, 57–59
  Columbus and, 77
  death of, 59, 104
Dias, Dinis, 35, 36, 37
Dias, Diogo, 104
Díaz, Juan, 173
Díaz del Castillo, Bernal, 167, 170
  López de Gómara and, 174–75
  True History of the Conquest of New Spain by, quoted, 171–77, 179, 181, 185–86, 188–89, 191, 193–4, 198
Discourse of a Discovery for a New Passage to Cathay (Gilbert), 319
Discourse of Western Planting (Hakluyt), 345–46
Discoverie of the large and bewtiful Empire of Guiana (Raleigh)
  literary success of, 271
  quoted, 272–74, 277–80
Diu, battle of, 117
Divers Voyages (Hakluyt), 344
Donne, John, 348
Doughty, Thomas, 310–11
Douro River, 6
Drake, Sir Francis, 142, 269
  circumnavigation by, in *Golden Hind*, 309–17
  death of, 327
  early life of, 307
  hatred of Catholics of, 335–37
  as member of Hawkins' Mexican expedition, 303–5
  San Felipe captured by, 326
Drake, Sir Francis (nephew), 311
  quoted, 311–16
Duarte, King of Portugal, 4–5, 20, 22, 83
Dulcert, Angelico, 33
Dutch
  capture of São Jorge da Mina by, 51
  as colonists of New World, 332
  as enemies of English, 327
  Spanish bullion fleet defeated by, 328
  spice trade and, 324–25

Eannes, Gil, Cape Bojador rounded by, 21
East India Company, English, 326, 346-48
  founded, 327
Eden, Richard, 297-98
Edward VI, King of England, 299-300
Egypt, 116
El Dorado
  legend of, 262
  search for, 262-68
    by Berrio, 267-68
    by Raleigh, 268-86
El-Edrisi, 16, 32
Elizabeth I, Queen of England
  death of, 281
  excommunication of, 306
  Raleigh's appeals to, concerning Guiana, 279-81
  Spain and, 287-88, 301, 305-6, 309, 317-20
  Turks and, 323-24
Encomiendas, system of, 168
English
  Columbus rejected by, 65, 287
  as defenders of Protestantism, 275, 306-7, 317, 319-20, 329-52
  as enemies of Dutch, 327
  as merchants in Spain and Portugal, 294-95
  Russian trading by, 299-301
  Spanish and, 287-88
    Armada, 317
    Eastern trade, 326-28
    illicit trade with Iberian possessions, 295-98, 301-3
    James I makes peace, 282, 284, 288
    open war, 288, 317
    Raleigh and Guiana, 268-86
    struggle for New World, 287-328
Enríques de Harana, Beatriz, 64
Ercilla, Alonso de, 261
Escalante, Juan de, 192
Escolar, Pero, 85
Es-Saheli, 33
Ethiopia, 54, 56, 125-26
Eugenius IV, Pope, 22, 26, 54

Faleiro, Ruy, 132-34
Federman, Nicolas, 259
Fenton, Edward, 337
Ferdinand, King of Aragon and Spain, 13, 16, 63, 96-97
  Christianization of Indians and, 167-168
  death of, 213
  Las Casas and, 210-11, 212
Fernandes, João, 29-30
Fernández de Córdoba, Gonzalo, 161

Fernández de Enciso, 165-66, 167
Fernández de Oviedo, Gonzalo, 164, 167
Fernando, Infante of Portugal, 4-5
  siege of Tangier and, 23-24
Fernando, King of Portugal, 4
Figueroa, Luis de, 213-15
Fletcher, Francis, 311, 313, 314, 336
Florence, wool trade of, 111
Fonseca, Juan, Bishop of Burgos, 132, 133, 135, 163, 200, 213
Foxe, John, 330-31
Foxe's Book of Martyrs and the Elect Nation (Haller), 331
Francis I, King of France, 78, 200, 269
French, 295
  See also Huguenots
Frobisher, Martin, 234-35, 321-22
Fugger, Jacob, 133

Gama, Estavão da (father of Vasco), 84
Gama, Estavão da (nephew of Vasco), 113
Gama, Gaspar da, 94-95
Gama, Paulo da, 85, 95-96
Gama, Vasco da
  cruelty of, 90-91
  as diplomat, 88
  early life of, 83
  first voyage of, 87-96
    East African coast, 88-91, 95
    India, 92-94
    preparations, 84-87
  death of, 123
  literature on, 86n
  marriage and temporary retirement of, 99-100
  reforming mission to India of, 122
  rewards of, 98-100
  second voyage of, 112-15
Gambia river
  Cadamosto's second voyage to, 44-45
  reached by Cadamosto, 43-44
Gao, 33, 34
Genghiz Khan, 13
Ghana, gold traffic in, 51
Gilbert, Sir Humphrey, 317, 330, 333, 339-41
  career of, 319-21
Ginés de Sepúlveda, Juan, 222
Goa, 118-19, 120-21, 122
  captured, 118
Gold
  African sources of, 38-40
    search for sea-route, 17-18
  Arctic, myth of, 321-22
  Europe's shortage of, 16-17
  in Hispaniola, 75-76, 79-80

Gold (*continued*)
trade in, at São Jorge da Mina, 51
See also El Dorado
Golden Hind, voyage of, 309–17
Gomes, Diogo, 47–49
Gomes, Fernão, discovery of African
gold traffic by, 50–51
Gómez Espinosa, Gonzalo, 141, 144,
154, 155–56
Gondomar, Count, 283–84
Gonzaga, Federico, Marquis of Man-
tua, 138
Gonçalves, Antão, 24–25
Goodwin, Hugh, 277–78
Gourgues, Dominique de, 318
Granada, Moorish kingdom of, 6, 13
reconquest of, 66
Grenville, Richard, 309
Gresham, Sir Thomas, 299
Grijalva, Juan de, 170–71
Guadeloupe visited by Columbus, 79
Guiana
Berrio's search for El Dorado in,
267–68
Raleigh and, 268–86
Guinea
discovery of, 35–37
legends about, 30–34
as source of African gold, 17–18
Guzmán, Fernando de, 264–65
Guzmán, Nuño de, 202

Hakluyt, Richard, 271, 317, 341, 343–
346, 350–52
Linschoten translated by, 325–26
quoted, 293–94, 303–5
on William Hawkins, 296
Haller, William, 331
Hanke, Lewis, 256
Harborne, William, 323–24
Harcourt, Robert, 348–49
Harlow, V. T., 266, 270, 285–86
Haro, Cristóbal de, 134
Hatton, Sir Christopher, 309, 334
Hawkins, Sir John, 296–97, 301–5, 307,
333, 327
Hawkins, "Old" William, 296–97
Hawkins, Richard, 333
Hayes, Edward, 340–41
Helps, Sir Arthur, 186
Henry, Prince ("the Navigator"), 4
Alcácer Ceguer captured by, 47
asceticism of, 12
Atlantic islands colonized by, 18–19
capture of Ceuta by, 5–11
created Duke of Viseu, 10
death of, 49
defeated at Tangier, 23–24
Order of Christ and, 11
Sagres built by, 19–20

Henry, Prince ("the Navigator")
(*continued*)
Saharan coast explored by, 20–22,
24–28
"school" of navigation of, 14–15
slave trade and, 25–27
West African coast opened up by,
35–45, 47–49
Henry VII, King of England
Columbus and, 65, 287
exploration and, 288–91
Henry VIII, King of England
exploration and, 291–92
Iberian interests and, 295–96
Hernán Cortés, Conqueror of Mexico
(Madariaga), 162, 164, 187–88,
202–3
Heyn, Piet, 328
Hindus taken for Christians by da
Gama, 94
Hispaniola
as center of New World expansion,
162–63
explored by Columbus, 74–76
settlement of, 75, 79–80
Historia General de las Indias (Las
Casas), 216
Hojeda, Alonso de, 80, 228, 291
career of, 163–64
Hormuz, 57, 117, 120
Hore, Master, of London, 293
Houtman, Cornelis, 326
Howard, Lord Charles, 271
Huascar, 238–39
Huayna Capac, 238–39
Hughes, Lewis, 349
Huguenots, 295
attempts to colonize Florida of, 318
Hulsius, Levinus, 271
Humabon, Rajah of Cebu, 150–51, 152,
154
Hutten, Philip von, 263

Ibn Battuta, 33–34
Ibn Majid, Ahmad, 91
Iconium, 13
Incas, 227, 232
fall of empire of, 242
religion of, 236–37
social system of, 238
See also Pizarro, Francisco, conquest
of Peru by
India
Arab merchants in, *see* Moslems in
India
East African trade with, 89–90
Portuguese in, *see* Portuguese, India
and
Innocent VIII, Pope, 55

Isabella, Queen of Castile and Spain, 13, 16, 63, 96–97
  Columbus's appeals to, 64–68
  on treatment of Indians, 208–10
Isalguier, Anselm d', 34–35
Islam, *see* Moors; Turks, Ottoman
Itinerario (Linschoten), 325–26
Ivan IV, Czar of Russia, 299–301

Jamaica
  Columbus marooned on, 81
  explored by Columbus, 79
James I, King of England
  Raleigh and, 281–84
  Spain and, 282, 284, 288
Jaramillo, Juan, 204
Jeronimos, church of the, 98, 114, 123
Jenkinson, Anthony, 300–1
Jews, expulsion from Spain of, 70
Jiménez de Quesada, Gonzalo, 258–59, 267
João I, King of Portugal
  accession of, 4
  capture of Ceuta by, 1–11
  death of, 20
  marriage of, 4
  sons of, 4–5
João II, King of Portugal, 4–5
  accession of, 51–52
  Columbus rejected by, 60–63
  death of, 84
  extension of African trade by, 52–54
  Indian explorations of, 54–59, 84
  papal division of world and, 78
  receives returning Columbus, 77
João III, King of Portugal,
  accession of, 122
  missionary zeal of, 125
John of Gaunt, Portugal and, 4

Keats, John, 166
Keymis, Lawrence, 281, 282–84
Kilwa, 104–5, 114
Kingsley, Charles, 308

La Cosa, Juan de, 69, 163
La Gasca, Pedro de, 253–54, 261
La Navidad, 75–76
  destroyed by Indians, 79
La Paz, 254
La Salle, Gadifer de, 16
La Vega, Garcilaso de, 238
Lagos as main port of the Algarve, 19–20
Lançarote, 27
  Guinea discovered by, 35–37
Lancaster, Sir James, 326
Laurentian Portolano, 16

Las Casas, Bartolomé de, 62, 73, 82, 169
  American Indians and, 205–26
  Cortés and, 185, 206–8, 219, 220, 225
  literature on, 205*n*
  on Negro slavery, 215, 217
  in Peru, 254
  at Valladolid, 222–23
Las Casas, Pedro de, 208
Laudonnière, René de, 318–19
Leicester, Earl of (Robert Dudley), 288, 302, 309, 317, 337–39, 343
Lemos, Gaspar de, 102
Lencastre, Jorge de, Duke of Coimbra, 99
León, Juan Ponce de, 170
Leonor, Queen of Portugal, 77
Letter Sent unto England from the Summer Islands (Hughes), 349
Levant Company, 324–25
Lima, 247, 250
Lincoln, Earl of (Edward Clinton), 309
Linschoten, Jan van, 325–26
Lobi goldfields, 51
Lok, John, 298
Lok, Michael, 321–22
Lombardo, Antonio, *see* Pigafetta, Antonio
López de Gómara, Francisco, 161
Los Cobos, Francisco de, 202
Los Rios, Pedro de, 231
Luque, Ferdinand de, 229, 234
Lusiads (Camõens), 126

Macao 123
Machim, Robert, and Anna d'Arfet, 16
Machodo, João, 87
Madagascar discovered, 104
Madariaga, Salvador de, 162, 164, 202–203
  on Cortés and Montezuma, 187–88
Madeira
  early voyages to, 16
  discovered by Portuguese, 18
Madox, Richard, 337–39
Magellan, Ferdinand
  achievements of, 158–59
  death of, 152–53
  early career of, 129–30
  literature on, 132*n*
  Manuel I of Portugal and, 130–31, 136
  marriage of, 132
  religious zeal of, 150–52
  Spanish backing for, 131–34
  voyage of, 134–59
    Philippines, 147–55

Magellan, Ferdinand (*continued*)
  preparations, 134–37
  mutiny at San Julian, 140–42
  traversing of Strait of Magellan, 143–45
Malacca, Portuguese in, 119, 122, 129–130
Malindi
  Cabral in, 105
  reached by da Gama, 91
Manco, 245
Manoa, mythical city of, 262–63
Mansa Musa, 32–33
Manuel I ("the Fortunate"), King of Portugal
  accession of, 84
  Asian power consolidated by, 112–122
  Cabral's Indian voyage and, 100, 108–10
  death of, 122
  eastern ambitions of, 97–98, 109–10
  da Gama's voyage and, 84–87, 93, 96–99
  Magellan and, 130–31, 136
  Spanish marriage of, 96
Manzanedo, Bernardino de, 213–15
Marchena, Antonio de, 63
Marina, "Doña," 175–76, 182
Martins, J. P. Oliveira, 19
Mary, Queen of England, 300
Medici, Lorenzo d', 111
Medina Celi, Count of, 64
Medina Sidonia, Duke of, 63–64
Mendoza, Antonio de, 220, 254
Mendoza, Francisca de, 202
Mendoza, Luis de, 137, 138, 141–42
Menéndez de Avilés, Pedro, 318
Menezes, Duarte de, 122
Mercenaries, 9–10
"Merchant Adventurers," 299
Mesquita, Alvaro de, 140–41
Mexico
  conquest of, 172–99
  See also Aztecs; Cortés, Hernán
Mexico City, *see* Tenochtitlán
Molino, Luís de, 142
Moluccas
  Drake in, 316
  Portuguese in, 119, 122, 129–30
  Spanish hopes of claiming, 132–33, 157–58
Mombasa reached by da Gama, 90–91
Montejo, Francisco de, 182
Montesinos, Antonio de, 211
Montezuma, 171
  Cortés and
    first contacts, 177–79
    Spanish in Tenochtitlán, 187–97
  death of, 196

Montezuma (*continued*)
  described by Bernal Diáz, 191
  as puppet of Spanish, 192–94
Moors
  divisions among, 13
  Portugal and, *see* Portuguese, Moors and
  Spain and, 6, 13
  reconquest of Granada, 66
Morison, Samuel Eliot, on Columbus, 60, 70
Moslems
  on East African coast, 89–91
  in India, 92–93, 106–7, 114–20
    decisively defeated at Diu, 117
  Portuguese and, *see* Portuguese, Moors and; Portuguese, Moslems and
  See also Arabs; Moors; Turks, Ottoman
Motolinia, *see* Benavente, Toribio de
Mozambique reached by da Gama, 90–91
Muscovy Company, 299–301

Narváez, Pedro de, 169, 194–95
Natal, 89
New Granada, 258–59
New Laws of the Indies, 218–21, 252, 254
Newfoundland, 290, 293
Nichols, Philip, 337
Nicuesa, Diego de, 162
Northwest Passage, 291–92
  Frobisher's voyages in search of, 321–23
  Humphrey Gilbert on, 319
Nova, João de, 112
Nowell, Charles E., 146
Nunes, Gonçalo, 85
Nuñez de Balboa, Vasco
  career of, 165–67, 169
  death of, 169
  in Peru, 228–29
  South Sea discovered by, 166
Nuñez de la Vela, Blasco, 252

Observations . . . in His Voyage into the South Sea (Hawkins), 333
Ojeda, Alonso de, *see* Hojeda, Alonso de
Olid, Cristóbal de, 171, 201
Order of Christ, 103
  Prince Henry and, 11
Orellana, Francisco de, 262–63
Ortelins, Abraham, 308
Ortiz, Bishop Diogo, 101
Osborne, Sir Richard, 324
Otumba, battle of, 197–98

Ovando, Nicolás de, 81, 161–62, 208–9
Oxenham, John, 308

Paiva, Afonso de, 55
Palacios Rubios, Dr., 167
Pedrarias, 167–69, 228–30
Pedro, Infante of Portugal, 4
  as regent, 20–21
  travels of, 13–14, 35
Pedro, King of Portugal, 4
Pembroke, 1st Earl of (Sir William
  Herbert), 302
Peraza, Beatriz de, 70
Pereira, Nun'Álvares, Constable of
  Portugal, 5
Perestrello, Bartholomew, 18, 62
Perestrello, Felipa, 62
Pérez, Juan, 66, 67
Peru, 227–56
Philip II, King of Spain
  American bullion and, 269, 272–74
  Elizabeth I of England and, 288, 317
Philippa, Queen of Portugal
  character of, 4
  death of, 7
Philippines, Magellan's expedition in,
  147–55
Pigafetta, Antonio, 137–38, 148, 158
  quoted, 139, 145–47, 149–53, 156–57
Pillars of Hercules, 15
Pinteado, Antonio, 297–98
Pinzón, Martín Alonso, 69, 71, 75–77
Pinzón, Vicente Yañez, 69
Piracy, 200, 269
Pizarro, Francisco, 164, 165
  Balboa executed by, 169
  character of, 169
  conquest of Peru by, 239–47
  Cuzco taken over by, 245
  death of, 251
  early life of, 228–29
  life in Lima of, 250
  Lima founded by, 247
  literature on, 231
  in Tumbes, 232–37
Pizarro, Gonzalo, 233, 247
  death of, 253–54
  defense of Cuzco by, 248–50
  as dictator of Peru, 252–53
  expedition of, to Land of Cinnamon,
    251, 262–63
Pizarro, Juan, 233, 247, 251
Pizarro, Pedro, 233
*Plain and True Relation of the Good-
  ness of God towards the Somers Islands* (Hughes), 349
Pliny, 16
Polo, Marco, 61, 64, 73

Portuguese
  African exploration by
    attitude of Pope, 20, 25–26
    East Africa, 58, 88–91, 104–5, 108–
      109
    Saharan coast, 20–22, 24–28
    West Africa, 29–45, 47–54
    See also Henry, Prince
  Asian empire of
    consolidation, 116–26
    decline, 126–27
  Atlantic islands colonized by, 18–19,
    20
  Columbus rejected by, 60–63
  in India, 54–59
    Cabral's voyage, 105–8
    Dias opens sea-route, 57–59
    first overland expedition, 54
    first trading, 92–93
    da Gama's first voyage, 83–99
    da Gama's second voyage, 112–15
    Manuel I's second and third ex-
      peditions, 112
    Moslems decisively defeated, 117
  Moors and, 4, 5, 13
    Alcácer Ceguer captured, 47
    Arzila and Tangier captured, 47
    Ceuta captured, 1–11
    Portuguese defeated at Tangier,
      23–24
    "Tawny" Moors enslaved, 24–25,
      35, 37
    trading on Saharan coast, 29–30
  Moslems and, in India, 92–93, 106–7,
    114–20
  Spain and
    Ferdinand and Isabella apprised of
      Portugal's achievements, 96–97,
      108–9
    marriage of Manuel I to Isabel, 96
    reactions to Columbus's First
      Voyage, 78–79
    Spanish rule, 47, 316
    Treaty of Tordesillas, 78–79, 132–
      133, 157–58
  Spice trade and, *see* Spice trade,
    Portuguese struggle for
Potato discovered by Quesada, 259
Potosí, Bolivia, 252, 254–56
Prester John, 10, 12, 17, 30
  equated with Mansa Musa, 33
  identified with Emperor of Ethiopia,
    54
  literature on, 54*n*, 56
Principal Navigations, The (Hakluyt),
  see Hakluyt, Richard
Ptolemy, 65, 67
Puertocarrero, Alonso Hernández, 176,
  181
Purchas, Samuel, 305

Quauhpopoca, 192
Quesada, Gaspar de, 137, 141–42
Quesada, Gonzalo Jiménez de, *see* Jiménez de Quesada, Gonzalo
Quevedo, Juan de, 167
"Quijote, Don," 5
Quintana, Gil de, 221
Quiroga, Rodrigo de, 261

Raleigh, George, 283
Raleigh, Sir Walter, 255, 268–86, 345
  execution of, 284–85
  Guiana and
    Discoverie of the large and bewtiful Empire of Guiana, The, 271–74, 277–80
    expedition of 1595, 268, 270–71
    expedition of 1617–18, 282–84
    "Of the Voyage for Guiana," 274–276
  in Virginia, 321
Raleigh, Walter (son), 282–84
Ravenstein, E. G., 96
Requerimiento, El, 167–68, 209–10
"Requisition, The," *see Requerimiento, El*
Reysgeschrift (Linschoten), 325
Ribaut, Jean, 318–19
Ridolfi, Roberto, 306
Roe, Sir Thomas, 282, 347
Roger II, King of Sicily, 16
Royal Commentaries of the Incas, The (La Vega), 238
Ruíz, Bartolomé, 230–32, 234
Ruminagui, 240, 246
Russians, English trade with, 299–301

Sá, João da, 95, 96
Sagres, school of navigation at, 13–14
St. Helena, 112
Salt traded for gold on Niger, 38–39
San Salvador discovered, 72–73
Sandoval, Tello de, 220
Santangel, Luis de, 67–68
Santiago de Chile founded by Valdivia, 260
Santo Domingo, 80, 82
Santo Domingo, Alonso de, 213–15
São Jorge da Mina, 51–53
Saris, John, 346
Saurez, Inés de, 260–61
Scurvy, 105
Senegal reached by Cadamosto, 40
Sequeira, Diogo Lopes de, 129
Serrano, Juan Rodriguez, 137, 142–43, 154–55
Serrão, Francisco, 129, 130, 137, 155
Seville, importance of, 131
Sforza, Ludovico, Duke of Milan, 289
Siaui, Rajah, 149

Sidney, Sir Philip, 344–45
Sigismund, King of Hungary, 13
Silva, Nuño da, 310
Simon, Fray Pedro, 264–67
Simpson, Lesley Byrd, 204, 208
Slave trade
  Arab tradition of, 30–31, 40, 90
  Christian justification of, 25–26, 31, 52–53
  East African, 90
  English, 302–3
  general remarks on, 31
  Portuguese
    in black Africa, 44–45, 50–53
    along Saharan coast, 24–28, 31, 35, 37
Sodré, Vicente, 113
Solís, Juan Diáz de, 140
Soto, Hernando de, 167, 235, 238, 240
Spain
  Columbus and, 63–82
  English and, *see* English, Spanish and
  expulsion of Jews from, 70
  Magellan backed by, 131–34
  Moors and, 6, 13, 66
  Portuguese and, *see* Portuguese, Spanish and
Sparke, John, 303
Sparrey, Francis, 277–78
Spice Islands, *see* Moluccas
Spice trade, 111–12
  Alexandria and, 109–10, 116
  Dutch and, 324–25, 326–27
  English and, 316
  Portuguese struggle for
    Moslems defeated, 116–17
    policy, 113, 115–16
    Red Sea traffic survives, 126
    Spice Islands controlled, 119, 122, 129–30
    Venetian fears, 109–10
  Spanish and, 128, 132–33
    Moluccan claims renounced, 157–158
Sudan, 29, 30–31
Suleiman the Magnificent, 14

Tabascans, 173–77
Tagus, 6, 7
Tainos, 73
Talavera, Hernando de, 64–66
Tamerlane, 13
Tangier, Portuguese repelled at, 23–24
Taureg, gold trade and, 17, 38–39
Teixeira, Tristão Vaz, 18
Tenochtitlán
  battle of, 199–200
  Cortés in, 187–97
  described, at Spaniards' arrival, 186

Terry, Edward, 347
Thorne, Robert, 291
Timur (Tamerlane), 13
Tlaxcalans, Cortés and, 183–84, 198–99
Tobacco
    discovered in Cuba, 74
    observed by English in Florida, 303
Toparca, 244
Tordesillas, Treaty of, *see* Treaty of
    Tordesillas
Torres, Luis de, 74
Toscanelli, Paolo, 64, 73
Totonacs, Cortés and, 181–82
Tovar, Sancto di, 108
Towerson, Gabriel, 346
Treaty of Tordesillas, 78, 132–33, 157
    England and, 282, 288
Trinidad, 267–68
Tristão, Nuno, 24–25, 26
*True History of the Conquest of New
    Spain, The* (Diáz), *see* Diáz del
    Castillo, Bernal
*True Report of the Late Discoveries
    and Possession Taken . . . of
    the Newfound Lands* (G. P.),
    341
Tumbes, 232, 235
Turks, Elizabeth I and, 323–24
Turks, Ottoman, as threat to eastern
    Europe, 13–14, 47

Ughtrede, Henry, 339
Unico Modo, Del (Las Casas), 217
Urre, Felipe de, 263
Urzúa, Pedro de, 264
Usselinex, Willem, 332

Valdivia, Pedro de, 260–61
Valverde, Vicente de, 241–42, 244
Vásquez Coronado de Valdés, Fran-
    cisco, 167
Velázquez, Diego, 169–72, 179–80, 194–
    195

Venezuela reached by Columbus, 80
Venice, 84
    as mart for Asian goods, 17
    reaction of, to Cabral's Indian voy-
        age, 110
Vera Cruz founded by Cortés, 180–81
Vespucci, Amerigo, 111–12, 163
    controversy over career of, 111*n*
Vienna threatened by Turks, 14
Villegagnon, Nicolas Durand de, 295
Virginia Company, 348
Vitoria, Francisco de, 218
"Voyage for Guiana, Of the" (Ra-
    leigh), 274–76

Waldseemüller, Martin, 33
Walker, John, 337–39
Walsingham, Sir Francis, 306, 309, 317,
    330, 343, 345
Watling's Island, *see* San Salvador
Welsers of Augsburg, 259
Westward Ho! (Kingsley), 308
Whiddon, Jacob, 270
Williamson, J. A., 296*n*, 298, 311
Willoughby, Sir Hugh, 299
Winter, John, 313–14
Winter, Sir William, 307, 309
Wolfall, Chaplain, 335
World Encompassed, The (Drake),
    311
    quoted, 311–16
*World's Hydrographical Description,
    The* (Davis), 342
Wyndham, Thomas, 297–98

Xavier, St. Francisco de, 125
Ximénes de Cisneros, Francisco, 213,
    214

Zarco, João Gonçalves, 18
Zumárraga, Juan de, 220
Zuñiga, Juana de, 201–2

Louis B. Wright

Louis B. Wright, *recently retired as Director of The Folger Shakespeare Library in Washington, D.C., is the author of numerous historical works. His two main fields of interest are Renaissance civilization and the transit of that civilization to colonial America. His first important book was* MIDDLE-CLASS CULTURE IN ELIZABETHAN ENGLAND (*1935*), *followed by* THE FIRST GENTLEMEN OF VIRGINIA (*1940*). *Other works illustrative of the history of civilization from the sixteenth to the eighteenth century are:* THE CULTURAL LIFE OF THE AMERICAN COLONIES (*1957*), THE DREAM OF PROSPERITY IN COLONIAL AMERICA (*1965*), *and* RELIGION AND EMPIRE (*1943*). *He has also edited a large number of texts, including all the works of Shakespeare in the Folger Library General Readers' Shakespeare,* THE PROSE WORKS OF WILLIAM BYRD OF WESTOVER (*1966*), *and* THE ELIZABETHANS' AMERICA (*1965*).

910.09
W951g   26715

AUTHOR Wright, Louis B.

TITLE Gold, glory and the
                        gospel.

910.09   26715
W951g
            Wright, Louis B.
Gold, glory and
        the gospel

MIDDLE AMERICA

- Tabasco
- San Luis Potosí
- Morelia

LAKE TEZCUCO
IZTACCIHUATL
Tenochtitlán
Tlaxcala
Cuernavaca
Cholula
POPOCATEPETL
Cempoala
Veracruz

M E X I C O

Oaxaca

Gulf of Mexico

- Mérida
YUCATÁN
- Campeche
COZUMEL IS.
PENINSULA

- Tehuantepec
- Chiapa

GUATEMALA

HONDURAS

San Salvador

South Sea (Pacific Ocean)

0   50   100   200
SCALE OF MILES

THE CARIBBEAN

(U.S.A.)

BAHAMAS

- Havana
- Matanzas

CUBA

CAPE HAITTIAN
Montecristi
(HAITI)
Santo Domingo
PUERTO RICO

VIRGIN IS.

LEEWARD IS.

GUADELOUPE

JAMAICA

HISPANIOLA

Caribbean Sea

WINDWARD IS.

TRINIDAD

MARGARITA

100   200   300   400
SCALE OF MILES

Coro

Nombre de Dios

VENEZUELA

PANAMA
GULF OF SAN MIGUEL

COLOMBIA